The Global Food System

The Global Food System

Issues and Solutions

William D. Schanbacher, Editor

 PRAEGER

AN IMPRINT OF ABC-CLIO, LLC
Santa Barbara, California • Denver, Colorado • Oxford, England

Library of Congress Cataloging-in-Publication Data

The global food system : issues and solutions / William D. Schanbacher, editor.
   pages cm
  Includes bibliographical references and index.
  ISBN 978-1-4408-2911-6 (print : alk. paper) — ISBN 978-1-4408-2912-3 (e-book)
1. Food sovereignty. 2. Food security. I. Schanbacher, William D.
  HD9000.5.G58284 2014
  338.1'9—dc23   2014014572

ISBN: 978-1-4408-2911-6
EISBN: 978-1-4408-2912-3

18 17 16 15 14   1 2 3 4 5

This book is also available on the World Wide Web as an eBook.
Visit www.abc-clio.com for details.

Praeger
An Imprint of ABC-CLIO, LLC

ABC-CLIO, LLC
130 Cremona Drive, P.O. Box 1911
Santa Barbara, California 93116-1911

This book is printed on acid-free paper ∞

Manufactured in the United States of America

Copyright Acknowledgments

Chapter 7, "Battles for the Soul of Organic: The Grassroots Versus the Suits," by Grace Gershuny, was originally published as a three-part series entitled "Conflicts Over Organic Standards," in *The Organic Standard*: Part 1 (August 2010), 13–15; Part 2 (September 2010), 16–18 ; Part 3 (October 2010), 16–19. Reprinted by permission.

Chapter 10, "Agroecology and Social Movements," by Peter M. Rosset and María Elena Martínez-Torres, was originally published in 2012 as "Rural Social Movements and Agroecology: Context, Theory, and Process," in *Ecology and Society* 17(3): 17. Reprinted by permission.

To Gary and Sherri for their unwavering support

Contents

Acknowledgments

I thank all of the contributors to the volume for sharing their expertise, activism, and research in our common effort to create a more just and equitable global food system. Moreover, I hope this volume will, in some small way, help the authors' respective causes and the people with whom they work. I also thank my editors, Beth Ptalis and Hilary Claggett, for all their insight, help, and patience while putting this project together. And I thank all my colleagues in the Department of Religious Studies at the University of South Florida for their support. In particular, Dell deChant and Michael DeJonge provided helpful advice during the final stages of production. Finally, a special thanks goes to Brett Bebber and Hollis Phelps for their valuable input, friendship, and unwavering comradeship.

Introduction

Today we live in a world in which billions suffer from extreme poverty and face pervasive inequality. Inequalities persist in multiple and interrelated dimensions of life, whether in terms of economics, gender, ethnicity, sexual orientation, or politics—among many other things. The suffering that accompanies poverty and inequality is exceptionally acute when experienced in hunger and malnutrition. To better understand world hunger and malnutrition, researchers and activists interrogate the global food system and its complex systems of production, distribution, and consumption to identify problems and potential solutions.

As the subtitle "Issues and Solutions" suggests, we hope this book will contribute to a growing chorus of voices of those who see the global food system for all its injustices. The title may sound bold in suggesting that all the problems present in the current global food system can be addressed in a single edited volume. This is not our intent. Rather, we hope the diversity of issues addressed in the volume can contribute to other, ongoing research and activist projects that share our desire to create a more equitable food system. Furthermore, the contributors in this volume come from a variety of disciplinary backgrounds, from research institutes to universities to industry activists. Thus we hope the diversity of contributor backgrounds can help inform us all about strategies, tactics, and issues that intersect with the common cause of creating more just institutions, practices, and power relations in the food system.

Chapter 1, by Annette Aurélie Desmarais, serves as an introductory reflection on how the concept or framework of food sovereignty might serve as a model for an alternative global food and agricultural system. As she highlights, the recurrent food crisis and growing environmental crisis compels researchers and activists to creatively and diligently search for alternatives to the current system. Based on her 20 years of research and involvement with La Vía Campesina, Desmarais presents questions and themes that are in many ways similar to threads of research and activist work found in all chapters in this volume. Although food sovereignty is a contested and evolving term that has sometimes been described as an "idea," a "concept," a "framework," a "mobilizing tactic," a "political project," a "campaign," a "movement," a "process," a "vision," or a "living organism," what is important is its desire to—drawing on the remarks of Elizabeth Mpofu—"change the food system, and the world."

Although the task of creating a more just global food system may seem an insurmountably utopian project to many, this should merely give us pause to reflect and draw on experiences, experiments, and lessons from food justice movements. Voices have been heard that are continuing to create social and political spaces in which activists, researchers, and small-scale farmers and peasants are bringing attention to problems in the current system. To this extent, food sovereignty and its various constituent groups worldwide symbolize and embody a hope that we can create an alternative to our unsustainable, unhealthy, unjust, and uncompassionate food system.

Chapter 2, by William D. Schanbacher, uses the work of human rights theorists to argue that issues pertaining to global hunger and malnutrition should be understood in the larger context of the responsibility, or lack thereof, of affluent countries to the global poor. Drawing on the central demand of global food justice movements that push for a global food system based on the concept and movement of food sovereignty, Schanbacher highlights the important distinction between positive and negative rights and the duties that arise from them. He argues that we should consider human rights in general and the human right to food in particular in a way that clearly understands the difference between positive and negative rights and duties. With respect to the human right to food, Schanbacher argues that rather than contextualizing access to food as a failure on the part of affluent countries to provide a framework for securing the right to food, affluent countries (and their citizens) should recognize how we are actively exacerbating global hunger and malnutrition.

Accepting this premise implicates all of us who are complicit in creating and perpetuating any coercive institutional order that denies global farmers the freedom from poverty, hunger, and malnutrition. Perhaps more important, this framework avoids some of the ethical conundrums associated with positive rights—namely, from whom (governments, charities, multilaterals, etc.) the global poor, hungry, and malnourished demand the right to food. In his chapter, Schanbacher argues for a more nuanced sense of duty that is required of affluent countries. We should focus on our negative duty to not impose agricultural practices and social structures that deny global farmers the freedom to chose how they wish to organize their own local communities' efforts to achieve food self-sufficiency.

Chapter 3, by Douglas H. Constance, Mary Hendrickson, and Philip H. Howard, examines the concentration of agribusiness with specific examples of Tyson Foods, Inc., Cargill, Monsanto, and Walmart. They argue that agribusiness concentration is a direct result of neoliberal economic policies that promote privatization, deregulation, and national and supranational policies that protect the interests and power of large corporations and consequently weaken and destabilize small-scale farmer production.

The authors organize the chapter around the following five questions: What is the problem with agribusiness concentration? Why is agribusiness concentration a problem for farmers, consumers, and communities? How did agribusiness concentration become a problem for so many groups around the world? What can be done to fix the problem? Why haven't we fixed the problem of agribusiness concentration and transformed the agrifood system?

The authors argue that these questions are grounded in the context of the historical debate between Marxian and Smithian versions of political economy. The battles over who controls the food system, whether small scale or large, that are waged between small-scale farmers, consumers, communities, and agribusinesses occur on the ideological spectrum of what the authors refer to as the "instrumental" or the "relative autonomy" view of the state. To fully understand the current concentration of agribusiness, we must analyze historical periods of the ebb and flow between a strong state that can wield power to regulate the market and the periods when plutocracy reigns and policy favors deregulation and privatization.

Ultimately, what is at stake is the quality of life for all the farmers, food system workers, and producers who daily bring food to our plates. The authors contend that the current concentration of agribusinesses has created a system that is harmful to these people as well as to consumers by having transferred wealth away from producers and workers into the hands of a few corporations. The result is the continuing deterioration of the livelihoods of workers and small-scale producers. The authors conclude the chapter with multiple examples of potential social movements or policy options that could challenge these harmful historical developments.

Chapter 4, by Joann Lo of the Food Chain Workers Alliance, addresses issues of race and gender discrimination in the five major sectors of the food system. Incorporating interviews with food system workers and data from the food production, food processing, food distribution, food retail, and restaurant workers sectors, Lo examines both the challenges these workers face and the successes they have achieved. Today, the food system is the largest employer in the United States and provides one out of five private-sector jobs. Employing more than 20 million workers, this employment sector represents one-sixth of the nation's entire workforce, a larger share than retail and health care combined. As one of the fastest-growing economic segments of the U.S. economy, food production, processing, distribution, retail, and service represent more than $1.8 trillion annually—13 percent of the U.S. gross domestic product (GDP). However, food system workers are among the lowest-paid workers and make an exponentially lower salary than the CEOs of the companies they work for.

As one major example of a food and labor-rights group, the Food Chain Workers Alliance is fighting for a more just and equitable food and agricultural system. A national coalition of unions, workers centers, and advocacy groups, the alliance advocates for higher wages, safe working conditions, and the end of workplace discrimination. Workers and advocates in these five major food sectors operate on the principles of social, economic, and racial justice with the guiding philosophy that everyone in the food chain should have access to healthy, affordable food. Highlighting the data with her experience of actual food system workers brings issues of race and gender into strong relief. Although challenges remain, the alliance has achieved victories through specific program strategies that can potentially network with similar food justice movements both nationally and abroad.

Chapter 5, by R. Dennis Olson, examines the unprecedented rise of Walmart's buyer power to illustrate the plutocratic nature of our food system and its harmful effects not only on consumers, but also on producers. Although Walmart did not sell food even as few as 30 years ago, by 2012 its grocery sales of more than $151 billion represented 55 percent of its annual sales in the United States. Moreover, as of 2012, the company controlled a quarter of the U.S. retail grocery market, more than its next three biggest competitors combined. This control over the retail grocery market presents an alarming situation for all stakeholders, including farmers and food processors, as well as all the employees who work along global food supply chains.

Walmart buys such large volumes of products that suppliers are forced to accept ever more exploitive terms for the privilege of selling to the company. Walmart's unprecedented buyer power (also known as monopsony) allows the company to squeeze suppliers to such a degree that it has forced the suppliers themselves to consolidate to survive. In effect, Walmart has driven market consolidation from the retail grocery level all the way back up the supply chain, to the detriment of all the stakeholders in those food chains.

Olson warns that Walmart's aggressive use of food items, both as part of a loss leader, and a greenwashing strategy, poses a dire threat to all stakeholders deriving their livelihoods from food supply chains. On the surface, Walmart's use of food as a loss leader may appear to be predatory pricing under earlier interpretations of U.S. antitrust laws. But Olson reviews the evolution of the consumer welfare doctrine in antitrust law from its origins in Robert Bork's 1978 book *The Antitrust Paradox* to its adoption by the U.S. courts. He argues that judicial activists, including some on the U.S. Supreme Court, have circumvented much of the original intent of Congress in passing antitrust laws, to the point of making it almost impossible for a predatory pricing claim against Walmart to prevail today.

In an illuminating critical analysis, Olson faults the Obama administration for failing to seize a historic opportunity to reevaluate Bork's consumer welfare doctrine on the food economy during an unprecedented 2010 antitrust investigation. In failing to act, the administration squandered the opportunity to develop viable reforms that could have taken into account the disturbing realities of Walmart's present-day buyer power abuses. He contrasts the failure of Obama's investigation with the success of a 2008 United Kingdom investigation that resulted in substantive reforms specifically designed to address buyer power abuses by large supermarket chains.

Olson concludes by identifying some potential paths forward to reform antitrust and other "market facilitation" laws to better protect all stakeholders in food supply chains. He closes by citing a 2010 United Nations report that concluded that anyone serious about ensuring the right to food enshrined in the UN's Universal Declaration of Human Rights must support measures to curtail buyer power abuses in global food supply chains.

Chapter 6, by Sara B. Dykins Callahan, examines *consumer* as a performance of identity integral to American culture. She argues that food, food industries, and food systems are all significant elements of our contemporary consumer culture and the identity politics of consumption. The identity *consumer*, as enacted through a set of practices informed and shaped by narratives of American nationalism and exceptionalism, directly engages systems that govern the production, distribution, and consumption of our foods. Dykins Callahan employs theories of cultural performance to investigate the construction and performance of consumer identity in the United States. She uses performance theory to examine how we consume: the processes and practices that embody our identity as consumers. These processes and practices provide insights into the troubling trajectory of the global food system. For instance, Dykins Callahan links the contemporary standard American diet, heavy in animal meats and dairy, to the American narrative of exceptionalism rooted in the principles of individualism, self-sufficiency, and territorial expansion articulated in the early 19th century. She then identifies the effects of this narrative, including on American foodways for both national and global food systems. The globalization of this American narrative has created increased international demand for animal meats and dairy that is currently being met through unsustainable and unethical agribusiness practices such as factory farming. Dykins Callahan notes that regulations of the food system by local governments for the stated purpose of improving the health of the community have been met with aggressive resistance. As Dykins Callahan observes, Americans interpret their constitutional rights to "life, liberty, and the pursuit of happiness" through the lens of consumerism. Restriction of the availability of food products has been perceived as a challenge to consumer-citizen choice and autonomy and thus, effectively, as a challenge to consumer identity and consumer culture. Although the identity of consumer has clearly contributed to the problems facing global food systems, Dykins Callahan does suggest that within the identity consumer there is also the potential for solutions to these problems. Understanding consumer as a *performance* of identity positions the citizen-consumer as an actor who possesses agency and who ultimately has the power to change the world.

Chapter 7, by Grace Gershuny, examines the historical roots, development, and current challenges of the organic food movement. Central to this story is the role of agribusiness, the role of the federal government, and consumer activism. Although these players are influential in creating policy and vying for food and health system change, Gershuny also highlights how their respective social, political, and economic interests are founded on different theoretical questions associated with the global food system.

Agribusinesses and agribusiness apologists highlight how the world population is on the rise and claim that if we are to feed the world we must use all the modern technologies available to us, whether fertilizers, industrialized farming techniques, or genetically modified crops. Supposedly unscientific, outdated farming techniques such as organic farming will never feed the world—they say. Alternatively, activists who oppose agribusiness underscore mounting evidence that organic farming can be just as productive as capital- and chemical-intensive farming. Moreover, it uses fewer nonrenewable resources, protects soil and water quality, treats livestock more humanely, and helps alleviate climate change. Activist also tend to oppose "industrial organic" or large-scale organic producers, believing that small-scale, local production and consumption models are the only way to maintain the integrity of the organic movement. Thus they often advocate for stricter standards in defining what can be considered certified organic. Today, many of these activists lament the industrial hijacking of organic standards by the hands of powerful agribusinesses, which they believe has left the organic label meaningless.

Gershuny contends that federal regulation of the organic label by the U.S. Department of Agriculture (USDA) has been a positive move with respect to stimulating growth of the market. Yet some activists continue to look on the USDA with suspicion—something that Gershuny admits is often justified. However, she says, a blanket condemnation of agribusiness or the USDA risks undermining public confidence in the integrity of the organic label. For Gershuny, this form of activism or uncritical condemnation has been a harmful historical development that in turn risks undermining the fundamental goals of the original organic movement.

Gershuny's chapter is organized in three sections: Part 1 traces the historical development of the organic standards and the various controversies and debates that fueled policy decisions. Part 2 maps the story of how organic standards have become law, highlighting how early discussions focused on various and often-conflicting ideological and scientific assumptions and objectives with respect to defining those standards. Part 3 asks what the future of organic will be. Even though policies have been formulated and put into practice, activists, agribusiness, and industrial organic continue to have a contentious relationship. Gershuny argues that some of these areas of contention need not be such, and that they potentially impede realization of certain goals of the organic movement.

Chapter 8, by Dell deChant, draws attention to the much-needed place of food in the curriculum and overall academic study of religion. The chapter is divided into four sections: The first section provides a brief description of the field of Religion and Ecology. It is followed by deChant's proposal for why the field of Religion and Food is rarely included in the subfield of Religion and Ecology. The third section offers reasons why this should not be the case, which naturally leads to possible ways in which scholars can continue to explore the "relationship of food to ecology, and both to religion."

By situating his argument in the context of the subfield of Religion and Ecology—a relatively new field in and of itself in broader academia—deChant provides an illuminating example of the intersections between food, religion, and ecology. As a subfield in Religious Studies, deChant argues that Religion and Ecology tends to focus on traditional methodologies that scrutinize beliefs and practices through critiques of formal doctrines, different religious cosmologies, and religious praxis. This is important for deChant, because this focus either outright ignores or lends itself to a dismissal of the relation between religion, ecology, and food. Though deChant hopes that one day Religion and Food will have its own niche in Religious Studies, much like the emerging subfields of Religion and Gender, Religion and Ecology, New Religious Movements, and Religion and Popular Culture, at present this does not exist. DeChant finds the subfield of Religion and Ecology to be one that lacks attention to religion and food but that has the potential to incorporate it into its curriculum, research, and course construction. The potential for the incorporation of Religion and Food into Religion and Ecology is apparent in their mutual concerns about environmental destruction, sustainability, and care for the natural world (including animals). As food studies programs increasingly find their way into colleges and universities, departments of Religious Studies will benefit by, and can in turn aid, new research and dialogue.

Chapter 9, by Brian Tokar, examines how the rising use of genetically modified organisms (GMOs) is presenting a grave threat to worldwide food justice and food sovereignty. Currently, it is believed that more than 365 million acres worldwide are cultivated with GMO varieties of soya, maize, and cotton, among other crops. The seeds of this expansion of GMOs were planted beginning in the mid-1990s when a handful of pesticide and agrochemical companies touted the potential for genetically modified crops and seeds to improve world agriculture. Companies such as Monsanto began aggressive consolidation campaigns and brought lawsuits against purported patent infringements. Concurrent with this, the biotech industry as a whole has waged campaigns demonizing independent scientists who question or are critical of the biotech industry. Both agribusinesses and the biotech industry argue that their technological advances are necessary for a growing global population, contrary to many recent studies that demonstrate how locally scaled peasant agricultures are far better equipped to feed the hungry.

Tokar organizes the chapter around a series of guiding questions that illuminate the historical rise of GMOs: How did a novel agricultural technology, advanced by just a handful of corporations, become such a powerful driver of the increasing global corporate control over the world's food supply? How did Monsanto and others achieve unprecedented dominance over the world's seed supplies? And what does independent science actually tell us about the track record of GMOs? Although these trends are alarming, Tokar also concludes by identifying potential alternatives that have emerged to help enhance people's ability to adequately feed themselves.

Chapter 10, by Peter M. Rosset and María Elena Martínez-Torres, examines how rural social movements have in recent years adopted agroecology and diversified farming systems as part of their discourse and practice. In this chapter the authors situate this phenomenon in the evolving context of rural spaces that are increasingly disputed between agribusiness—together with other corporate land grabbers—and peasants and their organizations and movements. Rosset and Martinez-Torres employ the theoretical frameworks of disputed material and immaterial territories and of repeasantization to explain the increased emphasis on agroecology by movements in this context. They provide examples from the farmer-to-farmer movement to show the advantages that social movements bring to the table in taking agroecology to scale and discuss the growing agroecology networking process in the transnational peasant and family farmer movement La Vía Campesina.

Chapter 11, by Ben McKay, Alberto Alonso-Fradejas, Chunyu Wang, and Saturnino M. Borras Jr., examines case studies from Brazil and China, two rapidly emerging BRICS (Brazil, Russia, India, China, and South Africa) countries, and two periphery countries—Bolivia and Guatemala—to situate contemporary dynamics of agrarian change in their specific historical contexts and point to new, but similar, trajectories of land access, control, use, and distribution emerging around the world. In Bolivia, a dual agrarian structure took shape throughout over 50 years of an "eastern landlord bias," institutionalizing a form of agrarian hegemony among the landed elites of Santa Cruz. Despite a seemingly proreform government with "redistributive" land policies, new forms of capital are penetrating into the Bolivian lowlands, with Brazilians now controlling almost 50 percent of cultivated land.[1] In Guatemala, where corporate deals over land and other natural resources have regained momentum, dominant forms of organizing agrarian production and of governing land resources are patterning and patterned by the balance of forces shaping relations of access to, control of, and use of land and other resources in historically and geographically situated conjunctures. In China, the gradual reconcentration of agricultural land use within the country and the pursuit to control more arable land overseas in recent years, perhaps as a result of increased demands among the Chinese population (for food, feed, and fuel), is presenting new challenges for the historically marginalized rural poor both inside and outside mainland China. Finally, in Brazil, despite strong demands from rural social movements in 1985 and 2003, MLAR and the continuing "agroindustrial bias" and "flex crop" concentration continue to threaten livelihoods of the rural poor and small-scale farmers even as state and societal (capitalist) actors are also looking abroad for newer and more lucrative investment opportunities.

These new demands and reconcentration of land and its productive resources have materialized in the context of the convergence of multiple crises—the global food crisis of 2007–2008, the ongoing climate crisis, the ongoing 2008 financial crisis, and the peak oil crisis—as well as a changing global economy with rapidly emerging economies such as BRICS and MICs (middle-income countries). Questions regarding land control, access, use, and distribution are thus extremely important and relevant in a rapidly changing global political and economic order. Although these changes and trajectories are alarming and require immediate solutions, the authors question the underlying logic of corporate social responsibility initiatives in addressing complex land-based social relations, arguing that investor-led strategies based on connecting the "poor" with markets or injecting capital into "marginal," "available," or undercapitalized areas will only exacerbate problems of poverty and hunger, reinforcing highly unequal agrarian structures and fostering the expansion of corporate control over land and the global food system. Land tenure relations must thus be understood in historical context and property rights as inherently relational—not as simply a tradable commodity in the de Sotoan[2] sense, but rather as a "social relationship."[3] Furthermore, following Herring, the authors understand that "land confers power in agrarian systems; reform policy must work through a system of power to restructure its base."[4] They thus emphasize the need to always historicize land-based social relations of access and control, so to better understand power relations within current agrarian structures. They conclude the chapter by turning to a "land sovereignty" alternative that takes a relational approach to the poverty problematic, considering relations of production, reproduction, property, and power.[5]

Chapter 12, by Heather R. Putnam and J. Christopher Brown, offers experiences from research in Latin America, in particular from a coffee cooperative in San Ramón, Nicaragua. The authors apply indicators from established food security frameworks and combine them with food sovereignty indicators to better take into account local contexts and cultures in the process of establishing food security. They argue that the food security model, though helpful to a certain extent, does not sufficiently capture the complex webs of interacting elements at the foundations of communities that need to be taken into consideration by researchers concerned with how local communities define and shape their own food security.

To this end, they employ the concept and practice of participatory action research (PAR). Rooted in the legacies of people such as Paolo Freire and Mohandas Gandhi, PAR is an interactive research methodology and practical model that is collaborative, that is participatory, and that requires political commitment. PAR emerged at a time when social theories were exploring how historical and cultural structures and institutions influence the production of knowledge and how we interpret different forms of knowledge. Moreover, if an analysis of social and political structures is done from within a particular structure, in what ways does this impede our ability to analyze them? To this extent, the practitioners of PAR argue, we need to engage communities outside historically dominant forms of knowledge creation. This is particularly apropos to agricultural and food security projects. As Putnam and Brown describe PAR, "the approach is rooted in a cyclical process of looking, reflecting, acting, and sharing between the investigators and the communities involved, resulting in a process of knowledge production in which reflections about actions are constantly monitored and reintegrated into actions in a dialogic process."

This model allows PAR to actively engage with various stakeholders, focusing first on the needs and knowledge of local communities. However, one of the unique features of the PAR model is that it opens space for avoiding what researchers call the "local trap," an approach to field research that tends to overromanticize local cultures and communities. Instead, PAR draws on input from various stakeholders, both those who are local and those who are outside the community. It is in this context that the problem of food security can be applied to the methodologies as well as contributing to the development of the food sovereignty framework. Putnam's and Brown's research with cooperatives in the coffee lands of San Ramón, Nicaragua, is offered as an illuminating case study of this methodology.

Notes

1. Miguel Urioste, "Concentration and 'Foreignisation' of Land in Bolivia," *Canadian Journal of Development Studies* 33, no. 4 (2012).

2. See Hernando De Soto, *The Mystery of Capital: Why Capitalism Triumphs in the West and Fails Everywhere Else* (New York: Basic Books, 2000).

3. Anna Tsing, "Land as Law: Negotiating the Meaning of Property in Indonesia," in *Land, Property, and the Environment*, ed. F. Richards (Oakland, CA: Institute for Contemporary Studies, 2000), 94–137.

4. Ronald Herring, "Beyond the Political Impossibility Theorem of Agrarian Reform," in *Changing Paths: International Development and the New Politics of Inclusion*, eds. Peter Houtzager and Mick Moore (Ann Arbor: University of Michigan Press, 2003), 58–87.

5. See S. Borras Jr. and J. Franco, "From Threat to Opportunity? Problems with the Idea of a 'Code of Conduct' for Land-Grabbing," *Yale Human Rights and Development Law Journal* 13 (2010): 507–523; and H. Bernstein, B. Crow, and H. Johnson, *Rural Livelihoods: Crises and Responses*, vol. 3 (Oxford: Oxford University Press in association with the Open University, 2010).

Food Sovereignty: Some Initial Thoughts and Questions for Research

Annette Aurélie Desmarais

> As peasants we believe that we are on this Earth . . . to grow food. Food for our families, food for our communities, food for our countries. . . . [W]e are not just resisting, we are also trying to build something new, a better world—with our ideas, and with our actions. . . . [O]ur gift to humanity . . . is the idea that we can all struggle together to build food sovereignty.[1]
>
> —Elizabeth Mpofu, General Coordinator, La Vía Campesina

In the context of the recurrent food crisis and growing environmental crisis the need for alternatives is more pressing than ever. But what does a real alternative look like? We can begin by analyzing the transformational potential of food sovereignty in creating socially just and environmentally sustainable food systems. This chapter offers some initial reflections on the meanings of food sovereignty and raises some questions that might help us build and strengthen a collective food sovereignty research agenda. This is a work in progress; it integrates some key points of learning from my 20-year involvement with La Vía Campesina and observations from research that I am just now starting on food sovereignty struggles in various countries.

The Urgent Need for Alternative Food Systems

The need for alternative rural development models, or alternative food systems, has been raised in a number of key international studies. For example, the International Assessment of Agricultural Knowledge, Science, and

Technology for Development (IAASTD) clearly stated that "business as usual [is] not an option."[2] This agriculture assessment, involving 400 experts including social and physical scientists from numerous countries, provided ample evidence to policymakers demonstrating the need for significant shifts in ways of thinking about agricultural development. It called for, among other things, changes to sustainable farming methods, adopting different ways of doing agricultural research to better include the participation and contribution of farmers, and emphasis on protecting and respecting human rights. The assessment also highlighted the potential of a new approach, that of food sovereignty.

Similarly, the United Nations Commission on Trade and Development's (UNCTAD's) *Environment and Trade Review*, released in September 2013—aptly subtitled *Wake Up before It Is Too Late: Make Agriculture Truly Sustainable Now for Food Security in a Changing Climate*—repeats some of these key messages.[3] But it does so with perhaps more urgency. *Wake Up before It Is Too Late* states that there is a need for a paradigm shift in agricultural development from a "green revolution" to an "ecological intensification" approach.[4] This, the authors argue, is not just about simply tweaking the industrial agricultural system. Instead, it "implies a rapid and significant shift from conventional, monoculture-based and high external-input dependent industrial production toward mosaics of sustainable, regenerative, production systems that also considerably improve the productivity of small-scale farmers."[5] Furthermore, the authors provide ample evidence challenging the wisdom of agricultural and trade policies that prioritize using industrial production under the slogan "growing more food at less cost to the environment."[6] As the authors point out, the fundamental problem is that "the current demand trends for biofuels, concentrated animal feed, excessively meat-based diets . . . are regarded as a given, rather than challenging their rationale."[7] This then leads the authors to question the assumption that there is a supply-side productivity, because, as the study goes on to argue, "Hunger and malnutrition are mainly related to lack of purchasing power and/or the inability of the rural poor to be self-sufficient. Meeting the food security challenge is thus primarily about empowerment of the poor and their food sovereignty."[8]

The two publications mentioned above are part of a substantial scientific literature on the need for a different kind of agriculture, one that moves us away from the industrial, highly capitalized, monoculture production model.[9] It is important to mention that the Office of the Special Rapporteur on the Right to Food has also contributed important insights on this issue from a human rights perspective.[10] Significantly, the special rapporteur's review of research of small-scale farming conducted in numerous countries argues that agro-ecological farming could increase world food production substantially within a decade and that it is an important way to ensure the full realization of the human right to food.

For over two decades, the millions of peasants, rural women, farm workers, indigenous peoples, and farm organizations belonging to the transnational agrarian movement La Vía Campesina have been demanding that governments and international institutions address the acute crisis occurring in the countryside around the world by developing policies to support the building of alternative food systems.[11] It is noteworthy, however, that the persistent displacement of peasants and small-scale farmers, and the 852 million hungry people apparently did not constitute a crisis before 2007. Instead, it took social unrest in approximately 40 countries and even the resignation of a president (in Haiti) before the global media began to pay attention. Subsequently, after being on the back burner for some years, agriculture was finally placed front and center when in 2008 the World Bank signaled the importance of redirecting national budgets, national governments began pledging more support to the sector, and international institutions reformed existing structures[12] and also created a new global structure—the High Level Task Force on Global Food Security—all of this in an attempt to address the world food crisis. But what kind of agriculture and food do these new efforts support?

Because the official food security response does not address the extent of dispossession, impoverishment, hunger, human rights violations, and threats to the environment as a result of climate change,[13] La Vía Campesina—along with a growing number of civil society organizations, human rights advocates, and researchers—claims that there is a need for radically different solutions.[14] All this points to the need for a paradigm shift in how we think about food and agriculture.

The Potential of Food Sovereignty

But what does a radical alternative look like? We can call it a radical or a common-sense alternative, but either way it must be transformatory: Viable alternatives must aim to transform, rather than tweak, existing and unjust social and political structures and relations. Many argue that food sovereignty is one such alternative and that it represents a path forward to socially just and environmentally sustainable models of agriculture.

First, let's clarify food sovereignty; Box 1 summarizes some key dimensions.

Some refer to food sovereignty as an "idea," "concept," and "framework"; others prefer to call it a "mobilizing tactic," a "political project," a "campaign," and a "movement"; still others refer to it as a "process," a "vision," and a "living organism." How do we make sense of these various ways of interpreting food sovereignty?

The Meanings of Food Sovereignty

In a nutshell, food sovereignty "is the right of peoples and nations to control their own food and agricultural systems, including their own markets, production modes, food cultures, and environments."[15] This alternative model of rural development is designed to keep small-scale producers on the land and enable them to make a living from growing food; it is a model of production, distribution, and consumption of food that is socially just and environmentally sustainable. As such, it is a radical alternative to the corporate-led, neoliberal, industrial model of agriculture. In the words of GRAIN, food sovereignty effectively "turns the global food system upside down."[16]

Food sovereignty is a prerequisite to the full realization of the human right to food and food security. It recognizes that the full realization of the human right to food is not possible under the current global trade framework in which agreements have expanded to include global governance over food, genetic resources, and agricultural markets. Food sovereignty demands that trade not be the first priority. Moreover, trade policies must respect, protect, and fulfill peoples' rights to sustainable and culturally appropriate production systems that yield safe and healthy food.

Going far beyond the concept of food security, food sovereignty stresses that it is not enough to ensure that a sufficient amount of food is produced nationally and made accessible to everyone. Equally significant is the issue of what food is produced, as well as who grows it and where and how it is produced, including at what scale. Most important, food sovereignty includes farmers' and peasants' "right to produce [their] own food in [their] own territory" and "the right of consumers to be able to decide what they consume and how and by whom it is produced."[17] In effect, it places those who produce and consume food at the center of decision making for agriculture and food policies. In many ways, food sovereignty is a social justice "counter-frame to food security": It emphasizes solidarity over individualism, insists that food is more than a commodity, rejects "free" markets, and demands state intervention and market regulation.[18]

In a world increasingly dominated by the ideals of liberalized trade governed by undemocratic and distant global institutions, food sovereignty proposes a radically different model. McMichael argues that as a mobilizing slogan, food sovereignty "serves to appropriate and reframe the dominant discourse, and as a political tactic to gain traction in the international political economy en route to a global moral economy organized around 'co-operative advantage.'"[19] He means that food sovereignty subordinates trade relations and transcends the fetishism for agricultural commodities as it reintegrates social, ecological, and cooperative production relations; revalues land, food, and those who work the land; and addresses questions of rights and social reproduction of agrarian cultures and ecological sustainability.[20] In fact, food sovereignty demands the "right to have rights"[21] and in the process expands our understanding of human rights to include the rights of peasants through the adoption of an International Declaration of Peasants Rights that includes, among other rights, the rights to food sovereignty, land, and natural resources.[22]

Perhaps most important, food sovereignty is fundamentally changing the ways we think about and relate to food, agriculture, and each other, because it politicizes the current global food system and agrarian policy.[23] Thus it is best understood as a radical democratic project that on the one hand exposes the power dynamics within the current global food system and that on the other hand cultivates new spaces for inclusive debate on food and agriculture. And as Patel argues, it does so in such ways that "the deepest relations of power come to be contested publicly."[24] If we remember Rosa Luxemburg's admonishment that "the most revolutionary thing one can do always is to proclaim loudly what is happening," then food sovereignty is nothing less than revolutionary.[25]

Although some lament the lack of a clear definition of food sovereignty, Elizabeth Mpofu, general coordinator of La Vía Campesina, provides some important insights:

[S]ome academics and analysts were concerned that La Vía Campesina seems to have a new and different definition of Food Sovereignty after every meeting and forum. Maybe they think this reflects a lack of seriousness on our part. But that would be a misunderstanding. We are not trying to create the perfect definition, for a dictionary or for a history book. We are trying to build a movement to change the food system, and the world. To build a powerful movement, you need to add more allies. And as you add more allies, you have more voices. More contributions. More issues to take into account. So your concept grows, it evolves, it broadens. To understand what Food Sovereignty is for La Vía Campesina, yes[,] it is a vision of the food system we are fighting for, but, above all, it is a banner of struggle, an ever evolving banner of struggle.[26]

Food sovereignty then, is about much more than agriculture and food—and therein lies its greatest potential. Instead, it is about social change writ large as it seeks "a transformation of society as a whole that can be achieved through the vehicle of food and agriculture."[27] As Desmarais and Wittman explain, at the heart of food sovereignty

> is a set of goals comprised of strengthening community, livelihoods, and social and environmental sustainability in the production, consumption and distribution of nutritious and cultural appropriate food. The pursuit of these goals is informed by a range of strategies: respect for place and diversity, acceptance of difference, understanding the role of nature in production, human agency, equitable distribution of resources, dismantling asymmetrical power relations and building participatory democratic institutions.[28]

Deepening and Strengthening the Food Sovereignty Alternative

Since the Nyéléni Global Forum for Food Sovereignty, held in Selingué, Mali, more rural- and urban-based movements and groups are embracing food sovereignty in their struggles for a different kind of agriculture, different societies, and a different world. How can we strengthen the diversity of social movements and groups working on food sovereignty? And what role can researchers and research play? What research questions might help deepen our understanding of the potential, politics, and challenges of food sovereignty?

Recently there has been a surge in the literature on food sovereignty, most notably as a result of "Food Sovereignty: A Critical Debate," held at Yale University and the Institute for Social Studies at The Hague in the Netherlands.[29] In the paper we presented at these events, we discussed some of the following theoretical dimensions of food sovereignty that informed our work.[30] Because food sovereignty has implications for what research is done and how it is conducted, it is worth summarizing some of the theoretical elements here.

First, we stressed that to analyze food sovereignty, we need to understand the social actors involved, and we need to understand their struggles. At the outset this means recognizing that, as some of the social movement literature argues, often when it comes to ideas that shape social change, academics and academia are the last to know. This is certainly the case with food sovereignty, a vision that was first introduced in the international arena some eighteen years ago by a movement of peasants and small-scale farmers—yet only recently spoken about in some academic institutions.

We suggested that to understand the great diversity of food sovereignty struggles occurring around the world, we "need to pay attention to the multiplicity of sites and the multifaceted nature of resistance to dispossession and inequality. . . . A range of factors, including history, social relations (class, race, gender, age), ecology, politics and culture, shapes the particular nature of each food sovereignty struggle in any given place."[31] This means addressing a series of questions such as the following:

- What are the nature of food sovereignty struggles in particular locales and countries? What food-producing resources and rights (environmental, productive, economic, social, political) are at the heart of these struggles? Which social actors are involved? What are these struggles rural and urban dimensions?
- What social justice claims are driving these struggles, and how do these relate to the International Declaration of Peasants Rights?
- How is food sovereignty conceptualized and practiced in different countries (as the chapters by McKay et al.; Putnam and Brown; and Rosset and Martinez-Torres illustrate in this volume)? What political conditions and public policies are necessary for the implementation of food sovereignty? How does food sovereignty strengthen the human rights to food, food security, and a safe environment in particular locales?

Second is the need to consider the different stages of struggles.[32] Analyzing the political and social significance of food sovereignty means examining the precise ways in which it can be a key driver of social change while also understanding the complexities of social change. It is critical to look at whether food sovereignty is anticapitalist (and if so, how), and also whether it is a counter-hegemonic strategy (and if so, how). In doing so, we might want to keep in mind the words of the editors of a recent edition of the geography journal *Antipode*: "Social change is usually not well organized, coherent and easily defined—and nor should it be. We are simultaneously in, against and beyond capitalism."[33]

We argue that to analyze food sovereignty as a driver of social change it might be best to "conceptualize it as a process involving persistent, diverse and interconnected struggles."[34] These multisited, multifaceted, and multiscale (local, national, and international) struggles often change over time, as most struggles do. At some points they may be more radical than at others. There may some flux in just how progressive or radical food sovereignty might be depending on the particular social and political dynamics at a given time in a given place. This suggests another series of research questions:

- What does food sovereignty mean for mainstream industrial agriculture and food? What are the human rights and social/environmental justice implications of the struggles between these two models?
- In what specific ways does the theory and practice of food sovereignty challenge or accommodate elements of existing agricultural production and consumption in specific locales?

- In what specific ways does food sovereignty lead to alternative social relations of production and consumption? Here I am thinking specifically of what it means when farmers in Spain tell me that they are in the process of deindustrializing agriculture and that they are not producing for the market, but rather for people.

Third, it is important to understand how the various place-based food sovereignty struggles are connected across time and space and thus are an expression of radical politics today.[35] Since food sovereignty was not conceptualized, nor does it function, in isolation, it is a mistake to read food sovereignty as a local/global binary. Instead, the local and global are deeply relational and feed off of each other. As such, food sovereignty reflects what David Featherstone[36] calls the "geographies of connection" and what Doreen Massey refers to as the "politics of place beyond place," by which she means "a politics both of places and of relations between them."[37] Food sovereignty as it was conceptualized and is practiced by La Vía Campesina, to use Michael Watts's[38] general discussion of resistance, is a "radicalism writ large" as it embraces the local, deeply situated struggles, then connects them and transforms them into a transnational organized politics of system change. It is a local, national, and transnational "organized politics of anti-enclosure."[39]

My research so far indicates that food sovereignty is fundamentally about the return to creating community— a permanent struggle to create, consolidate, and strengthen community. And this, too, is what makes it so radical. If we consider that the advancement of capitalism, historically, needed to destroy community, then food sovereignty, by creating and strengthening community, represents one of the strongest forms of resistance to the forces of global capital.

I want to stress here that I am speaking of community as a form of politicized radical public space, in the words of Simon Springer a "domain of contestation" where different social actors continually make their demands or "continually stake their claims."[40] And it is those struggles to create and strengthen community that need to be understood, analyzed, and supported— even when there are lapses, when nothing seems to be going forward, even when things look as if they are going backward. We need to understand just how difficult those struggles are, both internally and externally, understanding all the human failings of organizations and communities as well as the enormous pressure applied by external forces to try to crush collective action, to crush the consolidation of communities of resistance.

And what happens in cases in which the necessary political conditions are created and food sovereignty succeeds in carving out new democratic spaces? As Patel argues, because there is no universal perspective on food policy, food sovereignty in effect "calls for new political spaces to be filled with argument."[41]

This brings us to the complicated and messy daily struggles involved in building community and points to yet another set of key research questions:

- What alternative political, environmental, and cultural spaces and practices does food sovereignty help create? And in what specific ways does the practice of food sovereignty actually improve the well-being of rural and urban communities?
- How does the conceptualization and practice of food sovereignty help or hinder communities to negotiate the social constructs of gender, ethnic, and class differences? What mechanisms and processes can those advocating food sovereignty introduce to reconcile class interests and balance power dynamics to ensure that all voices are heard and acted upon? In other words, how does food sovereignty help build community, and how do those communities deal with internal power differences that historically have been key obstacles to the effective practice of social justice?

In conclusion, understanding food sovereignty as a permanent struggle to create and strengthen community poses, I think, all kinds of challenges for research and researchers. For example, in light of the diversity and complexity of food sovereignty struggles, can researchers read them accurately? Can we understand and analyze what is actually happening on the ground? Remember that a key point of learning from the social movements literature is that academics are often the last to know what is really going on (and even then they sometimes—often?—get it wrong). Some social movement theorists argue that if researches really want to play a more effective role in contributing to social change, we need to "get [our] hands dirty" and find creative and respectful ways of working more closely with social movements and community-based organizations, supporting their struggles.

Food sovereignty allows us to imagine and build communities of resistance that contribute to a kind of agriculture that can "feed the world and cool the planet." Research and researchers have an important role to play in deepening and strengthening the food sovereignty alternative. The peasants, small farmers, and farm communities of this world, with all their cultural, political, and organizational diversity, are challenging us all to engage in food sovereignty and thus to be drivers of social change. I, for one, am embracing this challenge with enthusiasm, imagination, and hope.

Notes

1. Excerpt from the keynote address given by Elizabeth Mpofu (2014) at "Food Sovereignty: A Critical Dialogue," International Institute of Social Studies, The Hague, January 24, 2014.

2. IAASTD (International Assessment of Agricultural Knowledge, Science, and Technology for Development), *Agriculture at a Crossroads: Global Report* (Washington, DC: Island Press, 2009).

3. UNCTAD (United Nations Commission on Trade and Development), *Environment and Trade Review: Wake Up before It Is Too Late: Make Agriculture Truly Sustainable Now for Food Security in a Changing Climate*, report released September 2013. http://unctad.org/en/PublicationsLibrary/ditcted2012d3_en.pdf

4. Ibid., i.

5. Ibid.

6. Ibid.

7. UNCTAD, Highlights of *Environment and Trade Review: Wake Up before It Is Too Late: Make Agriculture Truly Sustainable Now for Food Security in a Changing Climate*, report released September 2013.

8. UNCTAD, *Environment and Trade Review*, i.

9. See, for example, the report prepared by the New World Agriculture and Ecology Group (2009) and the IAASTD (2009), both of which refer to thorough lists of scientific literature.

10. Olivier De Shutter, United Nations Special Rapporteur on the Right to Food, "Agroecology and the Right to Food," report presented at the 16th Session of the United Nations Human Rights Council [A/HRC/16/49], March 8, 2011. www.srfood.org/en/report-agroecology-and-the-right-to-food

11. Annette A. Desmarais, *La Vía Campesina: Globalization and the Power of Peasants* (Halifax, NS: Fernwood Publishing, 2007).

12. The United Nations Committee for World Food Security, among other changes, now includes a civil society mechanism.

13. Annette Aurélie Desmarais and Jim Handy, "Food Sovereignty, Food Security: Markets and Dispossession," in *Controversies in Science and Technology*, vol. 4, eds. Daniel Lee Kleinman, Karen A. Cloud-Hansen, and Jo Handelsman (New York: Oxford University Press, forthcoming).

14. C. Rosin, P. Stock, and H. Campbell, *Food Systems Failure: The Global Food Crisis and the Future of Agriculture* (London/New York: Earthscan, 2012); S. Murphy and A. Paasch, eds., *The Global Food Challenge: Towards a Human Rights Approach to Trade and Investment Policies* (Bern, Switzerland: Brot fur die Welt, 2012).

15. Hannah Wittman, Annette Aurélie Desmarais, and Nettie Wiebe, "The Origins and Potential of Food Sovereignty," in *Food Sovereignty: Reconnecting Food, Nature and Community*, eds. Wittman et al. (Halifax, NS/Oakland, CA: Fernwood Publishing/Foodfirst Books, 2010), 2.

16. GRAIN, "Food Sovereignty: Turning the Global Food System Upside Down." *Seedling* (April 2005). www.grain.org/seedling/?id=329

17. "What Is Food Sovereignty?" La Vía Campesina (February 13, 2006). http://viacampesina.org/en/index.php/main-issues-mainmenu-27/food-sovereignty-and-trade-mainmenu-38/33-food-sovereignty

18. Madeleine Fairbairn, "Framing Resistance: International Food Regimes and the Roots of Food Sovereignty," in *Food Sovereignty: Reconnecting Food, Nature and Community*, eds. Wittman et al. (Halifax, NS/Oakland, CA: Fernwood Publishing/Foodfirst Books, 2010), 15–32.

19. Philip McMichael, "Peasants Make Their Own History, but Not Just as They Please..." *Journal of Agrarian Change* 8 nos. 2–3 (2008): 220.

20. Philip McMichael, "Peasant Prospects in the Neoliberal Age," *New Political Economy* 11, no. 3 (2006); Philip McMichael, "Food Sovereignty, Social Reproduction and the Agrarian Question," in *Peasants and Globalization: Political Economy, Rural Transformation and the Agrarian Question*, eds. A.H. Adram-Lodhi and Cristóbal Kay (New York: Routledge ISS Studies in Rural Livelihoods Series, 2008); Philip McMichael, "Peasants Make Their Own History, but Not Just as They Please..."

21. Raj Patel, "What Does Food Sovereignty Look Like?" in Wittman et al., *Food Sovereignty: Reconnecting Food, Nature and Community* (Halifax, NS/Oakland, CA: Fernwood Publishing/Foodfirst Books, 2010), 186.

22. UN Human Rights Council, Resolution on the Promotion of rights of peasants and other people working in rural areas. 21st Session of the HRC. A/HRC/21/L.23 (2012). http://ap.ohchr.org/documents/dpage_e.aspx?si=A/HRC/21/L.23; UN Human Rights Council, "Final Study of the Human Rights Council Advisory Committee on the Advancement of the Rights of Peasants and Other People Working in Rural Areas," prepared by the drafting group on the right to food of the Advisory Committee. A/HRC/AC/8/6 (2012); UN Human Rights Council, "Preliminary Study of the Human Rights Council Advisory Committee on the Advancement of the Rights of Peasants and Other People Working in Rural Areas"; P. Claeys, "The Creation of New Rights by the Food Sovereignty Movement: The Challenge of Institutionalizing Subversion," *Sociology* 46, no. 5 (2012); P. Claeys, "Claiming Rights and Reclaiming Control: The Creation of New Human Rights by the Transnational Agrarian Movement Vía Campesina and the Transformation of the Right to Food," unpublished PhD dissertation, Political and Social Sciences, University of Louvain, Brussels, Faculty of Economic, Social and Political Sciences and Communication (2013); M. Edelman and C. James, "Peasants' Rights and the UN System: Quixotic Struggle? or Emancipatory Idea Whose Time Has Come?" *Journal of Peasant Studies* 38, no. 1 (2011).

23. Hannah Wittman et al., *Food Sovereignty: Reconnecting Food, Nature and Community*; Madeleine Fairbairn, "Framing Resistance: International Food Regimes and the Roots of Food Sovereignty"; Philip McMichael, "Food Sovereignty, Social Reproduction and the Agrarian Question"; Raj Patel, "What Does Food Sovereignty Look Like?"

24. Raj Patel, "International Agrarian Restructuring and the Practical Ethics of Peasant Movement Solidarity," Centre for Civil Society Research, Report No. 35, University of Kwazulu-natal (2005), 113. http://ccs.ukzn.ac.za/files/CCS_RREPORTS2_REPORT35.pdf

25. Annette Aurélie Desmarais, "Building Food Sovereignty: A Radical Framework for Alternative Food Systems," in *Critical Perspectives in Food Studies*, eds. Koc, Sumner, and Winson (Don Mills, ON: Oxford University Press, 2012), 359–377.

26. Elizabeth Mpofu, keynote address at "Food Sovereignty: A Critical Dialogue," International Institute of Social Studies.

27. Annette Aurélie Desmarais and Hannah Wittman, "Farmers, Foodies and First Nations: Getting to Food Sovereignty in Canada," *Journal of Peasant Studies* 4. www.yale.edu/agrarianstudies/foodsovereignty/pprs/3_Desmarais_Wittman_2013.pdf

28. Ibid., 3.

29. A rich earlier literature is often referenced in this new wave of research. For a review of some of the earlier literature, see Hannah Wittman, "Food Sovereignty: A New

Rights Framework for Food and Nature?" *Environment and Society: Advances in Research* 2, no. 1 (2011): 87–105. For the papers presented at the two events, see www.yale.edu/agrarian studies/foodsovereignty/index.html and www.iss.nl/icas.

30. Annette Aurélie Desmarais and Hannah Wittman, "Farmers, Foodies and First Nations: Getting to Food Sovereignty in Canada."

31. Ibid., 5.

32. See Ibid.

33. Noel Castree, Paul Chatterton, Nik Heyen, Wendy Larner, and Melissa W. Wright (2010), "Introduction: The Point Is to Change It," *Antipode: A Radical Journal of Geography* 41, no. 1 (2010): 1–9.

34. Annette Aurélie Desmarais and Hannah Wittman, "Farmers, Foodies and First Nations: Getting to Food Sovereignty in Canada," 4.

35. Ibid., 5.

36. David Featherstone, "Common Sense beyond the Neo-liberal State," in *What Is Radical Politics Today?* ed. J. Pugh (London: Palgrave Macmillan, 2009), 243.

37. Doreen Massey, "Invention and Hard Work," in *What Is Radical Politics Today?* ed. J. Pugh (London: Palgrave Macmillan, 2009), 141–142.

38. Michael Watts, "Radicalism, Writ Large and Small," in *What Is Radical Politics Today?* ed. J. Pugh (London: Palgrave Macmillan, 2009), 23.

39. Michael Watts, "Then and Now," *Antipode* 41, no. 1 (2009): 23.

40. Simon Springer, "Public Space as Emancipation: Meditations on Anarchism, Radical Democracy, Neoliberalism and Violence," *Antipode* 43, no. 2 (2011): 528.

41. Raj Patel, "Transgressing Rights: La Vía Campesina's Call for Food Sovereignty," *Feminist Economics* 13, no. 1 (2007): 7.

2

Justifying the Human Right to Food in the Food Sovereignty Framework

William D. Schanbacher

As a college teacher I regularly incorporate in my courses issues associated with the ethics of global poverty, hunger, and malnutrition as they relate to the global food system. In particular, three things have struck me as particularly alarming: First, although my students have a vague sense of how fortunate their socioeconomic circumstances are, they are utterly unaware of the severity of global poverty. Second, and not surprisingly, they also lack a general awareness of the number of people who live malnourished and even starve each year. Finally, and perhaps most alarming, once they do acquire an awareness of our radical global socioeconomic inequalities, many—though disturbed and thus sympathetic with efforts to curb poverty and hunger—are still not convinced that we have a "human right" to food. I suspect much of this can be attributed to the need for further study, but through countless discussions I have found that it also may be tied to some potentially detrimental conceptual areas of grayness in why food should be considered a human right. Because this is at the core of the mission of food sovereignty (FS hereinafter) as well as FS's understanding of community and culture, this chapter contributes to the cause by offering a justification of human rights as they are understood in the FS framework.[1] Establishing a justification for human rights also lends some conceptual clarity to the relationship between human rights, culture, community, and self-determination, all of which are important features of the FS framework. Structurally, the first section of this chapter serves as a bookend beginning with a discussion of potential reasons why we, affluent global citizens, do not have an obligation to curb poverty and economic inequalities. To understand food justice movements such as FS, we must locate them in the wider context of global poverty. In the second portion of this chapter, I discuss several discourses—the right to food, food security, and FS—that researchers and activists have deployed when discussing how to eliminate global hunger and malnutrition. In the third section, I provide a potentially fruitful ethical justification for human rights, a justification that may aid FS against critics of the concept of human rights. In the next section, I apply the justification of human right to key features of FS—looking specifically at its language of rights and its understanding of the cultural importance of food—in an effort to identify some areas of future research. In the fifth and final section, the other bookend, I argue that we, affluent citizens, are complicit in a global violation of human rights in general and that we thus have the responsibility to remove policies that impinge on the ability of the world's poor to pursue their own ideas of food production, policy, and consumption.

Ethical Arguments for Why We Cannot or Should Not Do More for the Global Poor

Today we live in a world of radical socioeconomic inequality. According to 2004 World Bank estimates, 1.3 billion people live on less than $1.25 a day. On top of this, another 1 billion people live on less than $2 a day. Furthermore, 1.1 billion people lack access to safe water, 2.6 billion lack access to basic sanitation, 1 billion lack adequate shelter, 1.6 billion lack electricity, and 2 billion lack access to essential drugs.[2]

Compare these figures with the consumption patterns of the world's affluent as highlighted in the UN's 1998 Human Development Report:

> Inequalities in consumption are stark. Globally, the 20% of the world's people in the highest-income countries account for 86% of total private consumption expenditures—the poorest 20% a minuscule 1.3%. More specifically, the richest fifth consume 45% of all meat and fish, while the poorest fifth [consume] 5%. The richest fifth consume 58% of total energy, the poorest fifth less than 4%. The richest fifth have 74% of all telephone lines, the poorest fifth 1.5%. The richest fifth consume 84% of all paper, the poorest fifth 1.1%. Finally, the richest fifth own 87% of the world's vehicle fleet, the poorest fifth less than 1%.[3]

With respect to global hunger and malnutrition, even the optimistic 2012 State of Food Insecurity in the World report highlights that between 2010 and 2012, 870 billion people still went hungry or undernourished each year.[4] Global inequality in food consumption is further exhibited by this paradox: An equal amount of people are overweight (with estimates of up to 1 billion).[5] These numbers all occur within a changing global food system increasingly consolidated into the hands of a few agribusinesses, oriented toward large-scale homogenized farming that is chemical- and capital-intensive and that has caused volatile food prices that are particularly harmful to the poor.[6]

It is in this context that ethicists have asked the general question: Do we have a moral obligation to help the global poor?[7] Moreover, hunger and malnutrition being directly related to poverty, do people have a human right to food? If so, then what exactly is the ethical justification for the right to food? This brings us into a discussion on human rights and how they are to be conceived. Before returning to questions related to the human right to food, we must detail some of the pressing arguments surrounding our moral obligations to the global poor.

Drawing on Albert Hirschman's typology of reactionary rhetoric, Thomas Pogge highlights four standard arguments for ignoring world poverty. First, according to the "futility thesis," critics assert that "throwing money at the problem" is a futile (if not exacerbating) solution.[8] Unfortunately, humanitarian efforts to curb disease, hunger, poverty, and so forth often come up miserably short and, at worst, exacerbate the problems they aim to alleviate.[9] For example, if foreign donations depress incentives for local production, then we should direct aid elsewhere. Critics rightly ask whether foreign aid has caused more harm than good. However, as Pogge notes, we should recognize that much, if not most, official development assistance (ODA) goes to countries that will reciprocate: The aid goes to political elites in these developing countries. Similar to the harmful effects of misdirected aid, we can look at how U.S. agricultural policies historically have proved harmful to developing countries.[10] For instance, the well-known problem of dumping cheap food into countries has been particularly damaging to small-scale farmers worldwide.[11]

Second, arguments often focus on the notion that world poverty and hunger are so extensive that even affluent societies could not bear the costs of eradicating them completely. One of the ethical arguments associated with this line of reasoning contends that if well-off global citizens really tried to alleviate global poverty, doing so would require a revolutionary change in the status quo. In ethical terms, we would have an "overload" of duties to help the poor. Our obligations to the poor would be so great that we would be left helpless to find solutions for eradicating poverty. As Alan Gewirth explains, "How can the resident of Chicago help fulfill the pressing agency needs that the resident of Bosnia or Afghanistan or Somalia or Ecuador cannot fulfill for themselves or by their own efforts?"[12] Even if the responsibilities to radically change global economic inequality were placed in the hands of affluent governments, would this radically diminish our standard of living, perhaps to the point at which we, too, would become impoverished? If so, on what moral grounds are we to justify this reversal of economic fortune?

This leads to a third, somewhat related argument. In the 1970s Garret Hardin articulated the infamous notion of "lifeboat ethics." Metaphorically speaking, we might see each rich nation as a lifeboat out at sea; in the water swim the world's poor. Knowing the limited capacity of the lifeboat, we are forced to decide whether we will allow anyone else aboard the lifeboat and if so, then who. For Hardin, the answer is simple: We do not let anyone in the boat (even if we have some room), because this would risk drowning us all. To the "guilt-ridden" passengers who argue that we should try to save as many people as possible, Hardin answers: "Get out and yield your place to someone if you wish. The saved passenger will not feel guilty about his good fortune."[13] Though it may sound harsh, refusing to help the global poor will ultimately serve as a crude form of population control, a much-needed control considering that we face rising populations and limited natural resources. We should note how this position differs from the second argument mentioned above. The notion that we would have an overload of duties if we were to radically alter the global economic and power structure is not necessarily ethical in nature. Argument 2 simply states that we are at somewhat of a loss for how to strategically deal with the enormity of global poverty.[14] Hardin, on the other hand, argues that we have an ethical obligation to save ourselves rather than those who are drowning at sea.

Finally, and perhaps more commonly than we would like to admit, another position holds that we are making progress—and that thus nothing more should be done than is already being done: Progress in economic development, technology, health care, and so forth will eventually eliminate poverty and hunger. As we know, this is not the case. The FAO statistics highlighted above suffice as evidence that we are not making the progress we should.[15] And although these examples may seem tangentially related to FS, they provide helpful theoretical arguments pertaining to how we conceptualize global poverty, hunger, and malnutrition, as well as the potential obstacles we face in justifying our moral obligation to the global poor. I will not offer detailed responses to each of these four positions presently but will tackle all four when discussing Pogge's ethical argument later.

One final ethical position deserves mention: Many individuals and organizations recognize the massive socioeconomic inequalities and state of food insecurity in the world today. A simple look at the World Bank's mission statement, for instance, highlights two ambitious goals: "ending extreme poverty within a generation and boosting shared prosperity."[16] Similarly, the International Monetary Fund (IMF) asserts that it "works to foster global growth and economic stability" and provides "policy advice and financing to members in economic difficulties and also works with developing nations to help them achieve macroeconomic stability and reduce poverty."[17] Or, if we look at transnational agribusinesses like Monsanto, we find that in its ostensible mission to help fight global hunger, it is committed to "empowering farmers—large and small—to produce more from their land while conserving more of our world's natural resources such as water and energy."[18] The list could continue: Governments, multilateral organizations, NGOs, and corporations recognize the persistence of global poverty and hunger, couching their mission statements in terms of failing to prevent millions of deaths each year. But this is simply an admission of failure, not a confession that perhaps affluent countries pursue policies, both in terms of poverty reduction and food and agriculture, that actively harm the global poor. Underlying these ethical arguments against helping the global poor in general, and the hungry and malnourished in particular, is a tacit assumption that we do not have to protect rights to basic necessities. In the following section, I will introduce the call for the human right to food as it is expressed in the interconnected concepts of the right to food, food security, and FS.

Contrasting Concepts? The Right to Food, Food Security, and Food Sovereignty

The Right to Food

Windfhur and Jonsén have provided a helpful distinction between the concepts of the right to food, food security, and FS.[19] Of the three concepts, the right to food is the oldest, finding its first expressions in the United Nations Declaration of Human Rights in 1948. As a human right, individuals can demand that the state fulfill its obligation to provide sufficient and safe food. The state or the state's communities must respect, protect, and fulfill the right to food by *actively* pursuing policies that guarantee food security.

General Comment 12 of the UN's Committee on Economic and Cultural Rights takes this a step further by recognizing that the "roots of the problem of hunger and malnutrition are not lack of food but lack of access to available food" (point 5), adding the important notion of "access" to the definition of the right to food. The document further asserts that the right to "adequate food shall therefore not be interpreted in a narrow or restrictive sense which equates it with a minimum package of calories, proteins and other specific nutrients" (point 6). And, finally, strategies for obtaining the right to food need to include "cultural or consumer acceptability," thus needing to "take into account, as far as possible, perceived non nutrient-based values attached to food and food consumption and informed consumer concerns regarding the nature of accessible food supplies" (point 11) (UNESC 1999).[20] General Comment 12 builds upon the right to food by providing more substance to the definition of the right to food, including an implicit understanding of the cultural importance to food.

Food Security

Food security differs from the right to food in that it expresses more of a goal than a specific plan of action for securing the world with adequate food. Food security has been defined by the 1996 World Food Summit as "existing when all people at all times have access to sufficient, safe, nutritious food to maintain a healthy and active life."[21] The concept of food security, though well intended, does not specify a type of economic system nor a specific policy plan for use in achieving food security, nor does it clearly state how particular foods relate to a "healthy and active life." It should also be noted that the concept of food security has several differences from the right to food. As Windfhur and Jonsén note, even though it states a desired goal, there are no legally binding mechanisms through which a country's malnourished can demand that the state provide sufficient food. Second, there is a bias toward global, regional, or national food security "rather than individual access to food by deprived persons or groups."[22] Third, "the use of the term *food security* in many documents misses a crucial element of the right to food. Not only is it important to focus attention on the amount of food people are able to access, but [also it is important to focus on] *how* people access this food."[23] Fourth, the term food security fails to adequately set clear parameters for the implementation of particular policies. And, worse, many food policy documents (e.g., the 1996 World Food Summit Plan of Action) contain conflicting language, thus closing the widow for productive policy discussion.

Food Sovereignty

FS provides an illuminating contrast to our current global food and agriculture system. As Annette Desmarais elaborated in the previous chapter, FS is one of the world's largest and fastest growing grassroots social justice movements. As I argue elsewhere, FS is, in many ways, effectively challenging the food security paradigm, and specifically the economic system that supports it.[24] As defined by La Vía Campesina,

> [f]ood sovereignty is the right of peoples to healthy and culturally appropriate food produced through sustainable methods and their right to define their own food and agriculture systems. It develops a model of small-scale sustainable production benefiting communities and their environment. It puts the aspirations, needs and livelihoods of those who produce, distribute and consume food at the heart of food systems and policies rather than the demands of markets and corporations.[25]

Looking at how FS defines and understands food reveals some interesting contrasts to the concept of food security and also asserts a nuanced definition of human right to food. Broadly speaking, FS has parallel goals with food security in the sense that one of its fundamental aspirations is to provide the hungry with food. However, once we move beyond this simple goal, we start to see potential conflicts with respect to the implementation of specific policies. FS provides a more substantive definition of the conditions in which food is produced and for whom it is intended—namely, it prioritizes the needs of local communities. Broadly speaking, FS and its various global organizations and expressions fight against harmful neoliberal social and economic practices, including harmful global trade arrangements in agriculture,[26] inequitable access and ownership of land, blanket privatization of state institutions, unfair intellectual property rights laws, the imposition of unsustainable environmental practices, and the use of genetically modified organisms—among many other things. It also struggles for family and small-scale farms, sustainable alternatives to industrial agriculture, agrarian reform, and the human rights of peasants, indigenous peoples, and peasant activists.[27] Broadly speaking, what is at stake for FS communities is putting the production of food back into the hands of small-scale, both rural and urban, peasant, and family farmers.

Eric Holt-Giménez's work with the Campesino a Campesino Movement (Farmer to Farmer Movement or MCAC) provides one of many examples of what food sovereignty looks like in practice. In complete contrast to large-scale, corporate-driven agricultural production, MCAC focuses on local and regional farmers and farming techniques that generate knowledge, build communities, and educate farmers. Rather than rely on foreign professionals—whether agriculture "experts" or aid groups—MCAC stresses what Giménez calls a "campesino pedagogy" in which farming experiences and practices are shared with other local farmers in a way that reflects a "deeper culturally embedded exchange in which knowledge is generated and shared"[28] (Holt-Giménez 2006, 78). In this people-centered approach, farmers gather together in farmer-organized workshops, *enquentros* (gatherings), and *intercambios* (exchanges) that are punctuated by "songs, stories, jokes, poems, sayings and games" and, most important, food. It is in these events that "strong friendships are established that over time weave dense networks of reciprocity and solidarity."[29]

As the MCAC developed in the 1960s,

[t]he sharing of cultural wisdom produced a set of general normative principles that suggest that MCAC's technologies and methods are deeply rooted in meaning. Codified as a simple stick figure, MCAC is said to "work" with two hands: one for production of food and the other for protection of the environment. The Movement "walks" on the two legs of innovation and solidarity. In its "heart" it believes in love of nature, family and community, and it "sees" with a vision of campesino-led sustainable agricultural development.[30]

"This is a radically different vision for farming and farmers. In contrast to our current system that privileges large-scale, unsustainable, and capital and chemical intensive techniques, MCAC's approach re-envisions the future of farming that asserts the lives of those who produce the food we, but they often do not, get to enjoy in abundance."[31]

As just one example of what food sovereignty looks like on the ground, MCAC illustrates a paradigm shift in which identity and power relations are radically shifted. Community and individual identities are formed by the communities themselves rather than imposed from without. Self-determination, as opposed to dependency, is a key feature of MCAC.

Drawing a distinction between the right to food, food security, and FS has important implications for how to navigate the existing and potential internal conflicts within different expressions of FS.[32] It is natural to expect that we will find fragmentation, dissent, and conflict in such a diverse global movement, but we might question: Why is this so? The following section will examine some of the conceptual problems, both explicit and implicit, in the FS framework. Focusing on the larger context of global poverty—the umbrella under which FS does most of its work—will highlight certain ethical questions related to FS's demand for the human right to food.

Though it may seem elementary, it is necessary to establish that we live in a world of radical inequality and thus have a moral obligation to the global poor. Moreover, our moral obligation to the world's poor in general, and FS communities in particular, is rooted in the fact that we, affluent people of industrialized nations, are actively causing globally poverty, hunger, and malnutrition. A justification of the right to food will also introduce problems associated with FS's demand that this right also include a right to culturally appropriate food.

Ethical Foundations of Human Rights

Although FS has asserted the human right to food, it may be helpful to provide some conceptual clarity to this demand by asking what exactly are human rights and how they should be conceived and thus justified ethically. In addressing the question of what we mean by human rights, Jack Donnelly rightly notes that theoretical attempts to justify human rights have a variety of starting points. Theorists argue that they may arise from natural law,[33] from human needs,[34] from a notion of human flourishing,[35] and from human action[36]—to name a few ways. Part of the difficulty of justifying human rights is the prior need to articulate what it means to be human. Although this is outside the scope of this chapter, Donnelly correctly recognizes that there are few moral issues less conclusive than attempting to define human nature. However, for Donnelly, perhaps this conceptual "emptiness" is the most powerful aspect of it all. Donnelly's understanding of human rights is appealing because he makes a distinction between a scientific and a moral understanding of human nature. We can avoid the conundrums of attempting to establish an essentialist definition of the human nature by recognizing that humans are both animal and moral beings. As Donnelly puts it, "Human rights are 'needed' not for life but for a life of dignity."[37] To live a life of dignity entails understanding ourselves not simply as autonomous beings, but also as individuals who are shaped by our communities. Human rights philosopher Alan Gewirth offers a justification for human rights that fits particularly well with the FS framework.

For Gewirth, "the justification of rights requires the delineation of a basis from which rights can be logically generated," and the relevant foundation for human rights should be human action. Human action is basic to all forms of human behavior, whether in labor, in social and cultural interactions, or in ethical decision making, and "all moral precepts tell human beings how they ought to act." Furthermore, our moral precepts (whatever they may be) are founded on two features that relate to the actions to which they refer: On the one hand, they are voluntary or require freedom—namely, the persons to which moral demands are addressed have knowledge of relevant circumstances and are free to act accordingly. On the other, we act with intention or purpose; we direct all our actions toward some end, and we have some degree of confidence that we will achieve that goal. When purposiveness "is extended to the general conditions required for such success, it becomes the more general feature which [we] shall call *well-being* (author's emphasis).[38] Logically, then, well-being must also include the "various substantive conditions and abilities that are required either for acting at all or for having general chances of success in achieving one's purposes through one's actions."[39]

Gewirth discusses three hierarchical dimensions of well-being that provide more substance to the abstract concept well-being. *Basic well-being* refers to having the basic prerequisites such as life, physical integrity, mental equilibrium, and so forth necessary for action in general. *Nonsubstantive well-being* consists in having the general abilities and the proper conditions needed for purpose-fulfillment and includes examples such as not being lied to or stolen from. Finally, *additive well-being* is measured by our ability to increase our levels of "purpose-fulfillment" and our capability to achieve particular actions. It should also be noted that these concepts are increasingly showing up in literature and discourses on how we understand economic development, a key component in the fight to curb global poverty and for realizing the goals of FS groups in the developing world.[40]

With the necessary conditions of freedom and well-being thus established, Gewirth argues that a key component of well-being is *community* (author's emphasis). On the one hand, community is instrumentally important, because it is in the community context that we are nurtured, sheltered, and fed and thus obtain the conditions necessary for achieving our goals. On the other hand, drawing on Aristotle's notion that man by nature is a social animal, we recognize that communities are thus the only place in which we can achieve our full humanity. It is through mutual relationships and interactions (i.e., the community) that we bolster our chances of actually achieving our ends.

Before outlining a theory of the basis of human rights, it should be noted that FS has nuanced and multidimensional understandings of the right to food depending on context. As Desmarais and Wittman persuasively argue, FS conceives of rights as collective and decentralized, "with implementation depending not just on states, but also on communities, peoples, and international bodies"[41] (Desmarais and Wittman 2013, 3). This introduces an important conceptual project for FS—namely, clarifying exactly what it means to have a right to food. Three initial questions come to mind: Can we establish the source for human rights? Is the human right to food related to the cultivation of community cultures? And, finally, what class of rights are we discussing when we talk about human rights? Bringing conceptual clarity to these issues will prove beneficial to the FS framework.

One final note should be made with respect to rights in general. Drawing on the theorist Hannah Arendt, Raj Patel has identified an important, yet potentially difficult problem when discussing the FS right to food. Patel recognizes that a rigorous interrogation of the notion of rights reveals that they may not exist. We cannot simply pull claims for a right from thin air. They are a human creation that, moreover, requires individuals, groups, or nations to provide and protect them. Drawing from Arendt and Selya Benhabib, Patel suggests we need to begin with the idea of "the right to rights." In other words, we need to recognize contexts in which individuals or communities do not even have the social, cultural, and political spaces in which to assert a system of rights. Only after we have created conditions in which people can exercise a minimal amount of agency can we then assert some sort of system of rights, human rights in particular. With this said, many FS movements are creating social, cultural, and political spaces, and asserting creative ways, in which to challenge the global food system.[42] The following section will present an ethical argument justifying the foundations and existence of human rights.

The Argument for Human Rights

With the idea that human action is the basis for human rights now articulated, we can ask how human rights are derived from the generic features of human action. Gewirth employs a dialectical method that is *necessarily dialectic* (author's emphasis) insofar as the statements made by a purposive agent "logically must be accepted by every agent because they derive from the generic features of purposive action, including the conative standpoint common to all agents."[43] In other words, the argument for human rights and their concomitant duties is one that everyone must logically accept, because it is derived from the fundamental assertion that all human beings (purposive agents) need baseline conditions that allow for action (and generally successful action).

Gerwith's argument is technical, but it is worth explicating in detail. The argument proceeds with two theses: First, every agent or human "logically must accept that s/he has rights to freedom and well-being." Second, every agent "logically must also accept that all other agents also have these rights equally" with one another. In establishing this second thesis, we can posit the "existence of universal moral rights and thus human rights." The premises of the argument are as follows: (1) I do X for end or purpose E. From step (1) we logically must agree with step (2): E *is good*. The "good" need not be definitive, but the agent must recognize that he or she acts for some purpose that merits value and that thus is worth attempting to achieve. Subsequent to this, we recall that freedom and well-being create the basic conditions for an agent's acting. Therefore the agent must accept (3): *My freedom and well-being are necessary goods.* In other words, we must have freedom and well-being to act. Hence (4): *I must have freedom and well-being.* In other words, we recognize the practical necessity of freedom; it is a necessary condition for achieving our goals. Moreover, we recognize the prescriptive nature of freedom: If freedom is a necessary condition for achieving our goals, we will also endorse or advocate for its conditions. From (4) we must also accept (5): *I have rights to freedom and well-being.* For Gewirth, this is a crucial moment for the logical acceptance of the normative concept of rights—namely, what we ought to accept from the previous premises. The logic of step (5) can only be shown in light of (6): *All other persons ought at least to refrain from removing or interfering with my freedom and well-being.* If an individual rejects (6), then he or she must accept (7): *Other persons may remove or interfere with my freedom.* Furthermore, by accepting (7), he or she must also accept (8): *I may not have freedom and well-being.* However, here we notice that logically speaking, (8) contradicts (4). Finally, because (8) follows from the rejection of (5), every agent must reject that denial, and thus he or she must accept (5). At this stage in the argument, the existence of general rights is established. The universal nature of general rights can be established by the logical principle of universalization." Namely, "if some predicate P belongs to some subject S because S has a certain quality Q, then P logically must belong to all subjects that also have Q."[44] Therefore, if all humans are purposive agents (i.e., engage in human action, or quality Q), no rational being can be exclusively self-interested, because so being would contradict (5). Thus even self-interested people must accept the universal nature of generic rights in order to conform to the principle of non-contradiction, the fundamental principle of reason.[45]

Gewirth's derivation of human rights is particularly apt for theorizing human rights for two reasons. On the one hand, he provides a logically sound argument that does not need to appeal to human emotions such as compassion, care, and charity.[46] On the other, central to the argument is the idea that rights and community are intimately connected. In other words, we are not autonomous, isolated individuals acting out of pure self-interest, but rather we recognize the needs and desires of those in our communities. In my mind this resonates well with the FS framework and can strengthen the theoretical foundations of the right to food.

According to Bay, we need not clearly define any single, definitive type of community, but we must recognize that we do not live in complete isolation: Our identity is defined largely by the relationships we have both with each other and with the natural world. Although the need to be in community may derive from our desire to love and be loved, to have a sense of belonging and so forth, the need to be in community can be established on rational grounds as well. The need for community solidarity can be derived from a Rawlsian-like method. Generally stated, Rawls's original position is a hypothetical situation in which rational beings decide the framework for erecting a just institutional order. Without knowledge of economic status, time in history, gender, ethnicity, age, and so forth, Rawls asks us to determine what we would rationally chose as the most just institutional framework. Following Rawls, Bay concludes that "every rational person would be bound to opt for a social order in which people would see their need for community-solidarity as prior to their need for individual liberty." Why is this the logical conclusion? Bay suggests, rightly, that a social order of unconstrained liberty would result in a "capitalist-type social order, with permanent reward structures for enterprising individuals who choose to be free riders, exploiters, con artists, bullies, and the like."[47] In other words, rational beings deliberating on a just institutional order would not opt for unrestricted individual liberty. It is only after we posit the need for community that we can assert the need for individual liberty.

Local cultures and communities can remain diverse and heterogeneous (i.e., we do not have to assert the superiority of one culture or set of cultural values over another) as long as they do not violate access to basic needs, health, and the ability for others to gather in community. Recognizing the importance of both individual liberty and community-solidarity is central to FS's mission and framework. Although individual liberty is important (in fact it is a basic human need), FS's understanding of our communal nature is radically different from how the human is conceived in our current neoliberal capitalist order, an order that conceives of humans as cold, self-interested individuals eternally bent on conflict.

Global Poverty, Food Sovereignty, and Negative Rights and Duties

With the basis of human rights established, we should add a crucial distinction between two different types of rights. This distinction will also be important for my concluding argument in the fifth section.

For any given claim or demand for a right, we recognize there are three important parties involved: the individual or community making the claim, the right or object of the right demanded (e.g., the right to produce one's food for local consumption), and the respondent or individual, group, or organization (e.g., government, multinational corporation) responsible for protecting or providing the right. Negative rights are usually referred to as rights of noninterference—avoiding doing something that is harmful to an individual or group. An example of a negative right is the right to not have bodily harm inflicted upon us; for example, we have a right to not be tortured by officials of a tyrannical government. Or, we have a right not to be enslaved (which also entails fair remuneration for our labor). Conversely, a positive right is a right in which the claimant makes a demand on a certain individual or organization that requires the individual or organization to actively provide the object of the right. Examples of this might include the rights to education, adequate health care, and food for those who do not have access to these things. In other words, governments or organizations must provide these entitlements (availability of teachers, doctors, food, and so forth) to allow these rights to be realized. With this distinction in mind, the concluding section will respond to our original discussion about our responsibility to the global poor in general and about how a more just global food system can aid this effort.

An Argument for Our Moral Obligation to the Global Poor

Although we clearly live in a world of massive inequality, Thomas Pogge proffers a conceptual basis for establishing the existence and persistence of radical global inequality. According to Pogge, radical inequality exists if the following conditions are true:

1. The worse off are very badly off in absolute terms.
2. They are also very badly off in relative terms—very much worse off than many others.
3. The inequality is impervious: It is difficult or impossible for those worse off to substantially improve their lot, and most of those better off never experience life at the bottom for even a few months and have no vivid idea of what it is like to live that way.
4. The inequality is pervasive: It concerns not merely some aspects of life, such as the climate or access to natural beauty or high culture, but most or all aspects of life.
5. The inequality is avoidable: Those better off can improve the circumstances of those worse off without becoming badly off themselves.

Some argue that although the current state global economic inequality is a matter of concern, the scale of poverty as well as standards of living are much better than they used to be: Compared to 60 years ago, we are drastically reducing the number of people in extreme poverty.[48] Without delving into the debates over the rate of poverty reduction, Pogge persuasively argues that it is not the decrease in the number of people in extreme poverty that should give us cause to celebrate. From a moral standpoint, "the killing of a given number of people does not become morally less troubling the more the world population increases."[49] In other words, the persistence of poverty and, by extension, hunger and malnutrition remains a pressing moral dilemma. Again, the 2.3 billion people living on less than $2 a day, the 1.1 billion people lacking access to safe water, the 2.6 billion lacking access to basic sanitation, the 1 billion lacking adequate shelter, the 1.6 billion lacking electricity, and the 2 billion lacking access to basic sanitation conclusively demonstrates that criteria 1–4 are met.

Rather than asking why we have failed to achieve poverty reduction goals,[50] we might instead focus on the reasons poverty and hunger continue to exist: Are there policies in place that serve to perpetuate and exacerbate the conditions of the global poor?[51] Morally speaking, even if the radical inequality that exists today is considered problematic, many argue that we are not actively harming the poor. We might feel charitable and choose to give assistance in ways we feel fit, but we are not morally obliged to do so. Here the distinction between negative and positive rights and their concomitant duties is crucial. As Pogge comments, "there are two ways of conceiving such poverty as a moral challenge to us: we may be failing to fulfill our *positive* duty to help persons in acute distress; and we may be failing to fulfill our more stringent *negative* duty not to uphold injustice, not to contribute to or profit from the unjust impoverishment of others" (emphasis in original).[52] Again, we might feel we have good cause to help in meager ways, but we certainly do not have a moral obligation to help the global poor, those so distant from us that we have no real familial or communal connection.

However, the crux of Pogge's position is that we have imposed, and continue to impose, harmful policies and institutions on the global poor. Whether in the form of asymmetrical WTO and regional trade arrangements, support for corrupt political regimes, the lack of oversight in protecting harmful environmental and labor practices of transnational corporations (TNCs), and so forth, the affluent countries of the world have erected a global institutional order that thrives on the misery of nearly a third of the global population. In other words, we have created—and perpetuate—a coercive global institutional order that actively harms the poor. As affluent citizens of democratic countries, we have elected officials who are responsible for this institutional order and thus are complicit in what Pogge provocatively calls a massive violation of human rights. We either directly participate in or indirectly benefit from this harming of the global poor and thus are ourselves responsible for the current system. Ethically speaking, we, citizens in affluent countries, have not fulfilled our negative duty not to harm the poor.

In many ways FS advocates have implicitly recognized this. The call for food as a human right is directly connected to the call for eliminating harmful policies and practices that prevent communities—i.e., small-scale farmers, peasants, landless workers, fisherfolks—from exercising their right to self-determination. To use another example related to La Vía Campesina, "[La Vía Campesina] argues for a fundamental shift in who defines and determines the purpose and terms of knowledge, research, technology, science, production, and trade related to food."[53] The call for erecting a global institutional order that provides spaces for self-determination, particularly for those at the center of FS movements, can now be understood as a moral imperative, not simply something we choose whether to participate in.

Conclusion

As a growing movement and evolving concept, FS in its various global manifestations has not only challenged the neoliberal socioeconomic order, but also demonstrated viable alternatives to this system. It has additionally positioned the human right to food as one of its guiding principles. This right, moreover, is directly connected to a particular understanding of food, one that sees it as a cultural commodity that should not be haphazardly traded on a global scale without regard to the humans who produce it. Moreover, the right to food is built on a deep moral commitment that sees the right to self-determination as a necessary feature for living a life of dignity. Unfortunately, for much of the world's poor, this right is violated daily, to the toll of millions of deaths each year. I hope this chapter can contribute to ongoing efforts to clarify areas of conceptual ambiguity within FS's understanding of food, community, and human rights. Although Pogge's provocative suggestion that we, affluent citizens, are actively committing a massive violation of human rights may seem overtly polemical to some, it may compel us to, at the very least, ask how we are failing to fulfill our duties of noninterference. By positioning the argument in terms of our negative duties to the poor, FS is better equipped to respond to detractors who contend that although we may not be making as much progress in fighting world poverty and hunger as we would like, neither are we not morally obligated to do so at all. With specific respect to the global food system and our negative duties, Pogge's analysis directly addresses broad issues such as unfair, asymmetrical trade policies; IMF loan conditionalities; World Bank structural adjustment programs; and the corporate polluting of the environment. Pogge's argument provides a conceptual ground on which FS movements can avoid the ethical conundrums associated with positive rights—namely, from whom (e.g., governments, charities, multilaterals) do the global poor, hungry, and malnourished demand the right to food? In turn, Alan Gewirth's stringent argument for the justification of the existence of human rights firmly establishes the foundations for FS movements to assert the human right to food. Thus established, the core demand by FS movements for the human right to food and—in the context of community—can be posited as an essential condition necessary for living a life of dignity.

Notes

1. I realize that food sovereignty serves as an umbrella concept and movement for many global food and agricultural rights movements, but the argument contained in this paper attempts to assert and justify the human right to food and, by extension, community, culture, and self-definition.

2. Thomas Pogge, *World Poverty and Human Rights*, 2nd ed. (Cambridge: Polity Press, 2008), 2.

3. UNDP (United Nations Development Report), *Human Development Report 1998* (New York: Oxford University Press, 1998), 2.

4. FAO (Food and Agriculture Organization), *The State of Food Insecurity in the World, 2012* (Rome: FAO, 2012), 8. www.fao.org/docrep/016/i3027e/i3027e00.htm

5. Raj Patel, *Stuffed and Starved: The Hidden Battle for the World Food System* (Brooklyn: Melville House Publishing, 2007), 1.

6. Fred Magdoff and Brian Tokar, *Agriculture and Food in Crisis: Conflict, Resistance, and Renewal* (New York: Monthly Review Press, 2010). See especially their overview in chapter 1. See also William Heffernan and Douglas Constance, "Transnational Corporations and the Globalization of Agriculture and Food," in *From Columbus to Con Agra: The Globalization of Agriculture and Food*, eds. Alessandro Bonano et al. (Lawrence: University of Kansas Press, 1994), 29–51.

7. For an analysis that focuses on the concept of responsibility rather than obligation, see Iris Marion Young, "Responsibility and Global Labor Justice," *The Journal of Political Philosophy* 12, no. 4 (2004): 365–388.

8. *World Poverty and Human Rights*, 7.

9. See, for instance, Graham Hancock, *Lords of Poverty: The Power, Prestige, and Corruption of the International Aid Business* (New York: The Atlantic Monthly Press, 1989).

10. See, for instance, Walden Bello, *Dark Victory: The United States and Global Poverty* (Oakland, CA: Food First Books, 1999).

11. See, for instance, Eric Holt-Giménez and Raj Patel, *Food Rebellions! Crisis and the Hunger for Justice* (Cape Town, Dakar, Nairobi, and Oxford: Pambazuka Press, 2009).

12. Alan Gerwirth, *The Community of Rights* (Chicago: University of Chicago Press, 1996), 55. For an ethical response to this argument, see Peter Singer's well-known piece "Famine, Affluence, and Morality," *Philosophy and Public Affairs* 1, no. 3 (spring 1972): 229–243.

13. Garret Hardin, *Life Boat Ethics: The Case against Helping the Poor.* www.garrethardinsociety.org/articles/art_lifeboat_ethics_case_against_helping_poor.html

14. I use *necessarily* because positive rights ethicists must address this issue. I only bring the issue to light here.

15. For a slightly more optimistic analysis of our efforts and associated problems, see Jeffrey Sachs's *The End of Poverty: Economic Possibilities for Our Time* (New York: Penguin Books, 2005).

16. World Bank, "Mission statement." www.worldbank.org/en/about

17. IMF, "Overview." www.imf.org/external/about/overview.htm

18. Monsanto, "Monsanto at a Glance." www.monsanto.com/whoweare/Pages/default. aspx

19. See Michael Windfuhr and Jennie Jonsén, *Food Sovereignty: Towards Democracy in Localized Food Systems* (UK: ITDG Publishing, 2005). For a more detailed description of the evolution of the term, see Wittman, Desmarais, and Wiebe, "The Origins and Potential of Food Sovereignty," and Patel, "What Does Food Sovereignty Look Like?" in *Food Sovereignty: Reconnecting Food, Nature and Community*, eds. Hanna Wittman, Annette Desmarais, and Nettie Wiebe (Halifax & Winnipeg: Fernwood Publishing, 2010). See also William Schanbacher *The Politics of Food: The Global Conflict between Food Security and Food Sovereignty* (Santa Barbara, CA: Praeger, 2010).

20. CESCR (Committee on Economic, Social and Cultural Rights), "General Comment 12: The Right to Adequate Food" (Geneva, Switzerland: 1999). www.unhchr.ch/tbs/doc.nsf/0/3d02758c707031d58025677f003b73b9#Notes

21. World Food Summit (WFS), *Rome Declaration on World Food Security*. www.fao.org/wfs/index_en.htm

22. Michael Windfuhr and Jennie Jonsén, *Food Sovereignty: Towards Democracy in Localized Food Systems*, 22.

23. Ibid., 2–23.

24. Schanbacher, *The Politics of Food*.

25. La Vía Campesina, *The International Peasant's Voice*, http://viacampesina.org/en/index.php/organisation-mainmenu-44/what-is-la-via-campesina-mainmenu-45/1002-the-international-peasants-voice27. See also Annette A. Desmarais, *La Vía Campesina: Globalization and the Power of Peasants* (Halifax, NS: Fernwood Publishing, 2007).

26. Peter Rosset, *Food Is Different: Why We Must Get the WTO Out of Agriculture* (Halifax, NS: Fernwood Publishing, 2006).

27. See, for instance, Peter Rosset, Raj Patel, and Michael Courville, *Promised Land: Competing Visions of Agrarian Reform* (Oakland, CA: Food First Books, 2006).

28. Eric Holt-Giménez, *Campesino a Campesino: Voices from Latin America's Farmer-to-Farmer Movement for Sustainable Agriculture* (Oakland, CA: Food First Books, 2006), 78.

29. Ibid., 89.

30. Ibid., 104.

31. Will Schanbacher, "Conceptualizing the Human Right to Food in the Food Sovereignty Framework." Paper circulated at Food Sovereignty: A Critical Dialogue (Yale, 8/14–8/15/2013). www.yale.edu/agrarianstudies/foodsovereignty/papers.html

32. For a discussion of the difficulty organizing the diversity of FS and food justice organizations, see Eric Holt-Giménez ed., *Food Movements Unite!* (Oakland, CA: Food First Books, 2011) and Michael Windfuhr and Jennie Jonsén, *Food Sovereignty: Towards Democracy in Localized Food Systems*.

33. See, for instance, Jack Donnelly, "Human Rights as Natural Rights," *Human Rights Quarterly* 4, no. 3 (1982).

34. Christian Bay, "Self-Respect as a Human Right: Thoughts on the Dialectics of Wants and Needs in the Struggle for Human Community," *Human Rights Quarterly* 4, no. 1 (1982): 53–75.

35. Thomas Pogge, *World Poverty and Human Rights*.

36. Alan Gerwirth, *The Community of Rights*.

37. Jack Donnelly, *Universal Human Rights in Theory and Practice*, 2nd ed. (Ithaca: Cornell University Press, 2003).

38. Alan Gerwirth, *The Community of Rights*, 13.

39. Ibid., 14.

40. For instance, see Martha Nussbaum, "Capabilities as Fundamental Entitlements: Sen and Social Justice," *Feminist Economics* 9, no. 2 (July 2003); Martha Nussbaum, "Poverty and Human Functioning: Capabilities ad Fundamental Entitlements," in *Poverty and Inequality*, eds. David B. Grusky and Ravi Kanbur (Stanford, CA: Stanford University Press, 2006), 47–75; Amartya Sen, *Inequality Reexamined* (Cambridge, MA: Harvard University Press, 1992); Amartya Sen, *Development as Freedom* (New York: Anchor Books, 1999).

41. Annette A. Desmarais and Hanna Wittman, "Farmers, Foodies, and First Nations: Getting to Food Sovereignty in Canada," presented at Food Sovereignty: A Critical Dialogue (Yale, 8/14–8/15/2013). www.yale.edu/agrarianstudies/foodsovereignty/papers.html

42. Raj Patel, "What Does Food Sovereignty Look Like?" in Hanna Wittman, Annette Desmarais, and Nettie Wiebe eds., *Food Sovereignty: Reconnecting Food, Nature and Community* (Halifax and Winnipeg, Canada: Fernwood Publishing, 2010), 191–193.

43. Alan Gerwirth, *The Community of Rights*, 16.

44. Ibid., 17–19.

45. That people are contradictory presents somewhat of a problem here. However, I think the thrust of the argument is that we strive to be noncontradictory.

46. In my mind, these are obviously virtuous characteristics, but the argument here is directed more toward figures like Hardin who hold a strong position of self-interest. Even the radical egoist must accept the logic of this argument.

47. Bay, "Self-Respect as a Human Right," 60.

48. Laurence Chandy and Geoffrey Gertz, "Poverty in Numbers: The Changing State of Global Poverty from 2005 to 2015" (Washington, DC: The Brookings Institution, January 2011).

49. Thomas Pogge, *World Poverty and Human Rights*, 92.

50. See, for instance, Jeffrey Sachs, *The End of Poverty: Economic Possibilities for Our Time* (New York: Penguin Books, 2005).

51. For just two examples of an extensive literature, see Joseph E. Stiglitz, *Globalization and Its Discontents* (New York: W.W. Norton & Company, 2003), and Frances Moore Lappé, Joseph Collings, and Peter Rosset, *World Hunger: 12 Myths* (Oakland, CA: Food First, 1998).

52. Thomas Pogge, *World Poverty and Human Rights*, 203.

53. Desmarais, *La Vía Campesina*, 37.

3

Agribusiness Concentration: Globalization, Market Power, and Resistance

*Douglas H. Constance, Mary Hendrickson,
and Philip H. Howard*

In this chapter we document agribusiness concentration. By agribusiness we refer to agrifood corporations, most of them publicly traded and many of them with global operations. Notable examples are Tyson Foods, Inc., Cargill, Archer Daniels Midland (ADM), Smithfield Foods, Inc., and Monsanto. To define economic concentration, we borrow institutional economists' definition: The invisible hand of capitalism works up to the point at which the largest four firms control 40 percent of the market, after which an oligopoly or oligopsony has been formed. When the top four firms control 40 percent of supply in a market, an oligopoly is the result; an oligopsony arises when the top four firms control 40 percent of demand in a market. After market concentration passes 40 percent, competition decreases and market power contributes to predatory opportunism. The technical term for market consolidation is horizontal integration: Firms in the same business integrate horizontally to gain economies of scale and market share.

The social scientific concern about business concentration is grounded in the classical conversation between Adam Smith and Karl Marx. Smith's *Theory of Political Economy* argues that the heavy hand of government should be kept off the back of business; business markets should organize society. As long as there are many buyers and many sellers, the invisible hand of the market creates perfect competition, and there is no market power. Marx says that Smith's ideas are great in theory—and even work in practice sometimes—but the inherent need to grow in a capitalistic system will eventually result in competitive markets' giving way to concentrated markets and market power. Thus the state must regulate industries to limit economic concentration and thereby protect subordinate groups such as producers, workers, minorities, and consumers from the negative impacts of market power and predatory opportunism. This conversation continues today in both academia and politics.

This state-versus-market nexus regarding the regulation of capitalism can be analyzed from the "instrumental" versus "relative autonomy" views of the state. In general, the instrumental view sees the state as captured by elites, in particular economic elites. The wealthy use the state as the tool to control the masses, subsidize consumption, and minimize dissent. The relative autonomy position sees the state as having some relative freedom to advance and protect the interests of subordinate groups and support social movement resistance against the negative externalities of unregulated capitalism. The state/market nexus ebbs and flows over the course of time. From the New Deal through the Great Society, the United States had considerable relative autonomy to regulate capitalism and protect citizen groups. In the 1970s, this nexus changed, and the state became more instrumental as it implemented welfare reform. Market-centered approaches to social organization that favored deregulation and privatization replaced state-centered Keynesian approaches.

As part of the globalization of the economy and society based on neoliberal restructuring, agribusiness concentration accelerated during the 1980s and 1990s. Through mergers and acquisitions, some firms such as Tyson Food, Inc., Pilgrim's Pride, and JBS grew rapidly from family companies into transnational corporations (TNCs). Other established corporations such as Cargill and ADM solidified their global reach. During the Reagan administration, the U.S. government loosened antitrust regulations to allow U.S. corporations to expand and compete in global markets. Antitrust deregulation resulted in a wave of mergers and acquisitions and market consolidation in the general society as well as in agribusiness. During the same period, government deregulation reduced support for unions and the social safety net programs.

The processes of horizontal integration and commodity sector consolidation in agribusiness accelerated during the 1980s and 1990s, resulting in a concentrated market structure in the agrifood system wherein a few firms dominated across several commodity sectors both at the national and the global levels. The resulting structure has negative implications for farmers, consumers, and communities across the globe. Agribusiness concentration decreases quality of life for rural peoples as it transfers wealth from rural producers and communities to TNCs and their shareholders. New social movements resist and challenge market concentration through antitrust enforcement initiatives and efforts to create an alternative agrifood system.

We organize this chapter around five questions. The first section asks what the problem is with agribusiness concentration. We review work on the topic of market concentration in agrifood systems, including concentration data for the input, production, processing, and retailers sectors. This includes some commodity-specific information, noting that beyond the pattern of oligopolistic market structure, a global system of cross-commodity corporate integration exists and is dominated by a few firms. This section concludes with a discussion of the recent consolidation of the retailing sector, the driver of the global agrifood system.

The second section asks why agribusiness concentration is a problem for farmers, workers, consumers, and communities. We argue that agribusiness concentration extracts wealth from farmers and workers and their communities and shifts it to corporate actors. Vertical integration rationalizes the commodity chains, often to the detriment of producers, and horizontal integration limits producers access to competitive markets. Moreover, globalization and restructuring shift the balance of power in the agrifood system in favor of agribusiness TNCs, which negatively affects the lives of rural peoples.

In the third section we ask how agribusiness concentration became a problem for so many groups around the world. In this section, we interpret the changing levels of market concentration over time, as well as the specific sociohistorical events that influenced these changes. We apply an agrifood regimes framework and note three general periods of marginality, prosperity, and marginality for agrifood producers. We focus the discussion on the mechanisms of the globalization of the agrifood system as operationalized through the neoliberal restructuring of the economy and society in general and agrifood commodity systems and commodity chains in particular.

In the fourth section we ask what can be done to fix the problem. We discuss (1) farmer social movement resistance efforts to reduce market concentration and (2) alternative agrifood movements designed to create a more just and sustainable alternative to the current system. Farmer movements have resisted and continue to resist the economic power of agribusiness, often by demanding that the government protect them from the power of unregulated capitalism. Alternative agriculture movements work to reembed the agrifood system within community. At the global level, food sovereignty movements such as La Vía Campesina struggle for peasant rights. Alternative agriculture social movements combine issues of food security, environmental justice, economic and social justice, and nutrition. Collectively, these movements are an attempt to transform the agrifood system to one based on social justice rather than one based on corporate profit.

In the fifth section we ask why we haven't fixed the problem of agribusiness concentration and transformed the agrifood system. We discuss trends toward the conventionalization of alternative agriculture and the issue of agrifood governance, in particular the diminished ability of the nation-state to protect subordinate groups from the negative impacts of globalization and neoliberal restructuring. This section documents the political and economic environment of the global agrifood system in general and the commodity systems and commodity chains in particular. We focus on the power of the dominant agrifood TNCs to drive the chains and shape the environment to their advantage.

In the conclusion, we discuss the implications of what we see as disturbing trends related to agribusiness market concentration and their effects on quality of life for rural peoples and their communities.

What Is the Problem? Economic Concentration in Agrifood

William Heffernan and his associates have been researching the impacts of agribusiness concentration on rural quality of life for more than 40 years.[1] This long-term research project is known as the Missouri School of Agrifood Studies.[2] Heffernan's longitudinal research on the poultry industry revealed a progression of vertical and horizontal integration and declining quality of life. The Missouri School developed the CR4 table method to report the market shares of the largest four firms in major commodities (see Table 3.1). The market information is gleaned from trade journals, company annual reports, government documents, financial newspapers, and other sources. We focus on the top four firms in a market, because institutional economists generally agree that when four firms control more than 40 percent of a market, they can apply market power and have opportunities for predatory behavior.[3] The CR4 tables provide a visual summary of the dominant players across agrifood commodities.[4] In response to farmer pressure, the USDA Grain Inspection, Packers, and Stockyards Administration (GIPSA) now provides up-to-date information on CR4 ratios. The USDA percentages combined with the Missouri School names of the corporate actors reveals a pattern of agribusiness concentration within commodities and a pattern of cross-commodity integration.[5] For example, Table 3.1 reveals that Tyson provides a full array of protein—beef, pork, and broilers—while Cargill produces and processes an array of meats, provides feed, and trades and processes corn and soybeans. ADM is also dominant across several processing sectors.

Over 25 years of data reveals clear trends. First, horizontal integration has been a key component of agrifood system restructuring. Table 3.1 indicates that almost all commodity sectors have increased their CR4 ratios between 1990 and 2011, primarily as a result of acquisitions and mergers among dominant players. It also reveals that certain actors dominate across several commodities. For instance, the 1999 data report the top four beef packers as IBP (absorbed in 2001 by Tyson), ConAgra (now JBS, the world's top beef packer and meat company), Cargill (the world's largest agribusiness corporation), and Farmland National Beef Packing Company (a cooperative now dissolved, its packing operations remaining as National Beef)—all while the CR4 moved

only slightly, from 79 to 82 percent. Such horizontal integration and the resulting increase in CR4 mean that farmers have few choices when they sell their
commodities.

Farmers also face concentrated input markets. Global fertilizer companies
such as Yara, Potash Corp, Agrium, and Mosaic dominate the market. Three
cartels control 70 percent of the global trade in potash and potassium.[6] Consolidation in the seed industry after genetically engineered Roundup Ready
seeds entered the market in 1996 has also increased significantly. Up to 70
percent percent of corn seed and 60 percent of soybean seed in the U.S. are
controlled by two firms, DuPont/Pioneer and Monsanto.[7] About 29 percent
of global seed sales were controlled by DuPont/Pioneer, Monsanto, Syngenta,
and Limagrain,[8] with 53 percent of the global proprietary seed market held by
the same four firms (Monsanto 23%; DuPont 15%).[9] Since Monsanto entered
the seed industry in the mid-1980s, it has acquired more than 50 seed firms.
Cross-licensing agreements between Monsanto and the other "Big 6" chemical
and seed companies increase consolidation and barriers to entry.[10]

Vertical integration has also been a key factor in agrifood system restructuring. Food chain "clusters" of dominant corporations across input, production and processing, and manufacturing and distribution operate "seed to
shelf."[11] The clusters organized around Cargill/Monsanto, ADM/Novartis, and
ConAgra operate with minimal competition within the vertically integrated
cluster, but dynamic competition does exist between clusters. These actors
operate on a global scale, making it very difficult to document concentration
levels.[12] Cargill and ADM operate grain trading and processing enterprises
globally and dominate import/export activities at major ports. Similarly,
Tyson Foods, Inc., and Smithfield Foods operate vertically integrated meat
operations around the world.[13]

The retail sector exhibits the same trends toward horizontal integration
and globalization. Notably, Tyson reported that its acquisition of IBP in 2001
was driven by the changing food retail environment. It needed to add beef
and pork to its poultry portfolio to maintain leverage with retailers, especially
Walmart. Walmart entered the grocery business in the late 1980s; by 2000, it
was the second largest grocer in the United States. Walmart's entry prompted
rapid consolidation in the sector. In 1998, Kroger bought Fred Meyer, and
Albertson's bought American Stores, in a bid to compete with Walmart and
other discounters. But by 2006, Albertson's, the second most successful U.S.
grocer, decided to abandon the grocery business altogether.[14]

Table 3.2 presents consolidation in the U.S. grocery industry, rising from a
CR5 of 24 percent in 1997 to a CR4 of about 50 percent in 2011. Walmart has
over three times the sales of its nearest competitor.[15] Walmart uses market power
to lower prices paid to producers, manufacturers, and workers rather than forcing consumers to pay higher prices.[16] This is the classic behavior associated

TABLE 3.1 Concentration Ratio of the Largest Four Firms (CR4): 1990, 1999, 2011

Industry Sector and Representative Firms	CR 4 (2011)	Industry Sector and Representative Firms	CR 4 (1999)	Industry Sector and Representative Firms	CR 4 (1990)
Beef slaughter (Steer and heifer) • Cargill • Tyson • JBS • National Beef	82 percent	Beef slaughter (steer and heifer) • IBP • ConAgra • Excel (Cargill) • Farmland National Beef	79 percent	Beef slaughter (steer and heifer) • IBP • ConAgra • Excel (Cargill) • Beef America	69 percent
Beef production (feedlots) • JBS Five Rivers Cattle Feeding (838,000) • Cactus Feeders (relationship with Tyson) 520,000 • Cargill Cattle Feeders (350,000) • Friona Industries (275,000)	Top four have one-time capacity for 1,983,000 head	Beef production (feedlots) • Continental Grain Cattle Feeding (405,000) • Cactus Feeders Inc. (350,000) • ConAgra Cattle Feeding (320,000) • National Farms Inc. (274,000)	Top four had one-time capacity for 1,349,000 head	Beef production (feedlots) • Cactus Feeders • ConAgra (Monfort) • J.R. Simplot Co. • Caprock (Cargill)	Not reported
Pork slaughter • Smithfield Foods • Tyson Foods • Swift (JBS) • Excel Corp. (Cargill)	63 percent	Pork slaughter • Smithfield • IBP Inc.20 • ConAgra (Swift) 10 • Cargill (Excel)	57 percent	Pork slaughter • IBP • ConAgra (SIPCO/Armour) • Morrell • Excel	45 percent
Pork production • Smithfield Foods (876,804) • Triumph Foods (371,000) • Seaboard (213,600) • Iowa Select Farms (157,500)	Top four have 1,618,904 sows in production	Pork production • Murphy Family Farms (337,000) • Carroll's Foods (183,600) (8%) • Continental Grain/PSF (162,000) • Smithfield Foods (152,000)	Top four had 834,600 sows in production	Pork production • Murphy Farms • Tyson Foods • Cargill • National Farms	Not reported
Broiler slaughter • Tyson • Pilgrim's Pride (owned by JBS) • Perdue • Sanderson	53 percent	Broiler slaughter • Tyson • Gold Kist • Perdue • Pilgrim's Pride	49 percent	Broiler slaughter • Tyson • ConAgra • Gold Kist • Perdue Farms	45 percent

2011 data	1999 data	1990 data
Turkey slaughter — 58 percent • Butterball (Smithfield/Goldsboro) • Jennie-O (Hormel) • Cargill • Farbest Foods	**Turkey slaughter — 42 percent** • Jennie-O (Hormel) • Butterball (ConAgra) • Wampler Turkeys • Cargill	**Turkey slaughter — 31 percent** • Louis Rich (Philip Morris) • Swift (Beatrice/KKR) • ConAgra • Norbest
Animal feed — 44 percent • Land O'Lakes Purina LLC • Cargill Animal Nutrition • ADM Alliance Nutrition • J.D. Heiskell & Co.	**Animal feed — Unknown** • Cargill (Nutrena) • Purina Mills (Koch Industries) • Central Soya • Consolidated Nutrition (ADM/AGP)	
Flour milling — 52 percent • Horizon Milling (Cargill/CHS) • ADM • ConAgra	**Flour milling — 62 percent** • ADM • ConAgra • Cargill Flour Milling	**Flour milling — 61 percent** • ConAgra • ADM • Cargill • Grand Met (Pillsbury)
Wet corn milling — 87 percent • ADM • Corn Products International • Cargill	**Wet corn milling — 74 percent** • ADM • Cargill • A.E. Staley (Tate and Lyle) • CPC	**Wet corn milling — 74 percent** • ADM • Cargill • A.E. Staley (Tate and Lyle) • CPC
Soybean processing — 85 percent • ADM • Bunge • Cargill • Ag Processing	**Soybean processing — 80 percent** • ADM • Cargill • Bunge • Ag Processing	**Soybean processing — 61 percent** • ADM • Cargill • Bunge • Ag. Processors
Grocery — 42–51 percent • Walmart • Kroger • Safeway • Supervalu		

Sources: 2011 data—James, Hendrickson, and Howard (2012); 1999 data—Heffernan, Hendrickson, and Gronski (1999); 1990 data—Heffernan and Constance (1990).

TABLE 3.2   Changes in Food Retail Consolidation in the United States

1997	2000	2011
Kroger Co.	Kroger Co.	Walmart
Safeway	Walmart	Kroger
American Stores	Albertson's	Safeway
Albertson's	Safeway	Supervalu
Ahold USA	Ahold USA	
CR5 = 24% *	CR5 = 42% **	CR4=42–51%

Sources: Hendrickson et al. (2001) for 1997 and 2000 data; James et al. for 2011 data.

with buyer power (oligopsony), as contrasted to seller power (oligopoly), that concerns antitrust regulators interested in protecting consumers.[17] Seller power takes effect in highly concentrated markets, whereas buyer power can be exhibited in relatively unconcentrated markets.[18] Farmers are at the mercy of buyer power of highly concentrated processing firms in grains and livestock, whereas those firms' considerable selling power is no match for the buyer power of a firm like Walmart.[19] Walmart is one of a few global grocers, including Carrefour (the second largest retailer in the world) and Tesco, Britain's largest grocer. Walmart is the second largest grocer in the UK, the largest in Mexico, and the third largest in Brazil, while its competitor Carrefour is the largest food retailer in France, the second largest in Brazil, and the third largest in China.[20]

Why Is It a Problem? Tilting the Wealth Distribution Formula and Monopsony Opportunism

The Missouri School's position is that agribusiness concentration transfers wealth from producers and workers to the corporation and thereby reduces the quality of rural life.[21] Farmers are caught "betwixt and between" concentrated markets made up of powerful input suppliers and processors.[22] Heffernan's original concern centered on the situation contract poultry growers face with their integrators. His research revealed that as horizontal integration progressed, growers' quality of life decreased. Growers had fewer integrating firms in the region, and the quality of their contracts decreased.[23]

Heffernan's research focusing on the power of agribusiness is part of the New Rural Sociology (NSR) framework that emerged in the 1980s. From the 1940s to 1970s, rural sociological investigations employed modernist interpretations of social change that focused on the uncritical adoption and diffusion of new technologies. The systematic depopulation of rural America and the continuous farm crises were interpreted as the work of the invisible hand of the market that resulted in the natural processes of creative destruction.[24] The land grant university, the major technology transfer and agricultural education institution, was crucial to this process.[25]

The NRS framework challenged the conventional wisdom of uncritical technology transfer and socioeconomic progress with a critical framework that reengaged the "agrarian question," which asks: How does capitalism penetrate agriculture, and who benefits from this process?[26] Because agriculture has high fixed costs (land/machinery), long production periods (low profit/turnover rates), and episodic labor usage (planting and harvest), it tends to be unattractive to capital investment owing to its high risk and limited opportunities to generate labor value and extract surplus labor value—the source of profit and wealth.[27] There are detours around these obstacles to capitalist penetration of agriculture in the forms of debt, tenancy, contracting, vertical and horizontal integration, and corporate cooption of farming activities previously carried out on the farm.[28]

One way to extract wealth from rural producers is economic concentration of input, processing, and retail markets. The wealth of rural areas is primarily created through the labor of producers: farmers, ranchers, and farm workers. The farmers and ranchers are the owners of the means of production, and value is generated through their labor applied to the natural resource base. Producers self-exploit through long hours of work and an irrational desire to farm and ranch in the face of falling profits and declining equity.[29] This tendency for self-exploitation is capitalized upon by agribusiness corporations who extract the surplus labor value through opportunistic behavior, behavior that is enhanced by market concentration. Farmers are caught between these powerful agribusiness corporations.[30]

The wealth generated by the producers through labor value is then distributed among the actors that participate in the commodity system and commodity chain. Commodity systems and commodity chain analyses focus on the different aspects of production of particular products.[31] Commodity systems analysis includes the commodity chain focus on the power of the multiple actors directly along the chain but also incorporates the network of actors less directly linked to the production system, such as NGOs, state regulatory agencies, labor organizations, science institutions, and social movements. Commodity system analysis fits well with network analysis as a way to measure how the chains and systems are constructed and maintained through a network of power-laden interactions.[32]

How the wealth generated by labor value is apportioned among the actors in the commodity system influences the class structure in rural areas. The type of commodity chain influences the distribution of wealth in the system and along the chain. For example, grain producers have to compete as lowest-cost producers in global commodity chains dominated by powerful agribusiness TNCs, which have abundant spaces for opportunism. Conversely, fair trade is a value-chain initiative designed to eliminate the corporate middlemen and redistribute wealth to producers.[33] With the advance of globalization, the commodity systems are increasingly governed and driven by corporate actors. A result has been a tilting of the wealth distribution formulae away from producers and toward the corporate actors. As retailers consolidate their dominant position and further rationalize their upstream supply chains, they drive the chain through standard-setting to the exclusion of minor actors.[34]

Agrifood restructuring which transfers wealth out of rural areas negatively affects the quality of rural life. A middle-class structure of agriculture supports a higher quality of life for producers and their communities.[35] Independent family farms that provide the management, capital, and labor for their operations make the best citizens. The middle-class structure creates a higher community quality of life than the industrial structure. The negative effects of the industrialization of agriculture include greater income inequality or poverty, decreased retail trade and diversity of retail firms, population declines, and negative health effects of large livestock operations.[36] An agrifood system based on multiple horizontal linkages with better multiplier effects is replaced with a system of vertical linkages organized as global commodity chains that sends profits out of the community and into the global agrifood system.

The two main mechanisms that confer power to agribusiness TNCs at the expense of producers are horizontal and vertical integration.[37] Horizontal integration leads to market concentration within a commodity sector through mergers and acquisitions. Using the example of hogs, horizontal integration results in fewer firms buying hogs from producers. Fewer buyers put the producers at a market disadvantage relative to processors, increasing the likelihood that the pork packers will engage in predatory behavior (see Table 3.1).[38]

For grain farmers, this trend is especially problematic in the seed sector, which is dominated by just a few firms. Their dependency on proprietary seeds and the required specialized inputs puts them in an asymmetrical power relationship.[39] Both processes result in constrained choices for producers in the face of market power.[40] Our research shows market manipulations in beef and soybeans in the United States and milk in England.[41] The case of market manipulation by ADM and the lysine cartel provides details on the processes of collusion and market manipulation.[42]

The trend toward fewer and larger input and output corporations is matched by the trend toward larger production units linked to these firms as part of global commodity chains. The treadmill of production forces farms to adopt new technologies, increase size, and achieve economies of scale to survive the process of farm consolidation. Nonadopters (farmers who do not adopt the new technology) go out of business and get absorbed by the adopters. Larger production units result in fewer middle-class farm units on the land, exacerbate rural depopulation, and decrease diversified wealth generation. Consolidation at the production level results in fewer family farms overall and a structure of agriculture such that a small percentage of large farms produce most of the agricultural commodities and a large percentage of small farms produce a small percentage. The surviving farms buy their neighbors' operations to expand economies of scale to survive in precarious global commodity chains dominated by agribusiness. The surviving large-scale commodity producers compete precariously as least-cost inputs to global commodity chains driven by agribusiness TNCs, which are motivated by the maximization of quarterly short-term profits. Smaller-scale producers are relegated to marginal direct markets in alternative foods.[43]

Our research on the poultry industry provides a useful example of how vertical integration and horizontal integration combine to decrease the quality of rural life.[44] The modern broiler industry began in the Delmarva region of the U.S. Northeast in the 1930s and 1940s as a system of independent businesses that supplied urban markets. This form of the broiler industry had a positive influence on the quality of rural life. Early adopters benefited, and rural wealth was enhanced. By the 1960s this independent system of poultry production had been replaced by vertical integration in the U.S. South, which was based on nonunion processing labor and contract growers. Science supported by industry and land grant universities rationalized poultry production so that large numbers of animals could be grown indoors. By the 1960s, agri-industrial districts across the U.S. South dominated poultry production.[45]

Contract poultry growers perform the sharecropper function for integrators in the vertically integrated commodity system. The grower provides land, labor, and utilities; the integrator (the poultry corporation that coordinates the supply chain) provides feed, veterinary services, and chickens. Growers incur long-term debt when they mortgage their land to build single-purpose buildings to the specifications of the integrator, but the production contracts with integrators are short-term. The grower raises the chickens for the integrator and gets paid a piece rate based on his or her efficiency. This system has been criticized as a transitional status between independent farmer and farm worker whereby the producer loses autonomy over management decisions and steadily becomes a pieceworker for the poultry corporation. It has been referred to as "serfs on the land,"[46] "propertied laborers,"[47] and "debt slavery."[48] Integrators can exert control of the production processes without the responsibility and liability associated with formal labor relations and land ownership.[49] Neighbors to the poultry complexes report reduced quality of life.[50]

Contract poultry growers recently testified at the USDA/USDOJ hearings on economic concentration in agriculture that the integrators keep them in perpetual debt with constant upgrades and threaten them with contract termination if they complain or don't cooperate. Growers charged that the integrators were exercising predatory monopsony power. The burden of the single-purpose growout barns detrimentally affects the growers' negotiating power. As a result the grower gets held up by the integrator via coerced compliance with upgrades and less lucrative, more tenuous contracts. Through a system of efficiency ranking referred to as "the tournament," growers are threatened with contract termination.[51]

Poultry growers called on the government to protect them from monopsony opportunism that produced a declining quality of life in poultry production regions experiencing horizontal integration. For poultry growers, agribusiness concentration changed the poultry commodity system from one in which they made a good living to one in which they were exploited by monopsony opportunism. By the 1980s contract production was the norm, and into the 1980s poultry production contributed positively to household incomes.[52] But starting in the late 1980s, contracts favored growers less and integrators more. Vertical integration burdens growers with long-term debt and short-term contracts with agribusiness. This burden was exacerbated by horizontal integration among poultry integrators, as the CR4 for broilers remained flat at about 18 percent from the 1960s until the mid-1970s and eventually increased to 53 percent in 2011 (see Table 3.1).[53] This model is being exported around the world as the preferred model of agribusiness, one based on flexible accumulation: flexibility in the production contract and the nonunion processing labor.[54]

Both horizontal and vertical integration create dependencies that facilitate predatory behavior through asymmetrical power relationships. Poultry growers are dependent on the integrators, livestock growers are dependent on a few packing companies, and grain growers are dependent on a few millers and seed/input suppliers.[55] Our research on the pork industry reveals similar pattern.[56]

Agrifood firms are becoming larger and fewer in number in the United States and around the world. This consolidation and concentration has happened at the same time that rural populations across the United States and the globe have rapidly declined. Remaining farmers have fewer choices about where to buy their inputs or market their products. The increase in retailer concentration allows those firms to apply market power upstream through the system and thereby force restructuring at the worker and farmer levels, all the while decreasing choice of where consumers shop for food. These oligopolies and oligopsonies exercise their market power through predatory opportunism to the detriment of producers and consumers.

Globalization accelerates this process as dominant firms diffuse their business model to capture global market share.[57] Tyson's and JBS's global activities are evidence of this process. Today Tyson Foods, Inc., and JBS are the two largest meat companies in the world: JBS had over $40 billion in sales in 2011 and 125,000 employees worldwide, Tyson $33.3 billion in sales and 115,000 workers. Following a pattern of horizontal integration through mergers and acquisitions, JBS, which is based in Brazil, is expanding rapidly in the United States, Asia, and Europe as Tyson continues its expansion in South America and Asia. JBS controls 25 percent of the worldwide trade in beef.[58]

How Did It Get to Be a Problem? The Ebb and Flow of Market Concentration

Economic concentration in agricultural markets is not a new phenomenon. In this section we employ an agrifood regimes perspective to analyze the ebb and flow of economic concentration over recent history. Agrifood regimes frameworks organize history into stable periods of capital accumulation and social legitimization, which are divided by crisis and transition phased in between stable periods.[59] Symbiotic arrangements between institutional actors (laborers/producers, state, and market) create a stable regime that eventually decays into crisis, and a new regime emerges out of the contest between the major actors who shape and implement the new regime. Friedmann (2005) uses the metaphor of a pendulum swinging back and forth, representing broad historical periods of market regulation, state regulation, and market regulation again.[60]

The Frontier Regime emerged after the U.S. Civil War as industrialization and the wage relation spread across the United States. This First Regime was dominated by Great Britain, which combined tropical imports (fruits and sugar) with wheat and livestock from the settler states to provide low-cost foods for the European working class. The U.S. government supported capitalist development and agricultural modernization through the creation of the USDA and the land grant university system, the Homestead Act, and the subsidization of the railroads. An instrumental state combined with a laissez-faire approach to political economic relations supported the growth of large national corporations and trusts. By the late 1800s the robber barons of banking, railroads, milling, and meatpacking dominated their respective market sectors, to the detriment and marginalization of producers. Unions were not yet legal, and Henry Ford was warning other industrialists that capitalism was not sustainable if the workers were not paid enough money to buy the products they made. Social activism from farmer organizations led to national antitrust legislation, including the Packers and Stockyards Act and the Capper–Volstead Act, which protected producers from market power and provided them with countervailing power. The crisis of overproduction and underconsumption produced the stock market crash of 1929 and proved Ford correct. The global depression of the 1930s, combined with decolonization in Asia and Africa and the advent of World War II, eroded the stability of this regime.[61]

The Second Regime, known as the Fordist Regime, began during the New Deal and ended with the Great Society. Taylorism was applied to the labor process, and Keynesian policies balanced consumption with production. The diffusion of innovations modernized agriculture. In agrifood, the Second Regime emerged as the United States emphasized commodity programs and agricultural surpluses over rural development and exempted agriculture from the General Agreement on Tariffs and Trade (GATT). In this Second Food Regime, farmers prospered as the United States employed its food surplus generated by the New Deal commodity programs as a green weapon in strategic postcolonial efforts to combat the spread of communism. The Bretton Woods Agreement managed global development through the creation of GATT, the IMF, and the World Bank and by linking foreign currency exchanges to the U.S. dollar, at that time based on the gold standard. Food aid laws such as PL480 subsidized wages in support of industrialization in developing countries and created nascent global supply chains organized by U.S. multinational corporations. These processes further diffused the U.S. diet based on feed grains and animal protein and expanded markets for U.S. agricultural products as part of McMichael's Development Project.[62] As a result, many of the formerly colonized countries were transformed from food–self-sufficient to importing countries. At the domestic level, commodity support programs put a safety net under U.S. producers. The USDOJ and FTC regulated market power. Informed by a Keynesian economic perspective, the Great Compromise between big government, labor, and business matched mass consumption to mass production and facilitated a period of sustained prosperity in the United States. From the New Deal to the Great Society, the U.S. government exercised its relative autonomy to intervene in the political economy to protect subordinate groups from the negative effects of unregulated capitalism.[63]

Beginning the 1960s, the Fordist Regime began to unravel. Factors such as the demise of the Bretton Woods Agreement, the delinking of the U.S. dollar from the gold standard, the European Union's export subsidy system, OPEC and petrodollars in global banks, and emerging economies such as Brazil, China, and India, which challenged the legitimacy of the United States' agricultural exemptions, hastened the decline of U.S. hegemony internationally. The costs of the Cold War and the Great Society created a fiscal crisis for the U.S. government. At the same time, very high labor costs and strict business regulations limited capital accumulation for U.S. corporations. The environmental, antiwar, and civil rights movements also questioned the legitimacy of the regime. The Great Compromise was abandoned by capital and government when the Reagan administration did not support the federal air traffic controller strike. A surge of antiunion activities followed in the private sector, notably in the meatpacking industry. Similarly, antitrust regulations were loosened to allow U.S. corporations to compete with corporations from Europe and Japan, resulting in a surge in mergers and acquisitions. Just as Secretary of Agriculture Earl Butz was encouraging U.S. farmers to leverage and borrow to plow fence row to fence row to feed the world, the global petrodollars that had fueled the growth in U.S. exports dried up. When the U.S. Federal Reserve Board switched from a Keynesian to a monetarist fiscal policy and raised interest rates, the resulting farm/debt crisis squeezed billions of dollars and thousands of farms out of rural America. The era of prosperity was over, as was the era in which the state protected subordinate groups from the power of unregulated capitalism.[64]

Although there is debate regarding the characteristics of a Third Regime,[65] regimes theorists generally agree that during this transition phase flexible forms of accumulation are replacing the rigid forms associated with the Great Compromise and Fordism. The nation-state is reorienting its primary function away from social-democratic agendas toward global creditworthiness through deregulation and privatization.[66] McMichael describes the Globalization Project as an organized attack on the successes of the social-democratic movements. Neoliberalism provides the ideological underpinnings of these socioeconomic changes as TNCs drive the process of neoliberal restructuring that has transformed agrifood supply chains in favor of capital over subordinate groups.[67] This flexible accumulation system is diffused as new territories in the global south are integrated into the supply chains that service the global north. Agribusiness TNCs implement global agrifood integration in combination with governance provided by supranational statelike entities (IMF, EU, NAFTA, WTO). Forms of market-driven governance replace government as the regulator mechanism.[68] Producers linked to these global commodity chains driven by the retailers compete with each other as price takers in concentrated markets.

In 1991 we first documented the emergence of the global poultry agrofood complex.[69] Our recent research in Mexico shows how with the help of neoliberal policies implemented by the Mexican government post-NAFTA, Tyson and Pilgrim's Pride expanded their market position and are now second and third largest in Mexico, respectively, with a CR3 of over 60 percent.[70] NAFTA eliminated corn tariffs to the detriment of Mexican *campesinos* but the benefit of poultry integrators, who now had unlimited access to subsidized feed from the United States. Tyson now has the largest share of the value-added poultry market in Mexico and is the third largest poultry company overall. It followed its customers, such as McDonald's and Walmart, south in the post-NAFTA expansion. Tyson is expanding aggressively into Brazil, China, and India with joint ventures and acquisitions of major national firms. Pilgrim's Pride (now owned by JBS of Brazil) is JBS's major expansion into the North American poultry market and is the second largest in Mexico. In Asia, Tyson is in competition with Charoen Pokphand (CP), the dominant agribusiness TNC in the region.[71] CP is coordinating some cross-border regional poultry agrifood complexes in southeast Asia. JBS and Tyson are the dominant red meat firms in the United States as well as abroad. Following an aggressive pattern of acquisitions of poultry competitors through the 1980s and 1990s, Tyson's acquisition of IBP in 2001 made it the largest poultry, beef, and pork processor in the world. It has expanded aggressively in Brazil, where it produces for export to Europe. JBS followed a similar pattern with acquisitions of major brands and processing capacity (Armour and Swift) in the United States, Australia, and South America, and Pilgrim's Pride did the same with poultry in the United States and Mexico. Adopting Tyson's model, it became the largest in the world.

The innovation of the modern poultry model that developed in the U.S. South and that was based on contracting (as a remnant of sharecropping) and grounded in flexible accumulation relations of production is being diffused and adopted globally. The integrators exercise monopsony opportunism and extract wealth from rural areas. The flexible aspect of contract forms of agrifood production makes it very attractive to agribusiness TNCs and a central characteristic of flexible accumulation and globalization.[72]

How Can We Fix the Problem? Social Movement Resistance and Alternative Agrifood Systems

The exercise of economic power associated with agribusiness concentration and the restructuring of the agrifood system has not gone unchallenged. At the national level, farmer social movement resistance emerged in the late 19th century in response to the economic power of the grain and railroad trusts. It is expressed today by those who continue to advocate for a fair and open marketplace, and it culminated recently in a series of hearings on antitrust in agriculture held in 2010 by the USDA and USDOJ. At the international level, the global social movement La Vía Campesina pursues a food sovereignty agenda to counter the food security framework dominated by the agrifood TNCs and the WTO.[73] These movements have had some success in shaping international development discussions, and institutions such as the International Assessment of Agricultural Science and Technology for Development (IAASTD) have also become integrated into discussions with the United Nations Special Rapporteur on the Right to Food.[74]

Populist discontent with economic power emerged in the late 1800s. Laissez-faire capitalism had created concentrated markets in the banking, steel, railroads, meatpacking, grain millers, and other commodity sectors. Farmers and workers organized to resist what they perceived as unfair business practices. The agrarian movement charged the trusts with predatory business practices. The cooperative movement emerged as an attempt at countervailing market power. The populists were successful at securing antitrust legislation that created the Packers and Stockyards Administration (1921) and the Federal Grain Inspection Service (1916), both of which protected farmers from market power. The Capper–Volstead Act of 1922 granted farmers the right to organize in cooperatives exempt from antitrust laws. These and later New Deal policies provided government support for farmers. Land grant universities supported the modernization and mechanization of U.S. agriculture, and U.S. hegemony after World War II opened global export markets.

As market concentration and globalization accelerated, and as government protections contracted in the 1980s, farmer social movement activity reemerged. The farm/debt crisis of the 1980s demonstrated clearly the link between rural prosperity in the United States and harmful neoliberal economic policies at the national and global levels.[75] Producer organizations such as the National Farmers Union again called for the government to protect ranchers and farmers from corporate power. The recent USDA–USDOJ antitrust hearings provide a good example of this form of resistance. The 2002 Farm Bill contained a livestock competition title that was implemented in the 2008 Farm Bill, resulting in hearings on concentration in agriculture. Recall from Table 3.1 that the CR4 for beef packing is 82 percent and has increased to 63 percent in pork packing. In 2010 the Agricultural Competition Joint task force of the USDOJ and USDA conducted workshops on agrifood competition. At these hearings, farmers and ranchers provided testimony regarding their disadvantaged position vis-à-vis corporations in the U.S. agrifood system, and they were joined by consumers and environmentalists worried about the detrimental effects of concentrated agrifood systems.[76]

At the global level, La Vía Campesina challenges the Globalization Project.[77] It is at the center of the food sovereignty movement in the developing world, where it represents peasants and agricultural workers in their struggle against the negative impacts of corporate privilege. La Vía Campesina advances a counterposition to the food security viewpoint of dominant globalization actors such as the agribusiness TNCs, the IMF, and the WTO (see Desmarais, this volume).

Other significant forms of resistance to the dominant agrifood system include organics, fair trade, community supported agriculture (CSA), farmers markets, farm-to-institution, country of origin labeling, animal welfare, food-sheds, local/regional food systems, community gardens, slow food, and food policy councils.[78] Of these movements, the organics movement has proved to be a special example. The organic food movement emerged as a philosophical, economic, and agroecological counterpoint to the conventional system.[79] In the United States it began as a diversified system of producers linked to progressive restaurants and markets. These producers avoided participation in concentrated commodity markets and instead participated in direct markets, where they were rewarded for quality over quantity. The approach has been remarkably successful, with organic sales showing significant growth over the past 20 years (see Gershuny, this volume).[80]

To put these events in the context of our preceding discussion of the commodity chains conceptual frame, early organic producers were participating in a value chain instead of a commodity chain. Global commodity chains tend to be long chains dealing in undifferentiated commodities based on global sourcing, driven increasingly by dominant retailers. McMichael calls this "Food from Nowhere" as opposed to "Food from Somewhere."[81] Global commodity chains are problematic for rural prosperity, because agribusiness TNCs often externalize the social, economic, and ecological costs to the detriment of rural peoples. Alternative agrifood value chains often retain more value for the producer through a value premium attached to quality production, which contributes to an enhanced quality of rural life.

Fair trade is another example of alternative agriculture. Fair trade value chains can be local, regional, or global but originated globally as a way to link producers in the global south more directly to consumers in the global north.[82] Fair trade chains are built on a cooperative philosophy whereby the middle-man functions, normally dominated by corporations, are reduced or eliminated. In their ideal form, fair trade value chains promote transparency of economic activities for all actors along the value chain by advocating for "open books" and a "value in = profit out" model. With its focus on fair value and wealth redistribution fair trade provides a strong ethical dimension to agrifood chains. Local value chains tend to focus on direct sales, which are based on trust and are smaller in scale. Some chains might be certified organic and others noncertified organic, and the chains are often embedded in community. These types of value chains, referred to as Civic Agriculture, are more likely to support the ecological, economic, and social dimensions of sustainability.[83] As examples of Civic Agriculture, CSAs, farmers markets, and farm-to-institution can be seen as embryonic forms of democratic food that reembed the ethics of the cooperation between producers and consumers.

Agriculture of the Middle works to develop strategic partners and relationships in creating value-based value chains for those agriculture operations that are too large for direct sales and too small to compete in global commodity markets.[84] In this value chain, partnerships between producers, processors, distributors, and retailers emerge in a way that distributes risks and benefits along the chain. Any part of the chain may also be organized in a cooperative manner. By repopulating rural areas with moderate-sized operations, these chains could be a mechanism to support sustainable rural development.

The alternative agrifood systems are more likely to create horizontal linkages that retain money and build social capital in the community.[85] This system is more likely to be based on participatory research methods and holistic conceptual frameworks. An optimal structure for the agrifood system would include three dimensions: (1) the transparency in the wealth creation formula of fair trade, (2) a regional spatial form from Agriculture of the Middle, and (3) organizational support from a food policy council. Regional agrifood systems have more opportunities to support substantive rather than instrumental relationships among actors in the agrifood system.

Why Haven't We Fixed the Problem? Powerful Actors and Fragmented Resistance

We borrow from two perspectives to answer this question. First, we employ a complex organizations perspective to highlight the ability of agribusiness TNCs to pursue their agendas.[86] Second, we apply a social movement perspective based on logics of collective action to engage this question.[87] For Perrow, large organizations use their substantial power to shape their environments and solidify their market advantage. The primary mechanism for manipulating their environments is by influencing the nation-state and its regulatory regimes. The dominant actors in the agrifood system are agribusiness TNCs and their financial backers and political backers in government and industry. These actors defend the status quo of conventional agriculture and continue to consolidate their dominant positions both nationally and globally. Olson's work reminds us that the relatively monolithic interests of capital are much easier to organize than the varied oppositional/alternative organizations. We employ the examples of GIPSA and some alternative agriculture initiatives to support our position.

A key dimension of the discourse on the globalization of the agrifood system is the changing role of nation-state.[88] Nation-states still perform essential functions in balancing class interests internally, but must be creditworthy globally to attract investment. At the same time, some of the national coordination functions regarding economic policies are administered by supranational states such as the NAFTA and the WTO. Conceptually, we moved from the Fordist era, in which the nation-state exhibited relative autonomy and intervened in favor of subordinate groups, to post-Fordism, in which the instrumental nation-state implements the imperatives of the Globalization Project based on neoliberal restructuring and flexible forms of capital accumulation. In the United States this was manifest in post-Reagan policies of privatization, deregulation, and the decline of social safety programs for citizens and farmers. As monetarism replaced Keynesianism as the guiding political economic philosophy, neoliberal restructuring reoriented the nation-states' functions toward the financial and away from the social. Neoliberal economic policies empower corporate actors by eliminating competition and minimizing the effectiveness of the state. Neoliberal restructuring constrains the nation-state's ability to protect rural producers and their communities. Accumulation strategies of global agribusiness TNCs create an increase in legitimization crises and social movement resistance. But, as part of the neoliberal restructuring, the nation-state increasingly represents the interests of capital accumulation in global commodity chains rather than social legitimization.

Social movements attempt to increase enforcement of antitrust in agriculture and food have had limited success. No new enforcement policies have emerged from the USDA/USDOJ hearings in 2010. The proposed GIPSA rules have largely been a failure. In fact, many of the government officials responsible for the hearings have left their posts at both the USDA and USDOJ. Congress defunded any effective GIPSA rules or rule enforcement by the executive branch. Powerful agrifood lobbying groups were able to split farmers into those who are doing relatively well (especially those with ties to agribusiness firms) and those who are struggling, such as young farmers and small-scale farm operations. For example, beef farmers were split from contract poultry producers. The GIPSA process reveals that although farmer social movement action was able to force a state response regarding agribusiness concentration, the vested interest of powerful commodity groups prevented the government from protecting the vulnerable farmers.

A critical perspective of power and resistance in agrifood studies would place this discussion within the political economy of state/market relations. Agrifood TNCs' accumulation strategies create legitimization crises that generate social movement resistance, which is managed by the state.[89] Research from Texas on poultry and hogs provides another example of this phenomenon. Accumulation strategies of agribusiness TNCs in support of poultry and hog CAFOs fomented a legitimization crisis and the emergence of local social movement resistance. Hog industry experts warned state regulators that because of the lawsuits and tightened regulations, global hog integrators were expanding outside Texas and the United States. It was at this time that the public hearing process was eliminated, the CAFO permitting process was streamlined, and corporate agriculture was expanded. Or, as Governor Rick Perry announced, Texas was "open for business." These results point to a more general concern regarding the loss of substantive forms of democracy as the agrifood system continues to industrialize and globalize.[90] While social movement groups had some initial success at stalling the CAFO development, the corporate farming interests regrouped and were successful at streamlining the permit process by eliminating the public hearing for CAFOs. The loss of economic democracy for producers related to market concentration was accompanied by the loss of political democracy for opponents to corporate agriculture.

Organics is another good example of why it is hard to fix the problem of economic concentration. Though organics began as a local system based on direct sales and an anti-industrial philosophy, as demand outstripped supply, countries and companies all over the world mobilized to service the growing market and capture the green premium. National standards rationalized organic production, and major corporations increased their market share.[91] As a result, organics is increasingly taking on aspects of the dominant food system, a process described as conventionalization. If these trends proceed—and not all researchers agree that they will—then the majority of the organic foods sold in supermarkets will be sourced through global commodity chains dominated by the same agrifood TNCs as the conventional system.[92] Organics is therefore a good example of Friedmann's Corporate-Environmental Food Regime in which agribusiness TNCs mobilize to service the nascent green food economy. This corporate takeover has forced more movement-oriented actors to start over and create new alternative ecolabels that address values no longer embodied in organic (see also Gershuny, this volume).[93]

Fair trade is another example of an alternative agrifood system being coopted by agribusiness TNCs.[94] In recent years the market success of this ecolabel has attracted corporations like Nestle, J.M. Smucker, and Starbucks, albeit at token levels of participation. Nestle, for example, is the largest coffee company in the world, with sales of more than 1.7 billion pounds in 2008—but of this only 4.4 million pounds (or .0025%) was fair trade certified. Nestle strategically uses the fair trade seal in its marketing to burnish its image, a practice that some critics dub "fair-washing."[95] In addition, the appeal of increasing revenues through the participation of agribusiness TNCs has led the major U.S. fair trade certifier, Fair Trade USA, to weaken the standards in ways that appeal to these firms.[96] Most recently this includes certifying coffee and cocoa from plantations, something not allowed by the international certifying body. This has led more movement-oriented actors, such as 100 percent fair trade firms, to align with alternative certifications (e.g., "Fair for Life"), thus bifurcating the fair trade system.[97]

Together, these initiatives seek to create alternative economic relationships in agriculture and food.[98] But as they "scale up" to make healthy food available to more people, they are also conventionalized. As sustainable producers sell in "less direct" markets, they deal with food buyers in the existing system of commodity chains. And consumers often will not or cannot pay the prices that would ensure equitable distribution through the value chain.[99]

Conclusions

Agrifood concentration is a problem for rural areas. Globalization and market power allows corporations to shape the wealth distribution formulae of the commodity chain to their advantage. Because producers operate in asymmetrical power relationships with these agribusiness TNCS, increased wealth is extracted and quality of life declines. The emergent Third Agrifood Regime, based on neoliberal restructuring and flexible accumulation, has accelerated the process of horizontal integration and market consolidation. Social movement resistance challenges the Globalization Project as it spreads across the globe, but successes are difficult: Nation-states tend to favor fiscal over social demands, and conventionalization moderates the transformative dimensions of alternative agriculture movements.

Agribusiness TNCs such as Tyson, JBS, Cargill, and ADM, among others, control production and processing, and Walmart dominates the retail sector and drives the commodity chains. The poultry model based on vertical integration and flexible labor relations is being diffused around the world. The case of Mexico illustrates the process of nation-state neoliberal restructuring in support of diffusion of innovation. As Walmart drives the global commodity chains toward more efficiency, producers will increasingly perform the function of lowest-cost producers competing on a global scale.

The conversation between Marx and Smith continues. Neoliberal restructuring and concentrated markets signals the ascension of Smithian over Marxian perspectives. The global economy now transcends the sphere of influence of the nation-state, making it very problematic for the state to mediate class conflicts. Farmers and agricultural laborers are marginalized in the process and occupy precarious spaces in the global agrifood system.

Notes

1. William D. Heffernan, "Sociological Dimensions of Agricultural Structures in the United States," *Sociologia Ruralis* 12 (1972): 481–499.

2. See Anna M. Kleiner and John J. Green, "The Contributions of Dr. William Heffernan and the Missouri School of Agrifood Studies," *Southern Rural Sociology* 24, no. 2 (2009): 14–28.

3. Harold F. Breimyer, *Individual Freedom and the Economic Organization of Agriculture* (Urbana: University of Illinois Press, 1965); John Connor, John, Richard Rogers, Bruce Marion, and Willard Mueller, *The Food Manufacturing Industries: Structure, Strategies, Performance and Policies* (Lanham, MD: Lexington Books, 1965); Mary K. Hendrickson and Harvey S. James, "The Ethics of Constrained Choice: How Industrialization of Agriculture Impacts Farming and Farmer Behavior," *Journal of Agricultural and Environmental Ethics* 18, no. 3 (2005): 269–291; Bruce W. Marion, *The Organization and Performance of the U.S. Food System* (Lanham, MD: Lexington Books, 1986).

4. Harvey S. James, Mary K. Hendrickson, and Philip H. Howard, "Networks, Power, and Dependency in the Agrifood Industry," in *The Ethics and Economics of Agrifood Competition*, ed. H. James (New York: Springer Press, 2013).

5. William D. Heffernan and Douglas H. Constance, "Transnational Corporations and the Globalization of the Food System," in *From Columbus to ConAgra: The Globalization of Agriculture and Food*, eds. A. Bonanno, L. Busch, W. H. Friedland, L. Gouveia, and E. Mingione (Lawrence: University Press of Kansas, 1994).

6. Javier Blas, "End Looms for Fertiliser Cartels," *Financial Times*, August 19, 2010; Lauren Etter, "Lofty Prices for Fertilizer Put Farmers in a Squeeze," *Wall Street Journal*, May 27, 2008, A1; Robert C. Taylor, "Fertilizer Cartels: Market Power and Sustainability Issues," presentation at the annual meeting of the Organization for Competitive Markets (Omaha, NE, August 2010).

7. Andrew Pollack, "Monsanto's Fortunes Turn Sour," *New York Times*, October 5, 2010, Business Section.

8. UNCTAD, *Tracking the Trend towards Market Concentration: The Case of the Agricultural Input Industry* (Geneva: United Nations Conference on Trade and Development, 2006). http://unctad.org/en/docs/ditccom200516_en.pdf.

9. ETC Group, *Who Owns Nature? Corporate Power and the Final Frontier in the Commodification of Life* (ETC Group, 2008), www.etcgroup.org/content/who-owns-nature; UNCTAD, *Tracking the Trend towards Market Concentration: The Case of the Agricultural Input Industry*.

10. Philip H. Howard, "Visualizing Consolidation in the Global Seed Industry: 1996–2008," *Sustainability* 1, no. 4 (2009): 1266–1287.

11. William D. Heffernan, Mary K. Hendrickson, and Robert Gronski, "Consolidation in the Food and Agriculture System," report to the National Farmers Union, January 8, 1999. www.foodcircles.missouri.edu/whstudy.pdf

12. Mary K. Hendrickson, John Wilkinson, William D. Heffernan, and Robert Gronski, *The Global Food System and Nodes of Power*, prepared for Oxfam America, August 2008. http://papers.ssrn.com/sol3/papers.cfm?abstract_id=1337273

13. Douglas H. Constance, "Contested Globalization of the Agrifood System: A Missouri School Analysis of Sanderson Farms and Seaboard Farms in Texas," *Southern Rural Sociology* 24, no. 2 (2009): 48–86.

14. Mary K. Hendrickson, William D. Heffernan, Philip Howard, and Judith Heffernan, "Consolidation in Food Retailing and Dairy," *British Food Journal* 103, no. 10 (2001): 715–728.

15. Stephanie Clifford, "Groceries Fill Aisles at Stores Like CVS," *New York Times*, January 16, 2011.

16. Barry C. Lynn, *Cornered: The Monopoly Capitalism and the Politics of Destruction* (Hoboken, NJ: John Wiley and Sons, 2009).

17. Peter C. Carstensen, "Buyer Power, Competition Policy, and Antitrust: The Competitive Effects of Discrimination Among Suppliers," *Antitrust Bulletin* 53, no. 20 (2008): 271–331; Zhiqi Chen, "Defining Buyer Power," *Antitrust Bulletin* 53, no. 2 (2008): 241–249.

18. Albert A. Foer, "Agriculture and Antitrust Enforcement Issues in Our 21st-Century Economy" (Washington, DC: U.S. Department of Agriculture and Department of Justice, 2010), 219–252. www.justice.gov/atr/public/workshops/ag2010/dc-agworkshop-transcript.pdf

19. Mary K. Hendrickson et al., "Consolidation in Food Retailing and Dairy."

20. Ladka Bauerova, Chirs Burritt, and Joao Oliveira, "A Three-way Food Fight in Brazil," *BusinessWeek* 4172 (2010): 70–71.

21. William D. Heffernan, "Structure of Agriculture and Quality of Life in Rural Communities," in *Rural Society in the U.S.: Issues for the 1980s*, eds. D. A. Dillman and D. J. Hobbs (Boulder, CO: Westview Press, 1982); "Constraints in the Poultry Industry," in

Research in Rural Sociology and Development, vol. 1., ed. H. Schwarzweller (Greenwich: JAI Press, 1984), 237–260.

22. Oscar B. Martinson and Gerald R. Campbell, "Betwixt and Between: Farmers and the Marketing of Agricultural Inputs and Outputs," in *The Rural Sociology of Advanced Societies: Critical Perspectives*, eds. F. H. Buttel and H. Newby (Montclair, NJ: Allenheld, Osmun, 1980).

23. Mary K. Hendrickson et al. *The Global Food System and Nodes of Power.* http://papers.ssrn.com/sol3/papers.cfm?abstract_id=1337273

24. Joseph Schumpeter, *Capitalism, Socialism, and Democracy* (New York: Harper, 1975).

25. Jim Hightower, *Hard Tomatoes, Hard Times* (Cambridge, MA: Schenkman Publishing Co, 1973).

26. Frederick H. Buttel and Howard Newby, eds., *The Rural Sociology of Advanced Societies: Critical Perspectives* (Montclair, NJ: Allenheld, Osmun, 1980).

27. Susan Mann and James M. Dickenson, "Obstacles to the Development of Capitalist Agriculture," *Journal of Peasant Studies* 5 (1978): 466–481.

28. David Goodman, "Organic and Conventional Agriculture: Materializing Discourse and Agro-Ecological Managerialism," *Agriculture and Human Values* 17 (2000): 215–219; Patrick H. Mooney, "Labor Time, Production Time, and Capitalist Development in Agriculture: A Reconsideration of the Mann-Dickenson Thesis," *Sociologia Ruralis* 22, nos. 3/4 (1982): 279–291.

29. Harold F. Breimyer, *Individual Freedom and the Economic Organization of Agriculture* (Urbana: University of Illinois Press, 1965).

30. Oscar B. Martinson and Gerald R. Campbell, "Betwixt and Between: Farmers and the Marketing of Agricultural Inputs and Outputs."

31. William H. Friedland, "Commodity Systems Analysis," in *Research in Rural Sociology*, vol. 1, ed. H. Schwarzweller (Greenwich, CT: JAI Press, 1984); Gary Gereffi and Michael Korzeniewiez, *Commodity Chains and Global Capitalism* (Westport, CT: Praeger Press, 1994).

32. Harvey S. James et al., "Networks, Power, and Dependency in the Agrifood Industry."

33. Laura Raynolds Douglas Murray and John Wilkinson, eds., *Fair Trade: The Challenges of Transforming Globalization* (New York: Routledge, 2007).

34. David Burch, "Production, Consumption and Trade in Poultry: Corporate Linkages and North-South Supply Chains," in *Cross-Continental Agrifood Chains*, eds. N. Fold and B. Pritchard (London: Routledge, 2005); Mary K. Hendrickson et al., "Consolidation in Food Retailing and Dairy"; see *Agriculture and Human Values* 30, no. 2 (2013) for a detailed analysis of the role of retailers in global agrifood restructuring.

35. Walter Goldschmidt, *As You Sow* (Glencoe, IL: The Free Press, 1947); William D. Heffernan, "Constraints in the Poultry Industry"; Linda Lobao, *Locality and Inequality: Farm Structure, Industry Structure, and Socioeconomic Conditions* (Albany: The State University of New York Press, 1990); Thomas Lyson, *Civic Agriculture: Reconnecting Farm, Food, and Community* (Medford, MA: Tufts University Press, 2004).

36. Linda Lobao and Curtis W. Stofferahn, "The Community Effects of Industrialized Farming: Social Science Research and Challenges to Corporate Farming Laws," *Agriculture and Human Values* 25, no. 2 (2008): 219–240.

37. William D. Heffernan, "Concentration of Ownership in Agriculture," in *Hungry for Profit: The Agribusiness Threat to Farmers, Food, and the Environment*, eds. F. Magdoff, J. B. Foster, and F. H. Buttel (New York: Monthly Review Press, 2000).

38. Harvey S. James et al., "Networks, Power, and Dependency in the Agrifood Industry."

39. William D. Heffernan, "Consolidation in the Food and Agriculture System"; Philip H. Howard, "Visualizing Consolidation in the Global Seed Industry: 1996–2008."

40. Mary K. Hendrickson and Harvey S. James, "The Ethics of Constrained Choice: How Industrialization of Agriculture Impacts Farming and Farmer Behavior."

41. Mary K. Hendrickson, *The Global Food System and Nodes of Power*.

42. Alessandro Bonanno and Douglas H. Constance, "Corporations and the State in the Global Era: The Case of Seaboard Farms in Texas," *Rural Sociology* 71, no. 1 (2006): 59–84.

43. William D. Heffernan, "Concentration of Ownership in Agriculture."

44. William D. Heffernan, "Constraints in the Poultry Industry"; Concentration of Ownership in Agriculture"; Mary K. Hendrickson and Harvey S. James, "The Ethics of Constrained Choice: How Industrialization of Agriculture Impacts Farming and Farmer Behavior"; Mary K. Hendrickson et al., *The Global Food System and Nodes of Power*.

45. William Boyd William and Michael J. Watts, "Agro-Industrial Just-in-Time: The Chicken Industry and Postwar Capitalism," in *Globalizing Food: Agrarian Questions and Global Restructuring*, eds. D. Goodman and M. J. Watts (London: Routledge, 1997); Douglas H., Constance, Francisco Martinez, Gilberto Aboites, and Alessandro Bonanno, "The Problem with Poultry Production and Processing," in *The Ethics and Economics of Agrifood Competition*, ed. H. James (New York: Springer Press, 2013).

46. Harold F. Breimyer, *Individual Freedom and the Economic Organization of Agriculture*.

47. John E. Davis, "Capitalist Agricultural Development and the Exploitation of the Propertied Laborer," in *The Rural Sociology of Advanced Societies*, eds. Frederick H. Buttel and Howard Newby (Montclair, NJ: Allenheld, Osmun, and Co., 1980).

48. Harrison Wellford, *Sowing the Wind* (New York: Grossman Publishers, 1972).

49. Douglas H. Constance, "The Southern Model of Broiler Production and Its Global Implications," *Culture and Agriculture* 30, no. 1 (2008): 17–31; William D. Heffernan, "Concentration of Ownership in Agriculture."

50. Douglas H. Constance and Reny Tuinstra, "Corporate Chickens and Community Conflict in East Texas: Growers' and Neighbors' Views on the Impacts of Industrial Broiler Production," *Culture and Agriculture* 27, no. 1 (2005): 45–60; Douglas H. Constance, Alessandro Bonanno, Caron Cates, Daniel Argo, and Maranda Harris, "Resisting Integration in the Global Agro-Food System: Corporate Chickens and Community Controversy in Texas," in *Globalisation, Localisation, and Sustainable Livelihoods*, eds. R. Almas and G. Lawrence (Burlington, VT: Ashgate Press, 2003).

51. Douglas H. Constance, "The Problem with Poultry Production and Processing."

52. William D. Heffernan, "Constraints in the Poultry Industry"; Carl Weinberg, "Big Dixie Chicken Goes Global: Exports and the Rise of the North Georgia Poultry Industry," *Business and Economic History Online* 1 (2003): 1–32.

53. R. T. Rogers, "Broilers: Differentiating a Commodity," in *Industry Studies*, 3rd ed., ed. L. L. Deutsch (New York: M.E. Sharpe, Inc., 2002), 59–95; GIPSA (USDA Grain

Inspection, Packers Stockyard Administration), "2010 Annual Report of the Packers and Stockyards Program" (Washington, DC: USDA Grains, 2011). www.gipsa.usda.gov/Publications/psp/ar/2010_psp_annual_report.pdf

54. Douglas H. Constance, Francisco Martinez, and Gilberto Aboites, "The Globalization of the Poultry Industry: Tyson Foods and Pilgrim's Pride in Mexico," in *From Community to Consumption: New and Classical Statements in Rural Sociological Research*, Research in Rural Sociology and Development, vol. 16, eds. A. Bonanno, H. Bakker, R. Jussaume, Y. Kawamura, and M. Shucksmith (Bingley, UK: Emerald Group Publishing Ltd., 2010).

55. "Concentration of Ownership in Agriculture"; Mary K. Hendrickson, *The Global Food System and Nodes of Power*.

56. Alessandro Bonanno and Douglas H. Constance, "Corporations and the State in the Global Era: The Case of Seaboard Farms in Texas"; Douglas H. Constance, Anna Kleiner, and J. Sanford Rikoon, "The Contested Terrain of Swine Regulation," in *Fighting for the Farm: Rural America Transformed*, ed. Jane Adams (University Park: University Press of Pennsylvania, 2003).

57. William D. Heffernan et al., "Consolidation in the Food and Agriculture System"; Mary K. Hendrickson et al., *The Global Food System and Nodes of Power*.

58. Hoovers, "Tyson Foods, Inc.," www.hoovers.com/company/Tyson_Foods_Inc/rcsjhi-1-1njht4-1njhft.html; JBS, "JBS Is Now the World's Biggest Provider of Meat," www.jbssa.com/News/Archive/JBSFamilyBusiness.aspx

59. Harriett Friedmann and Philip McMichael, "Agriculture and the State System: The Rise and Fall of National Agricultures," *Sociological Ruralis* 29, no. 2 (1989): 93–117; David Harvey, *The Condition of Post-Modernity* (Hoboken, NJ: John Wiley and Sons, 1990).

60. Harriett Friedmann, "From Colonialism to Green Capitalism: Social Movements and the Emergence of Food Regimes," in *New Directions in the Sociology of Global Development: Research in Rural Sociology and Development*, vol. 11, eds. F. H. Buttel and P. McMichael (Oxford: Elsevier Press, 2005), 227–264.

61. Harriett Friedmann and Philip McMichael, "Agriculture and the State System: The Rise and Fall of National Agricultures"; Philip McMichael, "Global Development and the Corporate Food Regime," in *New Directions in the Sociology of Global Development*, Research in Rural Sociology and Development, vol. 11, eds. F. H. Buttel and P. McMichael (Oxford: Elsevier Press, 2005).

62. Philip McMichael, *Development and Social Change: A Global Perspective* (Thousand Oaks, CA: Pine Forge Press, 1996).

63. Harriett Friedmann and Philip McMichael, "Agriculture and the State System: The Rise and Fall of National Agricultures"; Philip McMichael, "Global Development and the Corporate Food Regime."

64. Alessandro Bonanno and Douglas H. Constance, *Stories of Globalization: Transnational Corporations, Resistance, and the State* (University Park: The Pennsylvania State University Press, 2008).

Harriett Friedmann and Philip McMichael, "Agriculture and the State System: The Rise and Fall of National Agricultures"; Philip McMichael, "Global Development and the Corporate Food Regime."

65. See *Agriculture and Human Values* 26, no. 4 (2009) for a detailed analysis of the regimes perspectives.

66. David Harvey, *A Brief History of Neoliberalism* (Oxford, UK: Oxford University Press, 2005).

67. Philip McMichael, "Global Development and the Corporate Food Regime."

68. Lawrence Busch, *Standards: Recipes for Reality* (Cambridge, MA: The MIT Press, 2011).

69. Douglas H. Constance and William D. Heffernan, "The Global Poultry Agrifood Complex," *International Journal of Sociology of Agriculture and Food* 1 (1991): 126–141.

70. Douglas H. Constance, Jin Young Choi, and Holly Lyke Ho-Gland, "Conventionalization, Bifurcation, and Quality of Life: Certified and Non-Certified Organic Farmers in Texas," *Southern Rural Sociology* 23, no. 1 (2008): 208–234.

71. David Burch and Geoffrey Lawrence, *Supermarkets and Agri-Food Supply Chains: Transformations in the Production and Consumption of Food* (Cheltenham, UK: Edward Elgar, 2007).

72. Douglas H. Constance et al., "The Problem with Poultry Production and Processing"; David Harvey, *A Brief History of Neoliberalism*.

73. Philip McMichael, "Global Development and the Corporate Food Regime."

74. Olivier De Schutter, "Towards More Equitable Value Chains: Alternative Business Models in Support of the Right to Food," report presented at the 66th Session of the United Nations General Assembly by the UN Special Rapporteur on the Right to Food, 2011, www.srfood.org/en/official-reports; Beverly D McIntyre, Hans R. Herren, Judi Wakhungu, and Robert T. Watson, eds., *Agriculture at a Crossroads: A Synthesis of the Global and Sub-Global IAASTD Reports* (International Assessment of Agricultural Knowledge, Science, and Technology for Development, 2009), www.unep.org/dewa/agassessment/reports/IAASTD/EN/Agriculture%20at%20a%20Crossroads_Synthesis%20Report%20(English).pdf

75. Philip McMichael, *Development and Social Change: A Global Perspective*.

76. USDA/USDOJ (U.S. Department of Agriculture/Department of Justice), "Agriculture and Antitrust Enforcement Issues in Our 21st-Century Economy" (Washington, DC: U.S. Department of Agriculture and U.S. Department of Justice, 2010).

77. Philip McMichael, "Global Development and the Corporate Food Regime"; Vía Campesina, "What is La Vía Campesina?" http://viacampesina.org/en/index.php/organisation-mainmenu-44/what-is-la-via-campesina-mainmenu-45

78. Clare C. Hinrichs and Thomas Lyson, eds., *Remaking the North American Food System: Strategies for Sustainability* (Lincoln: University of Nebraska, 2007); Kevin Morgan, Terry Marsden, and Jonathan Murdoch, *Worlds of Food: Place, Provenance, and Power in the Food Chain* (Oxford, UK: Oxford University Press, 2006).

79. Warren Belasco, *Appetite for Change: How the Counterculture Took on the Food Industry* (Ithaca, NY: Cornell University Press, 1989).

80. OTA (Organic Trade Association), "Industry Statistics and Projected Growth" (2011). www.ota.com/organic/mt/business.html

81. Philip McMichael, "Global Development and the Corporate Food Regime."

82. Laura Raynolds et al., *Fair Trade: The Challenges of Transforming Globalization*.

83. Thomas G. Lyson, *Civic Agriculture: Reconnecting Farm, Food, and Community*.

84. Mary K. Hendrickson, William D. Heffernan, David Lind, and Elizabeth Barham, "Contractual Integration in Agriculture: Is There a Bright Side for Agriculture in the Middle?" in *Food and the Mid-Level Farm*, eds. T. A. Lyson, G. W. Stevenson, and

R. Welsh (Cambridge, MA: The MIT Press, 2008); Thomas G. Lyson, G. W. Stevenson, and Rick Welsh, eds., *Food and the Mid-Level Farm: Renewing an Agriculture of the Middle* (Cambridge, MA: MIT Press, 2010).

85. Mary K. Hendrickson, "Creating Alternatives: A Participant's Observer Reflections on the Emerging Local Food System in Kansas City," *Southern Rural Sociology* 24, no. 2 (2009): 169–191; Clare C. Hinrichs and Thomas Lyson, *Remaking the North American Food System: Strategies for Sustainability*; Thomas G. Lyson, *Civic Agriculture: Reconnecting Farm, Food, and Community*.

86. Charles Perrow, *Complex Organizations: A Critical Essay* (New York: McGraw Hill, 1986).

87. Mancur Olson, *The Logic of Collective Action: Public Goods and the Theory of Groups* (Cambridge, MA: Harvard University Press, 1965).

88. Alessandro Bonanno and Douglas H. Constance, *Stories of Globalization: Transnational Corporations, Resistance, and the State*.

89. Alessandro Bonanno and Douglas H. Constance, *Stories of Globalization: Transnational Corporations, Resistance, and the State*; William H. Friedland, Lawrence Busch, Frederick H. Buttel, and Alan P. Rudy, eds., *Towards a New Political Economy of Agriculture* (Boulder, CO: Westview Press, 1991).

90. Alessandro Bonanno and Douglas H. Constance, "Corporations and the State in the Global Era: The Case of Seaboard Farms in Texas"; Douglas H. Constance, "Contested Globalization of the Agrifood System: A Missouri School Analysis of Sanderson Farms and Seaboard Farms in Texas."

91. Douglas H. Constance, "Sustainable Agriculture in the United States: A Critical Examination of a Contested Process," *Sustainability* 2, no. 1 (2010): 48–72; Julie Guthman, *Agrarian Dreams: The Paradox of Organic Farming in California* (Berkeley: University of California Press, 2004); Philip H. Howard, "Consolidation in the North American Organic Food Processing Sector, 1997 to 2007." *International Journal of Sociology of Agriculture and Food* 16, no. 1 (2009b): 13–30; Philip H. Howard, "Visualizing Food Systems Concentration and Consolidation." *Southern Rural Sociology* 24, no. 2 (2009c): 87–110.

92. Douglas H. Constance et al., "Conventionalization, Bifurcation, and Quality of Life: Certified and Non-Certified Organic Farmers in Texas."

93. Philip H. Howard and Patricia Allen, "Beyond Organic and Fair Trade? An Analysis of Ecolabel Preferences in the United States," *Rural Sociology* 75, no. 2 (2010): 244–269.

94. Daniel Jaffee and Philip H. Howard, "Corporate Cooptation of Organic and *Fair Trade* Standards," *Agriculture and Human Values* 27, no. 4 (2010): 387–399.

95. Philip H. Howard and Daniel Jaffee, "Tensions between Firm Size and Sustainability Goals: Fair Trade Coffee in the United States," *Sustainability* 5, no. 1 (2013): 72–89.

96. Daniel Jaffee and Philip H. Howard, "Corporate Cooptation of Organic and *Fair Trade* Standards."

97. Ibid.

98. Patricia Allen, *Together at the Table: Sustenance and Sustainability in the American Agrifood System* (University Park: The Pennsylvania State University Press, 2005).

99. Mary K. Hendrickson, "Creating Alternatives: A Participant's Observer Reflections on the Emerging Local Food System in Kansas City."

4

Racism, Gender Discrimination, and Food Chain Workers in the United States

Joann Lo

The food system is the largest employer in the United States, providing one out of five private-sector jobs. The almost 20 million people working in the U.S. food system constitute one-sixth of the nation's entire workforce, a sector larger than retail and health care combined.[1] The food system is also a large and growing segment of the U.S. economy. The industries of food production, processing, distribution, retail, and service collectively sell over $1.8 trillion dollars in goods and services annually, accounting for over 13 percent of the U.S. gross domestic product.[2] Core food occupations and industries include farmworkers (production), slaughterhouse and other processing facilities workers (processing), warehouse workers (distribution), grocery store workers (retail), and restaurant and food service workers (service).

Food system workers are among the lowest-paid workers in the United States and around the world. Front-line workers make up 86 percent of the 20 million people employed by the food system, earning a median salary of $18,889 a year.[3] CEOs, on the other hand, earn a median income eight times that: $151,833.[4] Overall, wages of workers in the food system are lower than those of workers in other industries. In fact, compared to data on all workers in the United States, the median hourly wage of food system front-line workers is about a third less than that of all front-line workers in the United States.[5]

In summer and fall 2011, 10 unions and workers centers, all members of the Food Chain Workers Alliance, surveyed over 600 workers throughout the food system. Workers and organizers asked workers about wages, hours, pay,

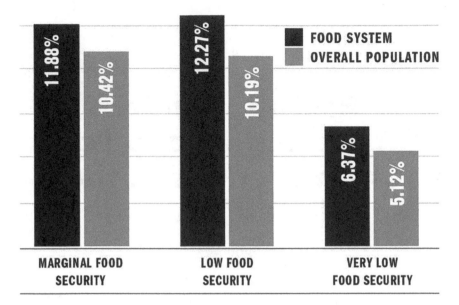

FIGURE 4.1   Food Security among Food System Workers v. Overall
Population, 2010

Source: Bureau of Labour Statistics, Occupational Employment Statistics 2010.

benefits, health and safety, training, career advancement opportunities, and
discrimination. We found that the median hourly wage of the surveyed workers was $9.65.[6] Owing to such low wages, the earnings of more than half of
food system workers—10 million—put them below the poverty line for a family of three.[7] Food system workers suffer higher rates of food insecurity[8] and
use food stamps at more than 1.5 times the rate of the general workforce.[9]

The food system both has historically been and continues to be one of the
largest employers of workers of color and women. In the early colonial days,
African slaves and indentured laborers from Europe were forced to provide
their free labor to produce food. After the Civil War, African American share-
croppers in the American South and Asian immigrants in the American West
became the low-paid workforce in the food system. The *braceros* program,
initiated during World War II, began providing seasonal Mexican agricultural workers to American growers. Beginning in the 1960s, when corporate
consolidation in the industry began to grow, immigrant workers increasingly
replaced African American and native-born workers in meat and poultry processing plants in the American Midwest and South. Now close to half of the
members of the U.S. food workforce are women, and almost 41 percent are
people of color.[10]

Due to this historical legacy, in its 2011 report "The Color of Food," the
Applied Research Center (ARC) reported that, on average, people of color

TABLE 4.1   Race/Ethnicity by Wage Segment

	SUBMINIMUM WAGE	POVERTY WAGE	LOW WAGE	LIVING WAGE
Black	21%	28.4%	36.9%	13.6%
Latino	24.4%	38.7%	22.9%	14%
Asian	37.5%	31.3%	18.8%	12.5%
Indigenous	28.6%	64.3%	7.1%	0%
White	13.5%	62.2%	8.1%	16.2%
Other	0%	50%	50%	0%
Total	23%	37.6%	25.8%	13.5%

Source: Food Chain Workers Alliance survey data.

earn less than whites working in the food chain. Half of white food workers earn $25,024 a year, whereas workers of color make $5,675 less than that.[11] Our survey of over 600 workers confirmed this difference in wages, with about one-quarter of Black and Latino workers and almost 40 percent of Asian workers, but only 13.5 percent of white workers, surveyed reporting earning less than the minimum wage.[12] Whites also hold three out of four management positions in the food system,[13] a higher rate than their representation in the food chain workforce (three out of five).

Women food system workers earn slightly less than men in the food system. In our survey, women earned median weekly wages of $400, whereas men reported a median weekly take-home pay of $421.[14] Women also reported suffering worse working conditions than men surveyed. Women reported feeling discriminated against at much higher rates than men (44 percent versus 32 percent).[15]

Immigrant workers are also more vulnerable to exploitation in the food system. Foreign-born workers reported earnings that were less per hour on average than those of U.S.-born workers surveyed ($10.55 versus $11.08). Undocumented workers were far more concentrated in lower-wage jobs, resulting in less than 1 percent of undocumented workers reporting earnings of more than 150 percent of the poverty line, compared to 20 percent of documented workers.[16] The median wage reported by undocumented workers—$7.60 per hour—was significantly lower than the median wage reported by all other workers: $10 per hour.[17]

The following sections on farm, food processing, food distribution, food retail, and restaurant workers provide data on racial and gender discrimination specific to each of these major sectors of the food system, as well as stories from workers who are facing such discrimination and who are organizing with worker centers to promote racial and gender justice.

Farmworkers

There was racism because [supervisors and growers] didn't treat us equally. They'd tell us we had to get an order in, so if you got hurt in the fields, it's like: Go on back to work.

—Linda Lee, former farmworker, Florida

The historical legacy of slavery continues to exacerbate the plight of farmworkers in the United States today. Farmworkers are excluded from the National Labor Relations Act, which provides most other workers the right to act collectively and to organize a union, as well as from the overtime provisions of the Fair Labor Standards Act. When both these laws were being negotiated in Congress during the 1930s, farmworkers (and domestic workers), who were predominantly African American at that time, were excluded in a bid to gain the support of Southern Democrats, who were afraid of the potential economic power of black workers[18] and who did not want to give them equal footing with white workers.[19]

This disrespect and disregard for the humanity of farmworkers is a lasting legacy of institutional slavery, forced labor, and modern-day slavery and continues to be a real problem in agriculture. For instance, the Coalition of

FIGURE 4.2   Farmworkers in Immokalee, Florida
(Photo by Forrest Woodward. Used by permission of the Food Chain Workers Alliance.)

Immokalee Workers (CIW) in Florida has assisted workers in seven cases of forced servitude in the past decade, involving more than 1,000 workers and more than a dozen employers. In these instances, workers were physically assaulted, shackled to prevent their escape, and forced to work with little or no remuneration. Fortunately, these cases have been successfully prosecuted by the Civil Rights Division of the U.S. Department of Justice.

Today, an estimated 1.4 to 3 million farmworkers—migrant, seasonal, and permanent—are employed in the United States.[20] About 400,000 to 800,000 of these farmworkers are children.[21] According to the National Agricultural Workers Survey (NAWS) data from 2009–2010, about 24 percent of farmworkers are female.[22] Eighty-three percent self-identify as Hispanic.[23] Most estimates project that a majority of farmworkers are undocumented immigrants. From 2005 to 2009, about one-third of all farmworkers earned less than $7.25/hour and only a quarter reported working more than nine months during the previous year; additionally, one-quarter of all farmworkers had family incomes below the federal poverty line.[24]

Female farmworkers not only face low wages and dangerous working conditions, but also are vulnerable to sexual harassment and sexual violence. Analysis of NAWS data from 2004 to 2006 by the Southern Poverty Law Center found that the average personal yearly income of female crop workers was $11,250, significantly lower than the average income of $16,250 for male crop workers.[25] A 2010 survey of 150 farmworker women in California's Central Valley found that 80 percent had experienced some form of sexual harassment, and a report by the Southern Poverty Law Center found that a majority of its 150 interviewees had also experienced sexual harassment.[26]

To fight these food worker inequities and abuses, food- and labor-rights groups such as the Food Chain Workers Alliance have rallied to create a more just and equitable food and agricultural system. The Food Chain Workers Alliance is a national coalition of unions, workers centers, and advocacy organizations joined together to improve wages and working conditions for all food workers. It also works toward a more sustainable food system that respects workers' rights, based on the principles of social, economic and racial justice, in which everyone has affordable, healthy food. The Alliance includes organizations such as the Farmworkers Support Committee (CATA) in eastern Pennsylvania, southern New Jersey, and coastal Maryland; the Coalition of Immokalee Workers (CIW) in Florida; the Farmworker Association of Florida (FWAF); and Rural and Migrant Ministry in upstate New York.

FWAF celebrated its 30-year anniversary in March 2013. FWAF's work includes voter registration; pesticide education, particularly as regards women's health; immigration reform; and policy advocacy, including anti-wage theft ordinances and paid sick days legislation. Although the majority of FWAF's membership of more than 10,000 are Latino, in the Apopka area near Orlando, FWAF's leadership group includes Haitians and African Americans. Since 1996, FWAF has been organizing with former African American farmworkers in Apopka who were displaced from their jobs when the state of Florida seized agricultural lands and ended agricultural production in the area. Many of the workers suffered and continue to suffer major health problems arising from their exposure to chemicals on the farms, but they have never been compensated and do not receive any health care assistance.

One such worker is Linda Lee. Linda started working on farms in the summers in the late 1960s, when she was about six years old. She harvested corn, cabbages, carrots, cucumbers, tomatoes, beans, hickory nuts, and potatoes. "When we were in the fields, there was no running water or bathrooms," she describes. "It was pretty tough trying to work, with cold, and then getting sunburned." Linda continued working in the fields through the mid-1980s. She says the wages remained stagnant over the course of the decades. "[We] were paid something like $1 something per hour for day labor, and piece work was—you make 12 cents a box or something like that," she explains. When she retired from farm work, "Pay was about the same. Because the growers, they never actually grow up. They kept the price down for them to make the money." The growers were all white, but the farmworkers were all African American. "There was racism because they didn't treat us equally," Linda says. "They'd tell us we had to get an order in, so if you got hurt in the fields, it's like: Go on back to work."

Linda's experience also illustrates the persistence of racism in terms of environmental and geographic context. In Apopka, a waste and wastewater plant disposes of toxic chemicals, leaving much of the community sick. This has had devastating health effects on Linda's family and community. "My whole family is sick. I just had a granddaughter last week who died of lupus. I have lupus. My mama had gout, so bad that you could hardly touch her. I had a sister who laid down and just died. We tried to figure out why, and they tried to tell us it was her heart, but young people don't just die," Linda says. "Down the street, a whole family died. I have grandkids who have skin problems. Cancer is big." But there has been no compensation for the farmworkers and the African American community. So Linda joined the Farmworker Association of Florida. "I've been fighting for healthcare. We've gone out and protested, signed different things, and went to Tallahassee." Linda also has been part of the Lake Apopka quilt project to bring awareness to the situation there.[27] Members of the Lake Apopka farmworker community have sewn individual squares that have been put together to create a number of quilts. Each square tells a personal story of tragedy or of a small victory. The quilts have been displayed around southern Florida to educate others about the history of the African American and farmworker communities in the region.

Food-Processing Workers

[The management] make us feel like we are only machines, and we feel like we don't have protection. It is a slaughterhouse for pork, but we at work, we call it a slaughterhouse for humans.

—Amelia Meza, meatpacking worker, Missouri

The nation's food system has become increasingly consolidated over the last 150 years. The food processing industry, especially in meatpacking and poultry processing, is a clear example of this corporate consolidation. Only a handful of companies, for example, still control the majority of the meat packing industry. Tyson, Cargill, and JBS now process more than 70 percent of all beef.[28] In pork, Smithfield Foods is the top packer, and Tyson, Swift (owned by JBS), and Cargill follow close behind. These four packers controlled an estimated 66 percent of the market in 2007.[29] Poultry is no different, with only a handful of companies dominating the processing of chicken broilers. Four companies control 58 percent of the chicken market: Pilgrim's Pride (owned by JBS), Tyson, Perdue, and Sanderson Farms; similarly, Butterball, Hormel Foods, Cargill, and Sara Lee control 55 percent of the turkey market in the United States.[30]

This corporate consolidation moved the meatpacking industry away from heavily unionized processing plants in urban centers in the American Midwest to massive, mostly nonunionized factories in rural areas in the American South and Midwest, where land, water, and labor were relatively cheaper. As a result, the median salary of meat- and poultry-processing workers is now $21,320 per year, as compared with $33,500 per year for workers in all manufacturing industries.[31] The shift in the geographic location of meat and poultry processing plants has been matched by a shift in the demographics of the workers. The industry, once dominated by African American male workers, has witnessed an increase in Latino and Southeast Asian workers. At least half of the 250,000 laborers in 174 of the major U.S. chicken factories are Latino;[32] more than half are women.[33]

Food processing overall provides roughly 1.3 million jobs in the United States,[34] and workers in food, meat, and poultry processing plants suffer from a high rate of workplace injuries owing to the repetitive and rapid nature of assembly line work. Coupled with the lack of training on how to operate dangerous slaughtering and processing machines, meatpacking is considered one of the most dangerous jobs in the United States. The rate of illnesses and injuries for workers in "animal slaughtering and processing" was more than twice as high as the national average for workplace injuries, and the rate of ill-nesses was about 10 times the national average.[35] In a survey of 200 food, meat, and poultry processing workers conducted by members of the Food Chain Workers Alliance, 65 percent reported experiencing injuries or illnesses on the job, and among those workers, the most frequently reported injuries were cuts (37.8% of injured processing workers), repetitive motion injuries (34.6%), slips and falls (26.8%), and back injuries (25.2%).[36]

Six of the member organizations of the Food Chain Workers Alliance organize meat, poultry, and/or food processing workers: Brandworkers International in New York City; CATA–Farmworkers Support Committee in New Jersey; the Northwest Arkansas Workers Justice Center; the Teamsters Joint Council No. 7 in northern California, the Central Valley, and north-ern Nevada; the United Food and Commercial Workers Union Local 770 in southern California; and the Health Action Council (HAC) of the Center for New Community in Milan, a small rural town in northern Missouri. The HAC organizes and educates workers and their families on issues such as worker's rights and health and safety issues within and without the workplace and is assisting the workers in asking the Occupational Safety and Health Adminis-tration (OSHA) for stronger enforcement of health and safety regulations in the meatpacking plants. Because many of workers speak English as a second language, the HAC also provides assistance at hospitals when workers suffer injuries on the job.

The majority of HAC's members are migrants and refugees of color and work in the meatpacking plants in the area of Milan, Missouri. One of these members is Amelia Meza, a Mexican immigrant, mother of four, and grand-mother of two. Amelia has worked in pork processing plants for over six years. In that time, she has experienced racial discrimination firsthand. "There are some positions that are very, very, very hard, and these jobs are being done by the people of color," she explains. The management also chooses who has to work overtime and who can go home. "If you're a mother, you want to go home to cook and see your children." But the supervisors are white, and they allow the white workers to go home first if they prefer. Amelia has also expe-rienced sexual harassment as a female worker in the industry. "The supervisor spoke to me a lot, came around to me a lot. He asked me out. I said no. I never went out with him, but I didn't like that he'd come so close to me. Later, this supervisor was fired for sexual assault [against another person]."

In the plant where she currently works, Amelia says that in addition to Latino immigrant workers, Haitian and Somali immigrant workers are also employed, and the management keeps them separated. In the same work area, "there is an undocumented, there is a colored person, they put someone from Haiti—they don't speak the same language" and therefore cannot com-municate with each other. "That is called structural racism," she says. "[The management] make us feel like we are only machines, and we feel like we don't have protection. It is a slaughterhouse for pork, but we at work, we call it a slaughterhouse for humans."

Amelia is organizing with the Health Action Council to improve the health and safety conditions in the plant. One major issue is the rapid line speed, which causes many injuries. Additionally, her employer only allows workers to take a bathroom break three times per week. "We have had cases that there are people that soil themselves number two in their clothing, right there standing in the line, and that is not right for the food," she explains. "I want to see a change."

Distribution Workers

> The men at the warehouse made comments like "Did you break a nail?" and "Are you going cry because the box fell on you?"
>
> —Uyolanda Dickerson, warehouse worker, Joliet, Illinois

Almost 1.7 million workers make up the distribution stage of the food supply chain.[37] They transport food from one destination to another and load and unload food at warehouses and distribution centers. Distribution workers also deliver food to intermediate locations for storage or further processing and to final points of sale. Essentially, distribution connects the material at each stage of the food system. Although a large component of this involves transportation, this stage also includes warehousing, refrigeration, logistics, and coordination.

Warehouse workers are often hired by temporary or staffing agencies to work in warehouses that are managed by logistics contractors for retailers like Walmart, Costco, and Amazon. According to data from the Bureau of Labor Statistics, the five largest occupations in warehousing and storage appear within the top 30 occupations in temporary services.[38] For example, the growth of temporary work in the Inland Empire region of southern California has been exponential. From 1990 to 2008, the number of temporary staffing agencies grew from 119 to 424, and as a result, the region has a higher concentration of temporary employment than any other in the state of California.[39] A recent report found that directly hired blue-collar warehouse workers earn a median annual wage of $22,000, but temporary warehouse workers earn a median annual wage of just $10,067.[40] Warehouse Workers for Justice (WWJ), a member of the Food Chain Workers Alliance, surveyed 319 workers in warehouses outside of Chicago in 2010 and found that 63 percent of the workers were temporary workers.[41] WWJ also found that a majority of warehouse workers made poverty-level wages, and temporary workers' median hourly wage was $9.00 per hour—$3.48 per hour less than directly hired workers.[42]

Temporary work results in higher rates of injury as well. According to a survey of 103 temporary workers conducted by Warehouse Workers United (WWU), an FCWA member group, nearly 65 percent of workers reported experiencing or witnessing at least one injury in the workplace within the last year. This rate of injury for temporary warehouse workers in the Inland Empire region of southern California was more than 10 times greater than the national average for temporary warehouse workers.[43]

Warehouse loaders and unloaders are also often paid a piece, or production, rate. A piece rate is a set amount of money workers receive for each box, pallet, or truck they load or unload at the docks. Although this practice is legal, employers are required by law to ensure that workers are paid the minimum wage if the production rate times the number of boxes, pallets, or trucks that are loaded or unloaded does not equal the minimum wage per hours worked. In reality, often this does not happen: Wage theft is a common occurrence.

High numbers of African Americans and Latinos work in the warehouse industry. In the case of the Inland Empire, about half the warehouse workers are immigrants, with Latinos representing 80 percent of the workforce.[44] In the Chicago area, 48 percent of warehouse workers are African American; 36 percent are Latino.[45] Nationally, 21 percent of warehouse workers are Latino.[46] In WWJ's survey, nearly 40 percent of warehouse workers reported being discriminated against, most commonly because of race, followed closely by speaking out for workers' rights at work.[47] In the survey conducted for the Food Chain Workers Alliance, African American workers experienced 76 percent of the cases of wage theft in warehouses.[48]

Women account for 30 percent of the workforce in warehouses nationally.[49] With a male-dominated workforce and management, women suffer sexual harassment, abuse, and discrimination. The case of Uyolanda Dickerson exemplifies the conditions that women warehouse workers face.[50] Uyolanda worked at a Walmart warehouse outside Chicago, Illinois, from 2009 to 2010. At the warehouse, she loaded and unloaded trailers and verified items on the trailer. While working at the Walmart warehouse as a temporary worker who was managed by a logistics contractor, Uyolanda says she was discriminated against for being a woman: The men at the warehouse made comments such as "Did you break a nail?" and "Are you going cry because the box fell on you?" She also feels that she was paid less than men and purposely given a heavy workload to prove a point. She also suffered sexual harassment on a daily basis. Some of her male coworkers called her "hot momma" and commented on her body. On one occasion, she was locked in a trailer with a male coworker, who said, "I'm going to do this and that to you," and then made sexual advances toward her. She went to management to report what had taken place, and Uyolanda reports, "[T]hey said, 'Stop being soft, you're just being a girl'; 'I

FIGURE 4.3   Uyolanda Dickerson at conference in New York City on June 6, 2012 to release the report "The Hands That Feed Us"

(Photo by Jake Ratner. Used by permission of the Food Chain Workers Alliance.)

didn't see anything, so I can't do anything about it.'" Uylonda also recalled, "I went to work sick a lot," because her employers made it clear that "if you don't come, you have no job." Toward the end of her employment, she received health insurance and paid $27 a week for it. At work, Uyolanda suffered from back pain, leg pain, and shoulder pain. When she requested to take time off, the management refused.

After a while, Uyolanda couldn't take the harassment any longer and left her job at the warehouse. She began organizing with Warehouse Workers for Justice (WWJ). She says that she wants to "let [other workers] know [there] are people out there like you and that you aren't alone." Uyolanda is now the head organizer of the steering committee of the WWJ workers committee and is also on the women's committee. She says, "Everything I went through at the warehouse made me want to tell others about their rights and that they could do something about it. I also want to better my community."

Food Retail Workers

When I complained about [sexual harassment] to my supervisor, he said, "[M]en do that" and "It's okay."

—Girshriela Green, retail worker, Los Angeles, California

TABLE 4.2 Percent of Industry Cases of Wage Theft by Race and Industry

	Farm/ agricultural and nurseries	Meat packing and poultry processing	Food processing, distribution, and packing houses	Restaurant and food services	Grocery	Warehouse	Total wage theft
Latino	92.9%	25.0%	68.2%	36.4%	78.6%	10.3%	57.9%
Black	0.0%	0.0%	18.2%	40.9%	14.3%	75.9%	27.8%
White	0.0%	0.0%	4.5%	4.5%	7.1%	6.9%	3.8%
Asian	0.0%	75.0%	9.1%	4.5%	0.0%	0.0%	4.5%
Indigenous	7.1%	0.0%	0.0%	4.5%	0.0%	0.0%	3.0%
Other	0.0%	0.0%	0.0%	9.1%	0.0%	6.9%	3.0%
TOTAL	100.0%	100.0%	100.0%	100.0%	100.0%	100.0%	100.0%

Source: Food Chain Workers Alliance Survey Data, 2010.

Note: The Food Chain Workers Alliance's national survey of over 600 workers throughout the food system analyzed whether workers had suffered wage theft—payment of wages that were lower than legally required for hours worked—in their previous two full weeks of work before they participated in the survey. Table 4.2 shows the percentage of cases of wage theft for workers in each major segment of the food chain in each racial/ethnic category.

Food and beverage stores provide about 2.9 million jobs in the United States.[51] These include workers at supermarkets, convenience stores, grocery stores, and buyers' clubs. These workers are increasingly facing new challenges under conditions of corporate consolidation. For instance, more and more jobs are being cut from full-time to part-time hours, and workers often do not know what the work schedule will be until a few days—or even the day—before the work week starts. Moreover, an increase in the number of nonunion stores has put pressure on wages. The average hourly wage of nonmanagerial grocery workers in June 2013 was $12.46; however, adjusted for inflation and based on the value of wages from 1982 to 1984, the real value of grocery workers' hourly wage in June 2013 was $5.42.[52] Seventeen percent of grocery store workers are covered by a union contract, compared to the 26.1 percent who were in 1990.[53]

Walmart currently commands approximately 28 percent of the share of the total supermarket sales, compared to 11 percent controlled by Kroger, the next largest competitor.[54] However, other big box stores such as Target and pharmacies such as CVS and Walgreens are expanding their retail sales into the grocery market. In 2010, Target invested $500 million to expand grocery operations, whereas CVS redesigned about 200 stores to include grocery sales.[55] Now, the four largest U.S. food retailers—Walmart, Costco, Kroger, and Target—control 50 percent of all grocery sales.[56]

The result of this corporate consolidation has been an increase in the retailer's share of the consumer dollar. Varying percentages of each dollar that a consumer spends to buy a retail item go to the retailer, the manufacturer, the transporter, and so on. For example, in 1990 the share of each consumer dollar spent on beef was distributed across the food supply chain as follows: $.59 for the farmer and rancher; $.08 for the packer and the packinghouse worker; $.33 for the retailer.[57] By 2009, the distribution of the consumer beef dollar had been significantly altered: The rancher/farmer's share had declined to $.42; the packer's share had risen slightly to $.09 (but still below its 1980 level); the retailer's share had risen to $.49[58] (as detailed in the chapter by the UFCW's Dennis Olson in this volume).

This increased share of the consumer dollar in the hands of retailers has not resulted in higher wages for food retail workers. According to the Bureau of Labor Statistics, the median wage for a front-line worker in food retail is $9.69 per hour.[59] In fact, a recent report based on worker surveys in New York City, Chicago, and Los Angeles found that 23.5 percent of grocery workers were paid less than the minimum wage, and 65 percent were not paid overtime.[60] Thirty percent of grocery-store workers are part-time, with the average work week for nonsupervisory workers at 29.4 hours, compared to 33.4 hours for all industries.[61]

With low wages and high levels of part-time employment, the average work week for nonsupervisory workers was 29 hours in April 2013,[62] and many workers lack health insurance because they do not have enough hours to qualify for employer-sponsored programs and they cannot afford it on their own. Half of the grocery workers surveyed by the Food Chain Workers Alliance who said they have health care coverage reported obtaining it through Medicaid or a state program.[63] Part-time work is also a particularly key issue at this time as the Affordable Care Act requires that employers with 50 employees or more pay for health insurance for all employees who work an average of 30 hours or more per week (or else pay a fine). Even before this act was passed, the grocery industry was increasing the number of part-time workers to avoid providing benefits such as health insurance; now the industry wants to avoid having to provide insurance as required by the law.

Two members of the Food Chain Workers Alliance represent grocery store workers: the United Food and Commercial Workers Union Local 1500 in Long Island, New York, and Local 770 in southern California. Both locals are supporting OUR Walmart—the Organization United for Respect at Walmart, a membership organization of Walmart employees around the country.

Girshriela Green, a 46-year-old single mother of seven children, is a worker organizer for OUR Walmart. She worked at the only Walmart Supercenter in the city of Los Angeles for four years. Even though she was a department manager, Girshriela was paid only $9.80 per hour. Because of the low pay at

FIGURE 4.4   Girshriela Green (left) with Ernestine Bassett and Cynthia Murray, fellow leaders of the Organization United for Respect (OUR), at Walmart in 2011

(Photo by United Food and Commercial Workers Union. Used by permission of the Food Chain Workers Alliance.)

Walmart, she says that most employees use SNAP benefits (formerly known as food stamps)—not only in her store, but all around the country. And in an extreme irony, Walmart provides a card to its employees so that they can receive discounts on all items sold in the store—except food.

Girshriela was injured on the job in 2011 and complained to her manager, but didn't receive treatment until after her injury worsened; even then she was rushed to the Walmart pharmacy rather than to the emergency room. After that, she had to go on medical leave for many months. Girshriela says that she also faced gender discrimination at Walmart, where she says women have a harder time moving up the career ladder and men generally make a dollar more per hour than women do. She says that she talked to the store managers about it, but nothing happened. She herself has also been subject to sexual harassment: "When I complained about it to my supervisor, he said, 'Men do that and it's okay.' I went higher up to management but got no response."

Girshriela joined OUR Walmart because she was tired of disrespect, low wages, and lack of benefits at Walmart. She participated in numerous protests, traveled to Bentonville, Arkansas, for Walmart's shareholder meeting, and went directly to Walmart headquarters there to confront executives about the mistreatment of store employees.

In June 2012, Girshriela was fired by Walmart because of her organizing activities. She proceeded to become a national organizer with OUR Walmart, traveling around the country to organize Walmart workers. She says, "It feels great after being broken and feeling hopeless that Walmart managers weren't going to be held accountable, but now we are holding them accountable! I can't imagine doing anything else now."

Restaurant Workers

> I didn't really get any breaks or lunch. I was paid less than the minimum wage—$7.
>
> —Oiko Opgonbeayar, restaurant worker, Los Angeles

The restaurant industry employs more than 10 million people, making it the largest fully private-sector employer in the nation (versus public-sector, government jobs) and the largest segment of the food chain. The restaurant industry is one of the fastest growing and largest industries in the United States. When other industries lost jobs during the recent recession, the restaurant industry added jobs.[64]

The presence of tips in the restaurant industry has allowed restaurant employer lobbying groups to prevent increases in the minimum wages in most states and at the federal level to keep pace with inflation. Additionally, the National Restaurant Association has successfully lobbied to keep the federal

FIGURE 4.5   Restaurant workers, Chicago
(Photo by The Restaurant Opportunities Centers United. Used by permission of the Food Chain Workers Alliance.)

minimum wage for tipped workers at $2.13 since 1991, a contributing factor in restaurant occupations' being named by the U.S. Department of Labor as 7 of the 10 lowest paid jobs in 2010 and the two absolute lowest-paid jobs in the United States. The median wage in the restaurant industry is only $8.89, which means that more than half of restaurant workers' earnings fall below the federal poverty line for a family of three.[65] As a result, restaurant servers have three times the poverty rate, and use food stamps at double the rate, of the rest of the U.S. workforce.[66]

The Food Chain Workers Alliance includes two member organizations whose membership exclusively comprises restaurant workers: the Restaurant Opportunities Center (ROC) of New York and ROC United. The ROC was initially founded after September 11, 2001, to provide support to restaurant workers displaced from the World Trade Center, and ROC United was formed in 2008 to organize restaurant workers nationally and has since grown to include over 10,000 members in 19 states.

ROC United has surveyed over 5,000 restaurant workers around the United States. An analysis of the surveys of workers in eight regions—New York, Chicago, Metro Detroit, Los Angeles, Maine, Miami, New Orleans, and

Washington, D.C.—found that workers of color are highly concentrated in the industry's "bad jobs," whereas white workers tend to disproportionately hold the few "good jobs" that provide living wages, benefits, and opportunities for advancement to higher-paying positions. Workers also reported discriminatory hiring, promotion, and disciplinary practices, resulting in a $3.71 wage gap between white restaurant workers and workers of color. The median hourly wage of all white workers surveyed in the eight localities was $13.25; that of workers of color was $9.54.[67]

ROC–NY also confirmed discrimination in the New York City restaurant industry. The organization sent in 139 pairs of white workers and workers of color with the same qualifications to apply for the same jobs in fine-dining restaurants. ROC–NY found that the job applicants of color were only 54.5 percent as likely as white applicants to get a job offer and were less likely than white testers to receive a job interview in the first place.[68] The work experience of white job applicants was also twice as likely to be accepted without proper vetting.

Female restaurant servers also face lower wages, not only because of discriminatory employment practices, but also because of the law holding the tipped minimum wage at $2.13 per hour. On average, full-time, year round, female restaurant workers are paid 79 percent of what male counterparts earn.[69] Servers constitute the largest group of all tipped workers, and 71 percent of them are female.[70] Full-time, year-round female servers are paid 68 percent of what their male counterparts are paid ($17,000 vs. $25,000 annually).[71]

Sexual harassment is also a major problem. According to ROC United, MSNBC reviewed data from the Equal Employment Opportunity Commission (EEOC) and found that from January to November 2011, almost 37 percent of all EEOC charges made by women regarding sexual harassment came from the restaurant industry, even though fewer than 7 percent of employed women work in the restaurant industry.[72] The EEOC has now targeted the restaurant industry as the "single largest" source of sexual harassment claims.[73]

Both locally and at the national level, ROC employs a tri-pronged strategy designed to improve low-wage restaurant workers' wages and working conditions and increase access to living-wage jobs. The three prongs of its strategy include (1) conducting industry research and policy work to lift conditions industrywide, (2) partnering with responsible employers to conduct workforce development work helping low-wage workers obtain living-wage jobs and to support policy proposals that improve conditions industrywide, and (3) organizing restaurant workers in workplace justice campaigns to confront exploitation in the workplace.

Twenty-seven-year-old Oiko Opgonbeayar is a member of ROC's affiliate in Los Angeles. She has worked as a cashier, waitress, and hostess in the restaurant industry for eight years. She was born in Mongolia and came to the United States 10 years ago. Oiko believes that she has been discriminated against because she is an immigrant and a woman. In one of her recent jobs, she says, "I didn't really get any breaks or lunch. I was paid less than the minimum wage—$7" (the minimum wage in California is $8 per hour). "Other servers got breaks and got to leave for emergencies and come back, but I always had to stay."

Oiko was looking for a better job and found a listing on Craigslist about the workforce development classes that ROC–LA offers for free to restaurant workers. She decided to attend an orientation and has since become involved with ROC–LA, attending bartending classes, helping with fundraising events, and supporting the Dignity at Darden Campaign, a campaign in which workers from the Capital Grille Restaurant are organizing to fight for payment of unpaid wages and to stop discrimination. Darden is the largest full-service restaurant corporation in the world, owning Red Lobster, the Olive Garden, and other chains, including the Capital Grille.

"I love working in restaurants, giving good hospitality service, but I want my rights respected in future work," Oiko says. She joined ROC–LA, and she has met many people who want this as a career and who should be happy in their work. One day, she hopes to open her own restaurant and treat her own employees fairly.

Conclusion

For workers throughout the food system, the vast majority are struggling for respect and a voice in their workplace and their community. Yet there is hope, and there are models, of food justice for food system workers. In our report "The Hands That Feed Us," 13.5 percent of the workers that we surveyed earn livable wages. And many members of the Food Chain Workers Alliance are winning union contracts and agreements with employers and corporations up the food chain.

For instance, the Coalition of Immokalee Workers has organized to win Fair Food Agreements with 12 major corporations, such as McDonald's, Whole Foods, and Trader Joe's. The agreements require that these companies pay 1¢ more per pound directly to the farmworkers who pick the tomatoes that these companies purchase in Florida. Moreover, the CIW has established a health and safety committee of farmworkers to ensure safe working environments, has worked to create a grievance procedure to resolve problems at the farm level, and requires buyers to have a zero-tolerance policy for the use of forced labor and slavery by its tomato suppliers, among much more.

Similarly, ROC United has achieved major successes since 2001 using its tripronged strategy described above. Restaurant workers organizing with ROC United have won 13 workplace justice campaigns against large, high-profile corporations, winning back more than $7 million in stolen tips and wages and discrimination payments, as well as agreements providing workers with paid sick days. Moreover, these agreements include a grievance procedure, training, and career advancement opportunities that address the racial and gender discrimination in the industry. ROC United has organized over 100 responsible employers to promote the "high road" to profitability in the industry and to provide an alternative voice to the National Restaurant Association (NRA), the powerful restaurant industry lobby. The organization has partnered with responsible restaurants around the country and has trained more than 3,000 low-wage workers, helping them to advance to livable wage jobs in the industry. ROC also played a leading role in raising the minimum wage for tipped workers in New York State and in winning a tip protection bill in Philadelphia.

ROC United has also opened two worker-owned restaurants called COLORS in New York City and in Detroit. The first location in New York City was opened in 2006 by some of the survivors of 9/11 who were displaced from their jobs at the Windows of the World, the restaurant at the top of the World Trade Center. These workers, who were also cofounders of ROC–NY, wanted to show bad restaurant employers that a restaurant could provide good food as well as a workplace in which workers have a voice, respect, and dignity. COLORS in both cities also provides a space for ROC to provide free training programs for workers to help them gain employment in higher-paying positions in fine dining restaurants. Both restaurants also focus on providing local, sustainably produced food.

Another example is the union UNITE HERE's Real Food Real Jobs Campaign, which is organizing food service workers at K–12 school districts, colleges, universities, and airports around the country. The workers organize not only to gain a union contract with improved wages, benefits, and working conditions, but to also cook real food for the students, rather than simply reheating processed food. Since the campaign launched in early 2011, hundreds of food service workers have organized together and joined the union, as well as renegotiated contracts so that workers have a voice in the workplace and concerning the food that they cook and serve. Through the Real Food Real Jobs Campaign, the union invites food justice groups and other organizations concerned about school food, nutrition, and health to work with the union to improve jobs and ensure healthy food is served in schools and airports. UNITE HERE's primary strategy is organizing workers and developing them into leaders who can talk to potential allies, such as students, professors, and community groups as well as to the media. UNITE HERE also conducts research and media work and organizes rallies and protests to promote the issues facing the workers as well as the solutions they want.

For example, in 2012, the Real Food Real Jobs Campaign worked with the UNITE HERE local union in Chicago as their members—3,200 lunchroom

FIGURE 4.6   Members of UNITE HERE Local 1 in Chicago rally to demand additional staff to be able to cook real food, winning 97 additional jobs in 2013

(Photo by Meghan Cohorst. Used by permission of the Food Chain Workers Alliance.)

workers—renegotiated an expired contract with the Chicago Public Schools. They named their local campaign "Let's Cook!" One of the workers' key demands was to cook real food again, not just reheat frozen processed food. The workers organized with parents to gain support for this demand. They released a report highlighting the growing amount of frozen and prepackaged food served in the schools. UNITE HERE Local 1 held press conferences and protests and started collecting parents' signatures on a petition supporting the union's demands for worker input on the school's food menu as well as advocated for cooking more food. On May 3, 2012, the workers and the union announced a victory. In addition to improvements in wages, protecting health care and job security, the contract halts any expansion of schools that have only warming kitchens for reheating frozen food. The Chicago Public Schools also agreed to actively solicit and incorporate input from lunchroom workers. A "Good Food Committee," with representatives from both the board of education and front-line workers, now meets monthly to identify best practices regarding healthful food. A biannual survey of lunchroom workers will also be conducted to ensure worker input on menu or program changes in schools.[74]

These are just a few examples of how food workers are organizing and strengthening power to improve their jobs and the food system. These organizations are also coming together in the Food Chain Workers Alliance, a national coalition of workers organizations. Those who want a more just food system should join with these workers. That is the only way to successfully organize for a food system that provides healthy, affordable food for all and that respects all who work to bring food to our tables.

Notes

1. Food Chain Workers Alliance, "The Hands That Feed Us: Opportunities and Challenges for Workers along the Food Chain" (June 6, 2012), 12.

2. Ibid., 9.

3. Ibid., 19.

4. Ibid., 19.

5. Ibid., 20.

6. Ibid., 4.

7. The Food Labor Research Center at the University of California–Berkeley, the Food Chain Workers Alliance, and the Restaurant Opportunities Centers (ROC–United), "A Dime a Day: The Impact of the Miller/Harkin Minimum Wage Proposal on the Price of Food" (October 24, 2012), 2.

8. "The Hands That Feed Us," 20.

9. Ibid., 5.

10. Ibid., 21.

11. Yvonne Yen Liu and Dominique Apollon, "The Color of Food" (Applied Research Center, February 2011), 9.

12. "The Hands That Feed Us," 42.

13. Liu and Apollon, 11.

14. Ibid., 43.

15. Ibid., 43.

16. The poverty level for a family of three in 2011, when we conducted these surveys of workers, was $18,530. The poverty line is used to determine eligibility for various federal programs, such as SNAP benefits (previously known as food stamps) and Women, Infant, and Children (WIC) programs, among others.

17. Ibid., 43.

18. Kyle Boyd, "The Color of Help," *American Prospect* (June 17, 2011). www.americanprogress.org/issues/race/news/2011/06/17/9783/the-color-of-help/

19. The New York Times, "Editorial: Farm Workers' Rights, 70 Years Overdue" (April 5, 2009). www.nytimes.com/2009/04/06/opinion/06mon1.html?_r=0

20. Bon Appétit Management Company Foundation and United Farm Workers, "Inventory of Farmworker Issues and Protections in the United States" (March 2011). Also, National Center for Farmworker Health, "Facts about Farmworkers." www.ncfh.org/docs/fs-Facts%20about%20Farmworkers.pdf

21. Association of Farmworker Opportunity Programs, "Children in the Fields: Learn the Facts." http://afop.org/children-in-the-fields/learn-the-facts/#AFOP_estimates

22. Human Rights Watch, "Cultivating Fear: The Vulnerability of Immigrant Farmworkers in the U.S. to Sexual Violence and Sexual Harassment" (May 2012), 16.

23. U.S. Department of Labor, "The National Agricultural Workers Survey (NAWS), 2001–2002: Chapter 6: Income, Assets, and Use of Public Programs" (January 11, 2010). www.doleta.gov/agworker/report9/chapter6.cfm

24. Bon Appétit Management Company Foundation and United Farm Workers, "Inventory of Farmworker Issues and Protections in the United States" (March 2011).

25. Human Rights Watch, 16–17.

26. Ibid., 23.

27. Lake Apopka Farmworker Memorial Quilt, http://apopkaquiltproject.blogspot.com

28. Tom Philpott, "Foodies, Get Thee to Occupy Wall Street," *Mother Jones* (October 14, 2011), http://motherjones.com/environment/2011/10/food-industry-monopoly-occupy-wall-street; Tom Philpott, "JBS: Industrial Meat's New Heavyweight Champ," Grist.org (September 23, 2009), http://grist.org/food/2009-09-22-meat-wagon-jbs-pilgrims/

29. Mary Hendrickson and William Heffernan, "Concentration of Agricultural Markets" (University of Missouri Department of Rural Sociology, April 2007). www.foodcircles.missouri.edu/07contable.pdf

30. Ibid.

31. Government Accountability Office, "Safety in the Meat and Poultry Industry, While Improving, Could Be Further Strengthened: Report to the Ranking Minority Member, Committee on Health, Education, Labor, and Pensions, U.S. Senate" (January 2005). www.gao.gov/new.items/d0596.pdf

32. William G. Whittaker, "Labor Practices in the Meat Packing and Poultry Processing Industry: An Overview" (Congressional Research Service RL33002, July 20, 2005), 14. www.nationalaglawcenter.org/assets/crs/RL33002.pdf

33. United Food and Commercial Workers International Union, "Injury and Injustice: America's Poultry Industry." www.ufcw.org/press_room/fact_sheets_and_backgrounder/poultryindustry_.cfm

34. "The Hands That Feed Us," 17.

35. U.S. Department of Labor, "Total Recordable Cases, Rate of Injury and Illness Cases per 100 Full-time Workers by Selected Industry, All U.S., Private Industry, 2003–2007: Animal Slaughtering and Processing (code 311600)" (Bureau of Labor Statistics Database). www.bls.gov/data/#injuries

36. "The Hands That Feed Us," 35.

37. "The Hands That Feed Us," 17.

38. Warehouse Workers for Justice, "Bad Jobs in Goods Movement: Warehouse Work in Will County, IL" (August 2010), 11.

39. National Employment Law Project, "Chain of Greed: How Walmart's Domestic Outsourcing Produces Everyday Low Wages and Poor Working Conditions for Warehouse Workers" (June 2012), 12.

40. Juan D. De Lara, "Warehouse Work: Path to the Middle Class or Road to Economic Insecurity?" (USC Program for Environmental and Regional Equity, September 2013), 4.

41. Warehouse Workers for Justice, 2.

42. Ibid., 2.

43. Jason Struna, Kevin Curwin, Edwin Elias, Ellen Reese, Tony Roberts, and Elizabeth Bingle, "Unsafe and Unfair: Labor Conditions in the Warehouse Industry," *Policy Matters* 5, no. 2 (summer 2012): 6.

44. Ibid., 2.

45. Warehouse Workers for Justice, 13.

46. National Employment Law Project, 14.

47. Warehouse Workers for Justice, 19.

48. "The Hands That Feed Us," 27.

49. "Bad Jobs in the Goods Movement," 13.

50. "The Hands That Feed Us," 31.

51. Bureau of Labor Statistics (BLS), "Industries at a Glance: Food and Beverage Stores: NAICS 445" (May 2013).

52. Data from Bureau of Labor Statistics, Current Employment Survey, and analysis of the real value of wages conducted by Basav Sen, United Food and Commercial Workers Union, August 2013.

53. Barry Hirsch and David Macpherson, "U.S. Historical Tables: Union Membership, Coverage, Density and Employment, 1973–2012." http://unionstats.com

54. The Reinvestment Fund, "Understanding the Grocery Industry" (September 30, 2011), 5. www.cdfifund.gov/what_we_do/resources/Understanding%20Grocery%20Industry_for%20fund_102411.pdf

55. Trefos Team, "Wal-Mart Could Get Wounded in Grocery Wars," *Forbes*, January 21, 2011.

56. Wenonah Hauter, *Foodopoly* (December 11, 2012). www.foodopoly.org/infographics/

57. United Food and Commercial Workers, "Ending Walmart's Rural Stranglehold" (August 31, 2010), 4.

58. Ibid., 4.

59. "The Hands That Feed Us," 19.

60. The National Employment Law Project, Center for Urban Economic Development at U of I–Chicago, and the Institute for Labor Research and Education at UCLA, "Report: Broken Laws, Unprotected Workers: Violations of Employment and Labor Laws in America's Cities" (2009), 31, 24.

61. BLS. "Industries at a Glance. Food and Beverage Stores: NAICS 445" (May 2013).

62. Ibid.

63. "The Hands That Feed Us," 35.

64. Restaurant Opportunities Centers United, "Executive Summary of Behind the Kitchen Door: A Multi-Site Study of the Restaurant Industry" (February 14, 2011).

65. "Research and Resources." http://rocunited.org/research-resources/#sthash.gmfftQhB.dpuf

66. "The Hands That Feed Us," 35.

67. "Executive Summary of Behind the Kitchen Door: A Multi-Site Study of the Restaurant Industry."

68. Restaurant Opportunities Center of New York, "The Great Service Divide: Occupational Segregation and Inequality in the New York City Restaurant Industry" (March 31, 2009), 1.

69. Restaurant Opportunities Centers United, "Tipped Over the Edge: Gender Inequity in the Restaurant Industry" (February 13, 2012), 2.

70. Ibid., 1.

71. Ibid., 2.

72. Ibid., 3.

73. Ibid., 3.

74. Kyle Schafer, "Chicago Public Schools Agrees with Lunch Workers, Moves toward Fresh Food!" Real Food Real Jobs (May 3, 2012). www.realfoodrealjobs.org/2012/05/cpsvictory/#sthash.NdXueP04.dpuf

5

Lessons from the Food System: Borkian Paradoxes, Plutocracy, and the Rise of Walmart's Buyer Power

R. Dennis Olson

In 1987 Walmart* did not even sell groceries.[1] Yet by 2012 Walmart's grocery sales of nearly $151 billion represented 55 percent of Walmart's annual U.S. sales of more than $274 billion.[2] Walmart's total 2012 combined grocery and nongrocery global sales reached nearly $444 billion.[3] The company controls nearly a quarter of the U.S. retail grocery market, more than its next three biggest competitors do combined.[4]

When Tesco—Walmart's chief grocery rival in Britain—breached the 30 percent market share threshold in that country, Walmart called for government intervention: "As you get over 30% and higher, I am sure there is a point where government is compelled to intervene," said Lee Scott, then president of Walmart, in 2005. "At some point the government has to look at it."[5] Ironically enough, Walmart has issued no such call for such government intervention in the United States, even though it had controlled more than a 30 percent market share in 44 percent of major U.S. grocery markets by 2009, including more than 50 percent in 29 of those markets.[6]

This unprecedented usurpation of a substantial share of the global food system by the world's largest retail corporation poses a dire challenge to all stakeholders who toil along the global food supply chains to produce goods

---

*Walmart was spelled "Wal-Mart" until 2008, when it formally lost the hyphen. Accordingly, I have used "Walmart" except in pre-2008 quotations, in which the previous spelling is retained.

under the boot of Walmart's monopsony.[7] These stakeholders include farmers, food processors, food distributors, and grocery retailers. It also includes the farmworkers and other employees who work in these sectors.

Usurpation is a strong word, but the history of U.S. antimonopoly policies stretching more than two centuries reflects the economic side of the instinctive distrust Americans have always had of centralized power, reflected politically in the separation of powers enshrined in the U.S. Constitution. Economic and political powers are two sides of the same coin, and we ignore Walmart's growing economic power only at the peril of our political democracy. The U.S. Supreme Court clearly demonstrated this peril in its disturbing *Citizens United* decision, which struck down century-old limits on corporate campaign spending and which now threatens the democratic underpinnings of our electoral system.

The danger posed to our democratic institutions can also be seen in the persistent bribery and corruption charges against Walmart in countries such as Mexico[8] and India.[9] This type of corruption is not limited to developing countries, as demonstrated by Walmart's returning gift cards it had donated to the 2012 Democratic Convention only after the *New York Times* exposed the company's use of the same type of gift cards in the Mexican bribery scandal.[10]

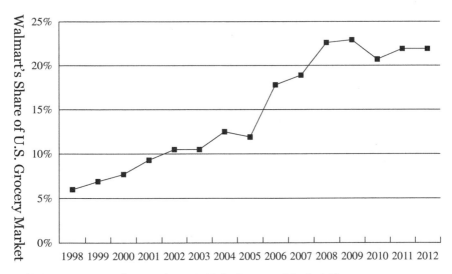

FIGURE 5.1   Trend in Walmart's U.S. Grocery Market Share

Source: "Ending Walmart's Rural Stranglehold" (UFCW, 2010). (Reprinted by permission of the UFCW.)

Note: Market share for Walmart was calculated as the ratio of the grocery sales obtained from the company's 10-K reports filed with Securities and Exchange Commission for each year analyzed to nationwide grocery sales for the respective year obtained from the annual Directory of Supermarket, Grocery and Convenience Store Chains, published by Chain Store Guide. The company reported grocery sales for both its Walmart Stores and Sam's Club segments starting in 1998.

Walmart has saturated U.S. markets to the point at which it is virtually impossible for the company to open a new store in rural or suburban markets without cannibalizing another of its already existing stores.[11] This market saturation helps explain why Walmart has launched three aggressive market expansion strategies to bolster its flagging growth.

First, the company wants to break into urban U.S. grocery markets heretofore shunned in favor of capturing rural and suburban markets. Second, Walmart has aggressively expanded into emerging economies like China, India, Mexico, and South Africa. And third, the company has recently launched a campaign to usurp the "sustainability mantle"—and the potential premiums that go with it—by increasing the volume of food products procured through vague and opaque certification protocols for fair trade, environmental friendly practices, and locally grown food from small- and medium-sized farmers.[12]

Smoke and Mirrors: Walmart's Dubious Claim to the Sustainability Mantle

Walmart's aggressive move to claim the sustainability mantle puts food in the crosshairs of the company's marketing strategy to revitalize its flagging sales:

> Following several consecutive years of moderate to strong growth, Wal-Mart Stores, Inc. appears increasingly challenged to sustain its momentum. As management has described its strategies for success going forward, food has a center stage role, with the effort and outcome holding important implications both for the world's largest retailer and its many food suppliers.[13]

Walmart outperformed the broader market over the past two years, posting impressive earnings-per-share growth for its shareholders, ranging from 9 to 12 percent from fiscal year 2009 through 2013.[14] Nonetheless, Wall Street's insatiable greed for ever higher rates of return can never be satisfied. "Rather than generating confidence in the investment community, the results have led some analysts to take a dimmer view of . . . Wal-Mart's prospects."[15]

"With the low-hanging fruit behind them . . . we believe [comparative sales] have peaked [and] will plateau following three straight years of acceleration," an analyst with JP Morgan said earlier this year as part of a downgrade of Wal-Mart stock.[16] So, under relentless pressure from Wall Street, Walmart's management has now set its sights squarely on food:

> The role food will play in Wal-Mart's efforts to generate growth was emphasized in a management update to the investment analyst community. Among retailers competing for consumer traffic, food aisles have become the principal battleground and are likely to remain so. . . .[17]

Consistent with this strategy, Walmart cloaks its intentions with the trappings of sustainability: locally grown, bought from small farmers both at home and abroad, and supplies of healthy food to poor people stranded in food deserts. Walmart advertises this all while claiming to save consumers billions of dollars.[18] Yet Walmart keeps tripping over the inconvenient truth that its model—based on the slogan of "Everyday Low Prices"—is antithetical to sustainability.

For example, faced with criticism that its produce is decrepit, Walmart recently announced that it would institute a money-back guarantee.[19] Additionally, the company announced that it would train 70,000 of its associates to better manage the store's produce.[20] Perhaps Walmart should instead reevaluate its policies of paying its produce managers poverty-level wages and intentionally manipulating employees' work schedules to ensure that they work fewer than 30 hours per week, thus disqualifying them for health care benefits. Walmart management might want to consider the possibility that being a good produce manager requires not only training, but also personnel policies that encourage dedication and commitment. Achieving such dedication and commitment requires treating employees with a minimum level of dignity, respect, and trust—all values that are sorely lacking in the exploitive Walmart model.

As one supermarket analyst put it, Walmart's approach to improving its produce departments is like "announcing [that] Walmart will now be cleaning their restrooms daily, and that employees will [be] (sic) receiving special training in bathroom cleaning. . . . It makes it sound like Walmart will have cleaner bathrooms, when this policy was actually already in place."[21]

Another analyst put it this way:

> This is an effort to get people to focus on positive things, rather than the $110 million in environmental fines[22] [Walmart] was ordered to pay last week or last quarter's international bribery scandal. . . . And have they really not been removing rotten produce from their shelves all along?[23]

In another sustainability initiative, Walmart has announced a goal of doubling its purchases of locally grown produce by 2015, which would represent 9 percent of its produce sales.[24] However, Walmart defines as "locally grown" produce sold in the same state where it was grown. In light of the company's vast volume of produce sales, Walmart could plausibly meet most of its 9 percent goal simply by opening new stores in California and buying produce from large corporate farms within the borders of this major agricultural state.[25] If such smoke and mirrors allows Walmart to claim the mantle of "locally grown," perhaps the public will forget about the company's claim of increasing purchases from small farmers.

This bait-and-switch strategy is also reflected in the opacity of how Walmart measures its progress at meeting its sustainability goals. For example,

Walmart's 2013 *Global Responsibility Report* simply says, "Despite widespread drought facing many of our vegetable farmers and early freezes that cut a swath through the eastern apple crops, we're still on course to continue expanding our purchases of locally grown fruits and vegetables and achieving our goal of doubling our local purchases by 2015."[26] However, Walmart provides no specific milestones to substantiate its claim to be "on course" toward achieving this goal. As is often the case with Walmart's sustainability claims, both the baseline and the progress reports are vague and opaque, making any meaningful verification by outside analysis virtually impossible. Walmart simply has not answered the question of how it intends to pay its suppliers enough to cover the unavoidable costs of concrete sustainability initiatives.

Walmart depends on using its monopsony power to squeeze its suppliers for its competitive edge, which makes the company's corporate model deeply antithetical to the values of true sustainability. Assuming that Walmart does actually implement substantive sustainability standards, and assuming that such sustainability standards carry a premium, will Walmart implement protocols to earmark those premiums for suppliers all the way up the food supply chain? Or will it just pocket them? If Walmart does actually guarantee suppliers a fair share of the premium, how will it meet the demands of its Wall Street investors for ever higher profit margins?

If Walmart does not guarantee the premiums to its suppliers, how can those suppliers pay for the sustainability standards when Walmart wields its formidable monopsony power to force them to pay the increased costs? And if the suppliers are unable to pay for the standards under the boot of buyer power abuse, how "sustainable" will Walmart's imposed standards be?

These questions of how to achieve sustainability have become more salient in recent years as Walmart's phenomenal growth has stagnated and Wall Street's relentless demand for ever higher returns on investment has increased the pressure on Walmart to wield its monopsony power even more ruthlessly in order to squeeze more profits out of the shrinking margins of its suppliers.

Food as a Loss Leader: The Key to Walmart's Growth Strategy

Walmart's sustainability claims are dubious, but it would be a mistake to underestimate the effectiveness of the company's greenwashing[27] strategy. To understand why food is pivotal to Walmart's growth strategy, it helps to understand how Walmart uses food as part of a *loss leader* strategy.

According to Investopedia, a loss leader strategy is one "in which a business offers a product or service at a price that is not profitable for the sake of offering another product/service at a greater profit or to attract new customers."[28] Although this strategy is employed by many businesses, Walmart has taken it a step further by using its advantage of selling nonfood items to wield power over its major grocery-sector competitors such as Kroger and Safeway, who primarily sell groceries.

In this context another retailing marketing term, *velocity*, comes into play. Velocity measures the frequency with which customers return to the store to purchase an item. As explained by William Simon, Walmart's CEO,

> the velocity of a pillow is one time every year or two years. . . . The velocity of bananas or milk is once a week or twice a week. You have to drive velocity through food. . . . And with the traffic . . . we're able to leverage [it] on the other side. If you double your traffic on sheets and towels, you won't have any measurable impact at all on bananas because of the raw numbers. So focusing on food . . . is focusing on the balance of the box.[29]

Selling produce at less than the cost of production can pay if it entices more customers to visit the store more often. If more customers come into the store more often to buy a loss leading food item, they are more likely to buy other nonfood items such as televisions and T-shirts. Walmart may then be able to recoup its loss of selling the food item below cost either by raising the prices on other nonfood items in the store or by simply increasing the volume of sales of those items even if prices are not raised.

Being able to raise prices on nonfood items that make up almost half its store inventory gives Walmart a potential competitive advantage over stores that primarily sell groceries. A supermarket that primarily sells groceries may be unable to match Walmart's food prices, because it cannot cross-subsidize food sales with nonfood sales. This means that supermarkets could lose market share to Walmart or even be forced out of business.

Evidence that Walmart's loss leader strategy is working can be found in the company's own quarterly reports touting the success of the loss leader strategy to Wall Street financial analysts:

> [W]e continue to execute our strategy [of] investing in [lower] retail price . . . in our food . . . so that we can drive traffic to our stores. . . . What you'll see is we've actually widened our price gap over the last 13 months, against our competition by 100 basis points.[30]
>
> —Duncan Mac Naughton, executive vice-president,
> Wal-Mart Stores, Inc.

Additional evidence of the success of Walmart's loss leader strategy can be found in statistics indicating that Walmart is gaining market share at the expense of its competitors. Between 2009 and 2011 Walmart opened 94 stores, whereas its major competitors—Kroger and Safeway—closed 6 and 25 stores, respectively.[31] Kroger and Safeway primarily sell groceries, so their store closings may indicate that they are unable to compete with Walmart's below-cost pricing in food.

Under current interpretations of antitrust law, it is not illegal for Walmart to sell below the costs of its competitors as long as it is not selling below its own costs. However, this is a crucial flaw in current antitrust policy, because it does not take into account Walmart's ability to cross-subsidize its food sales with nonfood items—an option unavailable to competitors like Kroger or Safeway. Additionally, it is extremely difficult to prove in court that a specific food item is being sold below cost.[32]

Nonetheless, on the surface Walmart's loss leader strategy appears to be a form of "predatory pricing," to use antitrust parlance. And there is some evidence to support a predatory pricing claim—e.g., a substantial number of Kroger and Safeway store closures[33] and Walmart's corresponding gain in market share. Unfortunately, because of several pivotal U.S. Supreme Court rulings, if Walmart is able to make a case that its loss leader strategy might ostensibly result in lower consumer prices, any potential plaintiff losing market share to Walmart would face a steep burden of proof in attempting to prove predatory pricing in court.[34]

> [I]t is unlikely that the current law of predatory pricing under . . . the Sherman Act will be violated [in the case of Walmart]. Even if there is evidence that Walmart targets particular competitors or entrants and it can be shown that Wal-Mart prices below costs . . ., Wal-Mart does not have sufficient market share to be considered a monopolist.[35]

Returning to Walmart's sustainability claims, we should also note that Kroger and Safeway are large union employers. So if Walmart's loss leader strategy is succeeding in taking market share away from them, then higher-paying union jobs with benefits are being displaced by nonunion jobs with lower salaries and fewer benefits. Such displacement erodes labor standards in the entire retail grocery sector. It reiterates the inherent contradiction between Walmart's corporate strategy of buyer power abuse and its sustainability claims that fail to provide fair living standards for workers.

To better understand the daunting challenges of mounting a successful legal challenge to prove that Walmart's loss leader strategy is illegal predatory pricing under current antitrust laws, it is first necessary to examine the current judicial prescription that has emerged over the last three decades around what is known as the "consumer welfare" doctrine.

The Borkian Antitrust Paradox[36]

For over three decades, U.S. federal courts have forged a prescription around the premise that the sole purpose of antitrust policy is to provide consumers with lower prices. The roots of this "consumer welfare" doctrine can be traced back to a book written in 1978 by Robert Bork, who was later nominated to the U.S. Supreme Court by President Reagan but whose nomination was rejected by the Senate. In his book, *The Antitrust Paradox*, Bork consolidated the relentless attacks on U.S. antitrust policy that he had been carrying out since the 1960s. He argued that the courts had misconstrued the original congressional intent of the Sherman Antitrust Act and that activist judges were misapplying antitrust laws to protect inefficient businesses from legitimate competition.[37]

Instead of couching his critique in terms of defending the predatory practices of large monopolistic corporations, Bork cleverly achieved a brilliant bait-and-switch. He argued that by protecting "less inefficient" companies against the predatory practices of bigger, "more efficient" companies through the enforcement of antitrust laws, the courts were forcing consumers to pay higher prices. In Bork's mind, the judicial approach at that time of protecting competitors from unfair market practices contradicted congressional intent in passing antitrust laws—namely, to provide the lowest prices to consumers.[38]

Ignoring nearly 200 years of bipartisan consensus in all three branches of government that antimonopoly laws had other objectives than merely lower consumer prices, the U.S. Supreme Court ultimately cited Bork's book in several pivotal antitrust rulings. Agreeing with Bork, the Supreme Court confirmed an already evolving legal prescription adopted by some lower courts that consumer welfare had been the sole goal of U.S. antitrust policy all along. That legal prescription prevails to this day.[39] It is a legal prescription because it is not a legal *consensus*: Many antitrust experts criticize the courts' approach in adopting the consumer welfare doctrine over the strong economic and legal arguments against it.[40]

The Antitrust Consumer Welfare Paradox

Antitrust scholar Barak Y. Orbach, in his article *The Antitrust Consumer Welfare Paradox*, challenges Bork's consumer welfare doctrine:

> [T]he antitrust consumer welfare standard was born in a rhetorical flourish and grew with illegitimate borrowing. Most antitrust lawyers and economists know that Bork was confused [or intentionally disingenuous] when he used the term "consumer welfare" in his analysis of the Sherman Act. The Supreme Court made a mistake in relying on his analysis. Over the years, dozens of articles and books have referred to Bork's "confusion" and debated

what meaning this mistaken labeling should have. The simple truth is that we, in the antitrust community, have failed to inform courts about the original mistake that Bork made. This article aims to correct that mislabeling.[41]

Although much of Bork's initial focus was on the Sherman Act, as the court rulings mounted over the decades in favor of the consumer welfare prescription, judges increasingly ignored the plain language of other U.S. antitrust statutes that had clearly articulated a multitude of other goals beyond consumer welfare.

For example, Congress passed the Robinson–Patman Act in 1936 to protect small independent grocers from predatory price discrimination by large grocery chains.[42] And the Packers and Stockyards Act explicitly prohibits meatpacking companies from engaging in price discrimination or price manipulation against farmers and ranchers who were suppliers.[43] Nonetheless, the U.S. Supreme Court uncritically adopted Bork's consumer welfare doctrine, which has since been expanded to other statutes.[44]

Bork is not a man of consensus. His analysis of the goals of antitrust laws is no exception: his views were fiercely debated by antitrust scholars and practitioners throughout the 1960s, 1970s, and early 1980s. The Supreme Court, however, quickly adopted Bork's "consumer welfare prescription," making it the stated law of the land.[45]

For more than 30 years the courts have used Bork's consumer welfare doctrine as a pretense for protecting the increasingly privileged position of corporate plutocracy. This inexcusable abdication by the U.S. courts has allowed corporate elites to consolidate unprecedented market power in a manner that dominates not only the U.S. economy at the expense of other stakeholders, but also the U.S. political system at the expense of democracy. The unprecedented rise of Walmart's strangulating buyer power epitomizes the former; while the U.S. Supreme Court's 2012 *Citizens United* decision elucidates the latter.

Taking the "Predatory" Out of Predatory Pricing

"Predatory pricing is . . . defined as sales below-cost by a dominant firm over a long enough period of time for the purpose of driving a competitor from the market; the predator firm then raises prices to supracompetitive levels to recoup its losses and render the practice profitable."[46] Although many critiques explain the devastating effects of the consumer welfare doctrine, the virtual nullification of antitrust restraints on predatory pricing is arguably the most pivotal.

Prior to Bork, the courts had established several tests for determining whether predatory pricing violations had occurred. For example, one test was whether the plaintiff could demonstrate that the alleged monopolist was selling a product below cost for a considerable period of time.[47]

However, Bork argued that Congress had never intended for antitrust policy to protect competitors in particular, but only competition in general for the purpose of providing lower prices to consumers. In Bork's view, harm to competitors caused by predatory pricing was usually not only irrelevant to the goal of consumer welfare, but also antithetical to it. He argued that by protecting competitors from predatory pricing, judges had been inadvertently protecting inefficient companies from competition and thereby unfairly forcing consumers to pay higher prices. Whereas earlier court interpretations had restrained predatory pricing if it damaged competitors under certain circumstances, eventually the courts adopted Bork's alternative view: They began rejecting previous predatory pricing tests that had been partially based on harm to competitors, because such harm to competitors had also been assumed to be detrimental to overall competition. Thus began the unshackling of the corporate plutocrats from previous legal constraints against predatory pricing.

Eventually, the courts also began requiring plaintiffs in antitrust actions to prove not only that the alleged monopolist was selling its product below cost, but also that the alleged predator would be able to recoup the losses incurred from the initial below-cost pricing. Ultimately, the courts came to the stunning conclusion that *it didn't even matter* whether the plaintiff could prove *that the predator had intended to drive the competition out of the business.* Instead, the courts created an almost impossible obstacle for plaintiffs to prove that such below-cost pricing was predatory: *They would have to prove that the predatory pricing would likely succeed.* Even if a plaintiff could prove in court that the price was below cost and that the predator had intended to drive competition out of business, that would not be sufficient to demonstrate an antitrust violation.[48]

According to former FTC commissioner Terry Calvani, the U.S. Supreme Court adopted this approach in a case called *Brooke Group Ltd.* In his written opinion, Justice Kennedy cited another court decision, *Matsushita Electric Industrial Co. v. Zenith Radio Corp.*:

(T)he success of such [predatory pricing] schemes is inherently uncertain: the short-run loss is definite, but the long-run gain depends on successfully neutralizing the competition. Moreover, it is not enough simply to achieve monopoly power, as monopoly pricing may breed quick entry by new competitors eager to share in the excess profits. The success of any predatory scheme depends on *maintaining* monopoly power for long enough both to recoup the predator's losses and to harvest some additional gain.[49]

Calvani goes on to cite another court decision, *A.A. Poultry Farms, Inc.,* expounding on the irrelevance of predatory "intent":

[I]ntent plays no useful role in this kind of litigation. Firms "intend" to do all the business they can, to crush their rivals if they can. . . . Rivalry is harsh, and consumers gain the most when firms slash costs to the bone and pare price down to cost, all in pursuit of more business. . . . Entrepreneurs who work hardest to cut their prices will do the most damage to their rivals. . . . If courts use the vigorous, nasty pursuit of sales as evidence of a forbidden "intent," they run the risk of penalizing the motive forces of competition.[50]

This ruling freed monopolists to predatorily price competitors out of business unless the victims could prove a priori that the predator would likely succeed for some vague amount of time in to the future—i.e., enough time for the predator to recoup its losses from below-cost pricing "and to harvest some additional gain," as Justice Kennedy put it. Only then could court intervention be justified. "Recoupment is the ultimate object of an unlawful predatory pricing scheme," according to the Supreme Court's majority opinion [in *Brooke Group Ltd.*]. "If prices don't ultimately go up, that means "predatory pricing produces lower aggregate prices in the market, and consumer welfare is enhanced."

Thus, the U.S. Supreme Court endorsed the Borkian rationale of justifying predatory pricing in the name of lower prices, thereby abandoning decades of bipartisan consensus that Congress had intended for antitrust policy to curtail predatory pricing at certain points prior to its causing harm to already existing competition as opposed to some theoretical future competition. Even if below-cost pricing would bankrupt all existing competitors, that would not necessarily be of concern to the courts unless the plaintiff can also prove that the alleged predatory pricing would also be likely to preclude some unknown, perhaps even non-existent, competitor from entering the market sometime in the future. Unfortunately, delaying action until a plaintiff can prove likely harm to future competition arguably means that in many cases judicial relief would likely come too late to prevent irreparable harm to sustainable, long-term competition. By setting such a high bar of proof for any plaintiff to prevail in court, this draconian interpretation of the consumer welfare doctrine has drastically curtailed practical access to predatory pricing protections under U.S. antitrust laws.

While predatory pricing remains actionable under U.S. federal law, the current case law is quite skeptical of the theory generally. . . . [T]he view [is] that the costs of intervention are particularly high since consumers are denied the benefits of tough competition. Current law embraces the cost/price tests suggested by Professors Areeda and Turner, which are not easy to satisfy. Moreover, the recoupment requirement imposed by the Court in *Brooke Group* requires [a] plaintiff to demonstrate that there is a likelihood of recoupment before going forward. The universe of actionable cases in U.S. federal courts may not be a null set, but it is not large.[51]

Given the courts' consumer welfare prescription, one obstacle to challenging Walmart's loss leader strategy is that the company does not disclose profit margins by specific product category, because it would be virtually impossible to allocate a whole array of costs below the gross margin level. For example, how would you allocate to a specific loss leader item certain costs such as advertising, office personnel, store and distribution center leasing costs; or nondepartment labor costs such as front-end cashiers or truck drivers?[52] This represents a significant challenge of proving that a loss leader was being priced below cost—and it is merely the first hurdle that must be cleared to prove predatory pricing.

Additionally, even if a plaintiff could prove that Walmart was selling certain grocery items below cost, doing so is not necessarily illegal, as previously discussed. Under the consumer welfare doctrine, the plaintiff must also prove that Walmart would likely be able to drive its competitors out of business long enough to raise prices high enough to recoup the initial cost of the initial below-cost pricing. Although Kroger and Safeway store closures provide some anecdotal evidence supporting a claim of predatory pricing, these companies are still in business. So their continuing competitive presence in the market continues to limit Walmart's ability to sustain below-cost pricing, thereby calling into question whether any below-cost pricing is lasting long enough to put them completely out of business. Thus a predatory pricing case would be unlikely to clear the final hurdle by proving that Walmart would be able to raise prices to the necessary monopoly levels to allow recoupment of its below-cost pricing.

On the other hand, in some regional markets—e.g., in those where Walmart controls more than 50 percent of a market—a predatory pricing case would be stronger than in the case of the national market, where Walmart's market share is "only" 25 percent. In such regions, there could be instances in which Walmart has been able to put all of its competitors out of business long enough to recoup losses through sustained monopoly pricing. If so, perhaps a predatory pricing action might prevail. Similarly, one could also make a stronger predatory price case if Walmart were using a specific grocery item as a loss leader in which the company dominated more than 25 percent of the market for that particular item.[53]

Another potential path to a successful antitrust action was a phenomenon identified by the UK Competition Commission 2008 investigation as the "waterbed effect."[54] The waterbed effect is an antitrust theory based on the assumption that a supplier might become so dependent on such a high volume of sales to a single large customer such as Walmart that the buyer would end up acquiring enough leverage to demand below-cost prices from that supplier. Because the supplier would have become so captive to the high sales volumes, it would then be forced to capitulate to Walmart's demand for below-cost prices. In order to try to recover its losses on the below-cost sales to Walmart, the supplier might then raise prices on its other customers causing a potential violation of the consumer welfare doctrine.

However, there are at least a couple problems with this theory. First, even if it could be proven in court that a supplier had raised prices to other customers under pressure from Walmart, and even it had been shown to cause the consumers buying from those customers to pay higher prices, it is unclear whether a court would find that this violates consumer welfare. Walmart's large sales volumes at the lower price may still benefit a greater number of consumers, thus compensating for the price increase incurred by that smaller group of consumers' buying from Walmart's retail competitor who is being charged a higher price by the supplier. In this case, consumer prices would not rise on average. Thus, because overall prices did not rise, the courts could still find that such an outcome does not violate the consumer welfare prescription even if some consumers did end up paying higher prices.

Second, even if Walmart secured, for example, a 10 percent discount from one of its suppliers, other competitors such as Kroger or Target could still retain enough buyer power of their own to be able to demand lower prices from that same supplier as well. Thus consumers would still not end up paying higher prices. So there would be no viable legal challenge under the consumer welfare test.

Consumer Welfare Obscures Basic Concepts of Economics: Consumers Are Also Producers

Although Orbach gives several other examples of how Bork's doctrine has "obscured basic concepts in economics,"[55] one is particularly relevant to the question of Walmart's excessive buyer power abuse:

> [M]any economists and lawyers argue that the goal of antitrust laws should be maximization of the aggregate welfare in a market, that is, the sum of consumer surplus *and producer surplus*, irrespective of the distribution of surplus between these groups.[56] [Emphasis added.]

Here Orbach exposes the myopic one-sidedness of the consumer welfare doctrine, which omits the second half of the societal welfare equation:

> The term "consumer" is conceptually confusing in various contexts. In many transactions, the identity of the parties as "consumers" is arbitrary and

subject to social traditions and marketing strategies. We normally identify "buyers" as "consumers," but in monopsonistic markets, most would identify the sellers as consumers. . . . Thus, the conceptual starting point of the stated goal of antitrust laws is somewhat ill defined. *The "consumer welfare" goal has never had a defined consumer to maximize her welfare.*[57] [Emphasis added.]

Borkian dogma doggedly ignores the dual interests of supply chain stakeholders—namely, not just as consumers, but also as producers. Thus antitrust policy should not solely be limited to protecting consumers. A sound antitrust policy must acknowledge and balance the interests of both consumers and producers if society as whole is to benefit from it.

Thus, the willful Borkian ignorance that forms the basis of the current prescription of U.S. jurisprudence around the consumer welfare doctrine must be challenged if antitrust law is ever to be restored to its original purpose: to balance the interests of both consumers and producers, and not simply to favor disingenuously the interests of corporate plutocrats over the interests of the rest of society under the guise of consumer welfare.

Unfortunately, Orbach admits that the outlook for reform remains bleak:

In recent decades, there are no attempts to persuade courts that antitrust laws have any goal other than "consumer welfare," so the economists and lawyers in this group must believe that courts will expand . . . the scope of the term to mean "total surplus [i.e., both consumer and producer surplus, not just consumer surplus]." In practice [however], probably very few judges have appreciation of the subtleties of the various interpretations that the consumer welfare standard may accommodate.[58]

The insidiousness of the Borkian consumer welfare doctrine is that it has been resoundingly successful in its unstated but underlying goal of unfettering corporate elites from the original intent of antitrust policy, which was in fact to restrict predatory tendencies and ensure fairness in the market place for all stakeholders. There is enough wealth generated in food supply chains to provide all stakeholders who work along it with dignified, humane, and fair livelihoods. However, if it is ever to be restored to its original societal purpose, U.S. antitrust policy must be liberated from its current narrow servitude to corporate plutocrats.

The methodology of antitrust law cannot maximize consumer welfare. Bork's rhetorical masterstroke is now an impediment to this progress. The phrase "consumer welfare" is confusing when the goal is all about [consumer, producer and total societal] surplus. Whatever good ends the phrase may have once served, antitrust law should now lay it to rest.[59]

Historic Antitrust Initiatives Promise Reforms

Despite the bleak outlook of the Borkian judicial landscape, many who had been concerned with excessive concentration in food supply chains had become cautiously optimistic by 2010. Then, opportunities for reforming archaic antitrust laws seemed plausible because of several investigations being launched in the United States and around the world.

The Obama administration had just launched a bold, unprecedented investigation led by U.S. Departments of Agriculture and Justice that would catalyze a spirited public debate on whether more antitrust enforcement was needed in agricultural markets. In Europe, the EU Parliament had just requested an investigation into buyer power abuse by large supermarkets.[60] Additionally, the UK Competition Commission had just begun implementing reforms that had come out of a three-year investigation of alleged buyer power abuses by large supermarkets.[61] Hope abounded on many fronts.

Under the banner "Agriculture and Antitrust Enforcement Issues in Our 21st Century Economy," Secretary of Agriculture Tom Vilsack and U.S. Attorney General Eric Holder convened five joint regional workshops to investigate whether more antitrust enforcement was needed in agricultural markets. A major impetus of this joint initiative was to identify not only what predatory, anticompetitive abuses might be occurring in light of the unprecedented consolidation of agricultural markets, but also what reforms might be needed to protect stakeholders in food supply chains from any abuses identified.

Never before had the USDA and Justice Department collaborated on such an ambitious undertaking to focus on critical issues related to rampant market consolidation in the food economy. It seemed as though President Obama was taking seriously his campaign promise of providing hope to restore fairness in the rural economy—including explicit promises to enforce antitrust laws in the food economy,[62] as well as making key appointments of individuals with a strong commitment to antitrust enforcement.[63]

Ending Walmart's Rural Stranglehold[64]

The United Food and Commercial Workers Union (UFCW) turned out hundreds of its food processing, meatpacking, and retail grocery members to testify at all five of the joint regional hearings and also provided panel speakers at two of the workshops. Additionally, the UFCW released a report, "Ending Walmart's Rural Stranglehold,"[65] that supported the Obama administration's antitrust inquiry while also urging that the Federal Trade Commission (FTC) be included in the investigation because it has jurisdiction over antitrust enforcement in the retail grocery sectors.[66]

Debate at the regional U.S. workshops focused on whether more antitrust enforcement was needed at the transactional levels, either between farmers and food manufacturers or between farmers and farm input providers. The UFCW, by contrast, concluded that the unprecedented consolidation of power in one company—Walmart—had given that company unprecedented monopsony power over many of its suppliers, and hence over the people who work for those suppliers. The UFCW therefore demanded that the FTC use its expertise to investigate whether Walmart was abusing its buyer power in ways that harmed the interests of workers, farmers, and other suppliers and to develop policy recommendations to address any abuses identified.

The UFCW asked the FTC to assess whether Walmart's buyer power abuse was driving market consolidation farther up food supply chains—i.e., were other retail grocers, as well as suppliers, consolidating as a reaction to Walmart's increasing monopsony power? Without the FTC's resources and expertise to investigate Walmart's alleged buyer power abuses, the UFCW feared that no progress could be made toward identifying meaningful reforms.

The UFCW report cited the 2008 UK Competition Commission's investigation of large supermarkets that had found evidence of buyer power abuse. The commission had responded by implementing a Groceries Supply Code of Practice (GSCOP) enumerating a suppliers' Bill of Rights against the growing buyer power abuse. The commission also recommended the creation of an independent Groceries Code Adjudicator to enforce the GSCOP more effectively.[67] The UK Parliament eventually passed legislation implementing this second recommendation.[68]

Case Study on Retail Grocers' Monopsony Power: Beef   The UFCW report documented that ranchers had indeed lost a substantial share of the beef retail dollar since 1990. However, the study also found that most of the ranchers' lost market share had been usurped by retailers; beef packers were able to hold on to most of their share owing to their rapid consolidation since the 1980s.[69] The UFCW concluded that there is enough wealth generated along food supplies to provide adequate livelihoods to all stakeholders who depend on those supply lines. However, with the rise of Walmart's unprecedented buyer power, retailers were usurping more than their fair share of the food dollar at the expense of others. For example, the Walton family—who now owns more than 50 percent of Walmart's stock[70]—has accumulated as much wealth as the bottom 41.5 percent of Americans, representing almost 49 million families. Meanwhile, from 2007 to 2010, median family wealth in the United States fell 38.8 percent, while the Walton family's income soared 22 percent, from $73.3 billion to $89.5 billion.[71]

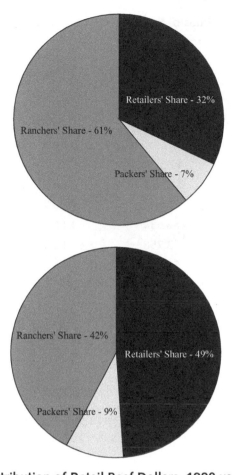

FIGURE 5.2   Distribution of Retail Beef Dollars, 1990 vs. 2009

Source: "Ending Walmart's Rural Stranglehold" (UFCW, 2010). (Reprinted by permission of the UFCW.)

No doubt the Waltons' exploitation of tax loopholes played an important role in causing this dramatic spike in inequity.[72] Nonetheless, there is also no denying that the rise of the consumer welfare doctrine over the past three decades has undermined antitrust enforcement, thereby aiding consolidation throughout the food supply chain. This consolidation includes the unprecedented growth of Walmart's monopsony power in retail groceries, which has undoubtedly contributed substantially to the Walton family fortune as well as to the widening gap income inequity in the U.S. economy as a whole. Thus antitrust policies should be recalibrated to help restore the balance of market power throughout the food supply chain to curtail the blatantly unfair market arrangements that facilitated the buyer power abuses exposed during the 2010

TABLE 5.1   Share of Sales of Selected Food Suppliers to Walmart

	Company Sales ($ millions)	Share of Sales to Walmart	Sales to Walmart ($ millions)
Kraft	$40,386	16.0%	$6,462
Tyson	$26,704	13.8%	$3,685
General Mills	$14,691	21.0%	$3,085
ConAgra	$12,731	16.0%	$2,037
Kellogg Co.	$12,587	21.0%	$2,643
Dean Foods	$11,158	21.0%	$2,343
Hormel	$6,534	13.0%	$849
Smucker	$3,758	24.0%	$902
Del Monte Foods Co.	$3,740	34.0%	$1,272
Flowers Foods	$2,601	20.5%	$533
Cott Corp.	$1,597	*	*
Cal Maine Foods	$929	32.9%	$306
Lance, Inc.	$918	22.0%	$202
Diamond Foods, Inc.	$571	21.0%	$120

*Cott Corp. has greater than 10% of its sales going to Walmart, but Cott does not disclose the exact share.

Source: "Ending Walmart's Rural Stranglehold" (UFCW, 2010). (Reprinted by permission of the UFCW.) Data gathered from companies' 10-K reports to the Securities and Exchange Commission.

antitrust hearings. Unfortunately, by primarily targeting on the meatpacking cartel, the agencies were focusing on the foreman rather than the plantation owner.

Captive Suppliers   Walmart controls nearly 25 percent of the national retail grocery market, more than 30 percent in every major region, and more than 50 percent in 29 markets across the country. Therefore, Walmart's successful loss leader strategy has dire implications not just for its retail grocery competitors like Kroger and Safeway, but also for food suppliers.[73]

> This domination by Walmart of the retail grocery market nationwide and in local markets makes the company an effective gatekeeper between food producers and consumers. Any food producer intending to sell their products nationally or in specific local markets needs to sell their products in Walmart's stores in order to reach a sizable number of consumers. This

gatekeeper role explains why Walmart accounts for such large shares of the sales of major meatpacking and food processing companies . . . . It also explains why Walmart's suppliers have no choice but to continue selling to Walmart in spite of the high-pressure negotiating tactic.[74]

Historic Antitrust Initiative Collapses under the Weight of Consumer Welfare

Without Federal Trade Commission (FTC) engagement, the UFCW worried that the investigation would develop recommendations for antitrust reforms that were limited only to transactions between farmers and food processors, or farmers and input dealers. Such recommendations might render a fairer share of the retail food dollar to farmers and ranchers, and even reduce some of the most egregious practices, such as the use of "tournaments" to promote competition among poultry farmers. However, absent reforms curtailing Walmart's buyer power, food processors would continue to be squeezed mercilessly. The net result of such piecemeal reforms would be that food processors would demand cuts in wages and benefits for their workers. So the UFCW insisted on a comprehensive approach to the investigation that assessed the entire food supply chain, not just disparate segments of it.[75]

The UFCW did finally succeed in convincing the Obama administration to bring the FTC to the table at the final hearing that focused on farm-to-retail prices spreads. Disappointingly, but predictably, the FTC's panelist, economist Howard Shelanski, deputy director for antitrust, testified that if Walmart's wielding of its buyer power against its suppliers reduced consumer prices, then no antitrust actions would likely be warranted:

> Monopsony . . . power . . . can benefit final consumers when benefit is measured in terms of their food bills. So . . . buying power that agricultural providers make in front along the supply chain may be beyond the scope of traditional antitrust enforcement.[76]

No matter how harmful monopsony power is to suppliers, the primary—if not the sole—criterion upon which the FTC decides its legality is whether that practice resulted in lower prices to consumers. Instead of taking up this historic challenge of curtailing the unprecedented dominance of Walmart's monopsony power, Shelanski signaled that the FTC would continue its decades-long history of complacency toward the company's growing abuse of that power because of the unproven assumption that it results in lower prices for consumers.

Other panelists did challenge Shelanski's position: Kyle Stiegert, director of the Food System Research Group at the University of Wisconsin-Madison, countered that what's been observed over the years in many . . . industries has been . . . that upstream cost increases . . . quickly get passed on to consumers, but cost decreases, for a variety of reasons, do not get passed on to the consumers. And so the firms that are in the vertical channel, retailers included, are taking a larger share of the pie, while those cost decreases are being noted. . . .[77]

So the retailer in this context is aware of that and can say "okay, I've got a price decrease today on ketchup, so I'm not going to lower the price to the consumer. I'll just take that as profit." But if they get an increase in the price of ketchup, they say "Hey, I'm not going to eat that. I'm passing it on, because frankly nobody really pays attention to a nickel or a dime change in the price of ketchup." Right? And that's really what's going on here.[78]

"[W]e say that competition is a good thing and it's a good thing for consumers to be able to buy from competitive sellers," added Albert A. Foer, president of the American Antitrust Institute, "[but w]hy is it that suppliers don't have a right to sell into a competitive market[?]" Foer pleaded that we should not give up on antitrust policy as a means for addressing buyer power abuse. He noted that Congress did in fact address buyer power in passing the Robinson–Patman Act as part of the New Deal response to the Great Depression: "When [the] A&P [grocery chain] and others were growing so strong as chains, we worried . . . about buyer power. We came up with a test regarding price discrimination and we said that abuse of buyer power to get discriminatorily low prices that would give you competitive advantage is illegal."[79]

Although Shelanski's response to Foer's question was disappointing, it was nonetheless revealing, given the U.S. federal courts' demonstrated bias in favor of the consumer welfare prescription. "I'll just say that antitrust is constrained ultimately not these days by its original purposes . . . but on what the Supreme Court has done in translating those original purposes into a very narrow set of constraints . . . within which the agencies must operate. So I think we need to look beyond antitrust."[80] He has a point, and we will return to it.

Historic Opportunity for Antitrust Reform Squandered

The Obama administration failed to seize the momentum from its 2010 antitrust initiative to mount a serious challenge to the Borkian hegemony over U.S. antitrust policy. The optimism initially fueled by the launch of these hearings deflated as the investigation first faltered and then collapsed under a withering corporate backlash.

By mid-2012 the high-profile officials who had displayed the most commitment to tougher antitrust enforcement during the workshops—Christine Varney, the U.S. assistant attorney general for antitrust, and Dudley Butler, head of the Packers and Stockyards Administration—had resigned. The

Obama administration had reneged on its promises to protect vulnerable stakeholders from retaliation for speaking out publicly against the predatory practices that they had helped document during the five regional hearings. Some, like the poultry growers, literally risked their livelihoods to testify, and it is unclear how many may have indeed lost their farms due to retaliation.[81] Thus the Obama administration's unprecedented and much-vaunted antitrust investigation came to an ignominious end.[82]

Instead of harnessing his courageous antitrust initiative to take the offensive against the alarming growth of corporate power in America's food system, President Obama and his cabinet members abandoned the battlefield at the crucial moment. In doing so, they squandered an historic opportunity to rally Americans to challenge the growing corporate power that was dangerously increasing inequality and threatening America's democratic institutions as evidenced by the *Citizens United* decision. History must someday be the judge of their disconcerting inaction.

The implications of the Obama administration's 2010 retreat were devastating on several fronts. The landmark U.S. trust-busting laws of the late 19th and early 20th centuries, which had empowered the state to intervene in markets to regulate or even break up concentrated economic power, and which had helped to facilitate the unparalleled prosperity of a growing middle class in the United States, were abandoned. The administration's abandonment of these unique laws to the disingenuous Borkian consumer welfare dogma became just one more disappointing capitulation to corporate plutocracy, allowing it to continue its alarming consolidation of wealth and power in the food supply chain at the expense of other stakeholders. This consolidation of economic power continues to facilitate the growing income gap between the richest and poorest in the United States, thus undermining the fundamental principles of liberty, equality, and justice—the fundamental underpinnings of American democracy.

Much as with the separation of powers that the Founders designed into the Constitution to protect people from the tyranny of centralized political power, U.S. antitrust laws originally intended to protect everyone in society—producers and consumers alike—from the tyranny of centralized economic power. In early 2010, President Obama had wisely and admirably taken the unprecedented step of publicly chastising the U.S. Supreme Court before Congress and the American people for unleashing unfettered corruptive power of corporate money into our political system through its devastating ruling in *Citizens United*. Yet by the end of that year he and his key cabinet heads were in full retreat from the corporate backlash against his historic antitrust initiative to return a semblance of justice to our food system.

Contrast this failure of the Obama administration to the UK government's adoption of key antitrust reform recommendations that came out of its 2008

Competition Commission investigation. Those reforms included a Groceries Supply Code of Practice (GSCOP) and a suppliers' Bill of Rights against the large supermarkets' buyer power abuses.[83]

Additionally, the UK Parliament also passed new legislation establishing an independent "Groceries Code Adjudicator" to investigate and arbitrate supplier complaints of buy power abuses that violate the GSCOP, as well as to fine supermarkets found guilty of such abuses.[84] It is a poignant lesson on the degree of corporate influence over the U.S. government to contrast this decisive UK parliamentary action to the U.S. Congress's appalling defunding of new rules proposed in 2010 that would have provided modest protections for poultry growers against the draconian production contracts imposed on them by big poultry processors.[85]

The capitulation of all three branches of the U.S. government—judicial, executive, and legislative—to the corporate plutocracy that dominates our food system leaves every stakeholder along Walmart's sprawling global food supply chains vulnerable to continued exploitation and abuse, and jeopardizes the Right to Food[86] of millions of people around the world who derive their livelihoods from those supply chains. As the current UN Special Rapporteur on the Right to Food, Olivier De Schutter said in his 2010 report on buyer power abuse, "There is . . . a direct link between the ability of competition regimes to address abuses of buyer power in supply chains, and the enjoyment of the right to adequate food."[87]

Prying Loose Walmart's Stranglehold: Overcoming the Consumer Welfare Prescription

After the Obama administration's failure in to seize the historic opportunity to challenge the consumer welfare doctrine through its historic antitrust initiative of 2010, and with dim hope for antitrust reform in the face of congressional gridlock, the U.S. courts' uncritical adoption of the Borkian consumer welfare prescription remains frustratingly intact. This bleak outlook for reform means that we must now regroup and reinvent new innovative approaches for challenging and loosening the stranglehold with which the Walmart model squeezes and exploits the livelihoods of those who work along food supply chains.

We cannot afford to surrender the power of government to corporate plutocracy. History has shown time and again that elites will not hesitate to wield the power of the state on their own behalf at the expense of everyone else, as we have recently seen in *Citizens United* as well as in other endless examples of corrosive corporate influence on our political system—such as Monsanto's passing a secret budget rider to exempt from court review the company's releases of genetically engineered organisms into the enviroment.[88]

In this vein, we must draw on our rich history of using antitrust laws to challenge and break up dangerous concentrations of economic power that inevitably lead to increasing concentration of political power into the hands of unaccountable plutocrats. Despite the steep challenges posed by the U.S. courts' adoption of the Borkian consumer welfare doctrine, we must heed Professor Obach's words: "Whatever good ends . . . [consumer welfare] may have once served, . . . [we] should now lay it to rest."

What Is to Be Done?

In his closing statement on a panel examining retail buyer power at the last USDA–Department of Justice hearing in 2010, Bert Foer, president of the American Antitrust Institute (AAI), proposed the creation of a blue ribbon study commission made up of a variety of stakeholders armed with subpoena power "to come out with specific recommendations . . . [that] would impact . . . [antitrust] enforcement [related to buyer power]."[89] How unfortunate that the Obama administration did not take Mr. Foer's advice! Although the devil would be in the details, such a commission could provide a constructive forum similar to that provided by the UK Competition Commission's 2008 investigation that culminated in the implementation of substantive reforms to curtail buyer power abuse by large supermarket chains.

In October 2008, the AAI had released a transition report that had included recommendations for antitrust reforms for the next president, who turned out to be Barack Obama.[90] The book dedicated an entire chapter to buyer power, providing valuable insights into the current status of U.S. antitrust policy with regard to this important topic, as well as recommendations for reform.[91]

In the report, the AAI recommended several reforms to the Robinson–Patman Act to refocus the law's emphasis on curtailing buyer power abuse in the context of the modern economy.[92] The AAI's recommendations to update Robinson–Patman stand in stark contrast to a 2007 recommendation by the Antitrust Modernization Commission to repeal the act.[93]

The AAI defends Robinson–Patman as a clear example of an antitrust law that Congress passed primarily to curtail buyer power abuse by retail chains against independent businesses.[94] One of the act's key provisions prohibits suppliers from giving better terms to large chains over small independent stores unless such a preference was based on real cost reductions such as those achieved through economies of scale. In other words, Robinson–Patman precludes big chains from pressuring their suppliers to give them a better deal than smaller independent business as a form of predatory pricing to put the smaller firms out of business.

The AAI notes that Robinson–Patman takes into account the differences between predatory pricing by a monopsony, as opposed to a traditional monopoly:

> [N]either below-cost pricing nor monopoly power is necessary [in a monopsony] to reduce consumer welfare. Most instances of harmful discrimination, therefore, would escape federal sanction if the Robinson–Patman Act were repealed.[95]
>
> In the ordinary [monopsony] case, the favored buyer is not a monopolist and is unlikely to acquire monopoly power through the discrimination. Instead, there may be several favored buyers, and though each may have significant buying power, none has a reasonable prospect of becoming a monopolist. Likewise, the typical case does not involve below-cost pricing by either the discriminating seller(s) or the favored buyer(s). Indeed, it is the big buyer's ability to use an unjustified concession to disadvantage smaller rivals without pricing below its own costs that makes the Robinson–Patman Act a potentially desirable policy instrument.
>
> Moreover, even if the plaintiff had some evidence of below-cost pricing and monopoly power, its chances of success in a Sherman Act action are likely to be low. [Ever s]ince the Supreme Court required proof of both below-cost pricing and recoupment, no plaintiff has won a final judgment in a predatory pricing case[,] and few plaintiffs have obtained settlements.[96]

Congress clearly passed Robinson–Patman in 1936 to protect competitors, albeit for the purposes of preserving competition on behalf of consumers. Unfortunately, the courts' narrowing of the scope of antitrust laws merely to provide lower prices for consumers has meant that federal agencies have virtually stopped enforcing this crucial law. Consequently, successful antitrust complaints filed under the act have plummeted over the past two decades.[97]

The courts' adoption of the consumer welfare doctrine has rendered Robinson–Patman nearly impotent by ignoring Congress's overarching intent of protecting competitors from unfair competition as an important strategy for ensuring lower prices to consumers. This apostasy stands as both testament to and indictment of the arrogant judicial activism that conservatives such as Bork incessantly rail against while hypocritically engaging in the same activism on behalf of the corporate plutocrats they serve. The AAI argues that a congressional initiative to amend Robinson–Patman may provide a potentially viable path toward a new strategy for effectively curtailing the even greater buyer power in today's retail grocery market as exemplified by Walmart.

The AAI's book contains another chapter focusing on a whole set of laws that redress buyer power abuses uniquely related to agriculture.[98] For example, the Capper–Volstead Act acknowledges the unique disadvantage faced by thousands of farmers selling to a few large processing companies. This situation leaves these unorganized farmers susceptible to buyer power abuse. So Capper–Volstead provides farmers with a limited exemption to antitrust laws if they choose to band together through associations such as cooperatives to market their products collectively. Such collective marketing counterbalances the excessive monopsony power caused by this market failure. Although the act does provide farmers with this exemption, it still imposes other aspects of antitrust laws on their associations to protect consumers from price fixing and other monopoly power abuses.[99]

In short, the Capper–Volstead Act is an example of Congress's acknowledging that sometimes markets fail and that in certain cases the government has a duty to intervene to correct such failures. In this case, the government intervenes to exempt from antitrust laws the farmers who are disadvantaged by the market failure of there being too few buyers for their products. This exemption allows them to market collectively, thereby providing them with more leverage to negotiate fair prices. Capper–Volstead is a good example of the principle of government playing the role of an impartial referee ensuring a level playing field in the market. Unfortunately, this sound principle has been eroded for more than three decades because the Borkian consumer welfare doctrine suffers from the erroneous assumption that markets never fail and that market deregulation is thus always preferable to government intervention.

One section of the AAI's agricultural chapter reviews a whole different set of laws, such as the Grain Inspection, Packers and Stockyards, Agricultural Fair Practices, and Agricultural Marketing Agreement acts. These laws, administered by the USDA, redress buyer power abuses through more of a regulatory, or market facilitation, approach, rather than through a strictly antitrust lens. "Taken as a whole, these statutes set forth a strategy of market facilitation intended to reduce exploitive, discriminatory and exclusionary practices and to authorize regulations that make markets in agriculture work more effectively." Unfortunately, as the AAI points out, "the USDA has basically failed to implement this regulatory scheme." Nonetheless, the AAI proposes several regulatory reforms for various sectors such as cattle, dairy, and poultry that the USDA could implement through rulemaking, thus providing an incremental path forward toward rolling back buyer power abuses against suppliers. By bolstering such a regulatory approach, the USDA may be more successful in curtailing buyer power abuses than by taking other approaches that rely on a pure antitrust enforcement, which is more likely to be derailed in the courts by the consumer welfare prescription.[100]

Importantly, reforming market facilitating regulations in agricultural markets could provide a model for addressing buyer power abuses by large supermarkets up and down the food supply chain. "Such regulations are a recurring feature of a workably competitive economy. They are used in a variety of consumer protection contexts, to constitute and regulate the market for corporate securities, both when initially issued and when traded in the public market, and in a variety of other contexts."[101]

This approach would also be consistent with Mr. Shelanki's comments at the last antitrust hearing of 2010 when he stated that "we need to look beyond antitrust." It could include addressing supermarket buyer power through a forum such as a blue ribbon commission like that proposed by Bert Foer. Such a commission could include a review of the UK Competition Commission's findings from its 2008 investigation of supermarket buyer power abuse. It could provide a forum for a thorough debate over whether the Grocery Supply Code of Practice, and the associated independent adjudicator law, both of which came out of that investigation, could be effectively adapted to the U.S. context. (Because this UK approach is a suppliers' Bill of Rights, it is more of a market facilitation than an antitrust approach to curtailing supermarket buyer power abuses.)

Additionally, exploring market facilitating regulation of food supply chains could potentially meet the challenge posed by Walmart's faux sustainability initiatives. It could open the door for building solidarity among stakeholders by working together to develop a broad range of sustainability criteria in food supply chains—e.g., food safety, labor, locally grown, humane animal treatment—and ensuring that such criteria meet enforceable minimum standards. Such an approach could include both advocating specific regulatory reforms and market-driven sustainability labeling and certification. It could appeal directly to consumers who are increasingly more willing to pay a premium to know where their food comes from and whether it was produced in a manner that doesn't exploit workers, animals, or the environment.

Another path forward could include a concerted effort to assess the feasibility of launching a successful predatory pricing case in any of those regional markets where Walmart has more than 30 percent of the market share for retail groceries. Twenty-four states have specific statutes banning below-cost sales,[102] and not all these states have adopted the Borkian consumer welfare doctrine as enthusiastically as the federal courts have. So perhaps some of the states in which Walmart has such high market concentrations may provide an opening to pursue a successful predatory pricing case or other antitrust actions.

Finally, Olivier De Schutter, the UN Rapporteur on the Right to Food, in his 2010 report "Addressing Concentration in Food Supply Chains," contends that global food supply chains are rapidly growing beyond the reach of national governments' capacity to enforce antitrust regimes against monopsony power abuse. He argues that this unprecedented development demands urgent and sophisticated international collaboration to curtail rampant buyer power abuse against stakeholders who derive their livelihoods from these supply chains. While providing concrete reforms in his report, De Schutter argues convincingly that anyone who takes seriously the Right to Food enshrined in the United Nations International Covenant on Economic, Social, and Cultural Rights (ICESCR) must also support strong antitrust enforcement against buyer power abuses in global food supply chains.[103]

Acknowledgments

I thank William Schanbacher for his invaluable guidance and patience in editing this chapter. I also express my appreciation to Albert A. Foer and Barry C. Lynn for their insightful comments based on their decades of experience with antitrust policy. Any errors are solely my own. The views expressed in this chapter are also my own and do not necessarily reflect the views of the United Food and Commercial Workers International Union.

Notes

1. Meredith Lepore, "Here's How Walmart Became the #1 Grocery Store in the Country," *Business Insider*, February 11, 2011. www.businessinsider.com/new-details-in-walmart-bribery-scandal-2012-12

2. Data obtained from Walmart company's 10-Ks.

3. Walmart 2012 Annual Report.

4. UFCWa (United Food and Commercial Workers International Union, CLC), Executive summary, "Ending Walmart's Rural Stranglehold" (2010), 1.

5. Richard Fletcher, "Wal-Mart Calls for Probe into Dominant Tesco," *The Sunday Times*, August 28, 2004. www.thesundaytimes.co.uk/sto/business/article146096.ece

6. UFCW, ibid.

7. Investopedia.com defines *monopsony* as "[a] market similar to a monopoly except that a large buyer, not seller, controls a large proportion of the market and drives the prices down. Sometimes referred to as the buyer's monopoly."

8. Kim Bhasin and Ashley Lutz, "7 Stunning New Details about Walmart's Mexican Bribery Scandal," *Business Insider*, December 18, 2012. www.businessinsider.com/new-details-in-walmart-bribery-scandal-2012-12

9. FirstPost Business, *Walmart India Head Quits amid Bribery Probe: All You Need to Know* (June 27, 2013). www.firstpost.com/business/walmart-india-head-quits-amid-bribery-probe-all-you-need-to-know-909117.html

10. Megan Hughes and Jonathan D. Salant, "Democratic Convention Panel Gives Back Wal-Mart Card," Bloomberg.com (May 8, 2012). www.bloomberg.com/news/2012-05-08/democratic-convention-panel-gives-back-wal-mart-cards.html

11. Trefis Team, "Wal-Mart Can Swell to $80 Riding U.S. Growth," Forbes.com (March 13, 2013). www.forbes.com/sites/greatspeculations/2013/03/15/wal-mart-can-swell-to-80-riding-u-s-growth/

12. See Walmart's Sustainability Index, including locally grown food: http://corporate.walmart.com/global-responsibility/environment-sustainability/sustainability-index

13. Josh Sosland, "Wal-Mart: Food Takes Center Stage," FoodBusinessNews.net (June 28, 2013). www.foodbusinessnews.net/articles/news_home/Food-Service-Retail/2013/06/Wal-Mart_Food_takes_center_sta.aspx?ID=%7BED727688-A8D5-41FA-A5DB-4746E281F17D%7D

14. Ibid.

15. Ibid.

16. Ibid.

17. Ibid.

18. Walmart.com, "Walmart Launches Fresh Produce Guarantee in U.S. Stores." http://news.walmart.com/news-archive/2013/06/03/walmart-launches-fresh-produce-guarantee-in-us-stores

19. Sarah Mahoney, "Deflecting Bad News, Walmart Talks Up Produce," Media Post Publications (June 4, 2013). www.mediapost.com/publications/article/201751/deflecting-bad-news-walmart-talks-up-produce.html#axzz2dlhPjyDl

20. Walmart.com, ibid.

21. Mahoney, ibid.

22. Brentin Mock, "Wal-Mart Smacked with $110 Million in Fines for Environmental Crimes," Colorlines.com (May 29, 2013). http://colorlines.com/archives/2013/05/wal-mart_smacked_with_110_million_in_fines_for_environmental_crimes.html

23. Ibid.

24. Brad Dorfman, "Wal-Mart to Boost Buying from Small and Local Farms," Reuters.com (October 14, 2013). www.reuters.com/article/2010/10/14/us-walmart-idUSTRE69C09V20101014

25. Mahoney, ibid.

26. Walmart 2013 Global Responsibility Report, "2012 Commitments and Progress." http://corporate.walmart.com/microsites/global-responsibility-report-2013/products OurProgress.aspx

27. Investopedia defines greenwashing as follows: "When a company, government or other group promotes green-based environmental initiatives or images but actually operates in a way that is damaging to the environment or in an opposite manner to the goal of the announced initiatives. This can also include misleading customers about the environmental benefits of a product through misleading advertising and unsubstantiated claims." www.investopedia.com/terms/g/greenwashing.asp

28. Investopedia.com. www.investopedia.com/terms/l/lossleader.asp

29. Sosland, ibid.

30. Josh Sosland, "Consumer Struggles Play to Wal-Mart's Strong Suit," Food BusinessNews.net (June 28, 2013). www.foodbusinessnews.net/articles/news_home/Food-Service-Retail/2013/06/Consumer_struggles_play_to_Wal.aspx?ID=%7B20DDDB7A-C5C3-4F52-B114-CB79532E0680%7D

31. Lepore, ibid.

32. Basav Sen, UFCW International Union senior research associate, e-mail exchange with R. Dennis Olson, September 5, 2013.

33. Lepore, ibid.

34. Albert A. Foer, "Mr. Magoo Visits Wal-Mart: Find the Right Lens for Antitrust," *Connecticut Law Review* (May 2007): 6–8.

35. Ibid.

36. Historical note: In 1987, Albert A. Foer, current president of the American Antitrust Institute, titled his testimony opposing President Reagan's nomination to the U.S. Supreme Court "Antitrust: The Borkian Paradox."

37. Barak Orbach, "The Antitrust Consumer Welfare Paradox," *Journal of Competition Law and Economics* 7 (February 28, 2011): 133–135.

38. Ibid., 133–136.

39. Ibid.

40. Patrick Bolton, Joseph F. Brodley, and Michael H. Riordan, "Predatory Pricing: Strategic Theory and Legal Policy," *Georgetown Law Review* (August 2000).

41. Orbach, ibid., 163.

42. Robert J. Toth, "A Powerful Law Has Been Losing a Lot of Its Punch," *The Wall Street Journal* (May 21, 2012). http://online.wsj.com/article/SB1000142405270230474660 4577380172754953842.html

43. See Packers and Stockyards Act of 1921, Title 2, Subtitle A, Section 202, which states: "It shall be unlawful for any packer or swine contractor with respect to livestock, meats, meat food products, or livestock products in unmanufactured form, or for any live poultry dealer with respect to live poultry, to:

. . . [m]ake or give any undue or unreasonable preference or advantage to any particular person or locality in any respect, or subject any particular person or locality to any undue or unreasonable prejudice or disadvantage in any respect. . . ." www.gipsa.usda.gov/Lawsandregs/PS_act.pdf

44. See "USA—Poultry Processors under Pressure," *Meat Trade Daily News* (June 1, 2012); and Toth, ibid.

45. Orbach, ibid., 135.

46. Terry Calvani, "Predatory Pricing and State Below-Cost Sales Statutes in the United States: An Analysis" (Canadian Competition Bureau, 2001). www.competition bureau.gc.ca/eic/site/cb-bc.nsf/eng/01292.html#Footnote40

47. See Calvani, ibid.; and Turner and Areeda, "Predatory Pricing and Related Practices under Section 2 of the Sherman Act," *Harvard Law Review* 88, no. 4 (February 1975): 697–733.

48. Calvani, ibid.

49. Ibid.

50. Ibid., footnote 39.

51. Calvani, ibid.

52. Sen, ibid.

53. Albert A. Foer, president, American Antitrust Institute, comment from his review of this chapter.

54. United Kingdom Competition Commission, "Appendix 5.4: The Waterbed Effect in Supplier Pricing," in *Grocery Market Investigation* (2009b). www.competition-

commission.org.uk/assets/competitioncommission/docs/pdf/non-inquiry/rep_pub/reports/2008/fulltext/538_5_4.pdf

55. Orbach, ibid., 133.

56. Ibid., 162.

57. Ibid., 163.

58. Ibid., 162.

59. Ibid., 164.

60. Olivier De Schutter, United Nations Special Rapporteur on the Right to Food, "Addressing Concentration in Food Supply Chains: The Role of Competition Law in Tackling the Abuse of Buyer Power" (December 2010), 1.

61. Hankey et al., "United Kingdom: Groceries Supply Code of Practice Comes into Force," Mondaq.com (February 8, 2010). www.mondaq.com/x/93598/Antitrust+Competition/Groceries+Supply+Code+Of+Practice+Comes+Into+Force

62. See the plank of the Obama Campaign's rural platform on Change.gov (http://change.gov/agenda/rural_agenda/), which states: "Prevent Anticompetitive Behavior against Family Farms: Pass a packer ban. When meatpackers own livestock they can manipulate prices and discriminate against independent farmers. Strengthen antimonopoly laws and strengthen producer protections to ensure independent farmers have fair access to markets, control over their production decisions, and transparency in prices."

63. President Obama appointed Dudley Butler, a trial lawyer who defended farmers against meatpackers, head of the USDA Packers and Stockyards Administration and supported Christine Varney, a former Federal Trade Commissioner appointed by President Clinton, as assistant attorney general for antitrust at the Justice Department.

64. Short title of the 2010 UFCW report released for the USDA–Justice Department antitrust workshops. The long title is "Ending Walmart's Rural Stranglehold: A Plan to Rebuild Rural America's Food Supply Chain with the Revival of Rural Economies for Workers, Ranchers and Farmers by Reinvigorating the Marketplace and Reining in Walmart's Anti-competitive Practices."

65. UFCWb, "Ending Walmart's Rural Stranglehold" (2010). http://grist.files.wordpress.com/2010/09/ag_consolidation_white_paper2.pdf?CFID=10082208&CFTOKEN=55376804

66. Ibid., 1.

67. United Kingdom Competition Commission, "Groceries Market Investigation—Final Report" (April 30, 2008), www.competition-commission.org.uk/assets/competition-commission/docs/pdf/non-inquiry/press_rel/2008/apr/pdf/14-08.pdf. For more extensive background on the Groceries Market Investigation, see www.competition-commission.org.uk/inquiries/ref2006/grocery/index.htm.

68. David Lowe and Michael Gledhill, "Groceries Code Adjudicator Bill to Become Law in June," Lexology.com (May 1, 2013). www.lexology.com/library/detail.aspx?g=3621493f-1c9a-40bd-bc01-742441388b54

69. UFCWb, ibid., 2–4.

70. Renee Dudley, "Wal-Mart Board Seen at Risk of Losing Independent Voices," Bloomberg (June 6, 2013). www.bloomberg.com/news/2013-06-06/wal-mart-board-seen-at-risk-of-losing-independent-voices.html

71. Tampa Bay Times, "Truth-O-Meter Says," PolitiFact.com (July 22, 2012). www.politifact.com/truth-o-meter/statements/2012/jul/31/bernie-s/sanders-says-walmart-heirs-own-more-wealth-bottom-/

72. Zachary R. Mider, "How Wal-Mart's Waltons Maintain Their Billionaire Fortune," Bloomberg (September 12, 2013). www.bloomberg.com/news/2013-09-12/how-wal-mart-s-waltons-maintain-their-billionaire-fortune-taxes.html

73. UFCWb, ibid., 6.

74. Ibid.

75. Ibid., 19–20.

76. U.S. Department of Justice, "Workshop on Agriculture and Antitrust Enforcement Issues in Our 21st Century Economy" (2010), 184–185, www.justice.gov/atr/public/workshops/ag2010/dc-agworkshop-transcript.txt. See also De Schutter, ibid., 3–4.

77. Ibid., 234.

78. Ibid., 235–236.

79. Ibid., 228–229.

80. Ibid., 246.

81. Lynn, Barry C., "Killing the Competition: How the New Monopolies are Destroying Open Markets," *Harpers Magazine* (February 2012), 30. http://harpers.org/archive/2012/02/killing-the-competition

82. Robert C. Taylor, "Too Big to Prosecute?" *The Daily Yonder* (July 11, 2012), www.dailyyonder.com/too-big-prosecute/2012/07/09/4178. See also the U.S. Justice Department's report and records of the five regional antitrust workshops, held jointly with U.S. Department of Agriculture: www.justice.gov/atr/pblic/workshops/ag2010/Y

83. Hankey et al., ibid.

84. Vidal et al., "The Grocery Code Adjudicator Act 2013," TaylorWeissing.com (June 26, 2013). www.taylorwessing.com/news-insights/details/the-grocery-code-adjudicator-act-2013-2013-06-26.html

85. Taylor, ibid.

86. The "Right to Food" was first recognized by the United Nations in the Universal Declaration of Human Rights (UDHR) of 1948, incumbent in the right to a decent standard of living. More recently, the UN Special Rapporteur on the Right to Food has defined it to mean "[t]he right to have regular, permanent and unrestricted access, either directly or by means of financial purchases, to quantitatively and qualitatively adequate and sufficient food corresponding to the cultural traditions of the people to which the consumer belongs, and which ensure a physical and mental, individual and collective, fulfilling and dignified life free of fear." For more background, see www.fao.org/righttofood/about-right-to-food/en/.

87. De Schutter, ibid., 1.

88. Ryan Grim, "Jeff Merkley Pushes 'Monsanto Protection Act' Repeal," Huffington Post.com (May 16, 2013). www.huffingtonpost.com/2013/05/16/jeff-merkley-monsanto-repeal_n_3288209.html

89. U.S. Department of Justice, ibid., 244.

90. American Antitrust Institute, "The Next Antitrust Agenda: The American Antitrust Institute's Transition Report on Competition Policy to the 44th President of the United States" (2008). www.antitrustinstitute.org/node/11001

91. Ibid., 95–137.

92. Ibid., 130–137.

93. Antitrust Modernization Commission, "Antitrust Modernization Commission Report and Recommendations: Letter to the President & Congress of the United States" (2007), iii. http://govinfo.library.unt.edu/amc/report_recommendation/letter_to_president.pdf

94. American Antitrust Institute, ibid., 130–132.

95. Ibid., 135.

96. Ibid., 135, footnote.

97. Toth, ibid.

98. American Antitrust Institute, ibid., 281–316.

99. David Volkin, "Understanding Capper-Volstead" (U.S. Department of Agriculture Rural Business and Cooperative Development Service, 1985). www.rurdev.usda.gov/supportdocuments/cir35.pdf

100. American Antitrust Institute, ibid., 309–311, 314–316.

101. Ibid., 309–310.

102. Calvani, ibid.

103. De Schutter, ibid., 6.

6

The Pursuit of Happiness: At the Intersection of Food, Performance, and Consumer Identity

Sara B. Dykins Callahan

consume[1] ► verb

1. eat, drink, or ingest (food or drink): *people consume a good deal of sugar in drinks.*
2. buy (goods or services): *accounting provides measures of the economic goods and services consumed.*
3. (of a feeling) completely fill the mind of (someone): *Carolyn was consumed with guilt.*

How do the choices people make in constructing and performing their individual and collective identities as *consumers* affect the global food system? Understanding ourselves as consumers, enacting certain practices based on a constellation of beliefs and values associated with consumerism, and participating in an increasingly global consumer culture positions food as a commodity to be purchased and thus subject to the market economy. This narrow positioning allows agribusiness and industrial food processors to dominate mass food production, compromising the viability of local farmers and food producers, endangering the sustainability of environmental resources, promoting a homogeneous global gastronomy, and interfering with the rights of communities to control their food systems. Performance theories and methods of inquiry provide particularly well-suited perspectives through which to investigate the complex relationships between individual and collective identity performances and the actuality of an increasingly unjust and danger-ous global food system.

To Consume

The first and foundational definition of "consume" is to eat or ingest. Con-suming is a physical action that integrates the matter of one being (animal, fish, plant) into the body of another (you are what you eat). We humans must consume to live; we are consumers because our survival depends on our ability to feed our bodies, to ingest energy and nutrients, to eat food. We are defined in part by this fundamental need. But in our contemporary world the word *consume* carries a multitude of definitions as well as popular associations. It is not surprising, then, that a word—an idea—with such primacy to the human condition would be appropriated to frame and make sense of the eco-nomic marketplace. In the *Oxford Dictionary of English*, the second definition of "consume" is to buy or purchase.[2] Through this rhetorical move, humans are positioned as consumers of products and services (to modify our earlier axiom: you are what you buy). The connotative conflation of meanings, to ingest and to purchase, is particularly important to understanding how people make sense of choices they make in their everyday lives. In our contemporary corporate capitalist society, replete with material-based freedoms (we have the right to own property and pursue happiness through the accumulation of material wealth), citizens are perpetually positioned as purchasers: vote with your dollar. The common national identity: *I am consumer.*

Our culture in the United States, and increasingly internationally, is a cul-ture of mass consumption enabled by the Industrial Revolution and Informa-tion Revolution of the 19th and 20th centuries, respectively, and perpetuated by our current Digital Revolution. Food, food industries, and food systems are all significant elements of our contemporary consumer culture and the inherent identity politics of consumption. Choices of what to eat and, often more important, what not to eat, as well as where to eat, how to eat, when to eat, and why to eat, are central to consumer identity and manifest the overtly political and social implications of consuming. This book is organized around issues faced by global food systems and investigates potential solutions for some of these issues. Specifically, the authors included in this collection are concerned with social justice in food systems, theorizing food concepts, food sovereignty, activism in new food movements, and community-based strat-egies for resisting globalization and industrialization of food systems. The activism involved in these alternatives and solutions to the mass production and consumption of foods becomes itself a product marketable to growing segments of our consumer culture. Food products marketed as "Fair Trade," "Organic," and "Sustainable" appeal to people who understand themselves as concerned consumers or responsible consumers and whose consumer choices (what to buy, what to eat) perform a particular identity. For instance, Grace Gershuny's chapter on "organic" labeling illustrates its complex history—one that has on occasion been coopted by the very economic ideologies and institutions the original organic movement sought to challenge. In this chapter, I am concerned with the intersections of the primary definition of "consume" (to eat) with the popular definition of "consume" (to purchase/acquire) and the manifestation of associated meanings (style, class, high culture, taste, refinement) as performances of identity directly engaging the systems that govern the production, distribution, and consumption of our foods. I highlight some of the tensions involved in the intersections of consumer culture, identity, and food. To investigate these tensions, I suggest employing theories of cultural performance articulated within the disciplines of performance studies, critical-cultural studies, communication, anthropology, and sociology.

To Perform, Perchance to Transform

performance[3] ▶ noun

1. a. The accomplishment or carrying out of something commanded or undertaken; the doing of an action or operation

"Performance" is in its broadest sense a doing, an action—for example, eating.[4] Popular uses of *performance* associate the term with theatrical and musical events and with skill-based job assessment (performance evaluations). As early as the 1950s, however, performance has been used in academia as a tool to critique and analyze cultural phenomena. Scholars working within the social sciences experimented with performance as a critical metaphor to analyze social ceremonies and ritual events. By the 1970s, several pivotal scholars, including Victor Turner and Edith Turner, Richard Schechner, Erving Goffman, and Dwight Conquergood, worked together across disciplines to advance performance studies as a site of converging interests between theater and the social sciences. One of the areas identified as fruitful for collaborative, interdisciplinary research was everyday life performance (practices and expressions in which people engage on a daily basis, such as preparing to go to work, ordering food from a restaurant, and going on a date). Goffman, in *The Presentation of Self in Everyday Life*, uses the language of theatrical performance (character, set, costume, script, audience, etc.) metaphorically to analyze the conscious and subconscious choices that people make in their daily lives to present themselves in certain ways to others. These individuals, Goffman suggests, perform specific culturally and socially derived behaviors based on the "scene" and the other "characters" involved.

Goffman's work is one of the foundations for a larger body of contemporary scholarship that positions identity as constructed and performed. Judith Butler, a definitive voice in performance discourse, examines gender identity through the lens of performance and argues that gender is performative as opposed to inherent or natural. People perform their gender identities through a citational process (the repetition of stylized bodily acts—the application or lack thereof of cosmetics, shaving legs vs. shaving facial hair, wearing dresses vs. a suit and tie, etc.) whereby "feminine" or "masculine" identities are achieved in relation to cultural and social norms. Norms, according to Butler, are not the same as rules or laws, but rather are implicit standards of normalization (of making something normal) that operate within particular social practices. "The norm governs intelligibility," argues Butler, "[and] allows for certain kinds of practices and action to become recognizable as such, imposing a grid of legibility on the social and defining the parameters of what will and will not appear within the domain of the social."[5] Drawing from the work of Barbara Kirshenblatt-Gimblett, performance studies scholar Cynthia Spurlock identifies the role of norms in the relationships between identity and food:

> Relationships formed with and through food are largely cultivated through a host of situated knowledges and discursive practices that are learned, rehearsed, enacted, resisted, and re/appropriated through performance in the constant re/negotiation of identities, positionalities, and desires.[6]

For example, we can examine various cultural texts, such as magazines, works of fiction, television shows, and events (baby showers, bridal showers, dinner parties, barbeques, etc.), to ascertain social understandings (situated knowledges and discursive practices) regarding the relationships between gender and food. These texts enact common practices that are organized by cultural and social norms. It is in relationship to these norms that food and food ways are given meaning. Certain foods become gendered (salads are feminine, steaks masculine); others are relegated to specific situations and distinguished by social class. For instance—champagne for celebrations, beer and hamburgers for tailgating, wine and cheese at the openings of art shows, turkey on Thanksgiving.

Within the last two decades, performance has been adopted by cultural studies scholars as a model for investigating and understanding everyday human actions, such as grocery shopping. Contemporary performance theories focus on the *how* of culture and society. As Marvin Carlson states, performance theories are concerned with "how human patterns of activity are reinforced or changed within a culture and how they are adjusted when various different cultures interact."[7] How are norms established? How do they become invisible (meaning normalized—so pervasive and entrenched in our daily lives that we cannot readily identify them as organizing powers)? What ruptures or transgressions make norms visible? How and why do norms change? To study the how of culture and society in order to understand the processes and the contexts of production, performance studies scholars often examine cultural products. Cultural products include artifacts such as visual art, music, and literature, as well as popular cultural expressions such as films, television programs, amusement parks, and social networking sites. Cultural products also include fast food chains, big box stores, factory farms, and food.

Performance studies positions the body as a site of knowledge production, meaning that we can develop different and deeper understandings of a subject we are researching through privileging sensory and kinetic (embodied) experiences. For instance, to better understand the phenomenon of food tourism, a researcher employing performance as a method of inquiry would engage in an actual experience of food tourism (e.g., attending an organized City Foodie tour). Through this performer-centered approach (similar to the anthropological method of participant observation, with the addition of classifying the physical, emotional, and psychological experiences of the researcher as data), the researcher would be able to include physical and emotional engagement in her analysis of the phenomenon. Using performance as a method of inquiry can also involve creating a staged performance of a particular text or set of texts (for example, Emily Post's chapter on table manners, an adaptation of Suzanne Collins' *The Hunger Games*, or preparing a Seder meal). Through the embodiment of the text, the performer-researcher may develop a better understanding of the motivations and decisions of a particular character, or of the author, or of the lived experience of an event (a formal seven-course meal, for example).

Performance, then, a perspective that examines the *how*, the process—the *doing*—of society and culture, is an excellent perspective through which to engage questions about the relationships between consumer identity and food systems. To consume (to eat and to purchase) is to perform (to enact) a set of values, beliefs, and knowledges within or against the norms of a particular society. How we consume—the processes and practices that embody our identity as consumers—can provide insights into the troubling trajectory of the global food system. Our identities as consumers shape the philosophies and ideologies that constitute and enable our food systems. Our actions as consumers engage and direct the systems that organize the production and distribution of foods. By positioning *consumer* as a performance of identity—an enactment of a set of choices, an embodiment of a set of beliefs—we can better understand ourselves as actors who possess agency, who can broaden the horizons of significance against which we make sense of our lives. If, as Ron Pelias asserts, "[p]eople are both products and producers of their cultures," then we have the power through what we choose to *do* to change our cultures and societies.[8] Performance offers the potential to transform ourselves and our worlds.

Purchasing as a Performance of Patriotism

The acts of consuming (eating and buying) are practices central to identity construction and performance in our contemporary society. Though the first definition of *consume* in the *Oxford English Reference Dictionary* refers to the embodied process of eating ("to eat or drink"), the first definition of *consumer* is "a person who consumes, esp. a person who uses a *product*" (emphasis mine).[9] The second definition is "a purchaser of goods and services."[10] Based on our social consensus of the definition of consumer, to understand one's self as a consumer is essentially to locate one's self within the economic marketplace. Zygmunt Bauman argues, "The way present-day society shapes up its members is dictated first and foremost by the need to *play the role* of consumer, and the norm our society holds up to its members is that of the ability and willingness to play it" (emphasis mine).[11] Bauman is pointing to the role of the consumer as purchaser, one who embraces consumerism: "a preoccupation with consumer goods and their acquisition."[12] He also situates *consumer* as a role, which people may or may not choose to enact. If, however, a member of our society desires to be considered "normal," then he or she must engage in the performance of consumer. Indeed, the practice of conspicuous consumption has been a requirement for identification as a "normal" citizen in the United States since the early 20th century. Our identities and positions within our social hierarchy are secured through performances of consumption: brand name clothing, electronics (Apple vs. PC), jewelry, shoes, the locations and sizes of our homes, our educational pedigree, the restaurants we frequent, the grocery stores we patronize (Walmart vs. Whole Foods). What norms, then, guide the practices that constitute the performance of American consumer?

In the United States, the identity *consumer* is subject to the frameworks of nationalism and patriotism. Nationalism is our psychological and emotional identification with the collective political and cultural identity of *American*, whereas patriotism is the actualization of our nationalism through conspicuous support (financially, physically, verbally) of our country. The Declaration of Independence proclaims the rights of Americans to life, liberty, and the pursuit of happiness. Consumer identity has been entwined with these inalienable rights arguably since the establishment of our nation. The pursuit of happiness has historically been interpreted in terms of material well-being, financial success, and purchasing power. If it wasn't already embedded in the psyches of Americans, the overt push to mass consumerism (especially as a patriotic duty) at the turn of the 19th to the 20th century, and the cultivation of a mass culture by the federal government and the new advertising industry in the early 20th century, unquestionably defined happiness and success in terms of material consumption of goods. These goods included food products, especially animal meats and dairy milk.

By the beginning of the 20th century, Americans, especially those belonging to the wealthier classes, were becoming accustomed to the constant introduction of new or improved products made possible by the mechanical advancements of the Industrial Revolution. The employment of assembly lines (or, rather, disassembly lines) in the process of butchering and dismembering animals by slaughterhouses and meatpacking industries as early as the middle 19th century, and the subsequent appropriation of the concept to construct (as opposed to deconstruct) vehicles by Henry Ford at the beginning of the 20th century, dramatically affected the rate at which products could be completed. The careful, skilled craftsmanship that had previously been the paradigm for the construction of consumer durables (furniture, clothing, coaches, farm equipment, and household tools) engendered respect and care for quality products that would survive years, if not a lifetime, but the shift in the production process to mass production privileged efficiency and quantity over quality and durability.

As commercial industries adopted technologies that enabled increasingly rapid production rates, they found themselves in need of large numbers of people willing to purchase these products. These industries often found themselves without sufficient demand for the surplus of goods. The surplus resulted in regular cuts in production, and thus laborers, and periods of stagnation. Ford would identify this as an inherent problem with Fredrick Winslow Taylor's theories of scientific management, a perspective that essentially advanced efficiency as the foundational principle of industrial production and dehumanized workers via automation. In general, from the late 19th century through the turn of the century, the transitioning and unstable industrial system included weeks of unemployment for workers when manufacturers needed to clean out their stock. Cuts in employment created economic recessions. The continued financial instability of the nation combined with these recessions resulted in multiple depressions from 1873 through the early 1900s. These regular periods of unemployment created an increasingly large and desperate population of working poor. Lack of job security resulted in anxiety, financial instability, and discontent.

While the early 20th-century industries suffered from overproduction leading to economic instability, corporations increasingly understood that to capitalize on the efficiency of industrial production, they had to create the counterbalance of a popular consumer demand. Influenced by the labor polices of Ford, who proposed that the wages of laborers be increased so that they could purchase the surplus of manufactured products, corporations began to increase the pay of employees and increased the amount of time off of work so that employees would have extra money and time to spend purchasing products.

The federal government understood the instability of the industrial economy as a matter of national security. Workers endured the seven-year depression of the 1870s and the massive collapse of the economy in 1893, which caused unemployment to soar to 20 percent. Class disparity had become apparent to workers suffering from industrialization and urbanization. In 1900, 1 percent of the population owned more of the nation's wealth than the remaining 99 percent combined. Indeed, 65 percent of the population owned only clothes and furniture and lived hand to mouth.[13] These conditions combined to incite violence and social instability. Class warfare erupted in the factories, plants, and yards of the major cities. Workers responded to the social inequity and the dangerous conditions of their workplaces by striking. Strikes, even those involving women and children, were usually violent and often brutal, resulting in deaths of workers. As the century progressed, the megacorporations that dominated the American industrial landscape and the U.S. federal government forged increasingly strong relationships, and worked to stabilize the nation's economy by promoting a new American dream bound up in the ideology of mass consumerism.

The government and these businesses collaborated in producing a cultural change that emphasized the importance of consumption—what we refer to today as consumer culture. The rationale for this cultural change was that it would save the national economy and create cultural unity by calming class conflict. In order to encourage mass consumption, however, the American citizenry had to be convinced that the careful saving they had been practicing, which was a part of the American dream (work hard, demonstrate good character, and save your way to wealth), was not appropriate or viable for this new modern era. The popular sentiment expressed by culture-makers and corporate leaders was that "the public must be reeducated to imagine how much it might pleasurably consume, rather than how little it might get by on."[14]

The challenge of "reeducating" the public fell to the early advertising industry. Advertisers were charged with selling a new narrative of "The Good Life" or "The American Way of Life." The rhetorical strategy developed by these advertisers advanced that Americans *needed* and *deserved* the products and luxuries supplied by manufacturers. Corporate advertisers also positioned themselves as patriots who were promoting American nationalism. By advocating for increased consumption, they were effactually saving the American people from a life of frugality and deprivation that was not suited to the modern era. "Advertising," stated Bruce Barton (superhero advertising executive of the 1920s), "is the spark plug on the cylinder of mass production, and essential to the continuance of the democratic process. Advertising sustains a system that has made us leaders of the free world: the American Way of Life."[15]

This "reeducation," however, posed a challenge. Although many well-to-do Americans had disposable incomes and substantial savings accounts, at least half the population was living at the poverty line. How could people who were barely able to make ends meet participate in a new narrative of consumption? Installment buying and credit became an integral part of sales promotions. The old taboos of debt had to be challenged, and Americans had to be convinced that purchasing on credit (time-based payments) was not shameful or excessive. Advertisers again invoked the frameworks of nationalism and patriotism. America's emerging international prominence as a world power demanded that citizens participate in both the actual financial support of the country and the cultivation of the appearance of success and power through the accumulation of material wealth.

What distinguishes modern advertising as it was developed in the early 20th century from 19th-century advertising practices is that modern advertising is not focused on the quality of the product, but on the self-image of the consumer. In the 1920s, advertisers began to emphasize style, which was linked to the increased importance of "personality." Personality, derived from *persona*, is a set of publicly performed practices and qualities of a person that are either socially attractive or not. The etymological derivation of *personality* as characteristics of the body or the physical appearance of a person, and its subsequent association with celebrity and fame, positioned this identity concept as easily alterable and superficial. Previously, character had been the primary identity concept. Character was understood as an inherent moral quality in an individual, an inner moral gyroscope that led people to make right or wrong decisions. Although both character and personality are etymologically associated with the theater and thus are plastic and achieved through performances, character was considered inherent (you were good or bad) and was a significant element in achieving the American dream. People of good character would thrive even when faced with adversity (witness Horatio Alger's stories of young protagonists who make choices that define their characters and who then reap the attendant rewards or detriments).

Considering that more than half the American population was far from thriving economically and that norms governing morality were in constant contestation in a diverse population enabled by immigration, urbanization, and increasingly visible and vocal gender and sexuality movements, character in its traditional sense no longer seemed relevant. By the 1920s, advertisers were promoting personality—what was socially attractive, how you presented yourself, how you got along with others—as being more important than character. How does one express one's personality? Through style. Style, from the literary derivation, refers to a particular manner and mode of expression "considered in regard to clearness, effectiveness, beauty, and the like."[16] This derivation positions style as the superficial features of expression (such as form) as opposed to the substance of content.[17] As early as the 18th century, style was used to characterize and judge individuals by their consumer choices, their public performances of self through material accoutrements. The value of style to the cause of mass consumerism is inestimable. Style is plastic, ever-changing. Early 20th-century advertisers linked style to professional trendsetters, which meant that for fashionable Americans to stay in style (which would be necessary to communicate a modern personality befitting a citizen of a world power), they had to continue to purchase products that were deemed stylish.

The other main advertising strategy in the early 20th century was to attack the individual's self-image. Advertisers manipulated the self-confidence of the consumer first by eroding that confidence and then by offering a product as a way to restore it. This tactic emphasized the need for people to care about a good (stylish) first impression. Because personality was now the most important aspect of an individual, people's first impressions of others were extremely important in determining relationships. Whereas character was an element that took time to determine, an individual's personality could be immediately ascertained by his or her consumer choices. Through this process, Americans came to understand conspicuous consumption as the primary performance of individual and American identity, and America became a consumer culture.

A consumer culture is a system of relationships between people and social, symbolic, and material resources mediated by a market economy. Central to the ideology of consumer culture is perceived freedom of choice, as well as the adjunct formation and expression of individual identity through those choices. Modern consumer practices are directed less by the relationship of substance (the thing consumed) to subsistence (an individual's survival) and more by the symbolic value of material goods (style). As consumers, people define themselves and give meaning to their lives through their choices in the marketplace. This ethic of consumption seemingly corrected the economic instabilities of the Progressive Era but created dramatic shifts in understandings of American identity and the elusive American dream. How, then, does this early history of mass consumerism in the United States intersect with current issues plaguing our global food systems?

The Effects of American Exceptionalism

As I have previously noted, to consume (to eat and to buy) is to enact certain practices that engage a constellation of values, beliefs, and commitments. Our acts of consumption of food, material goods, or services, whether intentionally or not, position us within certain systems of meanings and practices. Although many people can readily identify common systems in which they participate (educational, political, religious, economic, etc.), most people, at least until recently, have given little thought to their participation in food systems. A food system is a network of individuals and institutions that collaborate to produce, distribute, market, and consume food products (dairy, animal meats, vegetables and fruits, processed foods, fast foods, etc.). In the United States, and increasingly globally, food systems have been significantly influenced by principles of efficiency emphasizing speed, convenience, and low cost. These principles are consistent with the ideology of mass consumerism, enabled by the advances in industrial production technologies pioneered by Taylor and Ford at the beginning of the 20th century, and continue to buttress our contemporary consumer culture.

American national identity, as I have demonstrated, is bound up in narratives of consumption, specifically the consumption of material goods that perform style and personality. American national identity—what it means to be and to do American—is also inherently tied to the discourse of food. This is the land of plenty, where our perceived exceptionalism is enabled by our access to foods popularly understood as strengthening, such as milk and meat. Meat, notes Harvey Levenstein, has been "by far Americans' favorite food."[18] The process of consuming the animal body—meat—has been understood as a process of integrating the animal into oneself, thereby appropriating the animal's wild strength and cunning. As Roland Barthes notes of the mythology of meat, "Steak . . . is the heart of meat, it is meat in its pure state; and whoever partakes of it assimilates a bull-like strength."[19] Indeed, the consumption of animal flesh holds a distinct place in the American narrative of exceptionalism, tied to the Jacksonian ideal of rugged individualism, self-sufficiency (hunting and husbandry), and territorial expansion, as well as a new masculinity characterized by physical strength and stamina pioneered by Theodore Roosevelt. Contemporary American beliefs about the necessity and superiority of animal-derived protein to health and well-being are rooted in this national narrative that links meat consumption to exceptionalism, and so individuals and cultural and social institutions perform the reification of this narrative through contemporary practices of animal consumption.

In terms of the market economy, this narrative that links strength and national superiority to the consumption of animal flesh, specifically beef, dramatically increases the demand for cheap and abundant meat. This demand, then, fuels harmful land use practices (like deforestation) linked to pasturing livestock and the production of feed crops. Feed crop production has usurped approximately one-third of the world's arable land, and livestock are being raised on 26 percent of the world's ice-free land.[20] These land practices are contributing to global warming and world hunger. The continued importance of animal consumption as a performance of national identity is also responsible for the proliferation of Concentrated Animal Feeding Operations (CAFOs), or factory farms. CAFOs are well-documented hazards to the health of the environment, to people living near these operations, and to the global community.

Since the mechanization of the slaughter and meat-processing industries in the early 20th century, industrial meat production has become one of the most hazardous industries in the world. Feed and processing plants employ thousands of workers in assembly-line techniques to kill, inspect, decontaminate, dismember, and package tens of thousands of animals per plant per day. CAFOs are a product of the epidemic of industrial efficiency and are also an example of how the ethic of efficiency excludes consideration of factors and effects other than those that directly affect today's corporate profit margins. George Ritzer, in *The McDonaldization of Society*, defines "efficiency" as "the optimum means to a given end."[21] Who, then, determines the "given end"? Although the idea of efficiency is not inherently damaging (it is responsible for many innovations that make our lives more comfortable), when it is taken to an extreme and employed without other mitigating principles (such as ethics), efficiency can lead, and has led, to the degradation of work (mechanization, automation, and unskilled labor), cultural stagnancy (through standardization and homogenization), and dehumanization (both the devaluing of human beings themselves and the rising inhumanity of those same human beings). Besides the inherent cruelty of large animal feeding/processing operations, these CAFOs endanger food security, environmental sustainability, and the health of the global population.

CAFOs require enormous amounts of grain to feed the confined livestock. This grain is produced on monoculture fields through intensive synthetic farming methods that are fossil fuel–dependent and that privilege the use of toxic chemical fertilizers, pesticides, and herbicides. These billions of confined animals (more than 55 billion land animals are slaughtered each year) also produce waste.[22] In the United States, a typical cattle feedlot operation produces 344 million pounds of fecal waste per year.[23] The amount of total waste produced by all farmed animals in the United States is 130 times greater than that produced by the human population.[24] The management of this waste is poorly regulated—at best—and has been cited in the contamination of water and air supplies, as well as the contamination of vegetable crops (i.e., spinach). Industrially produced livestock are responsible for "thirty-seven percent of methane and sixty-five percent of nitrous oxide" production—greenhouse gases that significantly contribute to contemporary global warming trends.[25] These practices also compromise the long-term viability of the soil, usurp up to 70 percent of the world's available freshwater supply (contributing to the increased frequency of droughts), and introduce dangerous pollutants into the land and water.

CAFOs are also hotbeds for disease even as they employ upward of 35 million pounds of antibiotics each year in the United States alone (more than 11 times the amount administered to humans).[26] In 2005, the Council for Agricultural Science and Technology identified the practices of breeding genetically uniform poultry housed in factory farms as leading to an increasing risk of pathogen growth and mutation. These practices place the world at risk of another pandemic such as the Spanish flu of 1918, which infected approximately one-quarter of the U.S. population and killed more than 600,000 Americans and as many as 100 million people worldwide.[27] As early as 2004, the World Health Organization, in cooperation with the United Nations and the World Organization for Animal Health, identified the increase in global demand for animal meat as a "primary risk factor" for "emerging zoonotic diseases" such as H1N1 (traced to a North Carolina hog CAFO).[28] Ultimately, the organizations concluded that the "cost of increased efficiency" would be an increased likelihood of pandemics.[29]

Even with the increasing availability of information linking these practices to the contamination of our natural environments, climate change, the compromised safety of our foods, the dwindling fresh water supply, and the cultivation of new diseases, consumer demand fueled by "taste" and stories about who we are as a nation support the continued presence of this type of industrial farming. As we have seen, consumption, in its most basic embodied sense, is a performative practice foundational to American-ness. More disturbing, patterns of American consumption have been adopted globally. The narrative of American exceptionalism and its relationship to consumption (materialism and food systems) has become a model for developing countries. Our agribusinesses have become multinational monsters globalizing the same dangerous industrial farming practices that are compromising our food safety and food sovereignty.

The Palatable Is Political

Communication about food is always political and biased. Food, though intensely personal (we integrate its matter into our bodies), is also cultural and social and thus affected by and affecting the political. One of the challenges of creating a cultural shift that would combat the damaging practices of industrial food production is the intensity of individual identification with the dominant narrative of American identity: *consumer*. According to this narrative, consumption (to purchase/to ingest) is our patriotic duty as well as our inalienable right through which we pursue happiness. The connotative conflation of meanings (to purchase and to ingest) and the importance of food discourse to national identity (strength through the consumption of animal meat) has resulted in the deeply held belief that we are free to participate in the food system in any way we choose. Food is a consumer product. We have the inalienable right to purchase and eat what we want. When that perceived right is tested by an individual or group attempting to challenge the narrative of consumption, the resulting conflict makes visible the norms that govern our relationships with food as a consumer product. Take, for instance, a recent legislative initiative that targets food industries and food consumption in New York City.

In a controversial move, New York City Mayor Michael Bloomberg attempted to pass a law restricting the size of sodas (to a maximum of 16 ounces) that can be sold in most food establishments in the city. Harvard nutrition expert Dr. Walter Willet identifies soda as a key contributor to the obesity and diabetes epidemic currently plaguing the United States. "The evidence of harm for soda is longer than for anything else that we normally consume," Willett says. "And there's absolutely no benefit. Most foods, even if they are not the healthiest foods, have some nutritional value. Here it is all harm, no nutritional value. And the amounts being consumed are massive."[30] While the health benefits of reducing soda consumption are clearly documented, a state judge struck down the ban as arbitrary and potentially more damaging to society than the sugary drinks. Upon appeal, the court found the legislation unconstitutional. Mississippi lawmakers, reacting against potential public health initiatives similar to Bloomberg's NYC bill, have put forward the Anti-Bloomberg Bill, legislation that would prevent any local official from advancing any initiative that would regulate the food and beverage industries in the interest of public health (i.e., calorie labels, portion controls, or limitations on advertising to children).

Though laws forcing food industries to reveal potentially critical information to the public (ingredients, allergens, sodium content, and calorie counts most notably) are typically met with little resistance from the citizenry—even though the food industries themselves have launched massive multimillion dollar campaigns to prevent or reverse these laws—Bloomberg's initiative changes the focus of government intervention from enabling consumer-citizen access to information to preventing consumer-citizen consumption. This challenge to consumer-citizen choice and autonomy is effectively a challenge to consumer identity and consumer culture. Americans interpret their constitutional rights to "life, liberty, and the pursuit of happiness" through the lens of consumerism. We have the right to *purchase* health care that extends and increases the quality of our lives; we have the right to *purchase* products that we *choose* to purchase; and we have the right to pursue happiness through our *purchases*. Bloomberg's bill embodies the articulation of a different perspective; one driven not by consumerism but rather by social health. Consumer-citizen resistance to legislating restrictions on the availability of foods that have become staples in everyday life, such as soda, makes visible the norms that shape consumer identity, at least in the United States. Specifically, freedom is defined as freedom within the marketplace and performed through the purchase of products that assist individuals in constructing and performing their personalities (their selves). It is through this process of purchasing that Americans have come to make sense of their places in society and make meaning in their lives. This kind of legislation challenges the consumer-citizen's perceived right to define his or her own happiness and well-being and also destabilizes the individual's sense of self as an American.[31]

Globalization, McDonaldization, and the Performance of Plenty

The conflation of consumption (to purchase/to eat) with happiness is not unique to the United States. Nor is the popularity of industrially produced foods. Even as independent scientific research is linking the consumption of industrially produced foods, including soda, processed foods, and animal products such as meat and dairy, to obesity, cancer, and heart disease, and even as environmental activists are heralding the irreparable damage to the environment, the demand for these kinds of food products globally is growing. Multiple factors are at work in this phenomenon, but the two most relevant to this discussion are (1) the enduring power of stories of identity (nationalism, masculinity, virility, strength) and (2) the perceived rights of the consumer to purchase/eat whatever he or she desires.

We have previously examined the relationship between consumption and the narrative of American national identity. Specifically, we considered the American preoccupation with animal flesh as a symbol of strength, its relationship to CAFOs, and the global environmental effect of industrial animal farms. The availability of foods tied to American national identity, specifically milk and meat, has also been narratively linked to national health and security, and has affected American citizens' understandings of the global food economy.

In her article "Performing the Land of Plenty in the USDA's 1933–34 World's Fair Exhibits," Ann Folino White observes, "Access to staple foods such as milk and meat structures personal and national identities."[32] Through display techniques that involved citizen-visitors as participants, the USDA reassured citizens that even in this time of national crisis—the Great Depression—America continued to be the land of plenty where selecting "satisfying meats" was a "cultural right of ordinary life."[33] Indeed, these exhibits argued that daily consumption of dairy milk was imperative to the healthy development of individual citizens and to their physical superiority. Therefore, dairy milk was also imperative to the health and physical superiority of the nation, thereby ensuring national security. The dairy industry exhibit bore the slogan "Dairy Products Build Superior People" and was designed not only to celebrate the technological advances of the industry, but also to educate consumers about the health benefits of consuming dairy products.[34]

As early as the 1920s, the dairy industry adamantly promoted the benefits of consuming milk for older children and adults, a substance previously reserved for infants and toddlers.[35] By the 1930s, dairy milk was understood as integral to the health of the country, a national obsession seemingly supported by the new nutritional sciences and perpetuated by the USDA, as well as the dairy industry. A family of five was advised to consume at least 28 quarts (or seven gallons!) of milk per week to maintain optimal health and avoid serious illness.[36] Food security was measured in large part by children's access to milk. Levenstein notes that low-income families identified "consumption of milk [as] their most serious deficiency."[37] In the 1960 CBS documentary, *Harvest of Shame*, Edward R. Murrow asks Mrs. Doby, a migrant farm worker and mother of nine children, about their access to food:

MURROW. "How many quarts of milk do you buy for the children, Mrs. Doby?"

DOBY. "Well, we don't have milk, except maybe when we draw our paycheck we have milk about once a week."

MURROW. "For all these children you have . . .?"

DOBY. "The baby she is on the bottle and she uses about 15 cans of milk a week, but the older children have milk about once a week."

MURROW. "Do they like to drink milk, Mrs. Doby?

DOBY. "Yes, they like milk."

MURROW. "The only reason I ask that question is I was quite shocked that they had milk only once a week."

Murrow's line of questioning and his shock at the lack of access these children have to milk confirms the enduring position of milk as foundational to national health. A family is expected to perform care by providing its children access to dairy milk. The Doby family's inability to participate in this performance of consumption as care, then, compromises their identities as consumers, and therefore as normal Americans. The purpose of *Harvest of Shame* was to draw national attention to the plight of citizen-laborers, primarily migrant farm workers, who could not adequately perform the national identity of consumer (to purchase/to ingest) even as they participated in labor that enabled the production and distribution of staple foods to the nation. The presence of this group of people made visible the cracks in the national narrative of plenty and called into question domestic food security. And as exemplified by Murrow's shock, it also associated poverty and hunger with lack of access to dairy milk.

Indeed, even today dairy milk is a staple in public school cafeterias and lunch boxes. Contemporary advertising like the popular 1980s campaign

"Milk: It Does a Body Good" and, most recently, "Got Milk?"—launched in 1993 and famous for its milk-mustached celebrities—continue to position milk as an integral element to health, strength, fitness, and success. The "Got Milk?" commercial featured during the 2013 Super Bowl stars a well-muscled Dwayne "The Rock" Johnson who is faced with catastrophic events including an alien invasion. After securing milk for three young girls, he drinks a glass himself and says, "Ladies, gotta go to work," as he punches an alien. The caption reads: "Protein to start your day. Got Milk?" This advertisement clearly uses humor to convey the significance of milk. Just as clearly, we are presented with images of strength, heroism, and security. As the world faces destruction, The Rock consumes a fortifying glass of milk (reminiscent of Popeye's use of spinach) and nonchalantly announces his intention to save the world as going to "work." His punching of the alien performs his strength and power and foreshadows his unquestionable success. If we trace the logic, we find that milk provides The Rock with the foundational protein that supports his physique and allows him to save the world. Thus dairy milk saves the world.

Lack of access to dairy milk and animal meat has been understood, especially in the Western world, as being indicative of deficiency, poverty, or developing-nation status. Aid in the form of livestock, as exemplified by organizations like Heifer International, reify and promulgate the importance of milk and animal products as necessary for healthy and happy families. The genesis story of Heifer International includes protagonist Dan West, who, in his efforts to provide aid and relief to soldiers at the front lines of the Spanish Civil war, was dissatisfied with the meager ration of one "cup of milk" per soldier per day.[38] Inspired by the biblical proverb, "teach a man to fish," West asked, "What if they had not a cup, but a cow?" His mission to offer aid to families stricken by poverty and hunger is philosophically anchored in the American narrative of success—hard work, self-sufficiency, and morality (passing along "the gift" of animal offspring). It also advances the primacy of animal-based products to "hope and prosperity" and is indicative of the standards by which Americans assess global hunger and food security.[39]

As incomes rise, so does the consumption of products associated with success, luxury, and "the good life." In "Distinction: A Social Critique of the Judgment of Taste," Pierre Bourdieu examines how social class affects consumer participation in food systems. He notes, "Tastes in food also depend on the idea each class has of the body, and the effects of food on the body, that is, on its strength, health and beauty."[40] The positioning of dairy milk and animal meat as integral to the individual, social, and national health and security of Americans and America has influenced international understandings of the importance of these foods. In the past decade, consumption of milk has doubled and meat tripled in regions considered "developing" where urbanization is accompanied by population and income growth.[41] The Food and Agriculture Organization of the United Nations (FAO) states that "[f]ew countries are self-sufficient in milk" and that these countries therefore must import dairy milk from producers such as the United States and Australia to satisfy increasing demand.[42] Though it might seem the appropriate solution to satisfy consumer desire—importing a product demanded by consumers owing to lack of production at the local level—this trend makes visible the increasing international purview of norms that organize the performance of American consumer identity. As consumer culture goes global, the performance of consumer identity (to eat/to purchase) and its adjunct practices and meanings are appropriated and interpreted within the contexts of various cultural traditions and national agendas.

The increase in global demand for animal meat and dairy milk is, in part, a function of increasing globalization and what Ritzer refers to as McDonaldization. Globalization, as Frank Lechner defines it, is "the worldwide diffusion of practices, expansion of relations across continents, organization of social life on a global scale, and growth of a shared global consciousness."[43] Ritzer argues that McDonaldization is a process of globalization, as well as a revolutionizing force in the United States. McDonaldization is rooted in the practices of industrial efficiency standardized at the turn of the century and applied to the food industry in the mid-20th century. The success of the fast-food industry called the attention of other industries (travel, entertainment, education, etc.) to its guiding principles, which were then adopted and adapted by innumerable social institutions. McDonaldization, then, is "the process by which the principles of the fast-food restaurant are coming to dominate more and more sectors of American society as well as of the rest of the world."[44] The United States, according to Ritzer, is the source and center of this process.[45] Not only does McDonaldization affect technologies and processes of production, but it also affects culture. As values, beliefs, and performances of identity associated with McDonaldization (speed, convenience, efficiency, nutritional benefit of animal-based products, the right to consume, and consumption as happiness) are integrated into cultures throughout the world, the "norms common in the United States [. . .] are now replacing norms distinctive" to those other cultures.[46]

In the 20th and 21st centuries, consumer culture has been characterized by a rapid, constantly shifting spectrum of commercial products and services produced and marketed by an increasingly globalized culture-industry that includes advertisers, retailers, managers, brokers, culture-makers, and mediators (such as media figures and entertainment celebrities). Even dissidents, who posit alternative options to mass consumption, are active participants in this culture industry: Their alternatives are often assimilated into the market system as niche markets. The trend toward global consumer culture, globalization, and McDonaldization in recent years has led to the formation of movements that reassert the value of localization and heterogeneity, including groups interested in the foundation of consumer identity: food.

Conclusion: The Global Issue of Gross Consumption

There is an apparent paradox in the Western approach, particularly in the United States, to food systems. This paradox is directly related to the core belief of consumer identity and consumer culture: the right to purchase. Though Americans embrace their inalienable right as consumers to purchase freely, this right extends to the foundational definition of *consume*, the right to eat, only insofar as food is a purchasable product. Food, as a consumer commodity, is governed by our capitalist economy; supply and demand dictate availability, access, and purchase price. Yet, most people believe that access to food is a fundamental human right, thus the innumerable movements and organizations focused on ending world hunger. It is not the case, as so many social scientists and cultural critics have noted, that there is not enough food in the world. Central to the "food crises" of today is the imbalance of political and cultural power between the richest and most advantaged nations (such as those in North America, Europe, and Asia) and the poorest nations of the developing world. The increasing global dominance of large agribusinesses is harming farmers in developing nations. A recent report published by the FAO observes, "The rapid expansion and transformation of the global dairy sector contributes to growing threats to the environment and to human and animal health as well as to increasing pressures on the livelihoods of small scale dairy producers."[47] Danielle Nierenberg, director of the Worldwatch Nourishing the Planet project, notes that the increased global demand for meat and dairy products is being met by CAFOs and industrial dairy farms, resulting in increased environmental damage and posing global health risks.[48]

The Center for Disease Control identifies obesity as one of these health risks, a leading contributor to preventable illness and death in the United States, and has categorized obesity as a "national epidemic."[49] In 2010, more than 35 percent of adults (78 million) and almost 17 percent of children and adolescents (12.5 million) were obese.[50] The solution to obesity, according to the CDC, can be found in relationships between the obese person and his or her consumption of food and expulsion of energy via physical activity. The most important factor in this relationship as determined by the references on the CDC website is food. Individuals need access to, and must choose to consume, healthyful and nutritious foods (i.e., those low in fat and sugar).

The etymology of the word *obese* can be traced to the mid-17th century: from Latin *obesus* "having eaten until fat."[51] To eat is an action, a doing, a performance practice that engages values, commitments, and beliefs about the relationship between sustenance, pleasure, and sociocultural identity. This practice becomes literally embodied, and the body then performs the meaning of the practice: obesity. Obesity and its extant illnesses are no longer only a problem faced by the Western world. Globalization, and the globalization (McDonaldization) of food systems in particular, has contributed to shifting economies of food (access, diversity vs. homogeneity, cost, cultural capital) in non-Western and developing countries. A 2011 study of 9.1 million participants in 199 countries and territories identified a "globesity epidemic."[52] The global trends for body mass index indicate that 500 million people are currently obese and 1.5 billion either overweight or obese—and these numbers are increasing yearly. The study indicates that if current consumption trends continue to go unchecked, 60 percent of the global population will be obese by 2030.[53]

On a daily basis, we make choices about what to eat (or not eat), when and where to eat, and with whom we eat, as well as for what purposes (pleasure, sustenance, ritual) and in what amounts. These choices are informed by and in turn inform our social and cultural positions, and through the resulting cultural and material capital, these choices mark our bodies and function as identity performances. This premise extends beyond individual identity. Collective identity, especially our understandings of what it means to be—to do—American, is produced by our repetition of certain practices and our embodiments of particular beliefs that are closely tied to industrialization, modernity, and, ultimately, our consumption of food.

Although organized by the broader national identity *consumer*, a multitude of collectivities exist that offer Americans a perceived sense of choice and control in performing our "selves" and in making our lives meaningful. Americans negotiate their identification with and participation in these subgroups, which have their own defined systems of social and cultural engagement. A growing number of these groups are formed around food. Popular culture demonstrates the boom in interest in food and its production and consumption. Thousands of television shows clog networks worldwide featuring celebrity chefs, competitive cooking, and adventuresome eating. There is an entire network devoted solely to food programming—the Food Network—and a sister network, the Cooking Channel, recently launched. Food writers, too, have never been more popular. Even academia now includes an interdisciplinary field that focuses on the intersections of food and its contexts: Food Studies. Domestically and internationally, the consumption of food, food-based entertainment, and food systems have become essential to the food-centered identity politics that organize increasingly visible and powerful collectives of consumers.

Within the identity *consumer* are a plethora of options for citizens who have come to understand the importance of food systems. I want to briefly discuss one popular (and broad) performance of identity that revolves around food consumption: the Foodie. This performance offers a potential, if problematic, solution to the crisis facing our global food systems. Foodies, loosely defined, are people who engage in food-centered hobbies and recreational activities. Josée Johnston and Shyon Baumann define Foodies as, "well-informed, discovery minded, discerning *customers* [. . .] who lead food-focused lives and *present themselves to others* as uncommonly passionate about food" (emphasis mine).[54] Note that Johnston and Baumann refer to foodies as customers (consumers who *purchase*) who engage a particular set of markers and practices to perform the identity *Foodie*. People who perform the identity Foodie may or may not actually engage in the practices (being well informed, discerning, and discovery-minded) identified by Johnston and Bauman, but they do engage in practices of consumption that position food as style rather than sustenance.

The *Chicago Tribune*'s Food & Dining section recently featured an interactive segment titled, "Test Your Foodie IQ." James Fussell, the author of the brief introductory blurb, challenged readers to define a host of "50-cent food words" without cheating. His challenge, in the form of the question, "[. . .] do you know what they mean without looking them up?" was followed by his comment: "Liar."[55] This imagined conversation makes visible the characteristics of foodies (at least American foodies): Although they are fascinated by the production and consumption of foods socially positioned as gourmet, foodies are not food professionals and do not have the tools or knowledge of food professionals. Fussell points out that his readers are probably fans of cooking shows, and he concedes that they may be able to define a few of the technical terms. This passion, however, does not translate into a professional identity. Rather, as Fussell notes, "unless you *work in a restaurant*, you'll probably be stumped by the rest" (emphasis mine). We should note here that Fussell lets the reader off the hook—being a foodie is not predicated on a person's technical knowledge, knowledge that he clearly suggests can only be obtained through working in the field. Being a foodie, then, is about consumption and appreciation through consumption, as opposed to production.

A Google search for "Foodie" produces over 13 million results, emphasizing the pervasiveness of this identity marker in popular culture. It is in this pervasiveness that the potential for Foodie as a performance of consumer identity can contribute to solutions to the issues plaguing our global food systems. It is arguable that food, including its production and consumption, has never been more visible and central to Americans' performances of collective and individual identity. Awareness of the value (i.e., quality of contents and social significance) of food is the first step in cultivating awareness of the forces that are compromising that value, creating obstacles to accessibility, and creating the conditions for cultural and environmental degradation.

It is, however, the core characteristic of the identity foodie—consumption—that poses a problem, especially for Americans. As I have previously discussed, the American understanding of consumption is framed by nationalism:

Americans have the right to pursue happiness through their consumer practices. This kind of laissez-faire approach to food consumption functions as an obstacle to the promotion of ethical, responsible, and deliberate eating practices. Although foodies may be concerned with the aesthetic quality of their food products, and to some extent the designators that accompany gourmet, environmentally sustainable, or high-end food items ("Fair Trade," "Cage-Free," "Grass-Fed," etc.), they are ultimately seeking a pleasurable experience that performs their refined and cultured "tastes." It is the perceived right to the indulgence of these pleasures, and the adoption of this perspective internationally, that currently locates the consumer identity of foodie as counterproductive to the development of solutions to global food issues. Rather, this right to eat in the pursuit of happiness is contributing to the global epidemic of food-related illness.

The globesity epidemic is an embodiment of the conflation of the definitions of *consume* (to eat/to purchase) and of the complicated performance of consumer identity. Obviously it is only one of the multitudes of ills that accompany the globalization of industrial food production, the separation of producer/product/consumer in the marketplace, and the gross—"flagrant" and "total"—consumption that characterizes contemporary consumer identity. The increasingly pervasive belief in the inalienable right to consume is accompanied by overconsumption and consumption of damaging foods as well as potentially irreversible damage to our environment and the extinction of localized and culturally specific foodways. However, although foodie as a potential performance of identity does make visible the importance of food in our lives, it does not necessarily include issues of social justice and ethical production/consumption practices. Because of its contemporary relevance, however, this movement has the potential to positively affect looming global food issues. If we can shift the focus of food-centered identity performances from the pleasure of consumption to the integrity of the production of what is being consumed, can shift the definition of happiness from the instant gratification of "taste" to an understanding of happiness as social justice, and organize and activate the agency latent in the consumer identity (purchasing power!), we can work within the system to change the system. Although this is by no means an ideal or comprehensive solution, the mobilization of an already cohesive group of people bound together by a narrative of consumerism has the potential to significantly affect the practices that characterize our global food systems.

Notes

1. *Oxford Dictionary of English*, 3rd ed., ed. Angus Stevenson (Oxford: Oxford University Press, 2010).

2. "Consume," def. 2

3. "performance, n." OED Online, Oxford University Press. www.oed.com/view/Entry/140783?redirectedFrom=performance&

4. *Merriam-Webster Dictionary.*

5. Judith Butler, *Undoing Gender* (New York: Routledge, 2004), 42.

6. Cindy Spurlock, "Performing and Sustaining (Agri)Culture and Place: The Cultivation of Environmental Subjectivity on the Piedmont Farm Tour," *Text and Performance Quarterly* 29, no. 1 (2009): 6.

7. Marvin Carlson, *Performance: A Critical Introduction*, 2nd ed. (1996; New York: Routledge, 2004), ix.

8. Ronald J. Pelias and Tracy Stephenson Shaffer, *Performance Studies: The Interpretation of Aesthetic Texts*, 2nd ed. (Dubuque, IA: Kendall/Hunt Publishing Co., 2007), 5.

9. "Consumer," def. 1, *OERD.*

10. "Consumer," def. 2, *OERD.*

11. Zygmunt Bauman, *Globalization: The Human Consequences* (New York: Columbia University Press, 1998), 24.

12. *OERD.*

13. Thomas C. Reeves, *Twentieth-Century America: A Brief History* (New York: Oxford University Press, 2000), 10.

14. Roland Marchand, *Advertising the American Dream: Making Way for Modernity, 1920–1940* (Berkeley: University of California Press, 1986), 120.

15. Warren Susman, *Culture as History: The Transformation of American Society in the Twentieth Century* (1973; New York: Pantheon Books, 1984), 127–128.

16. OED Online. www.oed.com/view/Entry/192315?rskey=YbfvPq&result=1#eid

17. "Those features of literary composition which belong to form and expression rather than to the substance of the thought or matter expressed" (OED Online).

18. Harvey Levenstein, *A Paradox of Plenty: A Social History of Eating in Modern America* (New York: Oxford University Press, 1989), 74.

19. Roland Barthes, *Mythologies*, trans. Annette Lavers (New York: The Noonday Press, 1990), 62.

20. Anna Lappé, "The Climate Crisis at the End of Our Fork," *Food, Inc.*, ed. Karl Weber (New York: Public Affairs, 2009), 109.

21. Ritzer, 43.

22. "FAOStat," Food and Agriculture Organization of the United Nations. faostat.fao.org

23. Jonathan Safran Foer, *Eating Animals* (New York: Little, Brown and Company, 2009), 174.

24. Foer, 174.

25. Lappe, 111.

26. Foer, 140.

27. Foer, 124; Richard Knox, "1918 Killer Flu Reconstructed," NPR.org (2005).

28. 29. Foer, 142.

30. NBC News, "Nutrition Experts: Despite Ruling, Soda Ban Is Still a Great Idea," March 12, 2013. http://vitals.nbcnews.com/_news/2013/03/11/17274083-nutrition-experts-despite-ruling-soda-ban-is-still-a-great-idea?lite

31. Ann Folino White, "Performing the Promise of Plenty in the USDA's 1933–34 World's Fair Exhibits," *Text and Performance Quarterly* 29, no. 1 (2009): 25.

32. Ibid.

33. Ibid.

34. Cheryl Ganz, *The 1933 World's Fair: A Century of Progress* (Chicago: University of Illinois Press, 2012), 76.

35. Levenstein, 59.

36. Levenstein, 59.

37. Levenstein, 59.

38. Heifer.org. *Heifer International.*

39. Ibid.

40. Pierre Bourdieu, "Distinctions: A Social Critique of the Judgment of Taste," *Food and Culture: A Reader*, 3rd ed., eds. Carole Counihan and Penny Van Esterik (New York: Routledge, 2013), 34.

41. Christopher Delgado, "Rising Consumption of Meat and Milk in Developing Countries Has Created a New Food Revolution," *The Journal of Nutrition* 133, no. 11 (2003).

42. "Global Dairy Sector: Status and Trends," *Status and Prospects for Smallholder Milk Production: A Global Perspective*, eds. Torsten Hemme and Joachim Otte (Food and Agriculture Organization of the United Nations, 2010). www.fao.org/docrep/012/i1522e/i1522e02.pdf

43. George Ritzer, *The McDonaldization of Society*, rev. New Century ed. (London: Pine Forge Press, 2004), 160.

44. Ritzer, 1.

45. Ritzer, 166.

46. Ritzer, 183.

47. Stefano Gerosa and Jakob Skoet, "Milk Availability: Trends in Production and Demand and Medium-Term Outlook" (Food and Agriculture Organization of the United Nations, February 2012). www.fao.org/docrep/015/an450e/an450e00.pdf

48. Joe DeCapua, "Developing Countries See Sharp Rise in Meat Consumption," Voice of America. www.voanews.com/content/decapua-farm-animals-29mar12-144898655/179917.html

49. Centers for Disease Control and Prevention, "Healthy Weight: Introduction." www.cdc.gov/healthyweight/index.html

50. The CDC's definition of obese is related to body mass index and signifies being at least 20 percent in excess of an individual's "natural" or ideal weight. www.cdc.gov/nchs/data/databriefs/db82.pdf

51. "obese, adj.," Oxford Dictionaries. http://oxforddictionaries.com/us/definition/american_english/obese

52. Mariel M. Finucane, Gretchen A. Stevens, Melanie J. Cowan, et al. "National, Regional, and Global Trends in Body-Mass Index since 1980: Systematic Analysis of Health Examination Surveys and Epidemiological Studies with 960 Country-Years and 9.1 Million Participants," *Lancet* (February 2011).

53. Harvard School of Public Health, "Globalization." www.hsph.harvard.edu/obesity-prevention-source/obesity-causes/globalization-and-obesity/#References

54. Josée Johnston and Shyon Baumann, 67.

55. James A. Fussell, "Test Your Foodie IQ," *Chicago Tribune*, 2013. www.chicagotribune.com/features/food/chi-food-words-quiz,0,3799092.triviaquiz

Battles for the Soul of Organic: The Grassroots versus the Suits

Grace Gershuny

Agribusiness apologists ask us to consider how we can feed a world population that is expected to soon reach 9 billion. All the tools of modern scientific agriculture are needed, they tell us: We cannot return to the outmoded and unscientific methods represented by organic farming. Activists who oppose the agribusiness scenario point to mounting evidence that organic farms are as productive as chemical-intensive ones, use fewer nonrenewable resources and less energy, protect soil and water quality, treat livestock humanely, and help mitigate climate change by sequestering carbon in soil organic reserves. At the same time, many of the same activists attack "industrial organic" companies and demand stricter standards to maintain "organic integrity" and meet consumer expectations. As a result, young food system activists increasingly believe that the organic label has been hijacked by agribusiness and is thus now meaningless.

The History of Organic Standard-Setting and Attendant Controversies

The organic community in North America has long been divided along philosophical and ideological lines. Whereas the organic pioneers have mainly been identified with the counterculture and its associated political and social movements, increasing mainstream acceptance has resulted in the engagement of more pragmatic and business-oriented players. Many are unaware of the roots of some organic proponents in fascist ideologies.[1] Tension between the grassroots (small-scale, locally focused organic farming advocates), and the suits (middlemen, manufacturers, and distributors seeking to profit from the rapidly growing organic sector) has been a continual factor in drawing battle lines over organic standards and requirements, especially with the onset of federal regulation.

Regulation of the organic label by the U.S. Department of Agriculture (USDA) is now nearly universally recognized as a positive achievement stimulating market growth. Its introduction has seen increased organic production along with increased investment in research and public recognition of the benefits of organic agriculture. However, there are those who regard government regulation of the organic movement with suspicion and even hostility, always ready to assume the worst—and often finding their suspicions justified. The progressive social activist community has long held as given (not without justification) that the USDA is a captive of corporate industrial agribusiness interests, something documented by authors such as Marion Nestle.[2] This suspicion has created a self-fulfilling prophecy that is now threatening to undermine public confidence in the credibility of the organic label.

At the time of writing, the current economic recession has depressed the growth of the organic market, but that market is nevertheless still expanding, having grown by about 5 percent annually since 2009, with more recent rates of growth approaching the double digits. In comparison, conventional food sales have seen flat or even negative rates of growth. However, even though organic food (and nonfood products) now constitutes close to 4 percent of the food system in the United States, at less than 1 percent it still accounts for only a tiny fraction of domestic agricultural production.[3]

Many young activists, amplified by popular writers such as Michael Pollan[4] and by films such as *Food, Inc.*,[5] regard the USDA organic label as compromised at best—and possibly as meaningless. There is also increasing proliferation of—and confusion about—terms and ecolabels such as *natural, sustainable, green, fair trade, humane,* and *local*. Some of these labels include transparent standards and third-party verification, but most do not; many claim to be "beyond organic." A longtime administrator of a respected organic farming organization recently confided, "[I]t's almost embarrassing to refer to ourselves as organic."[6]

This three-part chapter will explore the history of organic standard setting in the United States, focusing on the role of social activist groups advocating for various forms of alternative agriculture, including family farm, environmental, and consumer protection agendas. How has this activity affected the development of the USDA National Organic Program (NOP)? To what extent do misconceptions and misleading information circulated by self-appointed watchdogs of organic integrity contradict the organic vision and work against the interests of small-scale organic farmers, including smallholder organic farmers worldwide?

Organic Standards before the U.S. Organic Foods Production Act

Organic certification in the United States began in the early 1970s, initiated through groups of like-minded farmers and would-be farmers in those regions, primarily on the west coast and a bit later in the U.S. Northeast, where the organic movement was seeking to define itself. Administration, inspection, and decision making were volunteer-based, with certified farmers approving standards and conducting peer reviews. Standards and certification procedures were borrowed freely from other organizations, and all had a local or regional focus.

Although there were some grain producers, particularly in Midwestern states such as Minnesota, the majority of certification in both western and eastern regions was for fresh produce. Initially there was little awareness of postharvest or handling concerns, let alone involvement by middlemen or processors. Very little attention was given to livestock or dairy standards, though the importance of including some livestock as part of the farming system was considered key from the start.

Consumers were rarely represented in early standards discussions, even though the rationale for farmer participation in certification included market development and consumer assurance. The focus was on what made sense ecologically in a given region, as well as the practicality of different requirements for working farms. The scientific justification for a given practice was key, and it was believed that consumers would neither understand nor care about the technical details. The promise of "food you can trust" was backed up by a system of farmers watching over each other.

In the U.S. Northeast, the first certification program for the Northeast Organic Farming Association (NOFA) was developed in 1977. However, primarily due to a lack of market demand for certification those early years were characterized by a low level of participation—about five producers registering per year through the early 1980s.

Markets in this region were almost exclusively local food cooperatives, restaurants, and small health food stores; direct sales also took place at farm stands and farmers markets. A few producer cooperatives and larger growers dealt with wholesale markets such as cooperative distributors, but those who sold direct to consumers, including early community-supported agriculture farms, generally saw no need for certification, although early experience with fraud convinced many of its importance.

The pivotal year for the organic community in the U.S. Northeast as well as the United States as a whole was 1984. Certification in the U.S. Northeast was substantially boosted by the arrival of a large organic produce wholesaler who sought suppliers from different states and required certification. Under its sponsorship, the Organic Crop Improvement Association (OCIA) was initiated as a pilot project. This became the first nationwide chapter-based certification program to operate under a single set of standards.

It was at this time that the International Federation of Organic Agriculture Movements (IFOAM) called a North American meeting of organic certifiers and businesses to consider developing unified standards. For the first time, representatives of grassroots organic organizations and organic processors and marketers met to work together on common concerns. From this meeting, the Organic Foods Production Association of North America (OFPANA), which later changed its name to the Organic Trade Association (OTA), was born. However, although the grassroots organic organizations played a central role in its formation, many of them have since abandoned the OTA, refusing to collaborate with corporate organics (e.g., Horizon Organic Dairy, Smuckers Foods), whom they view as now having control of the organization.

OFPANA/OTA's first project was to create a set of unified "Guidelines for the Organic Foods Industry,"[7] which were to form the basis for evaluating and then accrediting standards and certification programs. In the course of developing this document, standards from all known North American certification programs, including the handful of organic programs established by state agriculture departments, were compared. There was remarkable consistency among the standards, with only a few variations such as those concerning the use of Chilean nitrate and differing lengths for the conversion period. There were some regional differences as well, such as allowance for livestock medications in the case of illness and use of some nonorganic livestock feed.

These differences were generally treated as gray areas in which use of restricted or regulated practices and substances was allowed under certain conditions. Farm plans were universally required to document what practices were used and provide justification for use of any restricted practices (based on monitoring of conditions in the field), describing how the farmer would move away from reliance on them. This system provided a flexibility that allowed consistent application of clear organic principles to different ecological conditions, in contrast to a one-size-fits-all approach.

Meanwhile, the problems of multiple competing and inconsistent certification systems were mounting. Certifiers would not accept each others' certifications, and the various states' labeling rules conflicted with each other. Despite similarities in standards, every certifier called its standards the highest or strictest; mutual distrust was rampant. Producers often needed multiple certifications for different markets, and manufacturers of multi-ingredient organic products had considerable difficulty working with suppliers whose certificates were not accepted by their own certifier. It was, in short, a mess.

With a mission to unite the industry, OFPANA/OTA originally intended to develop an accreditation program for mutual recognition amongst certifiers. This idea was later picked up by IFOAM, although the reciprocity part never quite happened. Several meetings were held with the aim of promoting voluntary reciprocity agreements between certifiers, but without success.

Polarization and divisiveness in the U.S. organic community has, sadly, been one of its defining features, despite various attempts at unity. The failure of this voluntary reciprocity effort led directly to calls for federal legislation to facilitate interstate trade in organic products under consistent national standards.

Organic Standards Become Law

This part of the story begins with two controversies over organic standards that later determined the direction of the Organic Foods Production Act (OFPA). The newly formed Organic Trade Association (OTA, then known as OFPANA) had produced a set of "Guidelines for the Organic Foods Industry" in 1986. These guidelines were based on three overarching precepts distinguishing organic standards from other types of standards:

1. Organic standards address the process of producing an agricultural product, rather than any measurable quality of the product itself.
2. Organic standards encourage the most environmentally sound farm practices, with flexibility to allow for geographic and site-specific differences, referred to as agronomic responsibility.
3. Organic standards require producers to demonstrate continual improvement in the quality of their management system, as evidenced by improved soil and water quality, crop quality, biological diversity, and other factors outlined in a farm plan.

The first of these came into question when a laboratory owner argued that the absence of pesticide residues, and possibly also nutritional analysis of a product, should be the primary focus of organic standards. Several OTA/OFPANA members drafted a position paper arguing that the organic nature of a product resulted from a holistic set of attributes and production methods that could not be based on laboratory analysis of product quality. This position was affirmed by the board of directors.[8]

A second, more contentious issue turned on the question of whether the use of specific farm inputs should be allowed or prohibited based on their origin from either natural (e.g., botanical pesticides, mined rock powders) or synthetic (e.g., organophosphate pesticides, anhydrous ammonia) sources, or whether the criterion of agronomic responsibility was most important for evaluating farm inputs. This generated a heated debate, with the board split fairly evenly. Proponents of the origin of materials criterion acknowledged that this was neither scientifically valid nor consistent with prevailing norms for organic production methods. However, they argued that consumers had come to expect organic food to be produced without the use of synthetic chemicals, and that this expectation should not be violated.

The membership was asked to vote by mail for the position they favored. By a narrow margin the tally resulted in a majority favoring origin of materials as the basis for organic standards. The OTA/OFPANA board then changed the guidelines to prohibit all synthetic materials and to establish criteria by which some synthetics (e.g., dormant oil, a light petroleum-based oil sprayed on fruit trees when they are dormant in order to smother pests that overwinter in the bark) might be considered acceptable on a case-by-case basis. This approach was later enshrined in the OFPA, with the responsibility for determining which synthetics should be allowed and which "naturals" should be prohibited given to the National Organic Standards Board (NOSB).

Pressure Mounts for Legislation

Although a few members of Congress had previously sponsored organic labeling bills, none of these bills were supported by the organic community. Then, early in 1989, the popular television news magazine *60 Minutes* aired an exposé about the dangers of the synthetic growth regulator Alar, widely used on apples to allow harvest of the whole crop at once. Overnight, supermarkets started featuring displays of apples that were claimed to be "organic."

What came to be known as Alar Sunday resulted in a clamor by consumer groups for legislation to protect the public from fraudulent organic claims. It soon became known that Senator Patrick Leahy (D–VT), a strong supporter of sustainable agriculture, had taken up the task. With the threat of federal legislation looming, the grassroots organic organizations that had developed and refined the system of organic certification saw the need to band together to help shape the bill to reflect the farmer groups' understanding of what organic really meant.

Under the aegis of OTA/OFPANA, a national meeting of the grassroots organic producer groups was held in December 1989. Calling themselves the Organic Farmers Associations Council (OFAC), representatives from producer groups all over the United States met—many for the first time—to agree on common principles and definitions of organic agriculture and to dialogue with Senator Leahy's staffer, Kathleen Merrigan, about provisions that should be included in the law. This coalition was hardly unanimous in its support for federal organic legislation, but the leadership helped convince their members that if they didn't get involved it would be drafted without them—a potentially disastrous situation for organic farmers.

A Victory for the Grassroots Organic Producers

As legislative language was being hammered out, OFAC put together a coalition of consumer and environmental groups along with the organic farm constituency. Other players also got into the act, including a group of organic manufacturers and businesspeople who hired an expensive Washington lobbying firm. Credit for the passage of the law, however, truly belongs to the grassroots organizing effort—phone calls, letters, and personal testimony from organic farmers and consumer representatives from all regions of the United States put enough pressure on key members of Congress to force an unprecedented floor vote in the House of Representatives despite opposition from the House Agriculture Committee and the USDA (U.S. Department of Agriculture).

The law that was finally passed includes a blanket prohibition on synthetic substances and allowance for natural ones, with the possibility of exceptions as previously discussed. It also assigned to the USDA's Agricultural Marketing Service (AMS) the task of implementation, including developing programs to certify organic operations as well as to accredit organizations who could carry out the certification program on its behalf. Despite a number of internal contradictions and errors in the law, no technical corrections were requested by USDA, which had opposed the law and accordingly requested no funding from Congress for implementing it.

The law established the National Organic Standards Board (NOSB) as a federal advisory committee[9] charged with oversight of the national list of permitted synthetic and prohibited natural substances, as well as with offering general guidance to the USDA. The first 15-member NOSB was not appointed until 1992, when the administration changed in Washington. With only one half-time staff member assigned to manage the new program within the USDA, the NOSB's volunteer industry representatives took the initiative to begin drafting regulations—a task normally assumed solely by the agency staff. They circulated drafts of all aspects of the expected regulation and held a series of meetings to receive public comment, resulting in a set of final recommendations, submitted to the USDA in 1994.

Creation of the NOP

With a more sympathetic administration, some resources became available to begin implementation of the National Organic Program (NOP). The first couple full-time staff members were hired in 1993, and then in 1994 an additional handful were brought on—including one recruited from the organic community who was knowledgeable about organic principles and practices: this author.

The original few NOP staff members were career bureaucrats who had had some previous involvement in organics and who were committed to crafting a regulation that would honor the true spirit of the organic vision and be workable for small farmers while being legally airtight. Not an easy task!

The author's first assignment was to draft a set of organic principles,[10] which was ultimately approved by the NOSB with minor amendments and later condensed into a definition of a system of organic farming and handling, or SOFAH, included in the first regulatory draft:

A system that is designed to produce agricultural products by the use of methods and substances that enhance agroecosystem health within an agricultural operation and that maintain the integrity of organic agricultural products until they reach the consumer. This is accomplished by using, where possible, cultural, biological and mechanical methods, as opposed to using substances, to fulfill any specific function within the system so as to: maintain long-term soil fertility; increase soil biological activity; recycle wastes to return nutrients to the land; provide attentive care for farm animals; enhance biological diversity within the whole system; and handle the agricultural products without the use of extraneous synthetic additives or processing in accordance with the Act and regulations in this part.

This definition became the SOFAH on which the entire regulation was designed to rest, a yardstick for determining the compatibility of a given practice with the organic vision.

The first complete draft of the regulation took another three years to finish. In addition to the law itself (which, absent early technical corrections, included significant contradictory and ambiguous language), the NOSB's recommendations and the OFPANA/OTA guidelines were key reference documents.

Many battles were fought in the course of drafting the rules. Almost every agency within the USDA, as well as parts of the U.S. EPA (Environmental Protection Agency) and FDA (Food and Drug Administration), was affected by and had to approve the document. In addition to internal struggles, the relationship between the NOP staff and some members of the organic community, including the NOSB, was adversarial from the start. Many never wanted the law to begin with, and almost everyone distrusted the USDA to get it right. Ironically, a common accusation was that USDA was trying to "take over" organic standards. This antagonism created more delays and frustration for everyone.

Finally, in June 1997, a draft was approved by all necessary agencies, including the U.S. Secretary of Agriculture. The internal fight to prohibit both genetically modified organisms (GMOs) and irradiation for organic production—both of which were (and are) actively promoted in other branches of the USDA—had been won. Unfortunately, there was one more government hurdle to overcome—the Office of Management and Budget (OMB), which had to approve any new "significant" regulations and which was unwilling to accept the prohibitions on GMOs and irradiation, also demanding several other changes that effectively gutted the organic vision, represented by the SOFAH definition, embedded in the draft. The only option left to the staff was to make the changes required and then ask for public comment about the now missing prohibitions. The proposed rule was published in December 1997.

Although the staff had protested strongly at the changes and warned senior officials about the kind of response they could expect, nobody was prepared for the onslaught of public outrage that followed. Self-appointed "watchdogs of organic integrity" spread distorted information that whipped up hysteria about corporate agribusiness-controlled bureaucrats seeking to undermine the meaning of organic and "water down the standards." This was the first proposed rule to accept public comments via e-mail, and it generated a record more than 275,000 (mostly negative) messages—the majority of them form letters circulated through consumer networks and retailers. The extent of the personal attacks and utter nonsense coming from former colleagues and friends was crushing.

The uproar resulted in the scapegoating of the NOP staff members who truly cared about the organic vision and the impact of the new rules on small organic farmers. A new NOP program manager was hired in 1998, who responded to political pressure from the community by discarding the initial proposal and starting over. It took another year to create a new proposed rule, deleting the SOFAH definition and substituting "practice standards" for more flexible criteria of compatibility with a system of organic farming and handling, among other changes considered to be higher standards.

With the USDA hierarchy now chastened by public anger, the path to finalization was much smoother than it was the first time around. In fall 1999, OFPA author Kathleen Merrigan (who became deputy secretary of agriculture 10 years later) was appointed AMS administrator and was able to midwife the publication of the final rule at the end of the year, just before the next change of administration in Washington. Before an organic producer or handler could be certified in compliance with the NOP, an initial group of accredited certifying agents would first have to be accredited—the new rule would thus not be fully implemented until 2002.

The repercussions of these events continue to be felt in the ongoing regulatory approach that accedes to public demands for "stricter" standards, to the detriment of small organic producers and—in this author's opinion—the true organic vision. The third and final segment of this chapter examines the development of the NOP since implementation and the questions raised by younger generations of food activists as the organic industry appears increasingly dominated by global big business and incomprehensible regulatory complexity.

The Future of Organic

The general message communicated by the activist community was that the new regulation was far from perfect, but acceptable, but that the NOP (and of course the rest of USDA) was still not to be trusted. Since then periodic action alerts have stimulated a flurry of e-mails and public comments to avert another "sneak attack" on organic integrity, usually to be perpetrated by some corporate organic evildoer seeking to weaken the standards.[11] A few watchdog organizations have garnered substantial donations and foundation support to lead the charge to protect organic integrity by keeping the standards as high as possible.

Today the growth of the organic industry appears unstoppable. Despite the economic crisis and general downturn in sales of consumer goods, organic sales have continued to increase, albeit more modestly than before. Unquestionably, organic has entered the mainstream: It can be found in virtually any conventional store, available to consumers who would never patronize a natural foods market. Research funds have started to flow to organic-oriented farm technologies, and conventional universities offer coursework and concentrations in organic and sustainable agriculture.

To many in the activist community, including some pioneering organic advocates, this success represents a defeat of the vision of transformation of the food system—a sellout of true organic values (such as the social goals of small-scale, decentralized agriculture and agrarian independence) to the globalized industrial monoculture system that drives out small farmers and mass produces uniform, poorer-quality products that are processed and distributed via exploitive, profit-driven corporate entities. Though they may admit that there is much to celebrate in increased numbers of small organic producers and support for local, artisanal foods, they see this improvement as coming in spite of, not as a result of, the federal regulation of organic.

Organic Expansion at USDA

The NOP today has evolved from a minor program in a small division of the Agricultural Marketing Service (AMS) to its own division, with its budget and staff doubling in a single year. Miles McEvoy, former director of the Washington state organic program, became deputy AMS administrator in charge of the NOP in 2009. Kathleen Merrigan, author of the OFPA and the AMS administrator during the last months finalizing the NOP regulation, was appointed deputy secretary of agriculture that same year, serving until May 2013, and created the high-level position of organic program coordinator to better integrate organic into every aspect of the USDA.

NOSB (National Organic Standards Board) meetings are held twice a year, and the amount of time and effort needed by this all-volunteer committee to keep up with its responsibilities mounts geometrically. In the aftermath of the first proposed rule, when the relationship between NOP and the NOSB was strained, the NOP made a political decision not to act on any standards-related issue until it received a recommendation from the NOSB. (There remains widespread public misunderstanding of the NOSB's strictly advisory role, although the NOP–NOSB relationship has gradually become more collaborative.)

One topic that continues to occupy endless hours of committee time, public input energy, and industry concern is the question of classification of materials: Should a given substance be considered synthetic, or nonsynthetic?[12] If it is not synthetic, is it agricultural, or is it nonagricultural? As an example of the inordinate impact of these questions, in 2010 the NOSB Crops Committee voted to recommend classifying corn steep liquor (CSL), a byproduct of the wet milling of corn, as synthetic. CSL is widely used as an ingredient in commercial organic-approved fertilizer formulations owing to its high nitrogen content, and classifying it as synthetic would prohibit it for use as a fertilizer ingredient. A minority opinion of the Crops Committee opposed this determination, based on the technical reviews of the CSL production process, the OFPA definition of *synthetic*, and the secondary definition of *chemical change*;[13] the discussion involves fine distinctions about different types of chemical reactions. The full NOSB did not vote on the recommendation at its fall 2010 meeting, and in 2011 the NOP issued a memorandum stating that CSL would continue to be classified as nonsynthetic and therefore acceptable for use as an organic fertilizer ingredient until such time as the NOSB were to vote that it should be classified as synthetic. As of June 2013, the NOSB had not yet complied with this request, and the NOP issued a request for public comment about how to classify CSL, along with a list of other widely used organic waste products subject to some kind of chemical treatment. The question remains: What difference does this distinction make with respect to the principles and values of organic agriculture?

Harvey Splits the Organic Community

Shortly after NOP implementation, an organic inspector and blueberry producer named Arthur Harvey filed a lawsuit against the NOP, alleging that parts of the regulations were inconsistent with the law. Although the suit was at first overruled, Harvey persisted and convinced many of the grassroots organic and sustainable farm organizations to sign on as amici (supporters of his claims). An appellate court overturned much of the earlier decision and ordered the NOP to bring its standards and program into compliance.

The most significant impact of the *Harvey* victory was the interpretation that the law did not allow any synthetic substances to be used as ingredients in or on organically labeled products. This was one of the parts of the law that contained ambiguous and contradictory language, about which the consensus of the community had been to permit some synthetic substances to be used in handling and to later make appropriate technical corrections to clarify the law. Examples of these substances, all approved by the NOSB for inclusion on the national list, are ascorbic acid (Vitamin C), magnesium chloride (used to make tofu), and leavening agents used as ingredients in baking powder.[14]

The previous consensus was thus broken by those groups who signed on as amici to the *Harvey* case and who now came into direct conflict with the rapidly growing organic business sector represented by the OTA (Organic Trade Association). Numerous organic manufacturers had by this time begun to market hundreds, if not thousands, of products legitimately labeled "organic" that would no longer be able to use the USDA organic seal. For example, most organic sugar is filtered to remove impurities, using calcium hydroxide or slaked lime as a processing aid. The result of the *Harvey* decision would be that refined sugar could no longer be considered organic, but only represented or labeled as "made with organic ingredients." This would then disqualify many organic products that contain a significant percentage of refined sugar, such as sweetened drinks, chocolates, and cookies, from displaying the coveted USDA organic label.

Finally, the OTA decided to do something about the looming catastrophe unleashed by *Harvey* and lobbied successfully for a minor change in the OFPA in 2005. Once again the self-appointed watchdogs of organic integrity unleashed a barrage of attacks, charging that allowing use of synthetic chemicals in organic foods undermined confidence in the organic label and permitted the takeover of organic by corporate interests.

Not much later a genuine sneak attack on the OFPA occurred when an amendment was inserted allowing up to 20 percent of nonorganic feed to be given to organic livestock. A poultry company in Georgia had asked its senator to introduce this item via a routine budget bill, claiming it was necessitated by the high cost of organic feed grain. Senator Patrick Leahy (D–VT, original sponsor of the OFPA) was again enlisted by the community, including the OTA, to return the law to the way it had been, but doing so required political tradeoffs such as allowing organic certification for wild caught seafood.

Beating the Drum for Higher Standards

By the middle of the decade the NOP had grown considerably but was still vastly understaffed compared with the industry it was charged with regulating, which was growing by around 20 percent a year. Dealing with the *Harvey* lawsuit and the attendant mandated changes to the regulation had drained significant staff time and again created an atmosphere of hostility—not only between the organic community and the NOP, but also between different sectors within the community.

Since that time the activist sector has focused primarily on demands for stricter livestock and dairy standards. In 2007 a Wisconsin-based advocacy group sued a large organic dairy producer, as well as the USDA, for mislabeling milk as organic because animals were not being managed on pasture as called for in the regulation. Aggressive publicity fanned consumer concerns by painting a picture of the corporate-friendly USDA allowing deceptive practices by large animal confinement operations, calling into question the trustworthiness of the industry in general as well as the regulators.

The NOP responded with a proposed regulation on access to pasture for ruminants that included some draconian requirements, such as requiring animals to be outdoors year-round, with exceptions only for "hazardous" weather events. The tactic of forcing the community to request somewhat looser standards succeeded, with the final rule reflecting a much more moderate approach. The impact on small livestock producers remains to be seen, as the increased documentation of feeding practices and cost of verifying those practices is felt.

Conclusion: Questions to Consider

The pioneers of organic agriculture as well as the younger generation of organic producers continue to grumble about compulsory certification and USDA "stealing" the organic label. Many small organic producers have either dropped out of organic certification altogether or switched to labeling their products as consistent with the Farmers Pledge and as "Certified Naturally Grown"—indicators from other participatory guarantee systems. "Everything I want to do is illegal," proclaims Joel Salatin, a Virginia farmer featured prominently in the film *Food, Inc.*, whose book of that same title bemoans the encroachment of federal bureaucrats into regulation of the "O" word.

An article in the *New York Times* in April 2010 describes the situation of some organic farmers in upstate New York, who "can't make a living because it is so expensive for them to comply with the federal certification requirements for organic foods."[15] Food system activists almost universally focus on promoting local foods and more direct farmer-consumer relationships. Some denigrate "corporate organic" food that comes from far away or dismiss as not credible organic products obtained from large retail chains. An informal poll about perceptions of organic standards and regulation, conducted by the author in several classes and workshops, reveals that student activists who consider themselves well informed and concerned about food system issues generally agree that organic has been corrupted by corporate interests who have weakened the standards to the point of their being meaningless.

Other food system activists aim to go beyond organic and look to ecolabel schemes or social criteria such as animal welfare, fair trade, or sustainably harvested, often denigrating organic standards for failing to include preferences for small farmers or requirements for labor conditions. All such schemes involve similar concerns for maintaining strict or rigorous standards and involve costly and arduous third party certification requirements—all in the name of protecting consumer confidence in their label. Few question the assumption that more restrictive or complicated standards benefit smaller producers, although the reverse is generally shown to be true.

This misperception, referred to as the myth of higher standards, surely represents one of the biggest mistakes made by the alternative-sustainable-organic food systems activists. This is the explanation presented in the author's blog post of December 2008:[16]

> The gist of the problem is this: The activists have had it wrong all along. They believe without question that the only way to fend off the takeover of organic by global corporate evildoers is to keep up the pressure to make the standards as tight, strict, rigorous and undiluted as possible, and use consumer perceptions as their rationale. They mistakenly believe that regulation of the organic label is comparable to regulations that prohibit misdeeds by corporate polluters. Not true.
>
> The difference is one that very few outside of government and some rarefied academic fields seem to get, but which immediately makes sense to most people—even ignorant consumers—when it is explained. The short explanation is that, unlike a traditional environmental or consumer protection regulation that keeps giant corporations from threatening the health of consumers and the environment, the NOP is a marketing program that establishes minimum requirements for those wishing to enter the organic market.
>
> In marketing programs, tightening the standards is a strategy commonly used to benefit established players and limit competition by potential new entrants. It has nothing to do with protecting consumer interests, and works against consumers by maintaining high prices and limited supply for products that may not be demonstrably superior (e.g., spotless apples drenched in pesticides). It also has nothing to do with protecting the environment, and may even harm it, as may be seen in some of the provisions in the new proposed rule on access to pasture [discussed previously]. In fact, tightening the rules creates more obstacles for small players to enter the market than for large players, who are accustomed to meeting bureaucratic requirements and have paid compliance staffs. They actually prefer to have tighter standards, to protect the substantial investment needed to get in.

Monsanto was keenly aware of this mistake when it submitted its public comment in response to the 1997 NOP proposed rule. Although the corporation had lost its battle within USDA to allow the use of GMOs in organic food, it had triumphed through its influence on OMB. However, as discussed previously, nobody was prepared for the overwhelming negative public response to that initial draft regulation. Monsanto then reconsidered its position and suggested that it supported prohibiting GMOs in organic food, which would give consumers who wished to avoid these perfectly safe ingredients a choice. Monsanto also stressed its support for keeping organic standards as strict and rigorous as possible. This strategy paid off handsomely—conventional producers have seen little advantage to converting to organic production, GMO crops now account for a huge chunk of U.S. agricultural acreage, and the threat of mandatory labeling of GMO foods was defused for over a decade.

Besides the constant message of distrust of USDA organic, mostly from the political left, the opposition of conventional agribusiness to government support of organics has also intensified. Organic producers are portrayed as relying on unscientific, outmoded methods that cannot feed the world's growing population.

There are many questions to consider as the organic community and its regulatory mechanisms move forward. Does it make sense to restrict the organic label to those who have the wherewithal to meet ever-escalating bureaucratic requirements? Should consumer perceptions and expectations about organic purity and avoidance of synthetic chemicals dictate standards? Can the social and ecological damage done by a market-driven system that has turned food into a mass-produced commodity be reversed through a market-based strategy?

Without doubt organic agriculture represents an important part of the solution to the global climate crisis now confronting us along with myriad other problems of environmental degradation and human health consequences attributable to conventional agriculture. This potential can only be realized if organic production expands much faster than is currently happening—at least in North America, where still less than 1 percent of agricultural land is farmed organically.

Organic production alone cannot solve all the problems of the food system. Saddling organic producers and handlers with ever-"higher" standards and adding on desirable social criteria creates unnecessary obstacles to solving the problems that organic production can solve. Activists who are outraged at large corporations getting involved in organics should ask themselves to what extent they are bolstering the argument, often made by conventional agribusiness, that organic can never be more than a small niche market that caters to the elite and the fanatic—and that could never feed the world.

One corollary to the adage that we must not let the perfect be the enemy of the good is that we should not make the good into our enemy because it is not perfect.

Links

NOP: www.ams.usda.gov/AMSv1.0/ams.fetchTemplateData.do?template=TemplateA&navID=NationalOrganicProgram&leftNav=NationalOrganicProgram&page=NOPNationalOrganicProgramHome&acct=AMSPW

OFPA (as amended in 2005): www.ams.usda.gov/AMSv1.0/getfile?dDocName =STELPRDC5060370&acct=nopgeninfo

Chelsea Green author blog for Grace Gershuny: http://chelseagreen.com/ blogs/gracegershuny/

Notes

1. Philip Conford, *The Origins of the Organic Movement* (Edinburgh, UK: Floris Books, 2001).

2. Marion Nestle, *Food Politics: How the Food Industry Influences Nutrition and Health* (Berkeley: University of California Press, 2007).

3. Catherine Green, et al., "Emerging Issues in the U.S. Organic Industry," USDA Economic Research Service, Economic Information Bulletin No. (EIB-55), June 2009.

4. Michael Pollan, *The Omnivore's Dilemma: A Natural History of Four Meals* (New York: Penguin, 2006).

5. Robert Kenner, dir., *Food, Inc.*, 2008.

6. Personal conversation with Enid Wonnacott.

7. Grace Gershuny and Joseph Smillie, "Guidelines for the Organic Foods Industry," Organic Foods Production Association of North America (now Organic Trade Association), January 1986.

8. Harlyn Meyer, ed., "Laboratory Testing and the Production and Marketing of Certified Organic Foods," OFPANA Position Paper #1, December 1986.

9. In accordance with the Federal Advisory Committees Act or FACA. Despite the widespread belief that the NOSB has final authority over the national list, FACA clearly allows no such regulatory authority for federal advisory committees.

10. National Organic Program Staff, "Prologue: Moving Towards Sustainability," 1995.

11. See, for example, www.beyondpesticides.org/organicfood/alerts/index.php.

12. Although the OFPA used the term *natural* in contrast to *synthetic*, the regulations were written to avoid the use of this undefinable and meaningless term.

13. Synthetic is defined as "a substance that is formulated or manufactured by a chemical process or by a process that chemically changes a substance extracted from naturally occurring plant, animal, or mineral sources, except that such term shall not apply to substances created by naturally occurring biological processes." The term *synthetic* is not found in the EU organic regulations and is there generally equated with substances derived from petrochemicals.

14. Refer to Section 205.605(b) of the national list: nonagricultural (nonorganic) substances allowed as ingredients in or on processed products labeled as "organic" or "made with organic [specified ingredients or food group(s)]".

15. Devin Leonard, "Green Gone Wrong," *New York Times*, April 2, 2010.

16. See Grace Gershuny, "Are the Best Organic Standards the Toughest Organic Standards? Why the Activists Got It Wrong," Chelsea Green author blog, December 3, 2008. http://chelseagreen.com/blogs/gracegershuny/2008/12/03/are-the-best-organic-standards-the-toughest-organic-standards-why-the-activists-got-it-wrong/

8

Where's the Beef? Looking for Food in Religion and Ecology

Dell deChant

The relationship of religion and food is of enormous importance to understanding the relationship of religion and nature. This being so, we are given pause when surveying the emergent Religious Studies subfield of Religion and Ecology. Curiously, a review of research and curricula in Religion and Ecology reveals little engagement with food studies. Why? Why should it be otherwise? This chapter will respond to these questions in four sections.

The first two sections contextualize the questions as such. The first offers a brief sketch of Religion and Ecology; the second proposes an explanation for why Religion and Food as a research field is rarely included as a topic in Religion and Ecology. The third section presents reasons why this functional exclusion is not such a good idea. The final section introduces some provisional strategies for integrating Religion and Food into Religion and Ecology—thus, it is argued, allowing more complete and responsible inquiry into the relationship of food to ecology and of both to religion.

I

It is surprising how seldom Religion and Food appears in Religion and Ecology research and curricula. It is as though food and ecology were mutually exclusive fields or even alien inquiries when related to religion. This is a curiosity and a problem for both food studies and research on the relationship of religion and ecology. What makes the absence of Religion and Food from Religion and Ecology even more remarkable and problematic is the profound significance of food in the world's religions and, perhaps more important, the direct relationship of food production and distribution to the contemporary ecological crisis. To contextualize this curious problem, this section will briefly review the short history of Religion and Ecology as a field, and the next section will offer a possible explanation for the absence (or near absence) of Religion and Food from the field.

As noted, Religion and Ecology is an emerging subfield in Religious Studies. It has a relatively short history and is a young area of research in the larger field of Religious Studies, itself a young field in the academy, having originated in the 1960s. As a subfield or topical research area, Religion and Ecology is a natural fit with Religious Studies, which is best understood as an interdisciplinary field within the broader area of the humanities (as opposed to the social sciences).

As a subfield of Religious Studies, Religion and Ecology developed in the context of the maturation of Religious Studies as a recognized scholarly field and the emergence of environmentalism in American popular culture. In this regard, it has similarities with other Religious Studies subfields, such as Religion and Gender, Religion and Sports, New Religious Movements, and Religion and Popular Culture. Its specific point of origin can be located in a series of conferences on "Religions of the World and Ecology," hosted by Harvard Divinity School's Center for the Study of World Religions from 1996 to 1998. Organized by Mary Evelyn Tucker, among others, the conferences aimed to do the following:

> Provide a broad survey that would help ground a new field of study in religion and ecology. . . . Recognizing that religions are key shapers of people's worldviews and formulators of their most cherished values, this research project uncovered a wealth of attitudes and practices toward nature sanctioned by religious traditions.[1]

The Harvard conferences, and the resulting 10-volume collection of papers, launched Religion and Ecology. Prior to the Harvard conferences, various scholars had been working on questions related to Religion and Ecology, including Thomas Berry and, most notably, David Barnhill and Eugene Bianchi, who established Religion and Ecology as a regular topic area at meetings of the American Academy of Religion (AAR) beginning in 1989.[2] As critical as these initial institutional developments were, the foundational work in Religion and Ecology occurred independently of them—and more than 20 years earlier.

This, of course, was a single relatively short essay by Lynn Townsend White, Jr., a scholar of medieval culture and technology. White's seminal work, "The Historical Roots of Our Ecologic Crisis," was published in *Nature* in 1967.[3] Here, for the first time, contemporary ecological problems (in White's case, what he identified as "our ecologic crisis") were assessed in terms of their relationship to religion and the influence of religion on the worldview of the West. Although short, White's essay was a stunning and provocative inquiry and included a rather severe critique of the role and culpability of religion (especially Christianity) in bringing about the degradation of the natural world. Of all the many contributions White made to both the emergence and the development of Religion and Ecology, perhaps his greatest contribution is the establishment of the critique of religion as a valid (if not routine) feature of research in this area.

Following closely the publication of Rachel Carson's *Silent Spring* (1962),[4] which arguably initiated the environmental movement in popular culture, White's article traced the origins of the West's cavalier attitude toward the natural environment and disregard of ecological systems to Christianity and the sacred legitimization it gave to the aggressive exploitation of nature. Because sacred legitimization gives religious justification and powerful sociological support to worldviews and human actions, the West's abusive relationship with the environment is both deeply rooted and incredibly difficult to change. White's "Roots" continues to inform both the formal research agenda as well as the critical approach of contemporary scholars. It is an accurate assessment to recognize that few texts have had as great an effect on a field of study as this short article has had on Religion and Ecology.

By the end of the first decade of the 21st century, Religion and Ecology had become a robust, expanding, and very diverse area of scholarly activity. Today it is a well-established subfield in Religious Studies, featuring numerous academic texts, several substantial reference books, a number of collections, and two scholarly journals. Universities have created specific concentrations in Religion and Ecology (or Religion and Nature), and faculty at many schools of higher education have developed and continue to develop courses in this area.

II

As a rapidly expanding yet still emerging field, Religion and Ecology features research on a wide range of subjects at the intersection of ecology and religion. Not surprisingly, there is no established methodology, no definitive theories, and no formal curricula. There are, however, tendencies, and it is here that some insight into the absence of Religion and Food may be given. What, then, are these food-excluding tendencies?

When considering Religion and Ecology as an academic field, one must initially recognize that research in this area is remarkably normative, even "activist," in nature. This is atypical of Religious Studies, which usually features a neutral approach to inquiries. The second general tendency in this area is the presumption that the world is indeed on the verge of (or already experiencing) a massive ecological catastrophe. This tendency is directly related to the first, and the two really go hand in hand. Although the reality of the ecological challenges facing the planet are widely recognized, especially within the academic community, it is not so widely known (or even accepted) by the general public. Following on the second tendency, studies in Religion and Ecology seem largely insulated from popular culture and especially features of popular culture informed by conservative political ideologies. Fourth, and finally, Religion and Ecology tends to focus on traditional, well-established religions in what is referred to elsewhere as "the usual suspects approach."[5] These usual suspects are those best known and most highly researched—e.g., Christianity, Judaism, Islam, Buddhism, and Hinduism.

Although each of these tendencies tends to suppress studies of food, they do not necessarily preclude serious and extensive engagement with issues in religion and food. Together, however, the individual tendencies are more pronounced, and together they form a matrix in which certain elements, entries, and topics are featured and others ignored. Religion and food is the interest of this chapter, but others similarly overlooked are politics, popular culture, mythologies (sacred texts), and the media. On the other hand, a number of other topics receive considerable attention. Most notably, these include the major world religions, economics, ecojustice, globalization, sustainability, and gender. This is not to say that Religion and Food or any of the other marginalized topics are entirely absent, but rather to observe that their presence is minimal compared to their importance to the subject and subfield.

How, then, do these afore mentioned tendencies result in short shrift given to Religion and Food in Religion and Ecology? A tentative answer can be proposed by briefly considering the consequences of these tendencies.

The Perils of Activism

First, as a subfield in a generally nonnormative field, the activist approach of Religion and Ecology focuses on issues that appear to be most directly related to religious beliefs and practices—especially those most evident today. This results in critiques and calls for reform of specific cosmologies, formal doctrines, official pronouncements, and types of social action. Attention is directed more to broader positions taken by religious communities on general issues, rather than specific topics, such as myths, teachings, and rituals concerning food production and consumption. In a way, this is the safer approach in terms of research, and there are existing models to follow when developing such critiques. This activist-critical approach is first found in White's 1967 essay, but it appears routinely in current studies. For example, in the introduction to a recent textbook on Religion and Ecology, *Grounding Religion*, the editors observe the following:

Scholars in the field of religion and ecology seek to make a practical difference in the world. This field exists not just to develop theories and ideas, but also to contribute to the activist cause of building a more sustainable world. Scholars of religion and ecology help people to think critically about how religion has been shaped by the natural world and can be shaped by environmental degradation, and to imaginatively consider how religion and/or the study of religion might positively impact the future of our species and our planet.[6]

Although this approach is certainly laudable, and in many ways demanded, it has itself become something of a dogma in the subfield Religion and Ecology. In other words, it is hard to do work in Religion and Ecology without assuming an activist stance, typically expressed in the context of general issues related to religion. Food does not appear to be one of these issues for the activist scholars in Religion and Ecology.

The Crisis Circle

The activist tendency is clearly inspired by the widely held conviction that the planet is in peril, nearing the tipping point of ecological disaster and that the mainstream scientific community is essentially correct in its assessment of the contemporary environmental crisis and its *anthropogenic* origins. While the author and doubtless most readers of this book share this conviction, it is not nearly so widespread as the research-activists in this area presume. As noted elsewhere: "Robin Blumner reminds us (citing a Pew Research poll), in October, 2010, 'only 34 percent of respondents said global warming is caused by human activity.'"[7] As a consequence, Religion and Ecology specialists tend to develop their studies in a rather closed circle and around a somewhat orthodox set of issues. They are "preaching to the choir," oblivious to the considerable community of doubters, deniers, and whole-cloth rejecters of their critiques. In doing so, well-known and well-trod paths of the environmental crisis are reengaged in the context of religion. In this rather insulated community, food is not nearly as important as these more familiar concerns—climate change, species extinctions, wilderness destruction, and pollution of air and water.

In an important article, Roger Gottlieb cites "eight major dimensions" of the crisis, which together make for perhaps the most significant challenge human beings have ever faced.[8] The eight dimensions are instructive and are given here in Gottlieb's order:

1. climate change
2. accumulation of chemical and other wastes
3. loss of topsoil
4. loss of biodiversity

5. loss of wilderness
6. devastation of indigenous peoples
7. unsustainable levels of consumption
8. genetic engineering[9]

Notice the third dimension (loss of topsoil) and the eighth dimension (genetic engineering): Both relate directly to food and to its production and externalities and its distribution and consumption, yet food production itself does not appear on the list of the elements constituting "the most significant challenge human beings have ever faced." Many may beg to differ, and to his credit, Gottlieb does refer to agricultural practices in his analysis of these features. Nonetheless, as important as loss of topsoil or genetic engineering may be to the contemporary ecological crisis, listing them in the absence of food as such is an oversight.

Obviously, different scholars will have different lists, rankings, and assessments of critical issues. This is not the issue here. Noting the absence of food from Gottlieb's list is not intended to initiate a debate about lists of this sort, but merely to note that (1) this list does not feature food and (2) this list is representative of the topics engaged in Religion and Ecology. Clearly food, or something like food production and distribution, is not only as important as any of the other topics, but in fact could quite nicely capture several of the others. In fact, it is not a stretch to cite food production and distribution as perhaps the single greatest contributor to the ecological crisis and a (if not the) leading cause of each of the eight major dimensions. Still, it is left off the list as a primary dimension of the crisis, and not just off this list but also off the list of major research topics in the closed circle of Religion and Ecology.

Overlooking the Popular Culture Context

Although Gottlieb's alarming characterization of the crisis and this list of its eight features may well be accurate, many people are far from convinced—not withstanding the absence of food from the list. The presence of large-scale apathy and serious resistance to the ecological crisis, suggested in the Blumner passage cited previously, does not seem to be taken seriously or seriously engaged. This is the third tendency of the field—insulation from popular culture and especially that large swath of the population informed by conservative political ideologies.

A telling quote from Senator James Inhofe (R–OK) exemplifies the political opposition to the environmentalist position, and by inference the Religion and Ecology program. Commenting on climate change, Senator Inhofe has identified global warming as "the greatest hoax ever perpetrated on the American people."[10] Presidential candidate Rick Santorum reiterated Inhofe's position and nicely put it into a religious context by referring to environmentalism and the ecological crisis as a "phony theology."[11] It should be remembered that for those of us working in Religion and Ecology, this hoax and phony theology are largely accepted with little critical mediation. For us, it is certainly not a hoax, and there is nothing phony about it—it is a disclosure of reality about which there is little serious doubt and even less formal question. In short, it is not too farfetched to classify it as our faith claim. We do believe there is an ecological crisis, and we probably agree with Gottlieb that it is "the most significant challenge human beings have ever faced."

The downside of the ecological crisis faith claim is twofold. First, as noted, we do not consider environmentalism and the crisis it identifies a hoax or a phony theology (or even a faith claim). Like most other faith claims, it is simply the truth—a disclosure of reality. Moreover, rather than anything remotely resembling religious belief, it is probably recognized as a scientific fact, making it all the more convincing. This is not the appropriate venue to delve into issues about systems of sacred legitimization in secular culture, or how science has functional similarities to religion. Nonetheless, and this is a telling (if often ignored or dismissed) downside, it must be observed that there is a general absence of reflection on the way in which scholarship in this area (and most others) tends to accept scientific findings and assessments without too much critical mediation—and virtually no serious consideration of the possibility that the scholarly embrace of scientific assertions does in some way resemble a religious belief. So we may be a little negligent here.

The second problematic feature of the ecological crisis as faith claim is perhaps more significant than the first. This is the elitist trivialization of the criticism itself; a trivialization that renders us oblivious to the very favorable reception of the criticism by a distinct segment of the population. The phony theology charge may seem laughable to those of us doing higher critical inquiries into the ecological crisis (and I have observed more than a few sarcastic comments about the charge), but we ignore it at our peril, and with an arrogance that is self-defeating. By not taking the charge seriously, we may well forget that Inhofe and Santorum have a much larger audience than we do, and that tens of millions of culturally active, politically engaged individuals have heard and accepted their harsh dismissal of the claims upon which we base our research. It really does not matter what we think about the criticism, or whether we pause for a moment to critically reflect on the faith claim of the ecological crisis. What does matter, however, and it matters a great deal, is that Inhofe and Santorum represent and clearly articulate a position shared by tens of millions of Americans.

The general obliviousness to popular culture in Religion and Ecology both contributes to and is accentuated by the obliviousness to the powerful opposition offered to the entire environmentalist enterprise by political conservatives, their supporters in the media, and millions of conservative political activists. As a result, the relevance of the religious dimension of food is further marginalized. If researchers are not working in the context of popular culture and its political manifestation, they are unlikely to consider the political context of their work, except perhaps in some abstract manner. Moreover, absent engagement with popular culture, the political dimension of issues in religion and food, which is quite considerable, fails to surface as a meaningful research topic. Already overlooked for reasons noted above, the lack of sophisticated encounter with the ideological, political, and media opponents of environmentalism means that important topics in politics and food are ignored or not even recognized.

Ignoring "Un-usual Suspects"

The three challenges just analyzed are made all the more problematic by the focus of Religion and Ecology on "the usual suspects" approach to research. In practice, this means studies of the relationship of religion and ecology generally are concerned with various ecological issues and problems as they relate to and/or are encountered by traditional religions. This yields studies giving disproportionate attention to larger religious systems and their local manifestations (the "usual suspects," noted previously) while overlooking not only smaller traditions and new religions in general, but also some very promising strategies that consider the religious dimensions of seemingly secular traditions and movements.

Overlooking these "un-usual suspects" excludes a wide range of religious expressions and disregards important avenues of inquiry. The result is a compression of the range of Religion and Ecology itself, limiting it to the issues being addressed by larger traditions, which usually are the same issues already being addressed by Religion and Ecology, again to the exclusion of issues related to food. Additionally, by overlooking these less familiar manifestations of religion, Religion and Ecology does not encounter traditions that are especially focused on food-related concerns—e.g., Adventistism, Amish, International Society of Krishna Consciousness (ISKCON), and the Transition Movement.

Equally glossed by the usual suspects approach are seemingly secular groups and movements with significant religious characteristics (if not, in fact, being functional religions). Excluded here are Veganism, Vegetarianism, Neo-Agrarianism, Permacultualism, Survivalism, the Prepper movement, and any number of "back to the land" movements. Whether such groups are properly considered religions can be debated elsewhere. Suffice it to say that excluding them from consideration diminishes the range of research topics and, once again, misses an opportunity to bring food into the context of Religion and Ecology.

Finally, there is the disciplinary territorial problem, through which specific fields and disciplines carry more weight or are recognized as authoritative in specific areas. A somewhat humorous example of how this works in practice was a proposal developed by a colleague for a course in Religion and Ecology. Because it dealt with "ecology," the course needed concurrence from departments in the school of natural sciences. Those departments initially, and for some time, did not give concurrence, because in their view, ecology was a subject that could only properly be engaged in the context of natural sciences. Fields in the humanities generally encounter problems such as this when considering issues in any of the STEM fields, and smaller or younger fields face challenges from larger, older fields when they enter the territory of the older and larger fields.

As it pertains to our topic, the territorial problem restricts research on religion and food to generally accepted categories and contexts. Thus, when food is considered as an issue in religion, it is typically encountered in neutral studies of various religions' doctrines about food rather than in other contexts—except perhaps ethics, and even then it is more commonly considered relative to social justice or the treatment of animals relative to specific religious systems. Once again, the focus is on traditional religions, their sacred foods, food rituals, and food doctrines. So, to research food in the context of Religion and Ecology, one really has to make a case over and against more established approaches to food and religion. This can be tough going for younger scholars as well as those with a lower profile in their academic communities.

* * *

Any one of the four features noted in this section would be challenge enough to overcome on its own, but together they present a major obstacle to incorporating food into the subfield of Religion and Ecology. It is the contention of this chapter not only that Religion and Food should be included in Religion and Ecology, but that its absence is in fact a significant weakness in the research agenda and the curricula of this area.

III

On the face of it, excluding or marginalizing food studies from Religion and Ecology seems like a bad idea. Despite the challenges posed by the factors noted above, researchers and instructors in this area should make a concerted effort to include Food and Religion in the Religion and Ecology agenda. It may not be a celebrity topic, like climate change, species extinction, genetic modification, or exhaustion of natural resources, but it is of equal importance to these more celebrated and attractive academic topics. In fact, to not include

Religion and Food as a primary topic in Religion and Ecology compromises the entire subfield. Why?

To answer this question, a brief explication of four fundamental features of the relationship between religion and food can be considered in their ecological context. These features may help explain why Religion and Food must be part of the Religion and Ecology portfolio. These are not the only explanations, to be sure, but they are certainly among the most critical.

First, religion cannot be fully understood without understanding its relationship with food. One need but consider how central food is to the world's religious traditions. It relates to and defines numerous religious holy day celebrations, dietary doctrines and less formal menu options, fasting and feasting rituals, and even locations for eating. Food is and has always been a primary concern for religions throughout history, and this concern is and has always been mythically enshrouded and ritually expressed in ways that harmonize directly or indirectly with responsible ecological practices—i.e., sustainability, moderation in consumption, and respect for nature and its creatures. Although religions have been slow to respond to the contemporary ecological crisis, and although formal positions are only now beginning to emerge, religions have wide-ranging and longstanding de facto policies on the environment. They are not, however, usually presented as such. Instead, they are expressed in the context of myths, rituals, and doctrines pertaining to food, animals, agriculture, and stewardship of resources. One does not travel far in the study of religion without coming upon teachings and practices related to food. Failure to consider these teachings and practices does a disservice to religion and a disservice to Religion and Ecology.

Second, understanding the contemporary ecological crisis simply cannot occur absent a serious engagement with food production and consumption. Yet serious engagement is forgone nevertheless. Notably, Gottlieb's eight dimensions of the contemporary ecological crisis excludes food as such. Yes, "loss of topsoil" is on the list—and this is related to food, but only among other topics. There is a reference under that heading to how "chemical agriculture and the destruction of forests . . . threatens the production of food," but only among other environmental externalities, such "erosion and desertification. . . . [destruction] of ecosystem balance in rivers and costal fishing areas."[12] Food and its production does not get an independent listing.

Third, food is an ethical concern of great relevance to religions. In this regard, "Food Ethics seems to present itself as a viable vehicle for introducing food into the Religion and Ecology agenda. Nonetheless, despite being a valuable research area in environmental studies as whole, Food Ethics (like food itself) rarely figures prominently in Religion and Ecology research. This is unfortunate, because its concerns are vital to any serious reflection on the contemporary ecological crisis. Elemental to such reflections are the questions of food ethics: What do we eat? How is it produced? Who is producing it? What are the destructive environmental externalities of industrial agriculture? What are the consequences of the commodification of sustenance both to individuals and to the planet? As helpful as these questions are to environmental scholarship as a whole, to the extent that they marginalize the religious dimension of these questions (as they often do), they are not as helpful as they might otherwise be and are even less helpful to Religion and Ecology. So Food Ethics should certainly be a prominent feature of Religion and Ecology, but only insofar as Food Ethics includes reflection on the history and contemporary expression of religious ethics and religious practices as they pertain to food production and consumption—and as both pertain to the present ecological crisis. Omitting religion from the concerns addressed in Food Ethics omitting food Ethics from Religion and Ecology are as much oversights as is omitting food from lists of ecological problems.

Fourth, the production and consumption of food cannot be understood independent of religion and religion's relationship with the natural world. Religion was the first and most enduring human mediation of the natural world, and from primal cultures to postmodern New Age religions (and all the usual suspects in between), the sacredness of sustenance has been affirmed in myth and ritual. As a species, we have steadily and increasingly separated ourselves from nature, yet the connection with nature remains stunningly expressed throughout our lives every day. That connection is rooted in the most elemental of human needs—food. We must eat. This was true when we were hunter-gatherers living on the African savannas 50,000 years ago, true as well when the first large-scale farming cultures emerged in the river valleys of Asia, and true, too, when the transcendental religions first emerged—and is true to this day even in the seemingly secular West.

It is for good reason, therefore, that religion has always sacralized food and all that goes into its production and consumption. If there is an ultimate power, that power must in some way be responsible for supplying us with our daily bread. By sacralizing food, religion has affirmed a deep and perhaps at times unconscious connection with nature and its ecological systems. Without food we die, and without a healthy ecology we cannot produce food; thus religions ever remind the faithful (and the not-so-faithful) of the sacredness of food as well as, directly or indirectly, the sacredness of nature itself.

As with the other three ecological features of the religion and food relationship, failure to consider the ways in which religion sacralizes nature in and through the sacralization of food neglects one of the most important and most deeply rooted expressions of this relationship. Clearly, this oversight is unintentional. Those of us who work in Religion and Ecology know this history and understand these contexts. Even so, we give these topics little consideration and grant them little intentional significance in our research agendas. Instead, we go after the usual suspects, study doctrines and conciliar pronouncements, work to position various religions in the environmentalist matrix, do case studies of specific religions and sustainability or climate change, relate religions to secular activists, and, above all, critique religion and religions for their shortcomings and longstanding indifference to these major contemporary concerns. Then we go out and have a nice vegan whole food meal, perhaps saying grace or performing some other ritual before hand, enjoying wine from a local biodynamic vintner, and topping it off with USDA-organic dessert.

IV

Although it may not have been entirely evident here, I am as much an activist as my peers in Religion and Ecology. I, too, seek to prompt institutional and personal changes to respond to the ecological catastrophe that appears imminent if not already under way. For my part, I am interested in what we are missing in our research on Religion and Ecology—both theoretically and topically. Among other topics, as argued here, what appears to be missing is an understanding of the ecological dimensions of the relationship between religion and food. I would welcome its emergence as a distinct subject area in Religious Studies, akin to other more recent subject areas such as New Religions, Religion and Popular Culture, and Religion and Gender. There is certainly an abundance of important problems and concerns related to the relationship of religion and food and even more certainly a dearth of critical research on these problems and concerns.

Interestingly, what seems one of the primary subfields in which Religion and Food might find a place at the table has heretofore largely ignored the subject. That subfield is Religion and Ecology, and the absence of food studies in this subfield exemplifies this absence in Religious Studies as a whole. If we do not focus on religion and food in the context of religion and ecology, then where do we study it, really?

This chapter has offered an initial encounter with Religion and Food as a viable subject area in Religion and Ecology and has contextualized that encounter by relating it to issues and questions related to this subfield. Religion and Food has a natural place in Religion and Ecology, indeed in Religious Studies as a whole. Its relevance is independent of any other subfield, but that relevance seems best revealed in its relationship to Religion and Ecology.

This being said, what might be done to introduce Religion and Food to the subfield of Religion and Ecology? The short answer is anything we can, whenever we can—in research topics chosen, in public lectures, in professional papers, in topical collections, at academic conferences (such as AAR, where it has surfaced even as this chapter is being composed), in courses taught, in collegial conversations. Anything will do for now.

More specifically, there appear to be five distinct entry points for food studies into the Religion and Ecology subfield: (1) scripture studies, (2) popular culture, (3) politics, (4) course development, and (5) the religious dimension of seemingly secular food movements. Brief comments on the first three areas will be offered here.

Scripture

First, scripture studies offer a most appropriate opening for the introduction of Religion and Food to the study of Religion and Ecology. There is at present one outstanding example of how this might happen—Ellen F. Davis's *Scripture, Culture, and Agriculture.*[13] Davis's work is an exegetical study of those parts of the Hebrew scriptures that concern agricultural practices, giving attention to the sacred legitimization the text gives to responsible care for the environment. In a rather unconventional departure from traditional exegesis, Davis reads the biblical texts through the lens of contemporary agrarian critiques of current agricultural practices and today's technocapitalist consumer culture. The result is stunning and is an excellent example of how scriptural interpretation that might relate food issues quite directly to research in Religion and Ecology.

Throughout the book, Davis thoughtfully draws parallels between the admonitions to stewardship given in the ancient religious text and the contemporary ecological crisis, specifically relating to agriculture (food production). For example, in the section commenting on the inspiration for her research, Davis observes: "In recent years, I have come to believe that anyone who wishes to understand Israel's scripture deeply would do well to learn more about the ecological crisis, and especially about its agricultural dimensions.... The mutually informative relation between ecological awareness and biblical study rests not only on the land-centeredness of the Bible but also on the nature of the ecological crisis, which is principally moral and theological rather than technological."[14] Exemplifying this approach is an interpretation of Genesis 8:21–22, in which she links God's promise to "never again bring destruction upon the earth" to our present situation:

> Those poetic lines [Gen 8:21–22] sum up all that humans have for millennia taken for granted about the stability of our climate. . . . If we are now experiencing significant disruption of climatic patterns, then the divine promise itself condemns us, for it expresses the hollowness of claims that this is nothing more than natural fluctuation. . . . Our situation, then, is revealed to be one of complete vulnerability. We, "the rulers of the fertile soil on the soil"—have brought that vulnerability upon ourselves through our persistent refusal to heed the limits that God did indeed build into the created order, a refusal that dates back to the first human couple and escalates from there.[15]

Furthermore, reflecting on passages from Genesis and Leviticus, she writes: "If, however, most contemporary readers of Genesis overlook its concern for eating, that is because we belong to a culture characterized by unprecedented ignorance about where food comes from—our own food, let along that of other creatures."[16] She then introduces Norman Wirzba on our relationship with food today:

> Rather than seeing eating as the most intimate engagement with the life forms all around us, a sharing in the well-being and flow of all life, we have instead turned it into the purchasing of commodities that we can manipulate, control, and use according to convenience.... [In the past, food] carried immense symbolic power since food consumption was the concrete act in terms of which social relations, work life, *geographic identity*, and religious ritual came together.... [T]he act of eating, perhaps more honestly than our public piety, expresses our moral and religious sensibilities.[17]

Throughout this text, Davis vividly draws the clear, emphatic relationship between the religious dimension of food and the religious dimension of ecology. That Davis does so in the context of the Hebrew scriptures underscores the value of studies of religion and food to research in Religion and Ecology. The deployment of thinkers such as Wirzba and Wendell Berry accentuates its contemporary relevance to research in Religion and Ecology, which largely concentrates on current ecological issues and concerns.

In this regard, Religion and Ecology might well consider other sacred texts and their treatment of food. Headings might include animals, compassion, moderation, feasting and fasting, and stewardship, among many others. The key here would be to contextualize the exegesis through the use of contemporary authors who bring a religious sensibility to their writing, even if they are not explicitly religious. Authors to be considered in this context include Charles Russell Saunders, Wendell Berry, Margaret Atwood, Kij Johnson, and poet B. H. Fairchild.

Besides this, consideration of sacred texts from outside standard religious canons can be explored. Some of the classics in environmental writing would be a rich source for such "scriptures," with prime examples being works of such secular saints as John Muir, Henry David Thoreau, Aldo Leopold, Rachel Carson, and Al Gore. Again, the key is not the engagement of the texts simply in the context of ecology or Religion and Ecology, but also through the lens of food studies.

Popular Culture

As noted previously, popular culture, especially its political dimension, is largely overlooked in Religion and Ecology. To give even modest attention to popular culture would not only make Religion and Ecology more vital and more engaged, but also open up much more terrain to research. Of special interest here is food, but other areas that would also receive much needed attention would be film and media studies, gender studies, sports, economics (especially consumerism), holidays, and—of course—politics. As for food, it takes little research skill to recognize that food has an enormous presence in contemporary popular culture. Encounters with food are unavoidable: It is a dominant element in advertising, family budgets, recreational activities, visual and material culture, holiday celebrations, and increasingly large-scale cultural movements. It is so ubiquitous that it is no great stretch to cite food as one of the major categories of popular culture, with each of the other areas in which it appears affording easy access to issues and questions related to its meaning and implications—including its religious and ecological implications.

Notably, in their important text *Religion and Popular Culture in America*, Bruce David Forbes and Jeffrey Mahan introduce their study using a food analogy to characterize the three levels of culture. Dividing culture into three distinct classes—elite, folk, and popular—they use food to vivify the classes, explaining, "[H]igh culture is a gourmet meal, folk culture is [G]randma's casserole, and popular culture is a McDonald's hamburger."[18]

How, then, might we learn more about how fast food hamburger culture relates to the study of Religion and Ecology? We can start with the analogy itself and with the rather glaring absence of the ecological dimension of fast food culture in Religion and Ecology studies. In our pursuit of the really big, well-vetted issues in Religion and Ecology, we can easily enough miss the profound ways in which contemporary culture promotes fast food over healthy food, quick meals over wholesome ones, and processed provisions over natural and whole foods. Fast food restaurants are, again, only an example. The same cultural logic is manifest in the aisles of grocery stores, the shelves of convenience stores, in television and Internet advertisements, and in the cupboards and pantries of most American homes. Clearly the material and visual manifestations of our food logic engage us with consumer culture as a whole. More specifically, they demand that attention be given to corporatism, postmodern capitalism, the exploitation of labor, and alienation (in all the old Marxist senses of the term), among numerous other features and categories of contemporary popular culture. They also vividly engage us with the contemporary ecological crisis since each of those other features and categories have a direct bearing on the substance of the crisis. It does not take expertise in Theology of Culture or in Cultural Religion to find the religious context for the detrimental effects of these various cultural features and categories on the environment.

If Religion and Ecology considered the fast-not-healthy food logic so prevalent in popular culture, then whole new vistas of research, analysis, and critique would span out in all directions. Supporting texts and videos are abundant in this area, including Eric Scholosser's *Fast Food Nation*, Karl Weber's *Food, Inc.*, USC Canada's *The Story of Food*, Paul Robert's *The End of Food*, and Marion Nestle's

Food Politics, among many, many others. Any of these texts (print or visual) could serve as a departure point for specific research projects in Religion and Ecology, journal articles, or chapters in collections. They (or excerpts) could also immediately add food as a component to any course on Religion and Ecology.

Politics

Nestle's text *Food Politics* introduces another major domain of culture in which food is particularly prominent—politics.[19] As noted earlier, if researchers are not aware of popular culture in general, they are likely out of touch with its political dimension in particular. As a result, they probably do not consider the political context of their work except abstractly. Absent engagement with popular culture, the political dimension of food, which is considerable, does not present itself for inquiry, analysis, and critique. In the absence of a serious encounter with the ideological, political, and media adversaries of environmentalism, topics in politics and food are ignored or unrecognized. Rectifying this oversight is not difficult, and three good approaches can be used: farm policies, nutrition policies, and the GMO debate, further elaborated in Brian Tokar's contribution in this volume. As with the consideration of fast food, any of these topics immediately raises ecological issues.

Current U.S. farm policies favor industrial agriculture and its reckless assault on natural systems and their inhabitants. They also slight small farms, organic agriculture, local markets, and permaculture systems, all of which tend to operate in harmony with ecosystems. Though these policies favor the current economic order of the United States and the world, they bring disastrous externalities affecting both human culture and the environment. Religion and Ecology recognizes the way externalities work and how ecological destruction carries with it human misery. This existing recognition needs only take into consideration U.S. farm policies to isolate a critical food issue and its relevance to the field.

Nutrition is another policy area where relevance is evident and research slight. Closely tied to farm policies, nutrition policies struggle to articulate dietary norms that do not favor industrial agriculture—specifically the weight given to animal protein (dairy, fish, and meat) and grain products in a recommended diet. It is difficult to come by these items without relying on industrial agriculture. Even the notable stress given to fruits and vegetables glosses on the reality that most fruits and vegetables readily available are also products of industrial agriculture, not locally sourced, are nutrient-deficient, incur enormous food miles to deliver, and are most likely produced using liberal applications of synthetic fertilizers, pesticides, and preservatives. Again, this is a political issue, and one that many environmentalists consider critical.

Finally, the great GMO debate, heating up even as this book goes to press, reveals how political dimensions of food harmonize with ecological issues.

Here grassroots social action in the interest of human health and environmental stewardship is met head on with resistance from powerful agribusinesses and their political allies—e.g., ballot initiative 522 in Washington and Proposition 37 in California. Though national policies do not reflect the will of the vast majority of Americans to have GMO food labeled accordingly, and though the federal government has yet taken no action, a non-GMO not-for-profit organization has taken the initiative to at least label foods that do not contain GMOs.[20]

In each of these examples, a political food issue in popular culture is also a major ecological issue. If not already evident, reference to Gottlieb's eight dimensions will make it explicit. Presumably, researchers can make this case easily enough; if this is so, the relevance to Religion and Ecology naturally follows. Furthermore, if researchers really wanted to be activists in ways that mattered, they might point out how politics functions much like religion in contemporary culture, as well as how one of America's two major political parties not only rejects the broader environmentalist agenda but also stands fast with the agribusiness proponents of industrial agriculture. Robert Bellah's work on Civil Religion could be deployed in this regard, as could, even more tellingly, the work of Jacques Ellul.

The three areas considered in this section are put forward merely as suggested starting points for a fuller engagement with food studies in the subfield of Religion and Ecology. Besides the other two mentioned (course curriculum and the un-usual suspects), there are certainly many others. I am fairly confident that these five areas will bring food into Religion Ecology, if for no other reason than I have pursued them in my own research and have included them in my courses on Religion and Ecology.

*   *   *

Those of us who work in Religion and Ecology do indeed tend to be activists. At least we take seriously the contemporary ecological crisis, and we see in our professional research an opportunity to promote constructive responses, often through confrontational critiques and specification of distinct failures on the part of religion and religions. From my perspective, this is not often a helpful approach, especially when our own area of inquiry is so woefully nonconversant with the broader culture it proposes to change.

There are better, more effective methods to pursue our research agenda and also promote constructive responses of the environmental challenges the world is facing. This chapter has offered such a response.

The next step, of course, is to begin the hard (but immensely rewarding) work of rectifying the current situation. This next step might begin with the proposals suggested in the last section, but before that it must take into consideration the larger context in which we do our work. This larger context is that given to us not just as scholars of religion or food or ecology, but as scholars of a broader global culture, one that seems to have lost its understanding of the meaning and value of these elements to our world while remaining blissfully oblivious to the danger lurking in this loss.

Notes

1. Mary Evelyn Tucker, "Religion and Ecology: Survey of the Field," in *Oxford Handbook of Religion and Ecology*, ed. Roger S. Gottlieb (New York: Oxford University Press, 2006), 407.

2. Bron Taylor, "Religious Studies and Environmental Concern," in *Encyclopedia of Religion and Nature*, ed. Bron Taylor (London: Continuum, 2008), 1373.

3. Lynn Townsend White Jr., "The Historical Roots of Our Ecologic Crisis," *Science* 155, no. 3767 (March 10, 1967): 1203–1207.

4. Rachel Carson, *Silent Spring* (Boston: Houghton Mifflin, 1962).

5. Dell deChant, *Religion and Culture in the West: A Primer*, rev. prt. (Dubuque, IA: Kendall/Hunt, 2008), 77–79.

6. Whitney A. Bauman and Richard R. Bohannon, "Introduction," in *Grounding Religion: A Field Guide to the Study of Religion and Ecology*, eds. Bauman, Bohannon, and O'Brien (New York: Routledge, 2011), 8.

7. Robin Blumner, "Enough of Us, Already, Let's Think Smaller," *St. Petersburg Times* (January 30, 2011), 5P, cited in Dell deChant, "Religion and Ecology in Popular Culture," in *Understanding Religion and Popular Culture*, eds. Terry Ray Clark and Dan W. Clanton Jr. (Abingdon, Oxon, UK: Routledge, 2012), 34.

8. Roger S. Gottlieb, "Religion and Ecology—What Is the Connection and Why Does It Matter?" in *Oxford Handbook of Religion and Ecology*, ed. Roger S. Gottlieb (New York: Oxford University Press, 2006), 8.

9. Ibid., 4–5.

10. As noted in deChant, "Religion and Ecology," 34.

11. Rick Santorum, "When I Said Obama Believed in a 'Phony Theology,'" *Pensito Review* (February 20, 2012). www.pensitoreview.com/2012/02/20/santorum-when-i-said-obama-believed-in-a-phony-theology-i-was-referring-to-climate-change/

12. Gottlieb, 4.

13. Ellen F. Davis, *Scripture, Culture, and Agriculture* (Cambridge, NY: Cambridge University Press, 2009).

14. Ibid., 13.

15. Ibid., 19.

16. Ibid., 51.

17. Norman Wirzba, *The Paradise of God: Renewing Religion in an Ecological Age* (New York: Oxford University Press, 2003), 182–183; in Ibid., 51.

18. Bruce David Forbes and Jeffrey H. Mahan, *Religion and Popular Culture in America* (Berkeley: University of California Press, 2005), 2.

19. Marion Nestley, *Food Politics*, rev. ed. (Berkeley: University of California Press, 2013).

20. See ABC NEWS, "Poll: Skepticism of Genetically Modified Foods," June 19, 2013. http://abcnews.go.com/Technology/story?id=97567&page=1

9

The GMO Threat to Food Sovereignty: Science, Resistance, and Transformation

Brian Tokar

The expansive use of genetically modified organisms (GMOs) in agriculture is one of the most potent symbols of the worldwide threat to food justice and food sovereignty. Today over 365 million acres of land worldwide are believed to be planted in GMO varieties of soya, maize, cotton, and other crops.[1] Even though the vast majority of GMO crops are still raised in a small handful of countries, mainly in the Western hemisphere, they include agroexport giants such as the United States, Argentina, and Brazil. Much of the world, however, is continuing to resist this uniquely controversial and invasive form of genetic manipulation of our food.

A significant milestone in the global response to GMOs was achieved in July 2013, when after more than 17 years of popular campaigns, lawsuits, diplomatic maneuvers and political battles, Monsanto announced that it would cease its efforts to gain approval to grow any more GMO crop varieties in Europe.[2] Ten years before, the G.W. Bush administration in the United States had filed a lawsuit with the World Trade Organization seeking to pry open Europe's approval processes. After three years of deliberations, the WTO ruled that Europe's de facto moratorium on new approvals must be replaced by more specific case-by-case approval processes, but the transnational body upheld European countries' right to protect food safety and the integrity of local agricultures. In that ruling, countries retained the ability to consider all possible hazards of GMOs in their risk assessments, even those that are perceived to be "highly unlikely to occur."[3] By 2013, even Monsanto apparently conceded that

the unified opposition of European consumers, farmers, and many independent scientists was not likely to be overturned.

Opposition to GMOs also arose throughout the global South as soon as
the first engineered crop varieties were introduced in the late 1990s. Militant farmers campaigns in India with names such as Cremate Monsanto and
Monsanto Quit India made international headlines.[4] Farmers in Mali and
South Africa organized against the introduction of GMO maize varieties, and
Zambia took the unprecedented step in 2002 of refusing food aid shipments
containing GMO corn from the United States.[5] In Brazil, where food crops,
grazing lands, and vast tracts of former Amazon rainforest have been over-
taken by plantations of GMO soybeans grown mainly for export, farm activists and women's groups associated with the global La Vía Campesina alliance
have occupied seed facilities and research plots managed by Monsanto and
Syngenta on numerous occasions. A prominent leader of Brazil's renowned
Landless Workers' Movement (MST) was assassinated by Syngenta's private
security forces during one of these actions.[6]

A 2012 joint report on Monsanto by Vía Campesina and Friends of the
Earth International concluded, in part, that

> [a]s a result of Monsanto's presence, local seeds are becoming illegal,
> biodiversity is disappearing, land is being contaminated, and farmers and
> agricultural workers are being poisoned, criminalised and displaced from
> their land. Local food producers aiming to feed communities have to
> compete with huge corporations whose sole objective is to make profits.
>   . . . With the current economic and environmental crises, global resistance
> against transnational corporations has become an urgent necessity. A fair soci-
> ety organised to address people's needs and guarantee their rights cannot be
> built in co-existence with corporations that grab power and finite resources.[7]

Many years earlier, Vandana Shiva wrote that

> corporations that promote genetic engineering steal nature's harvest of
> diverse species, either by deliberately destroying biodiversity or by unin-
> tended biological pollution of species and ecosystems. They steal the global
> harvest of healthy and nutritious food. Finally, they steal knowledge from
> citizens by stifling independent science and denying consumers the right to
> know what is in their food.[8]

How did a novel agricultural technology, advanced by just a handful of
corporations, become such a powerful driver of the increasing global corporate
control over the world's food supply? How did Monsanto and others achieve
unprecedented dominance over the world's seed supplies, and what alternatives
have emerged to help enhance people's ability to adequately feed themselves?

The New Seed Cartel

Since the mid-1990s, a handful of corporations specializing in the production of pesticides and other agrochemicals have aggressively promoted the genetic engineering of crops and seeds, insisting that this technology is the key to improving world agriculture. Meanwhile, they have furthered the steady expansion of GMO technology by steadily increasing their control over the world's seed supply, mainly through outright purchases of major seed companies. Monsanto, one of the world's top chemical producers throughout the 20th century, is by far the most aggressive promoter of genetic engineering, and by 2005, it held patents to varieties grown on 88 percent of all GMO crop acreage.[9]

That same year, Monsanto became the world's largest seed company with its takeover of Seminis Seeds, a Mexican company that had become the premier supplier of vegetable seeds in the Western Hemisphere. A generation or two ago, seed production was a highly dispersed activity, one that still operated largely outside the commercial sphere in much of the world. Today, the informal sector in the seed trade still thrives in many areas, but it is under increasing economic and legal pressure from the new global seed cartel. Ten companies now control more than three-quarters of a worldwide seed market valued at $34.5 billion annually.[10] Five of those companies, Monsanto, Syngenta, Bayer, Dow, and DuPont, are also (along with BASF) the world's dominant producers of agricultural chemicals and are responsible for nearly all the genetically engineered seed varieties marketed around the world today. Monsanto itself became increasingly specialized in seeds and agrochemicals, spinning off its various industrial chemical and pharmaceutical divisions and spending much of the proceeds—at least $12 billion—buying up the world's leading seed companies, from DeKalb and Asgrow in the United States to Seminis in Mexico and India's flagship Mahyco, formerly the Maharashtra Hybrid Seed Company.[11]

All of these companies are, in their present form, the result of an extensive series of corporate mergers and divestments that shaped the emerging biotech era in the late 1990s and early 2000s.[12] Bayer, best known for aspirin and other common pharmaceuticals, is also the world's largest producer of insecticides. After a corn contamination scandal in 2000–2001 cost the food industry $1 billion—and forced the recall of hundreds of name-brand corn products due to contamination with a GE variety never approved for human consumption (discussed hereinafter)—Bayer bought the former CropScience division of the pharmaceutical giant Aventis. Syngenta is a perhaps a uniquely synthetic company, formed from successive waves of mergers, spinoffs, and recombinations of chemical companies from Switzerland, Britain, and Sweden; it is the second largest manufacturer of pesticides worldwide, after Bayer, and the largest producer of herbicides.

Monsanto remains the second largest producer of chemical weedkillers, so it is no coincidence that tolerance to herbicide treatments is by far the most dominant genetically engineered trait in commercial agriculture today; up to 90 percent of all GMO crops include some form of engineered tolerance to herbicides, especially Monsanto's various "Roundup" formulations. Engineered herbicide tolerance has made it easier for some growers to plant vast acreages of corn and soybeans on fields that are frequently doused with broad-spectrum herbicides such as Roundup that destroy most other plants. This has reduced the need for mechanical cultivation and helped popularize the spread of a highly chemical-dependent form of nominally "no-till" agriculture. This technology has led to such a rapid increase in herbicide use that superweeds with an evolved resistance to Monsanto's Roundup and other broad-spectrum herbicides have now come to dominate fields in many parts of the United States.[13] The other common category of GMO crops produce one or more pesticidal proteins, derived from Bt (Bacillus thuringiensis) bacteria; these insecticidal varieties of corn, cotton, and other crops are regulated as insecticides by the U.S. EPA. Current GMO crop varieties often combine both types of traits in multiple forms, a technique known as "gene stacking."

Farmers in the corn- and soy-growing regions of the United States report that Monsanto and other companies have leveraged their control over the seed market to make it increasingly difficult to obtain seeds with the latest agronomic improvements—traits introduced entirely through conventional plant breeding—unless farmers are willing to purchase patented GMO seeds. The latest products of U.S. breeding labs—also increasingly under corporate control—are often only available with various proprietary GMO herbicide tolerance and Bt insecticidal traits attached.[14] The remaining non-GMO seed supplies are often not reliably so: A 2004 study commissioned by the Union of Concerned Scientists detected transgenic DNA in 50–80 percent of the nominally non-GMO corn seed that was tested, in 50–80 percent of the soybeans, and in 80–100 percent of the canola seed.[15] Globally, companies have intervened in international trade negotiations to press for increased legal restrictions on farmers' ability to freely exchange seeds. For example, recent U.S. bilateral free trade agreements include provisions that force the adoption of "plant protection" rules that have long been advocated by GMO seed producers.[16]

Throughout North America, Monsanto has also pursued legal cases against hundreds of farmers who have been accused of illegally saving seeds and replanting patented GMO varieties without the company's consent. The Washington-based Center for Food Safety has been monitoring these lawsuits closely for over a decade and, as of late 2012, had documented 142 lawsuits against 410 farmers in 27 U.S. states.[17] The company has reportedly investigated as many as 4,500 farmers for so-called "seed piracy." Some of those growers openly defied the company's patents, asserting their right to the time-honored practice of saving and replanting seeds, whereas others were simply victims of inadvertent contamination of their seed stocks. In the most celebrated case of all, a Saskatchewan farmer named Percy Schmeiser replanted some canola (rape) seed that had apparently cross-pollinated with a neighbor's Monsanto Roundup-tolerant variety in an attempt to salvage the results of some 30 years of his own breeding research and crop development. The Canadian Supreme Court ultimately ruled that Monsanto had the right to sue Schmeiser to protect the company's patent rights, but it overturned all monetary damages imposed by a lower court. The Supreme Court affirmed in its decision that as a nonuser of Roundup-family herbicides, Schmeiser had obtained no tangible benefit from Monsanto's GMO traits.[18]

So it is that Monsanto and other companies, by virtue of their raw monopoly power, rather than any demonstrable advantages of GMOs, have come to dominate supplies of several important staple crops. It is clear that GMO crops have not been responsible for any reliable increase in yields over equivalent non-GM crops, and that they have generally increased farmers' dependence on agricultural chemicals.[19] Twenty years of claims that genetic engineering will "feed the world" by making crops more resilient and healthier have time and again proven false. Instead, they have created new oligopolies in key agricultural inputs, including seeds, and have helped advance the trend toward increasing mechanization and concentration of ownership of farmland.

Monopolizing Science

While Monsanto and other GMO developers often caricature their opponents as being antiscience, the biotech industry itself has significantly undermined the integrity of genetic science and worked to demonize independent scientists who raise criticisms of their technology. Some essential realities that the industry has worked hard to suppress include the following:

- The artificial insertion of new genes into the embryonic cells of our basic food crops is inherently disruptive of those cells' own internal processes of genetic regulation.
- The genetic material (DNA) that is forcibly introduced through genetic engineering is not merely extracted from other living cells, but rather is generally a wholly artificial construct, including added regulatory and marker sequences from viruses and other organisms. These added components are necessary to overcome living cells' evolved resistance to unfavorable genetic alterations and to help identify the minuscule proportion of cells in most experiments that actually express the inserted transgenic traits.

- Partly owing to these added components, genetic engineering is associated with very high levels of genome scrambling, disruption, and unusually high mutation rates.
- Most attempts to introduce agronomically significant traits through genetic engineering have not been successful, and conventional plant breeding is usually far better able to confer the advantages in crop yield, tolerance to environmental stresses, and other qualities that genetic engineers continue to tell us are just beyond the horizon.
- Monsanto, DuPont, and other companies have leveraged their patents over key GMO traits to limit independent scientists' access to important research materials.
- When studies appear that confirm significant health consequences from exposure to GMO crops, companies are often actively involved in efforts to demean and discredit the scientists involved, both within the scientific community and on the Internet.

Comprehensive studies of the health and environmental effects of GM crops remain relatively sparse. This is largely a consequence of Monsanto's unprecedented influence within some scientific circles and often covert involvement in aggressive smear campaigns against researchers who may publish objectionable findings. Researchers such as Arpad Pusztai in Scotland, Gilles-Eric Séralini in France, and Irina Ermakova in Russia, among many others, have published detailed studies showing that animals fed GMO grains suffer higher rates of organ damage, loss of fertility, suppressed immunity, and other negative health consequences. Instead of these studies' sparking additional research in these areas, as would normally occur in a climate of open scientific inquiry, each fell victim to organized campaigns to discredit the researchers and their findings in both the scientific and the popular press.[20] Combined with biotech companies' proprietary ownership of various GMO varieties, this has led to a situation where the effects of GMOs remain significantly underresearched. For example, entomologists engaged in studies of crop pests have complained to the EPA about numerous ways in which their research is undermined by corporate patent rules.[21]

Cellular- and molecular-level research, on the other hand, substantially affirms that technologies of gene splicing are inherently disruptive to cellular metabolism and the regulation of gene expression. In a detailed analysis of over 200 published research studies, researchers in the UK documented significant increases in genetic instability, higher mutation rates, large-scale deletions and translocations of DNA, and other disturbing effects at the sites of artificial gene insertion.[22] This study also helped reveal the extent to which research on the cellular and molecular consequences of genetic engineering tends to lag many years behind corporate-funded research focused almost entirely on the development and commercialization of new products.

Research on the environmental consequences of GMOs has also languished since the technology's early years. In 1999, scientists at Cornell University made world headlines with their announcement that pollen from a common variety of insecticidal *Bt* corn was lethal to monarch butterflies in their larval (caterpillar) stage.[23] Although later studies claimed to refute this finding, it was indeed confirmed that some *Bt* toxin proteins that had been used in commercial GMO crop varieties did kill monarch caterpillars. Studies suggesting harm to agriculturally beneficial insects such as ladybugs and lacewings were for the most part not followed up by subsequent researchers.[24] Meanwhile in 2011, a new study suggested that the main threat to monarch butterflies may indeed be an indirect consequence of the spread of GMOs. Monarchs' main feeding source in their larval stage is milkweed, which grows most abundantly in and around Midwestern cornfields. With the rapid spread of herbicide-tolerant corn varieties, weeds such as milkweed are eradicated due to the increased use of broad-spectrum herbicides such as Roundup throughout the main corn-growing areas of the country, hence depriving the caterpillars of their most important food source.[25]

Genetic Drift

The destabilizing environmental effects of genetic engineering are not limited to the laboratory nor to just a few charismatic organisms. One early study suggested that genetically engineered plant varieties may be inherently more likely to outcross than their non-GMO relatives, and the consequences of genetic contamination were demonstrated countless times in the first 15 years of the GMO era.[26] Since 2005, Greenpeace, in collaboration with GeneWatch in the UK, has maintained an online database of GMO contamination incidents: the GM Contamination Register.[27] An initial summary report in 2006 listed 142 publicly documented incidents in 43 countries since the introduction of commercial GMO crops in 1996. These included instances of contamination of food, seed, animal feeds, and wild relatives of crops, as well as illegal releases of unapproved GM varieties and documented negative agricultural side effects.[28] As of September 2013, the database contained a total of 384 entries.

Some of the better-known incidents that have alerted the world to the widespread contamination potential from GMO crops include the following:

- In 2001, researchers in the state of Oaxaca, Mexico documented the presence of DNA from GMO corn varieties in several indigenous corn crops.[29] A largely methodological dispute over the extent of contamination within the corn genome generated so much controversy that the journal *Nature* took the unusual step of withdrawing the original research paper, and Ignacio Chapela, the principal investigator, faced continued media attacks on his scientific reputation. Meanwhile, widespread corn contamination in Mexico has been confirmed by numerous independent and governmental studies.[30]

- In 2000, U.S. domestic corn supplies were widely contaminated with a GMO trait, known as Starlink (a *Bt* insecticidal protein known as Cry9C), which EPA regulators had previously declined to approve for human consumption. Some 300 consumer products were recalled, costing the food industry approximately $1 billion, including $110 million to settle claims from corn growers due to persistent marketing difficulties. Over 400 million bushels of corn were found contaminated with the Starlink trait, even though fewer than 40 million bushels of Starlink corn were harvested the previous year; 8.6 percent of all U.S. corn tested in 2000 was found to contain the Starlink trait.[31] Contaminated grain continued to be found in 1 percent of samples taken three years after the corn was withdrawn from the market, and a recent study published in the journal *Applied Biochemistry and Biotechnology* reported detection of numerous banned and discontinued GMO varieties, including Starlink, in samples of corn and soy products purchased in Saudi Arabia.[32]

- Researchers in the Canadian province of Alberta identified plots of oilseed rape (canola) that were simultaneously resistant to three common herbicide classes: glyphosate (Monsanto's "Roundup"), glufosinate (Bayer's, originally Aventis's Liberty) and imidazolinones (Cyanamid's imazethapyr formulations, Pursuit and Odyssey). A nearby grower had been cultivating GMO varieties demonstrating the first two resistances, as well as a non-GMO rape tolerant to imidazolinones.[33] A followup study detected resistant plants as far as 500 meters from the original plantings and confirmed through detailed DNA analysis that the multiresistant plants "were hybrids resulting from pollen transfer rather than inadvertent seed movement between fields."[34]

- In 2006, the U.S. Secretary of Agriculture announced that the U.S. long grain rice crop had been contaminated with an experimental glufosinate-tolerant variety (marketed as "LibertyLink") that was developed and field tested by Bayer CropScience. Even though no variety of GMO rice has yet been deregulated by the U.S. Department of Agriculture for commercial production, and field trials were reportedly less than an acre in size, glufosinate tolerance and two other GMO traits were subsequently identified in rice exported to Europe, the Middle East, Asia, and Africa.[35] The U.S. rice grower Riceland reported that the contamination was "geographically dispersed and random" throughout the long grain rice growing areas of the southeastern United States, and the U.S. Government Accountability Office later reported that the incident cost as much as $1.29 billion in lost exports, food recalls, and other expenses.[36] In 2011, Bayer agreed to pay 11,000 farmers in five U.S. states a total of $750 million to settle numerous pending lawsuits from this incident.[37]

- In at least two documented incidents, crops in the U.S. Midwest were contaminated with residues from prior-year experimental plantings of crops genetically engineered to produce pharmaceutical ingredients. In Nebraska, 500,000 bushels of soybeans had to be destroyed and 155 acres of corn burned when residues were detected from an experimental corn variety engineered to produce a pig vaccine. In Iowa, commercial corn crops were contaminated by residues of a previously grown GM variety that produced an experimental drug for cystic fibrosis.[38] These two incidents raised widespread concerns among U.S. food producers about potential pharmaceutical contamination of food, bankrupted the company (ProdiGene) responsible for these two incidents, and led others in the U.S. biotech industry to ultimately abandon the strategy of producing pharmaceuticals in GM food crops.[39]

- Plantings in Hawaii of a GMO papaya variety resistant to the ringspot virus led to widespread contamination of the islands' papaya crop. A sampling of 20,000 seeds from organic and wild papaya plantings found that 50 percent of the sampling sites were contaminated with the engineered trait.[40] Marketing problems drove the Hawaiian papaya crop to a 25-year low as many traditional papaya varieties were contaminated; beyond that, the engineered papayas were found to be unusually susceptible to other viral and fungal diseases.[41] Large-scale GMO contamination of papayas was also documented in Thailand, most likely from unapproved research trials, and samples of unauthorized GMO Hawaiian papaya appeared in several European countries in 2013.[42]

- In 2004, researchers from the U.S. Environmental Protection Agency investigated native grass contamination in the state of Oregon from a test plot of creeping bentgrass genetically engineered for Roundup tolerance. They found numerous grasses within 2 kilometers of the experimental plot, and two samples up to 13 miles away, that survived spraying with Roundup and that also contained major components of the inserted DNA imparting this trait.[43] Two years later, researchers determined that the transgene had established itself in resident grass populations, as well as in a non-GMO bentgrass that had been planted nearby to aid in monitoring potential gene flow.[44] They determined that the contamination had resulted both from the spread of pollen and from dispersed GMO seeds, a surprise in light of the minimal selective advantage of herbicide tolerance in areas that are not treated with herbicide.

- In 2013, several wheat plants resistant to applications of Roundup herbicide were found in a farmer's field in eastern Oregon. Monsanto had received approval from the U.S. Department of Agriculture to test herbicide-tolerant wheat varieties in 1998, but the tests were reportedly ended in 2005, when the company chose not to market GMO wheat in response to widespread opposition from farmers and consumer groups worldwide;

Monsanto had reportedly resumed testing GMO wheat varieties in Hawaii in 2012. Japan, Taiwan, and South Korea subsequently suspended imports of wheat from the northwestern United States for more than two months.[45]

Several researchers have reviewed the inherently disruptive character of genetic modifications for gene expression, ecological fitness, and production of potentially dangerous new gene products. In one review essay, Allison Snow of Ohio State University wrote:

Although crops and weeds have exchanged genes for centuries, genetic engineering raises additional concerns because it not only enables introduction into ecosystems of genes that confer novel fitness-related traits, but also allows novel genes to be introduced into many diverse types of crops, each with its own specific potential to outcross.[46]

Feeding the World?

Facing continuing opposition to GMOs on so many scientific, economic, and political grounds, Monsanto and other companies continue to assert the claim that their technology is necessary to feeding the world. Several recent studies affirm that locally scaled peasant agricultures are far better able to feed hungry people than all the innovations of global agribusiness.[47] Still, the promise of GMOs' "feeding the world" remains at the center of the industry's efforts to bolster its reputation. The GMO industry has supported numerous high-profile research efforts aimed at demonstrating its purported benefits for people in the global South, but each in turn has raised more questions than answers.

Many efforts to introduce GMOs to the global South have been generously supported by global institutions such as the World Bank. In the first few years of the GMO era, the World Bank provided some $50 million in direct aid for biotechnology research, with over 80 percent of research funding committed to six countries: India, Kenya, Brazil, Indonesia, Peru, and Ethiopia. India alone received a full 40 percent of the total, with $20 million in World Bank funds supporting the development of an insecticidal Bt rice, along with genetically engineered varieties of cotton, pigeon peas, chickpeas, and various horticultural crops.[48] In recent years, the Bill and Melinda Gates Foundation has invested heavily in agricultural technologies for the developing world, investing $1.3 billion in the late 2000s alone, and with a consistent focus on biotechnology applications.[49]

In one high-profile project, announced in 2003, genes from amaranth were spliced into the DNA of potatoes to increase their protein content for use in India. Although the protein content of the potatoes reportedly increased by nearly half, it was still only a small fraction of the amount found in whole amaranth, or even in wheat and rice. GMO opponents in India pointed out that the peas, lentils, and other legumes that are an important part of traditional Indian diets—but that have been marginalized in cash crop–oriented agricultural development projects—provide even more protein.[50] Many in India concluded that biotechnologists were promising a high-tech "cure" to hunger while ignoring far more realistic and readily available solutions, a recurring theme in many global South applications of genetic engineering.

In Kenya, the World Bank joined forces with the U.S. Agency for International Development (USAID), Monsanto, and private donors. There, the aim was to offer engineered varieties of sweet potatoes, a staple crop in rural areas that rarely attracts the interest of corporate researchers. After 11 years of research, which generated much international publicity for the Monsanto- and USAID-sponsored Kenyan researcher Florence Wambugu, only one local sweet potato variety had successfully been genetically engineered, imparting resistance to a virus that farmers routinely fend off by far less invasive means.[51] Under field conditions, the potato failed to demonstrate any significant virus resistance.[52]

Perhaps the most controversial GMO application in India has been the marketing of *Bt* insecticidal cotton varieties to small-scale growers in many parts of the country. Although *Bt* cotton has become dominant in regions of India where larger-scale cultivation is common, Monsanto has aggressively marketed its "Bollgard" brand to India's innumerable smallholders as well, promising crops that will resist infestations of the dreaded bollworm. From the first approved cultivation of *Bt* cotton in 2002, however, many farmers faced almost total crop failures, as their crops were found to be even more vulnerable to various other cotton pests, including budworms, mealybugs, and several fungi and viruses.[53] Some critics blame the rising use of GMO crops and the resulting unprecedented increase in seed prices and pesticide dependence for driving perhaps hundreds of thousands of Indian farmers to suicide in recent years, though others suggest that farmer suicides were a chronic tragedy in Indian communities even before the GMO era.[54]

Of all the various GMO crops developed for global South applications, perhaps the most worldwide attention has focused on so-called "golden rice," a rice genetically engineered with daffodil and bacterial DNA to produce elevated quantities of beta-carotene, a biochemical precursor to vitamin A. Researchers in Switzerland, Germany, and India reportedly spent $100 million developing this experimental rice variety, which in its initial iteration would require a person to eat 12 times his or her normal dietary intake of rice to receive the promised benefit.[55] The renowned food writer Michael Pollan thus described it as "the world's first purely rhetorical technology."[56] Even if current varieties produce significantly higher provitamin doses, as is claimed, critics continue to raise numerous questions about its metabolism, potential side effects, and whether the funds may have been better spent purchasing inexpensive vitamin A supplements and helping poor communities sustain their traditional dietary vitamin A sources, including leafy green vegetables, carrots, squashes, sweet potatoes, melons, mangos, eggs, and butter. Meanwhile, Brazil's public agricultural research agency, Embrapa, has announced varieties of eight staple crops with dramatically enhanced levels of provitamin A and other micronutrients, developed entirely through conventional plant breeding; they are already being introduced into local school lunch programs.[57]

Indeed a growing body of evidence suggests that scientific applications of traditional, time-tested crop improvement methods may have far more potential to help address the world's food needs than any of the biotechnology industry's proposed solutions. A study by Jules Pretty at the University of Essex (UK) surveyed more than 200 sustainable agriculture projects in 52 countries and showed how a variety of relatively familiar techniques have the potential to dramatically improve crop yields in the global South. Low-tech methods such as trap crops for insects, careful applications of compost, use of natural predators for common insect pests, and a wealth of traditional intercropping methods have demonstrable advantages, especially when applied in a systematic and consistent manner.[58] One Chinese study showed that simply interplanting two different rice varieties with distinctly different growing characteristics doubled yields.[59] Farmers in India have helped advance a system of "root intensification" through which yields of rice, wheat, and many vegetables are multiplied severalfold by adjusting methods of planting and cultivation, with the added benefit of requiring less water. The system combines some indigenous methods with others that were developed in Africa in the 1960s but that are often ignored by development officials with close ties to international foundations and research institutes.[60]

Miguel Altieri of the University of California at Berkeley, a central figure in the development of agroecology, writes:

The persistence of millions of agricultural hectares under ancient, traditional management in the form of raised fields, terraces, polycultures (with a number of crops growing in the same field), agroforestry systems, etc., document a successful indigenous agricultural strategy and constitutes a tribute to the "creativity" of traditional farmers. These microcosms of traditional agriculture offer promising models for other areas because they promote biodiversity, thrive without agrochemicals, and sustain year-round yields. The new models of agriculture that humanity will need include forms of farming that are more ecological, biodiverse, local, sustainable, and socially just. They will be rooted in the ecological rationale of traditional small-scale agriculture, representing long-established examples of successful community-based local agriculture. Such systems have fed much of the world for centuries and continue to feed people across the planet.[61]

The systematic advantages of traditional crop varieties and growing methods over those of agribusiness and biotechnology corporations may be even greater in the area of crop adaptation to disruptive changes in the earth's climate. For two decades, GMO proponents have suggested that biotech interventions would prove necessary for the world's food supply to withstand the stress of rising temperatures and erratic precipitation patterns associated with global climate change. In 2008 the Ottawa-based ETC Group identified over 500 patent filings for genes associated with climate-adaptive traits; just three years later the number of patents and applications had increased by an additional 50 percent.[62] In 2012, Monsanto released its first drought-tolerant GMO corn, but studies suggest that its ability to withstand modest droughts offered no discernable advantage over products of traditional plant breeding, nor various approaches focused on agroecosystem enhancement without genetic engineering.[63] In 2009, a major study on agriculture and climate by four UN agencies and the World Bank partly anticipated these outcomes, arguing that sustainable agricultural practices rooted in traditional and local agricultural knowledge are the primary strategies for both climate mitigation and reduction of poverty.[64]

Several comprehensive research efforts have confirmed that organic growing methods are generally associated with higher levels of stress tolerance in plants than conventional chemical-intensive methods. A 2005 study reviewing 22 years of organic crop trials at the Rodale Research Institute in Pennsylvania concluded that not only can organic growers achieve comparable yields with far less fossil energy and improved water conservation, but also organic corn yields were consistently higher in drought years than crops from conventionally cultivated fields.[65] A 2007 review compared over 100 studies each of conventional and organic growing methods and suggested an enhanced organic yield advantage in developing world applications.[66] In 1998, in the aftermath of a hurricane that devastated large areas of Central America, farmers who used cover crops, intercropping, and agroforestry methods suffered less damage than their neighbors utilizing agribusiness-approved methods, reporting less topsoil loss and lower economic losses overall.[67] Organic methods also demonstrate specific advantages for climate mitigation, including increasing soils' ability to sequester carbon, reducing nitrogen emissions associated with chemical fertilizers, eliminating energy-intensive pesticide production, composting instead of burning crop residues, and feeding ruminants less grain and more grass, thus helping reduce methane emissions.[68]

Despite overwhelming evidence to the contrary, proponents of genetic engineering continue to assert that GMO research is essential to feeding the world's hungry in an increasingly uncertain and unstable climate. They reiterate the promises they have offered since the dawn of the GMO era, insisting that numerous long-promised advantages will surely be revealed with further study. Meanwhile, the innovations that best serve the needs of both farmers and communities throughout the world continue to emerge mainly from applications of far less invasive methods. In some instances, laboratory techniques developed by biotechnologists are helping facilitate breeding research, offering useful diagnostic tools to better identify desirable traits and monitor the results of breeding experiments. These methods, for the most part, appear far less problematic than manipulations of crop genetics using genetic engineering and may continue to play a positive role in breeding research in various public and private settings.

Crop genetic engineering, on the other hand, may be a technology whose time is past. After more than 20 years of research and development, GMOs continue to present far more problems than benefits, and most of the purported advantages have proved limited at best; many simply do not withstand scientific scrutiny. Perhaps it is time to put this inherently problematic and invasive technology aside and instead redouble efforts around the world to advance far more benign and sustainable ways to improve the quality and availability of our food.

Notes

1. Joseph Zacune et al., "Combatting Monsanto: Grassroots Resistance to the Corporate Power of Agribusiness in the Era of the 'Green Economy' and a Changing Climate" (La Vía Campesina and Friends of the Earth International, March 2012). The source describes this as 3 percent of agricultural land, but the UN FAO's figure excluding pasture lands from its estimate brings it closer to 10 percent. See also J. Zacune, "Who Benefits from GM Crops? An Industry Built on Myths" (Amsterdam: Friends of the Earth International, February 2011).

2. Anna Meldolesi, "Monsanto Waves White Flag," *Nature Biotechnology* (September 2013).

3. WTO findings document WT/DS291-93/INTERIM (2006), 1031, quoted in B. Tokar, "WTO vs. Europe: Less—and Also More—Than It Seems." www.zmag.org/content/showarticle.cfm?ItemID=9734

4. Vandana Shiva, "Seed Satyagraha: A Movement for Farmers' Rights and Freedoms in a World of Intellectual Property Rights, Globalised Agriculture and Biotechnology," in *Redesigning Life? The Worldwide Challenge to Genetic Engineering*, ed. B. Tokar (London: Zed Books, 2001).

5. M. M. Lewanika, "GMOs and the Food Crisis in Zambia," in *Gene Traders: Biotechnology, World Trade and the Globalization of Hunger*, ed. B. Tokar (Burlington, VT: Toward Freedom, 2004).

6. Isabella Kenfield, "Expansion of Biotechnology in Brazil Brings Violence," Center for International Policy Americas Program Special Report, March 2008, http://americas.irc-online.org/am/5070. For background, see M. E. Martínez-Torres and P. M. Rosset, "La Vía Campesina: Transnationalizing Peasant Struggle and Hope," in *Latin American Social Movements in the Twenty-First Century: Resistance, Power and Democracy*, eds. R. Stahler-Sholk et al. (Lanham, MD: Rowman & Littlefield, 2008).

7. J. Zacune et al., *Combatting Monsanto*, 27.

8. Vandana Shiva, *Stolen Harvest: The Hijacking of the Global Food Supply* (Cambridge, MA: South End Press, 2000), 95.

9. ETC Group Communiqué No. 91, "Oligopoly, Inc. 2005: Concentration in Corporate Power" (Ottawa: ETC Group, November 2005).

10. ETC Group Communiqué No. 111, "Putting the Cartel before the Horse . . . and Farm, Seeds, Soil, Peasants, etc.: Who Will Control Agricultural Inputs, 2013?" (Ottawa: ETC Group, September 2013).

11. Brian Tokar, "Monsanto: A Profile of Corporate Arrogance," in *The Case against the Global Economy*, eds. Edward Goldsmith and Jerry Mander (London: Earthscan Publications, 2001).

12. Hope Shand, "Gene Giants: Understanding the 'Life Industry,'" in *Redesigning Life?*, ed. B. Tokar.

13. Charles M Benbrook, "Impacts of Genetically Engineered Crops on Pesticide Use in the U.S.: The First Sixteen Years," *Environmental Sciences Europe* 24, no. 24 (2012); Jerry Adler, "The Growing Menace from Superweeds," *Scientific American*, May 2011; Natasha Gilbert, "Case Studies: A Hard Look at GM crops," *Nature* 497 (May 2, 2013); Scott Kilman, "Superweeds Hit Farm Belt, Triggering New Arms Race," *Wall St. Journal*, June 4, 2010.

14. The same six companies that dominate global agrochemical production account for 76 percent of private expenditures in seed and agrochemical research and development. See ETC Group Communiqué No. 110, "Gene Giants Seek 'Philanthrogopoly'" (Ottawa: ETC Group, March 2013).

15. Margaret Mellon and Jane Rissler, *Gone to Seed: Transgenic Contaminants in the Traditional Seed Supply* (Washington: Union of Concerned Scientists, 2004).

16. ETC Group Communiqué No. 111, "Putting the Cartel before the Horse . . ."

17. "Monsanto v. U.S. Farmers 2012 Update" (Washington: Center for Food Safety, November 2012).

18. K. Makin and A. Dunfield, "Monsanto Wins Key Biotech Ruling," *Globe and Mail*, May 21, 2004; "Percy Schmeiser Claims Moral and Personal Victory in Supreme Court Decision," www.percyschmeiser.com/decisioncomments.htm; *Monsanto Canada Inc. v. Schmeiser*, May 21, 2004 (2004 SCC 34, File No.: 29437).

19. Doug Gurian-Sherman, *Failure to Yield: Evaluating the Performance of Genetically Engineered Crops* (Washington: Union of Concerned Scientists, 2009); Benbrook, "Impacts of Genetically Engineered Crops on Pesticide Use in the U.S."

20. Several such studies, and their political fallout, are summarized in Michael Antoniou et al., "GMO Myths and Truths: An Evidence-Based Examination of the Claims Made for the Safety and Efficacy of Genetically Modified Crops" (London: Earth Open Source, June 2012).

21. Andrew Pollack, "Crop Scientists Say Biotechnology Seed Companies Are Thwarting Research," *New York Times*, February 29, 2009.

22. Allison Wilson et al., *Genome Scrambling—Myth or Reality? Transformation-Induced Mutations in Transgenic Crop Plants* (Brighton, UK: Econexus, October 2004). See also Jonathan R. Latham et al., "The Mutational Consequences of Plant Transformation," *Journal of Biomedicine and Biotechnology* 2006 (2006): 1–7.

23. John Losey et al., "Transgenic Pollen Harms Monarch Larvae," *Nature* 399 (1999): 6733.

24. Early studies of the environmental effects of GMOs are reviewed in Ricarda Steinbrecher, "Ecological Consequences of Genetic Engineering," in *Redesigning Life?* ed. B. Tokar.

25. Andrew Pollack, "In Midwest, Flutters May Be Far Fewer," *New York Times*, July 12, 2011.

26. Joy Bergelson et al., "Promiscuity in Transgenic Plants," *Nature* 395 (September 3, 1998): 25.

27. www.gmcontaminationregister.org

28. Greenpeace International, "GM Contamination Register Report: Annual Review of Cases of Contamination, Illegal Planting and Negative Side Effects of Genetically Modified Organisms," February 2007. www.genewatch.org/uploads/f03c6d66a9b354535738483c1c3d49e4/gm_contamination_report_2006.pdf

29. David Quist and Ignacio Chapela, "Transgenic DNA Introgressed into Traditional Maize Landraces in Oaxaca, Mexico," *Nature* 414 (November 29, 2001): 541–543.

30. See, for example, ETC Group, "Genetic Pollution in Mexico's Center of Maize Diversity," *Food First Backgrounder* 8, no. 2 (spring 2002); E. Ortiz and J. Mainero, "Evidence of Gene Flow from Transgenic Maize to Local Varieties in Mexico," in *LMOS and the Environment: Proceedings of an International Conference* (OECD 2002), 289–295, www.oecd.org/document/18/0,2340,en_2649_34385_2509330_1_1_1_1,00.html

31. "StarLink Found in More Foods," United Press International, April 25, 2001; Paul Jacobs, "Banished Biotech Corn Not Gone Yet," *San Jose Mercury News*, December 1, 2003.

32. Sayer Ji, "Illegal StarLink GM Corn Resurfaces in Saudi Arabian Food Supply," *GreenMedInfo*, August 16, 2013. www.greenmedinfo.com/blog/breaking-illegal-starlink%E2%84%A2-gm-corn-resurfaces-saudi-arabian-food-supply

33. Mary MacArthur, "Triple-Resistant Canola Weeds Found in Alberta," *Western Producer*, February 10, 2000. www.producer.com/articles/20000210/news/20000210news01.html

34. L. Hall et al., "Pollen Flow between Herbicide-Resistant *Brassica Napus* Is the Cause of Multiple-Resistant *B. Napus* Volunteers," *Weed Science* 48, no. 6 (November 2000): 688–694.

35. *GM Contamination Register Report*, 15–19. Also Geoffrey Lean, "Rice Contaminated by GM Has Been on Sale for Months," *The Independent*, August 27, 2006, http://news.independent.co.uk/environment/article1222081.ece; Rick Weiss, "Rice Industry Troubled by Genetic Contamination," *Washington Post*, March 11, 2007.

36. Alan Bjerga and Jack Kaskey, "Rogue Oregon Wheat Stirs Foes of Monsanto Gene-Altered Crops," *Bloomberg Business Week*, May 30, 2013. www.businessweek.com/news/2013-05-29/rogue-oregon-wheat-inflames-foes-of-monsanto-gene-altered-crops

37. "Bayer Settles with Farmers over Modified Rice Seeds," *Bloomberg News*, July 1, 2011.

38. Justin Gillis, "Drug-Making Crops' Potential Hindered by Fear of Tainted Food," *Washington Post*, December 23, 2002.

39. Editorial, "Drugs in Crops: The Unpalatable Truth," *Nature Biotechnology* 22, no. 2 (February 2004): 133.

40. "Genetic Traits Spread to Non-Engineered Papayas in Hawaii," Environment News Service, September 10, 2004.

41. Sean Hao, "Papaya Production Taking a Tumble," *Honolulu Adviser*, March 19, 2006; Alan D. McNarie, "Papaya Problems: Scientists Square Off over How Safe Hawaii's Genetically Modified Papaya Is for Consumers," *Hawaii Island Journal*, April 1, 2003, http://hawaiiislandjournal.com

42. "GE Papaya Scandal in Thailand: Illegal GE Seeds Found in Packages Sold by Department of Agriculture," www.greenpeace.org/news/details?item_id=547563; www.gmcontaminationregister.org

43. Lidia S. Watrud et al., "Evidence for Landscape-Level, Pollen-Mediated Gene Flow from Genetically Modified Creeping Bentgrass with CP4 EPSPS as a Marker," *Proceedings of the National Academy of Sciences, USA* 101, no. 40 (October 5, 2004): 14533–14538.

44. Jay R. Reichman et al., "Establishment of Transgenic Herbicide-Resistant Creeping Bentgrass (Agrostis stolonifera L.) in Nonagronomic Habitats," *Molecular Ecology* 15 (2006): 4243–4255.

45. Andrew Pollack, "Modified Wheat Is Discovered in Oregon," *New York Times*, May 30, 2013; Jack Kaskey, "Monsanto Resumed Field Trials of Roundup Ready Wheat," *Bloomberg News*, May 31, 2013, www.bloomberg.com/news/2013-05-31/monsanto-resumed-field-trials-of-roundup-ready-wheat.html

46. Allison Snow, "Transgenic Crops: Why Gene Flow Matters," *Nature Biotechnology* 20 (June 2002): 542.

47. ETC Group Communiqué No. 102, "Who Will Feed Us? Questions for the Food and Climate Crises" (Ottawa: ETC Group, November 2009); Peter Rosset, "Fixing Our Global Food System: Food Sovereignty and Redistributive Land Reform," in *Agriculture and Food in Crisis: Conflict, Resistance, and Renewal*, eds. F. Magdoff and B. Tokar (New York: Monthly Review Press, 2010); Miguel A. Altieri, "Agroecology, Small Farms, and Food Sovereignty," in *Agriculture and Food in Crisis*, eds. Magdoff and Tokar.

48. Eija Pehu, "Biosafety Capacity Building: A World Bank Perspective," in *A Framework for Biosafety Implementation: Report of a Meeting*, eds. M. A. Mclean et al. (ISNAR [International Service for National Agricultural Research] Biotechnology Service, February 2003). For background, see B. Tokar, "The World Bank: Biotechnology and the 'Next Green Revolution,'" in *Gene Traders*, ed. B. Tokar.

49. Raj Patel et al., "Ending Africa's Hunger," *The Nation*, September 2, 2009.

50. "Providing Proteins to the Poor: Genetically Engineered Potatoes vs. Amaranth and Pulses" (New Delhi: Research Foundation for Science, Technology and Ecology, January 9, 2003). www.gene.ch/genet.html

51. Aaron deGrassi, "Genetically Modified Crops and Sustainable Poverty Alleviation in Sub-Saharan Africa: An Assessment of Current Evidence," Third World Network–Africa (June 2003), 6–10.

52. Gatonye Gathura, "GM Technology Fails Local Potatoes," *The Daily Nation* [Nairobi, Kenya], January 29, 2004. www.nationaudio.com/News/DailyNation/Supplements/horizon/current/story290120041.htm

53. G. S. Mudur, "Cotton Lessons for Bt brinjal," *The Telegraph* [New Delhi], February 15, 2010; "Failure of Bt. Cotton in India" (New Delhi: Research Foundation for Science, Technology and Ecology, September 2002); "The Marketing of Bt Cotton in India" (New Delhi: Greenpeace India and Centre for Sustainable Agriculture, September 2005); article archive from gaianet.org, October 2002.

54. Vivekananda Nemana, "In India, GM Crops Come at a High Price," *International Herald Tribune*, October 16, 2012; N. Gilbert, "Case Studies" (supra note 13).

55. Devinder Sharma, "The Great Trade Robbery: World Hunger and the Myths of Industrial Agriculture," in *Gene Traders*, ed. B. Tokar.

56. Michael Pollan, "The Great Yellow Hype," *New York Times Magazine*, March 4, 2001. Also Vandana Shiva, "Genetically Engineered 'Vitamin A Rice': A Blind Approach to Blindness Prevention," in *Redesigning Life?* ed. B. Tokar.

57. Fabiola Ortiz, "Brazil Develops 'Superfoods' to Combat Hidden Hunger," *The Guardian*, July 18, 2013.

58. Fred Pearce, "An Ordinary Miracle," *New Scientist* 169 (February 3, 2001).

59. Carol Kaesuk Yoon, "Simple Method Found to Increase Crop Yields Vastly," *New York Times*, August 22, 2000.

60. John Vidal, "India's Rice Revolution," *The Observer* [UK], February 16, 2013; Jonathan Latham, "The Next Green Revolution (This Time without Fossil Fuels)," *Solutions* 4, no. 2 (June 4, 2013), http://thesolutionsjournal.anu.edu.au

61. M. A. Altieri, "Agroecology, Small Farms, and Food Sovereignty" (supra note 47), 255.

62. "Patenting the 'Climate Genes' . . . and Capturing the Climate Agenda" (Ottawa: ETC Group, May/June 2008); ETC Group Communiqué No. 107, "Who Will Control the Green Economy?" (Ottawa: ETC Group, November 2011).

63. Doug Gurian-Sherman, "High and Dry: Why Genetic Engineering Is Not Solving Agriculture's Drought Problem in a Thirsty World" (Washington: Union of Concerned Scientists, June 2012); Tiffany Stecker, "Drought-Tolerant Corn Efforts Show Positive Early Results," *Scientific American*, July 27, 2012, www.scientificamerican.com/article.cfm?id=drought-tolerant-corn-trials-show-positive-early-results

64. Beverly McIntyre et al., "Synthesis Report: A Synthesis of the Global and Subglobal IAASTD Reports" (Washington, DC: International Assessment of Agricultural Knowledge, Science and Technology for Development Secretariat, 2009).

65. David Pimetel et al., "Environmental, Energetic, and Economic Comparisons of Organic and Conventional Farming Systems," *Bioscience* 55, no. 7 (July 2005): 573–582.

66. Catherine Badgley et al., "Organic Agriculture and the Global Food Supply," *Renewable Agriculture and Food Systems* 22, no. 2 (2007): 86–108.

67. M. Altieri, "Agroecology, Small Farms, and Food Sovereignty," 261.

68. Adrian Muller and Joan S. Davis, "Reducing Global Warming: The Potential of Organic Agriculture" (Emmaus, PA: Rodale Institute, 2009).

10

Agroecology and Social Movements

Peter M. Rosset and María Elena Martínez-Torres

At the beginning of the 21st century, the rural areas of the world constitute spaces that are hotly contested by different actors with opposing interests. Organizations and social movements of rural peoples—peasants, family farmers, indigenous people, rural workers and the landless engaged in land occupations, rural women, and others—increasingly use agroecology,[1] based on diversified farming systems (DFS), as a tool in the contestation, defense, (re)configuration, and transformation of contested rural spaces into peasant territories in a process that has been termed repeasantization.[2] On the other hand, financial capital, transnational corporations, and domestic private sectors are reterritorializing spaces with abundant natural resources through megaprojects such as dams,[3] large-scale strip mining,[4] and monoculture plantations.[5] These corporate interests, aided by neoliberal economic polices and laws, have generated the growing land grabbing problem in many countries in the global South.[6]

In this chapter we seek to provide a framework for understanding the increasing adoption of agroecological farming and diversified farming systems by rural social movements. We first paint the changing rural context with broad strokes, then provide a theoretical framework for understanding how this has translated into an increased emphasis on agroecology in both the practice and the discourse of social movements as they seek greater autonomy and control over their territory and try to bring agroecology to scale. Finally, we illustrate this with examples from the Campesino a Campesino movement and from organizations belonging to the transnational peasant movement La Vía Campesina (LVC).

Context: Renewed Capital Flows into Rural Areas

In recent decades, neoliberal policies—characterized by deregulation, privatization, open markets, and free trade—have opened avenues for transnational financial capital and transnational corporations to invest in new and old enterprises all over the world. The collapses of the mortgage, dot-com, biotechnology, finance bank, and other speculative bubbles have helped usher in the first generalized world economic crisis of this century.[7] This has created a somewhat desperate search for new investment opportunities, pushing investors to increasingly look to the global South, especially focusing on rural natural resources. This is driving a new boom of export crops, agrofuels, mining, and industrial monoculture plantations.[8] Although transnational agribusinesses already had a major presence in Latin America, for example, since at least since the 1980s,[9] this new wave of investment is much larger owing to the bigger injection of crisis-driven capital. In most countries, both in the global North and the global South, domestic corporations are being partially or totally bought by transnational corporations, and finance banks or are being newly (re)capitalized by large loans so that they effectively become subsidiaries of large transnational lenders.[10]

The recent wave of investment and capitalization is putting agribusiness and other sectors that exploit rural resources in direct and growing conflict with the peasantry and other rural peoples,[11] where each side represents a different model of development and way of life. Peasant agriculture follows a pattern typically based on short, decentralized circuits of production and consumption, with strong links between food production and local and regional ecosystems and societies. Agribusiness, on the other hand, has a centralized pattern based on corporate producers of inputs, processors and trading companies, with production that is decontextualized and delinked from the specificities of local ecosystems and social relations.[12] In this system, production and consumption are delinked in both time and space, and operations act on a global scale with strategic alliances between input suppliers, processors, traders, supermarket chains, and finance banks to form agrifood complexes in what Phillip McMichael[13] and others call the corporate food system or regime and what Jan Dowe van der Ploeg calls food empires.[14]

Social movements composed of peasants and other rural peoples are actively defending spaces from, and contesting them with, these agribusinesses and other private sector actors and their allies in government. Because the private sector is typically transnational in nature, peasant social movements have increasing organized themselves into transnational alliances, the most important and largest example of which is LVC.[15] LVC is a global alliance of organizations of family farmers and peasant farmers, indigenous people, landless peasants and farm workers, rural women, and rural youth representing at least 200 million families worldwide.

Both agribusiness and rural social movements are attempting to reterritorialize spaces—that is, to reconfigure them to favor their own interests, whether those are maximum extraction of profits or are defending and building communities. A key aspect is that we are speaking not just of a battle over land per se, but also very much of a battle over ideas.

Theory: Agroecology, Disputed Territories, and Repeasantization

Definitions: Agroecology and Diversified Farming Systems

Wezel et al. have observed that the word *agroecology* is variously used to refer to a science, a movement and a practice.[16] In a book written by, and largely for, LVC, Machín Sosa et al. similarly note the following (translated from the Spanish):

> For many, agroecology is a science: the science that studies and attempts to explain the functioning of agroecosystems. For others, the word agroecology refers to the principles—not recipes—that guide the agronomic and productive practices that permit the production of food and fiber without agrochemicals. . . . For the social movements that make up La Via Campesina, the concept of agroecology goes much farther that just ecological-productive principles. In addition to these, LVC incorporates social, cultural and political principles and goals into its concept of agroecology.[17]

In the movements' position on "sustainable peasant agriculture," LVC argues that

> [w]e can find examples of sustainable peasant and family farm agriculture all over the planet, though the names we use vary greatly from one place to another, whether agroecology, organic farming, natural farming, low external input sustainable agriculture, or others. In La Via Campesina we do not want to say that one name is better than another, but rather we want to specify the key principles that we defend. Truly sustainable peasant agriculture comes from a combination of the recovery and revalorization of traditional peasant farming methods, and the innovation of new ecological practices. . . . We do not believe that the mere substitution of "bad" inputs for "good" ones, without touching the structure of monoculture, is sustainable. . . . The application of these principles in the complex and diverse realities of peasant agriculture requires the active appropriation of farming systems by peasants ourselves, using our local knowledge, ingenuity, and ability to innovate. We are talking about relatively small farms managed by peasant families and communities. Small farms permit the development of

functional biodiversity with diversified production and the integration of crops, trees and livestock. In this type of agriculture, there is less or no need for external inputs, as everything can be produced on the farm itself.[18]

Here we see references to what in this special issue are called diversified farming systems (DFSs) based on the integrated management of functional biodiversity. DFSs fall somewhere under agroecological principles and agroecological practices and are a key part of what Machín Sosa et al.[19] and Rosset et al.[20] call agroecological integration. Furthermore, Rosset et al.[21] and Holt-Gimenez[22] show clearly how the movement form of agroecology is key to bringing agroecological practices (including DFS) to scale (this will be examined in greater detail below).

Part of the broader definition of agroecology for LVC is to see it as a key pillar in, and inseparable from, the construction of "food sovereignty," defined as

the right of peoples to healthy and culturally appropriate food produced through ecologically sound and sustainable methods, and their right to define their own food and agriculture systems. It puts the aspirations and needs of those who produce, distribute and consume food at the heart of food systems and policies rather than the demands of markets and corporations. It defends the interests and inclusion of the next generation. It offers a strategy to resist and dismantle the current corporate trade and food regime, and directions for food, farming, pastoral and fisheries systems determined by local producers and users. Food sovereignty prioritizes local and national economies and markets and empowers peasant and family farmer–driven agriculture, artisanal fishing, pastoralist-led grazing, and food production, distribution and consumption based on environmental, social and economic sustainability. Food sovereignty promotes transparent trade that guarantees just incomes to all peoples as well as the rights of consumers to control their food and nutrition. It ensures that the rights to use and manage lands, territories, waters, seeds, livestock and biodiversity are in the hands of those of us who produce food. Food sovereignty implies new social relations free of oppression and inequality between men and women, peoples, racial groups, social and economic classes and generations.[23]

Social movements such as LVC are taking agroecology very seriously. One reason (more are explored hereafter) is that when land is acquired through struggle, it is often degraded land. And when peasants have used industrial farming practices, they have themselves incurred significant degradation. Faced with this reality, peasants are finding ways to manage or recover soils and agroecosystems that have been severely degraded by chemicals, machines, excessive mechanization, and the loss of functional biodiversity caused by the indiscriminate use of Green Revolution technologies.[24] Severe degradation means that even the ability to mask underlying causes with ever higher doses of chemical fertilizers and pesticides is limited,[25] and the cost of doing so is in any event becoming prohibitive, as prices of petroleum-derived farm inputs have soared in recent years.[26] This often leaves agroecology and DFS as the only alternatives open to small farmers.[27]

In this paper we have chosen to use the word agroecology in preference to DFS, simply because we believe it to be the broader, more inclusive term form for the following discussion.

Agroecology and Disputed Territories

The theoretical work of critical geographers in Brazil and elsewhere on contested territories helps us understand territorial conflicts such as those between peasants and agribusiness.[28] Fernandes,[29] for example, argues that social classes and relationships generate different territories and spaces that are reproduced under conditions of continual conflict; as a result, there are spaces of domination and spaces of resistance. Territorial disputes are carried out in all possible dimensions: economic, social, political, cultural, theoretical, and ideological. In the case of rural areas, this gives rise to disputes between grassroots social movements and agribusiness with its government allies over what he calls both material and immaterial territories.[30]

The dispute over material territories refers to the struggle to access, control, use and shape, or configure land and physical territory consisting of communities, infrastructure, soil, water, biodiversity, air, mountains, valleys, plains, rivers, and coasts. The opposing extreme outcomes of this kind of dispute might be viewed as a landscape consisting of a mosaic of diversified peasant farms intermingled with community managed forests on the one hand versus a region devoid of families, trees, or other biodiversity, dedicated to enormous export monoculture plantations based on hired labor rather than peasant families on the other.[31]

For Fernandes,[32] immaterial territory refers to the terrain of ideas, of theoretical constructs, and he posits that there are no material territories that are not associated with immaterial territories. Therefore the dispute over real and tangible territories and the resources they contain necessarily goes hand in hand with the dispute over immaterial territories or the space of ideology and ideas.[33] Contestation over immaterial territories is characterized by the formulation and defense of concepts, theories, paradigms, and explanations, all of which are used to convince others. In other words, the power to interpret and to determine the definition and content of concepts is itself a territory in dispute.[34]

Agribusiness and its ideological and financial support infrastructure in the World Bank, governments, finance banks, think tanks, and elite universities, as well as advertising agencies and media specialists, creates and puts forth a framing language of efficiency, productivity, economies of scale, trade liberalization, free markets, and the need to "feed the world" to build the consensus needed in society to gain control over territories and (re)configure them for the needs of industrial agriculture and profit-taking.[35]

Rural social movements respond in this discursive battle over immaterial territories with framing arguments[36] based on the benefits of family-based diversified agroecological farming in terms of feeding the world with healthy, local food; good stewardship of the rural environment; the preservation of cultural heritages and the peasant or family farm way of life; and resilience to climate change.[37] At the same time, they put forth a critique of agribusiness and industrial agriculture for producing unhealthy food and generating inequality, greenhouse gases, hunger, environmental devastation, GMO contamination, pesticide poisoning, and the destruction and loss of rural cultures and livelihoods. In this struggle to (re)configure the immaterial territory of ideas and ideology, they seek to (re)construct a consensus in society for the defense of peasant and indigenous material territories against corporate land grabbing, build support for land occupations by landless peasants, and change public policies toward food sovereignty based on agrarian reform, local markets, and ecological farming.[38]

Here it is important to note that agroecology is playing an increasingly central role for these social movements in both arenas of territorial dispute. In the discursive struggle, social movements contrast agroecological farming by peasants and family farmers with the destructive practices and unhealthy food produced by industrial agriculture and agribusiness. This becomes more difficult when agribusiness responds with organic, GMO-free, and other types of "labeling games,"[39] in turn forcing social movements to draw ever finer and more political distinctions between "true agroecology" and corporate "green washing" (see, for example, LVC 2011d).[40]

In the defense or conquest of material territory (through, for example, land occupations or via policy victories in favor of land redistribution), there is a growing tendency to promote agroecological farming as part of (re)configuring a space as a clearly peasant or family farm territory. This promotion is part of the reconfiguration of both material and the immaterial territory. For example, Martínez-Torres[41] has recently analyzed the case of the Landless Workers' Movement (MST) in Brazil, one of the most important and militant peasant organizations in the Americas and a leading member of LVC. In the past, the MST appealed to public opinion to back its occupations of the idle lands of absentee landlords based on the injustice of a few having more land than they could use while others went landless. But recent waves of transnational investment have capitalized Brazilian agribusiness, which in turn is turning once idle land into export, pulp, and agrofuel monocrop plantations of soy, sugar cane, *Eucalyptus*, and pine, with associated environmental degradation caused by excessive use of chemicals and heavy machines and the elimination of biodiversity. As idle lands dry up, the landless are left only with the option of occupying the "productive" lands of agribusiness. As a result, they have had to reframe their arguments as they seek the support of public opinion. Now they do so by contrasting the ecological and social wasteland of agribusiness plantations (green deserts) with a pastoral vision of agroecologically farmed peasant lands, conserving biodiversity, keeping families in the countryside, and producing healthy food for local markets (food sovereignty).

This example shows how social movements must promote and implement agroecology in a much more overtly politicized and ideological manner than do other actors in the sphere of alternative farming practices, such as nongovernmental organizations (NGOs), researchers, government agencies, and private companies. We say "more" overtly political and ideological because any technological choice brings political and ideological baggage with it. But that their use is politicized in no way means that the families who belong to these organizations and movements are not engaged in everyday practices of cultivation and harvest, nor that the organizations themselves are not involved in the complicated task of building processes to promote and support the transformation of productive practices. In promoting the transition from Green Revolution–style farming—in which families depend on input markets—to more autonomous agroecological farming, thus reconfiguring spaces as peasant territories, social movements engage in the process of repeasantization.

Repeasantization and Agroecology

Jan Dowe van der Ploeg has put forth a theoretical proposition about the peasantries of today. Rather than defining *peasant*, he chooses to define what he calls the peasant condition or the peasant principle, characterized by the constant struggle to build autonomy:

> Central to the peasant condition, then, is the struggle for autonomy that takes place in a context characterized by dependency relations, marginalization and deprivation. It aims at and materializes as the creation and development of a self-controlled and self-managed resource base, which in turn allows for those forms of co-production of man and living nature that interact with the market, allow for survival and for further prospects and feed back into and strengthen the resource base, improve the process of co-production, enlarge autonomy, and thus reduce dependency. . . . Finally, patterns of cooperation are present which regulate and strengthen these interrelations. (van der Ploeg 2008:23)[42]

Two characteristics of this definition stand out: (1) that peasants seek to engage in coproduction with nature in ways that strengthen their resource base (soil, biodiversity, etc.) and (2) the struggle for (relative) autonomy via the reduction of dependence in a world characterized by inequality and unequal exchange. According to van der Ploeg,[43] peasants may pursue agroecology to the extent that it permits them to strengthen their resource base and become more independent of input and credit markets (and thus indebtedness) while improving their condition. This use of agroecology to move along a continuum from dependency toward relative autonomy—from being the entrepreneurial farmers they in some cases had become toward being peasants again—is one axis of what he calls repeasantization.[44] Another axis of repeasantization is the conquest of land and territory from agribusiness and other large landowners, whether by land reform, land occupations, or other mechanisms.

The overall process of repeasantization is analogous to the (re)configuration of space as peasant territory, and agroecology can be, and increasingly is, a part of both.[45] When farmers undergo a transition from input-dependent farming to agroecology based on local resources, they are becoming "more peasant." Agroecological practices are similar to, and frequently based on, traditional peasant practices, so in this transition, repeasantization takes place. And in marking the difference between the ecological and social wasteland of agribusiness land, and ecological farming on land recovered by peasants, they are reconfiguring territories as peasant territories as they repeasantize them through agroecology.

Conversely, when peasants are drawn into greater dependence, use of Green Revolution technologies, market relations, and the debt cycle, this is one axis of depeasantization. Another axis of depeasantization is when land-grabbing corporations or states displace peasants from their land and territories and reconfigure these as territories for agribusiness or mining, tourism, or infrastructure development.

Along similar lines, Paola Sesia[46] found in her research in Oaxaca that when market conditions and fluctuations generate situations in which the value of income from the sale of cash crops and family labor drops relative to the value of production for subsistence and family self-provisioning, many peasant families shift the mix of land devoted to coffee versus subsistence crops. She coincides with van der Ploeg in judging that repeasantization is based on reducing external dependence, part of an overall process that Barkin et al. call a "new communitarian rurality" because it also includes a renewed emphasis on cooperation and strengthening rural communities.[47]

The twin processes of re- and depeasantization move back and forth over time as circumstances change.[48] During the heyday of the Green Revolution in the 1960s and '70s, the peasantry was incorporated en masse into the system, many of them becoming entrepreneurial family farmers.[49] But today, faced with growing debt and market-driven exclusion, the net tendency is the reverse, according to van der Ploeg.[50] He presents convincing data to show that even those farmers in Northern countries most integrated into the market are in fact taking (at least small) steps toward becoming "more peasant" through relatively greater autonomy from banks, input and machinery suppliers, and corporate middlemen. Some even become organic farmers. In other words, there is net retreat from some or many elements of the market.[51]

Numerical repeasantization can be seen in the end of the long-term decline in the number of farms and the number of people dedicated to agriculture, and even a visible uptick, in countries such as the United States[52] and Brazil.[53] In fact, one observes an increase in both the number of small family-size farms and an increase in large-scale commercial farms (agribusiness), with a decline in the numbers of intermediate-size classes. In other words, in today's world, we are essentially losing the middle (entrepreneurial farmers) to both repeasantization and depeasantization. And we are increasingly witness to a global territorial conflict, material and immaterial, between agribusiness and peasant resistance.[54] In this context we see the post-1992 emergence of LVC as arguably the world's largest transnational social movement,[55] promoting agroecologically diversified farming as a key element in resistance, repeasantization, and the reconfiguration of territories.[56] (Of course, this somewhat stylized dichotomy should in no way be taken to imply that there no longer are a very significant number of medium-scale farmers who still maintain both agribusiness and peasant identities.)

Process: Taking Agroecology to Scale

A persistent debate in the literature on agroecological farming, and on the effect of agricultural research in general, has been the question of scaling out (broad adoption over wide areas and by many farmers) and scaling up (institutionalizing supportive policies for alternatives) successful experiences.[57] This is paralleled in the literature concerning the effectiveness and appropriateness of conventional agricultural research and extension systems for reaching peasant families in general[58] and, more specifically, for promoting agroecology rather than the Green Revolution.[59]

Whereas conventional top-down agricultural research and extension has shown a negligible ability to develop and achieve broad adoption of the practices of agroecological diversified farming, social movements and socially dynamizing methodologies appear to have significant advantages.[60] Social movements incorporate large numbers of people—in this case large numbers of peasant families—in self-organized processes that can dramatically increase the rate of innovation and the spread and adoption of innovations.

The fact that agroecology is based on applying principles in ways that depend on local realities means that the local knowledge and ingenuity of farmers must necessarily take a front seat: Farmers cannot blindly follow pesticide and fertilizer recommendations prescribed on a recipe basis by extension agents or salesmen. Methods in which the extensionist or agronomist is the key actor and farmers are passive are, in the best possible cases, still limited to the number of peasant families who can be effectively attended to by each technician, because there is little or no self-catalyzed dynamic among farmers themselves to carry innovations well beyond the last technician. Thus these cases are finally limited by the budget—that is, by how many technicians can be hired. Many project-based rural development NGOs face a similar problem. When the project funding cycle comes to an end, virtually everything reverts to the preproject state, with little lasting effect.[61]

The most successful methodology for promoting farmer innovation and horizontal sharing and learning is the *campesino-a-campesino* (farmer-to-farmer, or peasant-to-peasant) methodology (CAC). Although farmers innovating and sharing goes back to time immemorial, the more contemporary and more formalized version was developed locally in Guatemala and spread through Mesoamerica beginning in the 1970s.[62] CAC is a Freirian horizontal communication methodology[63] or social process methodology based on farmer-promoters who have innovated new solutions to problems common among many farmers or who have recovered/rediscovered older traditional solutions and who use popular education methodology to share them with their peers, using their own farms as classrooms. A fundamental tenet of CAC is that farmers are more likely to believe and emulate a fellow farmer who is successfully using a given alternative on his or her own farm than they are to take the word of an agronomist of possibly urban extraction. This is even more the case when they can visit the farm and see the alternative functioning with their own eyes. In Cuba, for example, farmers say that "seeing is believing."[64]

Whereas conventional extension can be demobilizing for farmers, CAC is mobilizing as they become the protagonists in the process of generating and sharing technologies. CAC is a participatory method based on local peasant needs, culture, and environmental conditions that unleashes knowledge, enthusiasm, and protagonism as a way of discovering, recognizing, taking advantage of, and socializing the rich pool of family and community agricultural knowledge that is linked to their specific historical conditions and identities. In conventional extension, the objective of technical experts all too often has been to replace peasant knowledge with purchased chemical inputs, seeds, and machinery in a top-down process wherein education is more like domestication.[65] Eric Holt-Giménez has extensively documented the Mesoamerican CAC social movement experiences with CAC as a methodology for promoting agroecological farming practices, which he calls peasant pedagogy.[66]

Agroecology in La Vía Campesina

Cuba is where the CAC social methodology achieved its greatest effect, when the National Association of Small Farmers (ANAP), a member of LVC, adopted it along with a conscious and explicit goal of building a grassroots movement for agroecology inside the national organization.[67] In fewer than 10 years, the process of transforming systems of production into agroecological integrated and diversified farming systems had spread to more than one-third of all peasant families in Cuba, a remarkable rate of growth. During the same period when peasants became agroecological, the total contribution of peasant production to national production jumped dramatically, with other advantages in reduced use of farm chemical and purchased off-farm inputs (more autonomy) and greater resiliency to climate shocks.[68]

In southern India, a grassroots agroecological movement has grown rapidly that cuts across the bases of some member organizations of LVC, which is now facilitating exchanges with farmers from other countries across Asia.[69] The Zero Budget Natural Farming (ZNBF) movement is partially a response to the acute indebtedness in which many Indian peasants find themselves. The debt is of course from the high production costs of conventional Green Revolution–style farming, as translated into budgets for bank credit, and is the underlying cause of the well-known epidemic of farmer suicides in that country.[70] The idea of ZBNF is to use agroecological practices based totally on resources found on the farm, such as mulching, organic amendments, and diversification, to break the stranglehold of debt on farming households by purchasing zero off-farm inputs. According to LVC farmer leaders in south Asia, several hundred thousand peasant families have joined the movement.

In Zimbabwe, the Zimbabwe Organic Smallholder Farmer's Forum (ZIM-SOFF) is a recent member of LVC. The current president of ZIMSOFF is an agroecology promoter from Shashe in the Masvingo agrarian reform cluster. Shashe is an intentional community created by formerly landless peasants who engaged in a two-year land occupation before being awarded the land by the government's oft-maligned but basically misunderstood land reform program.[71] A cluster of families in the community are committed to practicing and promoting diversified agroecological farming. Through ZIMSOFF, they are having a national effect; through LVC, an international effect. When Shashe hosted a regional agroecology encounter in 2011 of LVC organizations from southern, central, and eastern Africa, the participants noted in their final declaration that

[w]e have been meeting at the Shashe Endogenous Development Training Centre in Masvingo Province, Zimbabwe to plan how to promote agroecology in our Region (Southern, Eastern & Central Africa). Here we have been privileged to witness first hand the successful combination of agrarian reform with organic farming and agroecology carried out by local smallholder farming families. In what were once large cattle ranches owned by three large farmers who owned 800 head of cattle and produced no grain or anything else, there are now more than 365 small holder peasant farming

families with more than 3,400 head of cattle, who also produce a yearly average of 1 to 2 tonnes of grain per family plus vegetables and other products, in many cases using agroecological methods and local peasant seeds. This experience strengthens our commitment to and belief in agroecology and agrarian reform as fundamental pillars in the construction of Food Sovereignty.[72]

They also decided to establish an international agroecology training school in Shashe to train peasant activists from LVC organizations in the region as agroecology promoters using the CAC method.

These are examples of what is a burgeoning agroecology process in LVC and its member organizations. Part of the process (described in this section on the basis of participant-observation by the authors) has consisted of holding regional and continental "Encounters of Agroecology Trainers."[73] These have been held in the Americas (2009 and 2011), Asia (2010), southern, central, and eastern Africa (2011), west Africa (2011), and Europe (2012), in addition to a first Global Encounter of Peasant Seed Farmers, held in Bali (2011). The declarations from some of these meetings illustrate the growing discursive place of agroecology in LVC.[74]

This process has served several important purposes so far. One has been to help LVC itself collectively realize the sheer quantity of ongoing experiences with agroecology and sustainable peasant agriculture currently being gained inside member organizations at the national and regional levels. The vast majority of organizations either already have some sort of internal program to promote agroecology or are currently discussing how to create one. Another purpose these encounters are serving is to elaborate detailed work plans to support these ongoing experiences and to link them with one another in a horizontal exchange and learning process. It also has been a space in which to collectively construct a shared vision of what agroecology means to LVC—that is, the philosophy, political content, and rationale that links organizations in this work.

As participant-observers in this process, it has been possible for us to identify a number of clear, shared rationales for the transition to agroecological farming and local seeds among the peasant and farm families that belong to the member organizations of LVC and among the organizations themselves. Above all, the shared vision that is emerging sees agroecology as a socially activating tool for the transformation of rural realities through collective action and as a key building block in the construction of food sovereignty.

Another central rationale is based on the relationship between peasants and nature. We can think of LVC as a space of encounter among different cultures, whether East and West, North and South, landed and landless, or Hindu, Muslim, Buddhist, animist, Christian, and atheist. Among these exchanges, one that has profoundly affected attitudes toward nature has been the encounter between the indigenous and nonindigenous worlds inside

LVC. The nonindigenous organizations have learned from indigenous people about the importance of thinking in terms of territory rather than just land and about the imperative to live in harmony and to take good care of the mother Earth. The indigenous people inside LVC were the first to sound the alert about climate change, now a priority issue, and their influence is felt strongly in the growing rejection of industrial farming practices that "damage the mother Earth" and in the consequent embracing of agroecology. A closely related rationale is the need to use agroecological practices to restore degraded soils. Here we see both the coproduction with nature and the construction of peasant/indigenous territories, both material and immaterial, wherein the mother Earth is defended rather than injured.

Van der Ploeg's emphasis on the struggle for autonomy is echoed time and again as organizations and families stress the advantages offered by agroecology in terms of building relative autonomy from input and credit markets (by using on-farm resources rather than purchased inputs), from food markets (greater self-provisioning through mixing subsistence and market crops), and even by redirecting outputs toward local and ecological or organic markets where farmers have more influence and control (and thus greater autonomy from global markets). Not only are these clear steps toward repeasantization, but they are also increasingly part of creating peasant territories.[75]

Driven by these motivations and rationales, LVC and its members have in recent years set up CAC agroecology programs in many countries in the Americas, Asia, and Africa, have produced agroecology training materials, and have sponsored seed fairs and seed saving and exchange networks in a number of regions and countries. One enormously successful national program (Cuba) has been developed under which farmers breed and select their own varieties, with smaller-scale programs in other countries. LVC has not only organized national and international exchanges so that farmers can see for themselves ("seeing is believing") and learn from the best cases, but it has also recently begun to identify, self-study, document, analyze, and horizontally share the lessons of the best cases of farmer-led climate-robust agroecology and food sovereignty experience. LVC has opened regional agroecology training schools and peasant universities in Venezuela, Paraguay, Brazil, Nicaragua, Indonesia, and India, with others on the drawing boards for Mozambique, Zimbabwe, Niger, and Mali (in addition to dozens of national- and subnational-level schools).

LVC has also created political leadership training academies in many countries and several regions to prepare peasant leaders to pressure governments for needed policy changes. It has taken steps to engage in an ongoing, critical but constructive way with "peasant-friendly" policymakers in local, provincial, and national governments in diverse countries, and with select programs and functionaries in international agencies, to promote the implementation of alternative, more agroecology-, climate-, farmer-, and consumer-friendly public policies. In countries with less friendly governments and policymakers, member organizations have organized massive mobilization political pressure to encourage serious consideration of alternatives.

A number of LVC member organizations in the Americas, Asia, and Africa have peasant-owned and peasant-run cooperative seed enterprises that multiply and distribute local seed varieties, and some of these and other member organizations have pressured and cooperated with other actors and local governments to open farmers markets for ecologically produced food and have experimented with other systems of direct sale to consumers.

LVC believes that it now has a sufficient number of pioneering experiences under way—particularly in training—to be able to effectively synergize them to achieve a significantly enhanced multiplier effect and scaling out and scaling up of agroecology by integrating and networking them into regional systems for exchanges of experiences and lessons, mutual support, and coordinated lobby and pressure work to push governments to implement policies more favorable to peasant farming, agroecology, and food sovereignty (and, by extension, repeasantization and the construction of peasant territories).

In the continual dispute over the immaterial territory of agroecology, the latest arena is that of solutions to climate change. LVC has been actively denouncing so-called false solutions to climate change—agrofuels, GMOs, carbon markets, and REDD and REDD+[76]—and has more recently sounded the alarm about the possible cooption of agroecology by the World Bank and others via the creation of soil carbon markets using slogans such as "Our Carbon Is Not for Sale" and "Agroecology Is Not for Sale" (LVC 2011d).[77]

Conclusions

The theoretical frameworks of disputed territories and repeasantization help us understand the empirical phenomenon of the growing interest, practice, and discourse of agroecology among rural social movements, especially LVC, in the context of growing corporate land grabbing and rising input costs. For peasants and family farmers and their movements, agroecology helps build autonomy from unfavorable markets and restore degraded soils, and social processes and movements help bring these alternatives to scale. Finally, this (re)invention of peasant practices is part of the (re)configuration of contested material and immaterial spaces as peasant territories in the process of repeasantization.

Notes

1. M. A. Altieri and V. M. Toledo, "The Agroecological Revolution in Latin America: Rescuing Nature, Ensuring Food Sovereignty, and Empowering Peasants," *Journal of Peasant Studies* 38, no. 3 (2011): 567–612; La Vía Campesina (LVC); "Sustainable Peasant and

Family Farm Agriculture Can Feed the World," Vía Campesina Views no. 6 (2010), http://viacampesina.org/downloads/pdf/en/paper6-EN-FINAL.pdf; P. M. Rosset, B. Machín Sosa, A. M. Roque Jaime, and D. R. Ávila Lozano, "The Campesino-to-Campesino Agroecology Movement of ANAP in Cuba: Social Process Methodology in the Construction of Sustainable Peasant Agriculture and Food Sovereignty," *Journal of Peasant Studies* 38, no. 1 (2001): 161–191; A. Wezel, S. Bellon, T. Doré, C. Francis, D. Vallod, and C. David. "Agroecology as a Science, a Movement and a Practice: A Review," *Agron. Sustain. Dev.* 29 (2009): 503–515.

2. B. M. Fernandes, "Sobre a tipologia de territórios," in *Territórios e territorialidades: Teoria, processos e conflitos*, eds. M. A. Saquet and E. S. Sposito (São Paulo, Brazil: Expressão Popular, 2009); J. D. Van Der Ploeg, *The New Peasantries: Struggles for Autonomy and Sustainability in an Era of Empire and Globalization* (London: Earthscan, 2008); J. D. van der Ploeg, "The Peasantries of the Twenty-First Century: The Commoditization Debate Revisited," *Journal of Peasant Studies* 37, no. 1 (2010): 1–30.

3. B. M. Fernandes, "Sobre a tipologia de territórios," in *Territórios e territorialidades: Teoria, processos e conflitos*, M. A. Saquet and E. S. Sposito (São Paulo, Brazil: Expressão Popular, 2009): 197–215; World Commission on Dams (WCD), *Dams and Development* (London: Earthscan, 2000).

4. A. Bebbington, ed., *Minería, movimientos sociales y respuestas campesinas: Una ecología política de transformaciones territoriales* (Lima: Instituto de Estudios Peruanos, 2007); E. Holt-Giménez, "Land—Gold—Reform: The Territorial Restructuring of Guatemala's Highlands," Institute for Food and Development Policy, Development Report no. 16 (2007), www.foodfirst.org/fr/node/1770

5. M. S. Emanuelli, J. Jonsén, and S. M. Suárez, *Red Sugar, Green Deserts: Latin American Report on Monocultures and Violations of the Human Rights to Adequate Food and Housing, to Water, to Land and to Territory* (Sweden and El Salvador: FIAN International, 2009).

6. Genetic Resources Action International (GRAIN), *The New Farm Owners: Corporate Investors Lead the Rush for Control over Overseas Farmland* (Barcelona: Genetic Resources Action International, 2009); D. Hall, "Land Grabs, Land Control, and Southeast Asian Crop Booms," *Journal of Peasant Studies* 38, no. 4 (2011): 837–857; A. Zoomers, "Globalisation and the Foreignisation of Space: Seven Processes Driving the Current Global Land Grab," *Journal of Peasant Studies* 37, no. 2 (2010): 429–447; P. M. Rosset, "Food Sovereignty and Alternative Paradigms to Confront Land Grabbing and the Food and Climate Crises," *Development* 54, no. 1 (2011): 21–30.

7. J. P. Stédile, "La ofensiva de las empresas transnacionales sobre la agricultura," *Rebelion* (2008), www.rebelion.org/noticia.php?id=77961; R. W. Cox, "Transnational Capital, the U.S. State and Latin American Trade Agreements," *Third World Quarterly* 29, no. 8 (2008): 1527–1544; P. M. Rosset, "La Guerra por la tierra y el territorio," in *Primer Coloquio Internacional In Memoriam Andrés Aubry: Planeta tierra: movimientos antisistémicos*, ed. Centro Indigena de Capacitacion Integral Universidad de la Tierra (CIDECI–UNITIERRA) (San Cristobal de las Casas, Chiapas, Mexico: CIDECI–UNITIERRA Ediciones, 2009), 159–175.

8. D. Humphreys, "Life Protective or Carcinogenic Challenge? Global Forests Governance under Advanced Capitalism," *Global Environmental Politics* 3, no. 2 (2003): 40–55; K. Barney, *Power, Progress and Impoverishment: Plantations, Hydropower, Ecological Change and Community Transformation in Hinboun District, Lao PDR*, York Center for Asian Research Papers no. 1 (Toronto, Canada: Political Ecologies Series and (Re)making

Governance Series, York Center for Asian Research, 2007); J. P. Stédile, "La ofensiva de las empresas transnacionales sobre la agricultura"; P. M. Rosset, "La Guerra por la tierra y el territorio"; P. McMichael, "Agrofuels in the Food Regime," *Journal of Peasant Studies* 37, no. 4 (2010): 609–629.

9. R. Burbach and P. Flynn, *Agribusiness in the Americas* (New York: Monthly Review Press, 1980); M. Teubal, "Internationalization of Capital and Agroindustrial Complexes: Their Impact on Latin American Agriculture," *Latin American Perspectives* 14, no. 3 (1987): 316–364; T. Marsden and S. Whatmore, "Finance Capital and Food System Restructuring: National Incorporation of Global Dynamics," in *The Global Restructuring of Agro-Food Systems*, ed. P. McMichael (Ithaca, NY: Cornell University Press, 1994), 107–128.

10. J. P. Stédile, "La ofensiva de las empresas transnacionales sobre la agricultura"; P. McMichael, "A Food Regime Genealogy," *Journal of Peasant Studies* 36, no. 1 (2009): 139–169; L. Bruszt and R. Holzhacker, eds., *The Transnationalization of Economies, States, and Civil Societies* (Berlin: Springer, 2009).

11. B. M. Fernandes, "Questão Agraria: Conflictualidade e desenvolvimento territorial," in *Luta pela Terra, Reforma Agraria e Gestão de Conflitos no Brasil*, ed. A. M. Buainain (Campinas, Brazil: Editora Unicamp, 2008), 173–224; B. M. Fernandes, "Entrando nos territórios do territoório," in *Campesinato e territórios em disputas*, eds. E. T. Paulino and J. E. Fabrini (São Paulo, Brazil: Expressaão Popular, 2008), 273–301; J. F. Gerber, J. F., S. Veuthey, and J. Martínez-Alier, "Linking Political Ecology with Ecological Economics in Tree Plantation Conflicts in Cameroon and Ecuador," *Ecological Economics* 68, no. 12 (2009): 2885–2889.

12. J. D. Van Der Ploeg, *The New Peasantries: Struggles for Autonomy and Sustainability in an Era of Empire and Globalization*.

13. P. McMichael, "A Food Regime Genealogy"; P. McMichael, "Agrofuels in the Food Regime."

14. J. D. Van Der Ploeg, *The New Peasantries: Struggles for Autonomy and Sustainability in an Era of Empire and Globalization*; J. D. van der Ploeg, "The Peasantries of the Twenty-First Century: The Commoditization Debate Revisited."

15. A. A. Desmarais, *LVC: Globalization and the Power of Peasants* (Halifax, Canada: Fernwood Publishing, 2007); M. E. Martinez-Torres and P. M. Rosset, "La Vía Campesina: Transnationalizing Peasant Struggle and Hope," in *Latin American Social Movements in the Twenty-First Century: Resistance, Power, and Democracy*, eds. R. Stahler-Sholk, H. E. Vanden, and G. D. Kuecker (Lanham, MD: Rowman and Littlefield, 2008): 307–322; M. E. Martinez-Torres and P. M. Rosset, "La Vía Campesina: The Birth and Evolution of a Transnational Social Movement," *Journal of Peasant Studies* 37, no. 1 (2010): 149–175.

16. A. Wezel, S. Bellon, T. Doré, C. Francis, D. Vallod, and C. David, "Agroecology as a Science, a Movement and a Practice: A Review," *Agron. Sustain. Dev.* 29 (2009): 503–515.

17. B. Machín Sosa, A. M. Roque Jaime, D. R. Ávila Lozano, and P. M. Rosset, *Revolución agroecológica: El movimiento de campesino a campesino de la ANAP en Cuba. Cuando el campesino ve, hace fe* (Havana, Cuba: ANAP and La Vía Campesina, 2010), 16. www.viacampesina.org/downloads/pdf/sp/2010-04-14-rev-agro.pdf

18. La Vía Campesina (LVC), "Sustainable Peasant and Family Farm Agriculture Can Feed the World," *Vía Campesina Views* no. 6 (2010): 2–3. http://viacampesina.org/downloads/pdf/en/paper6-EN-FINAL.pdf

19. B. Machín Sosa et al., *Revolución agroecológica: el movimiento de campesino a campesino de la ANAP en Cuba*, 16.

20. P. M. Rosset, B. Machín Sosa, A. M. Roque Jaime, and D. R. Ávila Lozano, "The Campesino-to-Campesino Agroecology Movement of ANAP in Cuba: Social Process Methodology in the Construction of Sustainable Peasant Agriculture and Food Sovereignty," *Journal of Peasant Studies* 38, no. 1 (2011): 161–191.

21. P. M. Rosset, "The Campesino-to-Campesino Agroecology Movement of ANAP in Cuba: Social Process Methodology in the Construction of Sustainable Peasant Agriculture and Food Sovereignty."

22. E. Holt-Giménez, *Campesino a Campesino: Voices from Latin America's Farmer to Farmer Movement for Sustainable Agriculture* (Oakland, CA: Food First Books, 2006).

23. "Food Sovereignty." www.grassrootsonline.org/publications/multimedia/slideshows/food-sovereignty

24. R. Lal, "Soil Degradation as a Reason for Inadequate Human Nutrition," *Food Security* 1 (2009): 45–57.

25. P. P. Marenya and C. B. Barrett, "State-Conditional Fertilizer Yield Response on Western Kenyan Farms," *American Journal of Agricultural Economics* 91 (2009): 91–106.

26. Economic Research Service, U.S. Department of Agriculture, "Farm Income and Costs: 2011 Farm Sector Income Forecast" (August 31, 2011). www.ers.usda.gov/briefing/farmincome/nationalestimates.htm

27. La Vía Campesina (LVC), "Sustainable Peasant and Family Farm Agriculture Can Feed the World."

28. B. M. Fernandes, C. A. Welch, and E. C. Gonçalves, "Agrofuel Policies in Brazil: Paradigmatic and Territorial Disputes," *Journal of Peasant Studies* 37, no. 4 (2010): 793–819; Fernandes, "Sobre a tipologia de territórios: Fernandes"; "Questão Agraria: Conflictualidade e desenvolvimento"; Fernandes, "Entrando nos territórios do territoório"; A. Escobar, "Development, Violence and the New Imperial Order," *Development* 47, no. 1 (2004): 15–21.

29. Fernandes, "Questão Agraria: Conflictualidade e desenvolvimento"; Fernandes, "Entrando nos territórios do territoório."

30. Fernandes, "Sobre a tipologia de territórios."

31. I. J. Perfecto, J. Vandermeer, and A. Wright, *Nature's Matrix: Linking Agriculture, Conservation and Food Sovereignty* (London, UK: Earthscan, 2009).

32. Fernandes, "Sobre a tipologia de territórios."

33. Fernandes, "Sobre a tipologia de territórios"; K. R. Bezner, "The Land Is Changing. Contested Agricultural Narratives in Northern Malawi," in *Contested Development: Critical Struggle for Social Change*, ed. P. McMichael (New York: Routledge, 2007): 98–115; *Contested Development: Critical Struggle for Social Change*, ed. P. McMichael (New York: Routledge, 2007).

34. Fernandes, "Sobre a tipologia de territórios."

35. M. C. Nisbet and M. Huge, "Where Do Science Debates Come From? Understanding Attention Cycles and Framing," in *The Public, the Media and Agricultural Biotechnology*, eds. D. Brossard, J. Shanahan, and T. C. Nesbitt (Wallingford, UK: CABI, 2007).

36. See R. D. Benford and D. A. Snow, "Framing Processes and Social Movements: An Overview and Assessment," *Annual Review of Sociology* 26 (2000): 611–639.

37. See S. M. Borras, M. Edelman, and C. Kay, "Transnational Agrarian Movements: Origins and Politics, Campaigns and Impact," *Journal of Agrarian Change* 8, no. 23 (2008): 169–204; La Vía Campesina (LVC), "Small Scale Sustainable Farmers Are Cooling Down

the Earth," *Vía Campesina Views* no. 5 (2009): 24, http://viacampesina.net/downloads/PAPER5/EN/paper5-EN.pdf; La Vía Campesina (LVC); "Sustainable Peasant and Family Farm Agriculture Can Feed the World"; M. E. Martinez-Torres and P. M. Rosset, "La Vía Campesina: The Birth and Evolution of a Transnational Social Movement," *Journal of Peasant Studies* 37, no. 1 (2010): 149–175; A. Starr, M. E. Martínez-Torres, and P. M. Rosset, "Participatory Democracy in Action: Practices of the Zapatistas and the Movimento Sem Terra," *Latin American Perspectives* 38 (2011): 102–119.

38. Desmarais, *LVC: Globalization and the Power of Peasants*; M. E. Martinez-Torres and P. M. Rosset, "La Vía Campesina: The Birth and Evolution of a Transnational Social Movement"; M. E. Martinez-Torres, "*Territorios disputados: Tierra, agroecologia y recampesinización. Movimientos sociales rurales en Latinoamerica y agronegocio,*" paper presented at the 2012 Conference of the Latin American Studies Association, San Francisco, California, May 23–26, 2012, http://lasa.international.pitt.edu/members/congress-papers/lasa2012/files/4305.pdf

39. M. E. Martinez-Torres, *Organic Coffee: Sustainable Development by Mayan Farmers* (Athens: Ohio University Press, 2006).

40. La Vía Campesina (LVC), "LVC: Call to Durban" (2011). http://viacampesina.org/en/index.php?option=com_content&view=article&id=1109:la-via-campesina-call-to-durban&catid=48:-climate-change-and-agrofuels&Itemid=75

41. M. E. Martinez-Torres, "*Territorios disputados: Tierra, agroecologia y recampesinización*"; M. E. Martinez-Torres, unpublished manuscript, *Disputas en la Construcción de Territorios Campesinos: Tierra, Agroecologia y Mercado.*

42. J. D. Van Der Ploeg, *The New Peasantries: Struggles for Autonomy and Sustainability in an Era of Empire and Globalization,* 23.

43. J. D. van der Ploeg, "The Peasantries of the Twenty-First Century: The Commoditization Debate Revisited."

44. J. D. van der Ploeg, *The New Peasantries. Struggles for Autonomy and Sustainability in an Era of Empire and Globalization.*

45. M. E. Martinez-Torres, "*Territorios disputados: tierra, agroecologia y recampesinización*"; M. E. Martinez-Torres, unpublished manuscript, *Disputas en la Construcción de Territorios Campesinos: Tierra, Agroecologia y Mercado.*

46. P. Sesia, "Repeasantization and Decommodification of Indigenous Agriculture: Coffee, Corn and Food Security in Oaxaca," in *The Social Relation of Mexican Commodities: Power, Production and Place,* eds. Casey Walsh, Elizabeth Emma Ferry, Gabriela Soto Laveaga, Paola Seisa, and Sara Hill San Diego (University of California: Center for US–Mexican Studies, 2003), 81–126.

47. D. M. Barkin, E. Fuente, and M. Rosas, "*Tradición e innovación: Aportaciones campesinas a la orientación de la innovación tecnológica para forjar sustentabilidad.*" *Trayectorias* 11, no. 29 (2009): 40.

48. J. D. Van Der Ploeg, *The New Peasantries: Struggles for Autonomy and Sustainability in an Era of Empire and Globalization.*

49. Alain de Janvry, *The Agrarian Question and Reformism in Latin America* (Baltimore: John Hopkins University Press, 1981).

50. J. D. Van Der Ploeg, *The New Peasantries: Struggles for Autonomy and Sustainability in an Era of Empire and Globalization;* J. D. van der Ploeg, "The Peasantries of the Twenty-First Century: The Commoditization Debate Revisited."

51. C. Muñoz, *"La reinvención de la comunidad: cambio social y estrategias de adaptación en el México rural: Un caso de estudio,"* in *¿Ruralidad sin agricultura? Perspectivas multidisciplinarias de una realidad fragmentada,* eds. K. Appendini and G. Torres (Mexico City: El Colegio de México, Centro de Estudios Económicos, 2008).

52. U.S. Census Bureau, Section 17, Agriculture, "Statistical Abstract of the United States 2010." www.census.gov/prod/2009pubs/10statab/agricult.pdf

53. Ministério do Desenvolvimento Agrário, *Agricultura familiar no Brasil e o Censo Agropecuário 2006* (Brasilia, Brazil: Ministério do Desenvolvimento Agrário, 2009).

54. J. D. van der Ploeg, "The Peasantries of the Twenty-First Century: The Commoditization Debate Revisited"; M. E. Martinez-Torres, unpublished manuscript, *Disputas en la Construcción de Territorios Campesinos: Tierra, Agroecologia y Mercado.*

55. Desmarais, *LVC: Globalization and the Power of Peasants*; M. E. Martinez-Torres and P. M. Rosset, "La Vía Campesina: The Birth and Evolution of a Transnational Social Movement."

56. E. Guzmán Sevilla and J. M. Alier, "New Rural Social Movements and Agroecology," in *Handbook of Rural Studies,* eds. P. Cloke, T. Marsden, and P. Mooney (London: Sage, 2006); E. Guzmán Sevilla, E., *De la Sociología Rural a la Agroecología* (Barcelona: Ediciones, 2006), 468–475.

57. J. M. Von Der Weid, *Scaling Up, and Scaling Further Up: An Ongoing Experience of Participatory Development in Brazil* (São Paulo: Brazil Assessoria e Serviços a Projetos em Agricultura Alternativa, AS–PTA, 2000), www.fao.org/docs/eims/upload/215152/AS-PTA.pdf; E. Holt-Giménez, "Scaling-Up Sustainable Agriculture," *Low External Input Sustainable Agriculture* 3, no. 3 (2001): 27–29; D. Pachicho and S. Fujisaka, eds., *Scaling Up and Out: Achieving Widespread Impact through Agricultural Research* (Cali, Colombia: Centro Internacional de Agricultura Tropical, 2004); M. A. Altieri and C. Nicholls, "Scaling Up Agroecological Approaches for Food Sovereignty in Latin America," *Development* 51, no. 4 (2008): 472–480; Rosset et al., "The Campesino-to-Campesino Agroecology Movement of ANAP in Cuba: Social Process Methodology in the Construction of Sustainable Peasant Agriculture and Food Sovereignty."

58. P. Freire, *Extension or Communication?* (New York: McGraw, 1973).

59. See R. Chambers, "Farmer-First: A Practical Paradigm for the Third Agriculture," in *Agroecology and Small Farm Development,* eds. M. A. Altieri and S. B. Hecht (Ann Arbor, MI: CRC Press, 1990): 237–244; R. Chambers, *Challenging the Professions: Frontiers for Rural Development* (London, UK: Intermediate Technology Publications, 1990); E. Holt-Giménez, *Campesino a Campesino: Voices from Latin America's Farmer to Farmer Movement for Sustainable Agriculture*; Rosset et al., "The Campesino-to-Campesino Agroecology Movement of ANAP in Cuba: Social Process Methodology in the Construction of Sustainable Peasant Agriculture and Food Sovereignty."

60. Rosset et al., "The Campesino-to-Campesino Agroecology Movement of ANAP in Cuba: Social Process Methodology in the Construction of Sustainable Peasant Agriculture and Food Sovereignty."

61. Ibid.

62. E. Holt-Giménez, *Campesino a Campesino: Voices from Latin America's Farmer to Farmer Movement for Sustainable Agriculture.*

63. P. Freire, *Pedagogy of the Oppressed* (New York: Seabury Press, 1970).

64. Rosset et al., "The Campesino-to-Campesino Agroecology Movement of ANAP in Cuba: Social Process Methodology in the Construction of Sustainable Peasant Agriculture and Food Sovereignty."

65. P. Freire, *Extension or Communication?*; Rosset et Al., "The Campesino-to-Campesino Agroecology Movement of ANAP in Cuba: Social Process Methodology in the Construction of Sustainable Peasant Agriculture and Food Sovereignty."

66. E. Holt-Giménez, *Campesino a Campesino: Voices from Latin America's Farmer to Farmer Movement for Sustainable Agriculture.*

67. B. Machín Sosa et al., *Revolución agroecológica: el movimiento de campesino a campesino de la ANAP en Cuba*; Rosset et al., "The Campesino-to-Campesino Agroecology Movement of ANAP in Cuba: Social Process Methodology in the Construction of Sustainable Peasant Agriculture and Food Sovereignty."

68. Ibid.; M. A. Altieri and V. M. Toledo, "The Agroecological Revolution in Latin America: Rescuing Nature, Ensuring Food Sovereignty, and Empowering Peasants."

69. Palekar, S. *The Philosophy of Spiritual Farming: Zero Budget Natural Farming*, rev. 4th ed. (Amravati, Maharashtra, India: Zero Budget Natural Farming Research, Development & Extendion Movement, n.d.); R. Y. Babu, *Action Research Report on Subhash Palekar Zero Budget Natural Farming* (Mysore, India: Administrative Training Institute, 2008).

70. B. B. Mohanty, "We Are Like the Living Dead: Farmer Suicide in Maharashtra, Western India," *Journal of Peasant Studies* 32, no. 2 (2005): 243–276.

71. For excellent analysis of the agrarian reform in Zimbabwe, see I. Scoones, N. Marongwe, B. Mavedzenge, F. Murimbarimba, J. Mahenehene, and C. Sukume, *Zimbabwe's Land Reform: Myths and Realities* (Suffolk, UK: Boydell & Brewer, 2010); S. Moyo, "Three Decades of Agrarian Reform in Zimbabwe," *Journal of Peasant Studies* 38, no. 3 (2010): 493–531; L. Cliffe, J. Alexander, B. Cousins, and R. Gaidzanwa, "An Overview of Fast Track Land Reform in Zimbabwe," *Journal of Peasant Studies* 38, no. 5 (2011): 907–938.

72. La Vía Campesina (LVC), "1st Encounter of Agroecology Trainers in Africa Region 1 of LVC," Shashe Declaration, 2011. http://viacampesina.org/en/index.php/main-issues-mainmenu-27/agrarian-reform-mainmenu-36/1071-1st-encounter-of-agroecology-trainers-in-africa-region-1-of-la-via-campesina

73. See K. M. DeWalt and B. R. DeWalt, *Participant Observation: A Guide for Fieldworkers* (Walnut Creek, CA: AltaMira Press, 2002).

74. La Vía Campesina (LVC), "1st Encounter of Agroecology Trainers in Africa Region 1 of LVC"; La Vía Campesina (LVC), "Peasant Seeds: Dignity, Culture and Life—Farmers in Resistance to Defend their Right to Peasant Seeds"; LVC—Bali Seed Declaration, 2011, http://viacampesina.org/en/index.php/main-issues-mainmenu-27/biodiversity-and-genetic-resources-mainmenu-37/1030-peasant-seeds-dignity-culture-and-life-farmers-in-resistance-to-defend-their-right-to-peasant-seeds; La Vía Campesina (LVC), "2nd Latin American Encounter on Agroecology: Final Declaration," 2011, http://viacampesina.org/en/index.php/main-issues-mainmenu-27/agrarian-reform-mainmenu-36/1078-2nd-latin-american-encounter-on-agroecology

75. J. D. Van Der Ploeg, *The New Peasantries: Struggles for Autonomy and Sustainability in an Era of Empire and Globalization*; J. D. van der Ploeg, "The Peasantries of the Twenty-First Century: The Commoditization Debate Revisited."

76. "Peasant Seeds: Dignity, Culture and Life—Farmers in Resistance to Defend their Right to Peasant Seeds."

77. La Vía Campesina (LVC), "LVC: Call to Durban."

11

Contested Land Politics and Trajectories of Agrarian Change within an Emergent World Agro-commodity Regime: Insights from the BRICS and the Periphery

*Ben McKay, Alberto Alonso-Fradejas, Chunyu Wang,
and Saturnino M. Borras Jr.*

Questions around land—of access, control, use, and distribution—remain a focal point of development dialogue around the world. This should come as no surprise since 86 percent of people living in rural areas depend on agriculture—and therefore land and its productive resources—as a primary source of income and subsistence.[1] Of the estimated 1.4 billion people living in extreme poverty and acute hunger worldwide, around 70 percent reside in rural areas and depend on access to land and other resources (such as water, forests, flora, and fauna) to support their livelihoods.[2] This condition is undergoing rapid contextual changes in recent years: Newer challenges have emerged concerning land access, control, use, and distribution with a rising global interest in farmland and the World Bank estimating a 14-fold increase in land deals from 2008 to 2009 compared to previous years.[3] These new demands for land have materialized in the context of the convergence of multiple crises—the food price spike of 2007–2008, the climate crisis, the 2008 financial crisis, and the realization of a peak oil—as well as a changing global economy with rapidly emerging economies such as those of the BRICS (Brazil, Russia, India, China, South Africa) countries and some of the

MICs (Middle-Income Countries). Questions regarding land control, access, use, and distribution are thus extremely important and relevant in a rapidly changing global political and economic order. Some have explored possibilities of new land investments yielding sustainable results through win–win solutions based on a voluntary code of conduct for transnational land transactions.[4] Others point to the "problems" with the idea of a code of conduct[5] and argue that a more critical perspective on land deals must be considered to understand its multiple forms and effects on rural livelihoods, poverty, and hunger.

In this chapter, we use case studies from Brazil and China, two rapidly emerging BRICS countries, and two countries in the periphery—Bolivia and Guatemala—to situate contemporary dynamics of agrarian change in their specific historical contexts and point to new, yet similar, trajectories of land access, control, use, and distribution emerging around the world. Although these changes and trajectories are alarming and require immediate solutions, we question the underlying logic of corporate social responsibility initiatives in addressing complex land-based social relations. We argue that investor-led strategies based on connecting the poor with markets or injecting capital into marginal, available, or undercapitalized areas will only exacerbate problems of poverty and hunger, reinforcing highly unequal agrarian structures and fostering the expansion of corporate control over land and the global food system. Land tenure relations must thus be understood in historical context and property rights as inherently relational—not as simply a tradable commodity in the de Sotoan[6] sense—but as a social relationship.[7] Furthermore, following Herring, we understand that "land confers power in agrarian systems; reform policy must work through a system of power to restructure its base."[8] We thus emphasize the need to always historicize land-based social relations of access and control to better understand power relations within current agrarian structures.

This chapter will be organized as follows: In the next (second) section, we will provide a very brief overview of the socioeconomic and political importance of land issues in recent history and the renewed interest in the contemporary period. This will be followed by cases studies featuring Bolivia, Guatemala, China, and Brazil that will be used to illustrate the importance of historicizing land-based power relations in order to understand contemporary dynamics and future trajectories of agrarian change. Though the cases present diverse historical developments, contemporary dynamics are exposing the system of power within such structures. Considering these differences and complexities, section 4 points to the threats posed by the current land governance proposals of the World Bank, FAO, IFAD, UNCTAD, and IFPRI. We conclude the chapter by turning to a land sovereignty alternative that takes a relational approach to the poverty problematic, considering relations of production, reproduction, property, and power.[9]

Recent Historical Context of World Land (Re)distributive Efforts

Land—and, more specifically, land reform—has been and continues to be a central pillar for many struggles for social justice around the world. Access to land, for example, was a key pillar for peasant-led revolutionary regimes from Mexico (1910), Bolivia (1952), Cuba (1959), and Nicaragua (1970). Land was also central to reforms in China (1950s) and Vietnam (1960s). In South Korea and Taiwan, state-led agrarian reform processes by authoritarian regimes were necessary strategies for the developmental state. Further, democratically elected governments in Puerto Rico (1940s), Guatemala (1952), Venezuela (1960s), and Chile (1960s) also implemented important land reforms seeking "increased electoral support from low-income rural voters as well as being pressured by a wide range of other clients and allies with frequently conflicting interests in land reform."[10] During the period following World War II up until the neoliberal turn (1943–1973), what McMichael calls the development project, we can highlight six broadly interlinked sociopolitical reasons for which land reforms were carried, as highlighted by Akram-Lodhi, Borras, and Kay: (1) the post-WWII decolonization process by emerging nationalist governments (Algeria, Egypt, Indonesia, Zimbabwe); (2) Cold War ideological warfare between capitalists and socialists (United States in Japan, South Korea, Taiwan; Alliance for Progress in Latin America); (3) national projects of victorious peasant-based revolutions (Mexico, Bolivia, Guatemala, Nicaragua, Vietnam); (4) state reaction to manage rural unrest and political pressure (external/internal) (Kenya, Peru, Philippines, northern Mexico, Indonesia, Italy, Portugal, southern Spain); (5) legitimization/ consolidation of state power and reach (Peru, Philippines, Chile, Kerala and West Bengal, India); and (6) state-building process and tax-base development.[11] These different land reforms produced different outcomes for a variety of reasons. However, the importance of land—socially, politically, economically—cannot be overlooked. Questions of land must always be situated in their historical contexts so as to understand past struggles and land-based social relations of property and power. Although land reform was therefore an important issue for development, neoliberal policies that kicked in beginning in the 1980s facilitated its being edged out of the policy agendas.[12] Despite being undermined by food aid and free trade policies that allowed highly subsidized food staples from the global North to flood domestic markets of the global South,[13] the increased concentration of land through land markets, the debt and dependency created through green revolution technologies,[14] and the supermarketization of food markets by corporations,[15] land reform "never left the 'political agendas' of peasants and their organizations."[16]

By the mid-1990s, peasant movements once again began to mobilize against such exploitation and to regain control and access over their land resources. In 1994, the same day the North American Free Trade Agreement (NAFTA) came into effect, the Zapatista Army of National Liberation (EZLN) in Mexico launched a series of coordinated attacks on the government in the name of "tierra y libertad" (land and freedom) and in memory of revolutionary leader Emiliano Zapata.[17] In Zimbabwe, black landless peasants invaded white commercial farms to regain control over their lands, and Brazil's Landless Workers' Movement (MST) exercised militant land occupations on unused land.[18] Issues regarding land were thus back on the international stage, as governments and international agencies alike reconsidered the issue of land reform, particularly in terms of what to do with the large state and collective farms and how to capitalize on the resource-rich, labor-abundant developing countries of the South.[19] Over the past decade or so, land issues have been revitalized in key academic and policy circles, particularly over how, for whom, and for what purposes land reform should be carried out.[20]

Although there has been a renewed interest in land issues among development academics, practitioners, and policymakers, new actors and mechanisms of land concentration have also emerged. The financialization and heightened corporate interests in agriculture has increased the number of actors involved in global agrifood commodity chains and "abstracts food from its physical form into highly complex agricultural commodity derivatives."[21] These challenges have emerged in the context of what has been called contemporary global land grabbing, understood here from the following three interlinked dimensions: (1) the power to control land and its productive resources (i.e., control grabbing); (2) large scale, in terms of either relative land size or capital involved; and (3) financial capital's response to the convergence of multiple crises and the emerging needs for resources by newer hubs of global capital, particularly BRICS and MICs.[22] Although land grabbing has been facilitated through new means of accumulation, these are manifested in diverse and complex ways around the world. The following section presents case studies from Bolivia, Guatemala, China, and Brazil to provide diverse and wide-ranging examples of land-based social relations in the current agrocommodity food regime. Although Friedmann and McMichael's food regime concept links "international relations of food production and consumption to forms of accumulation broadly distinguishing periods of capitalist transformation since 1870,"[23] the agrocommodity food regime goes beyond the politics of food relations to an analysis involving crops used for animal feed, raw materials for nonfood industries, agrofuels, and food. As we will discuss hereafter, this emergent agrocommodity food regime presents multiple continuities from the "corporate neoliberal food regime"[24] and also involves new actors (transnational capitalists, financial investors, BRICS, MICs), new acquisition and control mechanisms (agro-financialization),[25] and new drivers (heightened global demand for farmland and natural resources as capital's response to the convergence of multiple crises, the growth of the flex crops[26] complex).

Bolivia

After almost 60 years and three agrarian reform programs, Bolivia's land distribution remains extremely unequal: Roughly 13 percent of farm units control 86 percent of arable land in the country, and the remaining 87 percent (or 574,200) of farm units, on average, occupy just 0.7 hectares of land each.[27] Moreover, of the nearly 10 million people living in Bolivia, 33.5 percent reside in rural areas—one of the largest rural–urban ratios in Latin America.[28] With 29 percent of the workforce employed in agriculture, farming remains a key source of livelihood for many Bolivians.[29] Furthermore, land access and resource control are of critical importance for rural livelihood viability, as well as for overcoming poverty and inequalities.[30] This is very apparent in Bolivia, where the sharp inequalities in land distribution coincide with a rural poverty rate of 66 percent (45 percent extreme poverty).[31] This data represents a severe structural problem in rural Bolivia. It is thus necessary and crucial to critically analyze and historicize Bolivia's agrarian reform policies to understand why such inequalities persist as well as the possible trajectories of agrarian change in the contemporary period.

Past Agrarian Reform Policies: Key Features   Bolivia's first agrarian reform in 1953 was a state-led process that attempted to dissolve the *latifundia* (large agricultural estates) and redistribute small plots of land to landless or near landless peasants. In what was referred to as *la marcha al oriente*, peasants in the western Andean region were offered plots of land between 20 and 50 hectares in the eastern lowlands of Santa Cruz to produce food for domestic consumption.[32] This coincided with the distribution of large-scale landholdings between 500 and 50,000 hectares—known as enterprises, *not* as *latifundia*[33]—to capitalist entrepreneurs and local elites to produce for export. This two-track agricultural development strategy was largely designed by the United States after Bolivia accepted a $25 million loan from the U.S. Export–Import Bank to promote economic development, channeled through the Inter-American Agricultural Service.[34]

This dual agricultural development model managed to dissolve the *latifundia* in the western Andean region, redistributing small plots to landless peasants even as it created a new regime of *latifundia* in the east distributing huge tracts of public lands.[35] However, driven by the interests of the Inter-American Agricultural Service, an eastern landlord bias emerged, favoring large-scale, export-oriented agriculture. As an export-oriented agricultural development model was pursued, technology, low-interest credit, and infrastructure investment policies were directed toward modernizing large-scale agriculture.[36] Whereas the agrarian structure in the western Andes became plagued with "economically and technically unsustainable" *minifundios*, the eastern lowlands were characterized by an increasingly dominant agricultural enterprise regime.[37]

Agrarian reform policies of 1953 demonstrate the insufficiency of redistributing land without providing complementary policies to sustain the reform. Increasing discontent among the peasantry, prevalent and widespread corruption, and the lack of property rights legibility led to Bolivia's second agrarian reform—the 1996 INRA[38] Land Law—which sought to formalize property rights (*saneamiento*) to make society legible.[39] The concept of a social and economic function (FES) was established to redistribute unused/fallow land as well as to distribute community lands of origin (TCOs) to indigenous populations.

According to the INRA Law, small and communal landholdings must fulfill a social function by supporting the reproduction of households and the economic development of individuals. Land that is abandoned or that is not visibly being lived on is subject to expropriation.[40] As of 2006 however, only 10.7 percent of the land subject to titling had been titled, 32.6 percent was in process, and 56.7 percent had not yet been surveyed. Moreover, only 11.1 percent of the land in Santa Cruz had been titled.[41]

This second agrarian reform combined policy elements of both market-led agrarian reform (MLAR) and state-led agrarian reform (SLAR) as the *saneamiento* process formalized landholdings to develop a land market system while simultaneously distributing and protecting collective land rights of indigenous peoples through TCOs. The failure to challenge the unequal agrarian structure by allowing the existence of large-scale landholdings to maintain land and resource control did not address the problems of poverty and inequality. Instead, the period marked by neoliberal reforms and political discontinuity[42] allowed existing capital to increasing its exploitation over resources and labor. As such, the outcomes of the two agrarian reforms from 1953 to 2002 resulted in 81.78 percent of total beneficiaries' (peasant plots, small farms, communal property and indigenous territories, TCOs) receiving 50.86 percent of total land distributed, while the medium- and large-scale farmers, representing just 16.79 percent of total beneficiaries, received 51.11 percent of total land distributed.[43]

Agrarian Reform under Evo: A "New Left Turn"?   In 2006, President Evo Morales officially launched the "Agrarian Revolution" in Santa Cruz by immediately presenting over 7.5 million hectares of land to 60 indigenous communities.[44] These land titles had actually already been processed but had remained inactive in the INRA database for the past 10 years. Furthermore, Morales also promised that an additional 20 million hectares would be distributed to Bolivia's 2.5 million rural poor over the following five years.[45]

This 2006 Ley de Reconducción 3545 (Extension Law) redefines natural resources as state property and puts more emphasis on state control and oversight over land consolidation and labor relations.[46] Law 3545 seeks to end exploitative labor relations. Landowners must register salaries, length of hire, and benefits for their wage-laborers. If exploitative behavior by a landowner over laborers is present, then land is subject to expropriation. Furthermore, the state can also draw on historical land tenure records to ensure that no fraudulent activity has previously taken place. Any previous fraudulent activity also makes land subject to expropriation.

The new agrarian reform is characterized by four main policy aims: (1) distribution of state-owned land and redistribution by expropriation of land not in compliance with FES to indigenous peoples and peasant communities; (2) mechanization of agriculture; (3) subsidized credits for small-scale producers; (4) markets for the products of peasant origin.[47]

As of 2010, the agrarian reform appeared to be one of the most successful in Latin America—titling more than 31 million hectares and distributing over 100,000 titles to 174,249 beneficiaries since 2006.[48] However, in the department of Santa Cruz—where over two-thirds of total cultivated land is located, including 98 percent of large-scale soy plantations—a mere 12 percent of the territory has been regularized.[49] In addition, 91 percent of titled lands "have been endowed by the State and are composed entirely of forest reserves."[50] Thus, the seemingly impressive *saneamiento* not only fails to challenge the prevailing unequal agrarian structure, but also has led to widespread deforestation as new frontiers expand into Bolivia's rich biodiverse areas of the Amazonian, Andean, and Chaco forests.[51]

Furthermore, in the contemporary period of global land grabbing,[52] the flex crop complex, and the rise of Brazilian capital as an emerging global and especially agroindustrial power, newer processes are shaping Bolivia's agrarian transformation that require immediate attention. Despite there being no regulation for foreign land ownership before the 1996 INRA Law, during the last 15 years foreigners—specifically, Brazilians—have rapidly increased their access to and control over Bolivian agricultural land and resources. In 2006–2007, for example, Brazilians controlled 40.3 percent of total soy plantation area in Bolivia, up from 19.6 percent in 1994–1995.[53] Although no official data exists on the total amount of land controlled by Brazilians, the most reliable and recent study conducted by Miguel Urioste of Fundación Tierra suggests that "in oilseeds alone, Brazilians own approximately half a million hectares of the best agricultural lands, both category I (intensive agricultural use)[54] and category II (extensive agricultural use),[55] without counting those that are in fallow or rotation, nor those that are directed toward other crops or ranching, which usually comprise larger areas." It is thus extremely likely that Brazilians control much more of Bolivia's land than actually recorded.

Locating these developments within the changing international political economy of food and land provides a better understanding of why Brazilians control an estimated 1.2 million hectares (and likely more) of Bolivia's 2.86 million hectares of total cultivated land.[56] In the past decade, farmland appreciated 278 percent in Brazil, outpacing the cumulative inflation of 88 percent.[57] This average annual inflation of 14 percent in farmland prices is indicative of the rising global interest in farmland whereby "over the past two decades, Brazil's Cerrado experienced the world's fastest expansion of the agricultural frontier,"[58] combined with increased domestic and foreign land grabs.[59] With the Cerrado now accounting for over 50 percent of Brazil's soybean area, land use change has adapted to international demand and new geographies of meat consumption in the context of a food regime in transition.[60] For example, China's 23-fold increase in soybean imports from 1990 to 2009 has coincided with its rapid increases in both meat production and meat consumption during this same period.[61] These increasing demands from China have been met with Brazilian supply—with Brazilian soy exports to China increasing an average of 30 percent per year and projections that by 2019–2020, 86 percent of Brazil's total soy production will be sent to China.[62]

These changing global patterns in the production and consumption of food have reverberating effects. As demand and prices for Brazilian farmland continues to increase rapidly, the expansion and accumulation of land and resources becomes increasingly scarce and more expensive. As a result, capital is expanding into newer areas with a relative abundance of unexploited factors of production—in this case, in rural Bolivia. Consequently, alliances have been formed between Bolivian and Brazilian capitalist agroentrepreneurs, creating a new wave of land appropriation for expanded accumulation. These processes are rooted in the historical developments of Bolivia's agrarian structure, in which the concentration of territorial control has been solidified since the very first agrarian reform in 1953.

Although the Morales regime has regularized and distributed land titles to many beneficiaries in comparison with the past two agrarian reform programs, the lands have largely been state-owned and forested areas. This fails to challenge the existing agrarian structural dynamics and power relations that exist between classes and the environment. Instead, the prevailing structure is maintained even as new frontiers become regularized and distributed to new land beneficiaries.

This section has attempted to shed light on the structural dynamics of land control in Bolivia. Social and environmental problems are inextricably linked to larger agrarian structures that encompass the unequal social relations within societies. Thus, without altering the structural dynamics of resource, land, and, ultimately, power control, exploitative tendencies on labor and the environment are likely to persist. The underlying mechanisms through which exploitation and domination over nature and society are driven must be identified and targeted in policy design and implementation, but, more important, through restructuring the unequal land-based social relations of access and control.

Guatemala

Corporate deals over land and other natural resources in Guatemala regained momentum from the mid-2000s on.[63] Most distinctive, a domestic oligarchy-controlled mix of agrarian, financial, and industrial corporations, usually allied with transnational financiers and social and environmental certification bodies, has been aggressively grabbing control[64] over land, water, and other natural resources (hereinafter land resources) for sugar cane and oil palm plantations. These converge with afresh land resources control grabs in the fields of mining, oil extraction, fast-growing tree plantations, conservation enclosures and carbon trading, hydropower generation, cattle ranching, special economic zones, mass tourism, and even to launder moneys from drug-trafficking.[65]

Such deals have a determining influence over the nature, character, and directions of agrarian change and the food system. State and social forces involved in these land resources deals are critical in constituting and reproducing dominant forms of agrarian production and of governing land resources. The former is approached here beyond its possible technological particularities as the ideas and practices embedded in land social relations and condensed in labor regimes.[66, 67] The latter entails enquiring how changing politico-economic conditions influence ideas, discourses, and practices of different state and social actors (inter)acting in the government of land resources at national, territorial, and local levels. Arguably, then, dominant forms of organizing agrarian production and of governing land resources are patterning and patterned by the balance of forces shaping relations of access, control, and use of land and other resources in historically and geographically situated conjunctures.[68]

Thus, we will briefly historicize here main dynamics of contemporary agrarian change in Guatemala that are shaping the food system critically and at multiple scales. In so doing, we will discuss some relevant premises inherited from the (orthodox) neoliberal globalization times before the mid-2000s, considered very telling of how current dominant forms of agrarian production and of governing land resources were constituted and are being reproduced and contested.

Precedents of Contemporary Dominant Forms of Organizing Agrarian Production   From a world perspective, it is interesting to situate contemporary agrarian transformation in Guatemala within the politico-economic dynamics shaping dominant food regimes[69] in different historical junctures. This concept "links international relations of food production and consumption to forms of accumulation broadly distinguishing periods of capitalist transformation since

1870."[70] In Guatemala, this includes discussing the heritage of liberal takes on agrarian forms and social relations production. These were arguably pervasive from the last quarter of the 19th century until the second half of the 1980s, when the relative scale-down of genocidal violence coincided with a flourishing neoliberalism. But it is especially relevant to understand how the "corporate neoliberal food regime"[71] laid fertile material and ideational grounds in the world and Latin American trade and investment patterns from the early 1970s onward (the late 1980s on in the case of Guatemala). Some fundamental examples include World Trade Organization economic (and extraeconomic) regulations shaping food systems globally; the Washington Consensus's structural adjustment programs that resulted in public agricultural trade boards, postharvest management and extension services' being cancelled; mushrooming free trade agreements from the mid-1990s on;[72] changing directions and patterns in agricultural foreign direct investment (FDI)[73] and other domestic, regional and international regulatory instruments influencing agriculture;[74] and the (racialized) urban imaginary representing indigenous cultivators as backward and inefficient that gained momentum in the neoliberal 1990s.

Precedents of Contemporary Dominant Rationality and Mechanisms of Governing Land Resources   As with the analysis of changing forms of agrarian production in Guatemala across different world food regimes, the analysis of change and continuity in the dominant political rationality and associated mechanisms of governing land resources demands a historical perspective. This includes accounting for the initial processes of land resources commoditization in the main liberal postindependence period (from the 1870s onward) and for its particularities within the internal armed conflict from 1962 to 1996. Most important, once again, it implies analysis of how recent neoliberal rationality and mechanisms of land resources government laid appropriate material and ideational grounds to accommodate contemporary land resources control grabs.

Among these mechanisms it is worth considering the mushrooming environmental enclosures from 1989 onward[75] that spread over 31 percent of the national territory, the energy and infrastructure megaprojects included in the "Mesoamerican Integration and Development Project" from 2008,[76] and other attributes within the previously commented (racialized) urban imaginary picturing indigenous rural dwellers in general as unruly, disrespectful of property and the rule of law, and destroyers of the rainforest. To this it is necessary to add the lack of agrarian courts and legislation in the face of "1,214 cases of unresolved agrarian conflicts in the country [involving] 1,000,055 peasants claiming rights over 338,935 hectares of land" (Guatemalan Secretary of Agrarian Affairs in Prensa Libre, September 4, 2012). Arguably, though, the two most relevant mechanisms of governing land resources originated in this period are the land titling programs and the Market Assisted Land Reform.

Under advice and funding from the World Bank, a land fund (FONTIERRAS) was institutionalized during the 1996 Peace Accords (1) to grant subsidized credit, nonrefundable financial support, and technical assistance to facilitate access to land to groups of landless and near landless families and (2) to manage the official land regularization and titling program, together with the National Cadastral Registry from 2005 onward. FONTIERRAS redistributed just 4 percent of the arable land in Guatemala to fewer than 5 percent of the (near) landless families from 1997 to 2008. Moreover, many of the families who accessed land through a FONTIERRAS credit have already sold their land entitlements; most who have not are incapable of coping with their (growing) debt owed to FONTIERRAS. There are several reasons behind these regressive outcomes of the MALR in Guatemala[77]—notable among them farming difficulties due to the low-quality/overused lands redistributed and the political-economic obstacles, previously depicted, to peasant food production under neoliberal structural adjustment.

Nonetheless, FONTIERRAS's outcomes regarding land titling, together with the National Cadastral Registry, have been paradoxically successful. The historical and comprehensive claim of peasant and indigenous families and peoples to increase their abilities to maintain and control their access to land resources through a state-sanctioned document was narrowly understood by FONTIERRAS as a claim for individual freehold land titling (over other legally binding forms of ownership) to generate private property rights over indigenous peasants' land (without considering other alternative, practiced, and legally binding rights of land tenure and use). Accordingly, many community common lands over which farming rights used to be collectively distributed were split up, privatized, and titled under individual property rights. State-sanctioned, private land ownership in a milieu in which peasant farming faces critical limitations has often resulted in the paradox of owning an inaccessible property. Conditions were laid then for "safe property rights [to] allow for markets to transfer land toward more efficient uses and producers,"[78] which ended up meaning the legally sanctioned dispossession of the indigenous peasantry, and not necessarily for the sake of productive efficiency.[79]

Contestation and Resistance to Dominant Directions of Contemporary Agrarian Change   As aforementioned, state and social forces embodying dominant accumulation interests and political rationalities of government create and reproduce consenting subjects in their struggle for hegemony. But through expected and unexpected outcomes in their original plans, dominant state and social actors also constitute (new) rejections of particular forms of being exploited, oppressed, or governed more broadly.

To the marginalization of the (indigenous) peasantry from food, commodities, and credit markets during the previous period of orthodox neoliberalization is added, from the mid-2000s on, their marginalization from labor markets and territorial land resources. It is in this context that resistance is increasingly framed as defense of territory. Most distinctively, this "frame of contention"[80] emerges in the national political arena from below. It is from there that national militant peasant, indigenous, or women's organizations adopt the concept. The strategic interest of defense of territory lies in "moving from practices of cultural resistance to the full exercise of collective rights in the territory."[81] Ethnic identities intertwine with class-based ones (peasants, rural laborers) to dignify, encourage, and justify resistance to corporate land resources from below.

Defense of territory involves both "everyday practices of resistance,"[82] such as foot-dragging in plantation work, a wave of arsons in plantations from two distinct areas, women from different villages' hiding the land title away from their partners to complicate the sale of the family plot, and widespread gossiping and critique of the agribusinesses in trust networks.[83] Additionally, there are more organized struggles to maintain access to and control over land resources, as well as to gain access to them and for repossession. The former usually entail the creation or strengthening of community systems to manage land resources, community politics, and justice, together with the promotion of economic alternatives often linked to low external-input farming and increased control over local food markets in search of more favorable terms of trade.[84] The latter struggles to gain access to land resources and for repossession are inherited from decades of struggle for a redistributive land reform aimed at taking back the land, essentially through land occupations and other pressing collective actions.

All these are relatively well-known strategies among contending actors, and many were originated earlier in history. A distinctive feature within the current cycle of contention is that very often resisters deploy these strategies not as an end, but rather as a means of strategic litigation processes. Such processes relate diverse grassroots practices of material and ideological resistance that pair political pressure from below with politico-juridical lobby and advocacy from above as well as with systematic research and social communication. Accordingly, struggles in defense of territory are reshaping the frames and repertoires of contention of many historical rural social movements by integrating the land to the tiller and food sovereignty frames within.[85]

China

We must admit that a description of China's agrarian changes is in danger of oversimplification even when confining its span to three decades. Significant and interrelated changes could be observed in farming systems, in the composition and movements of peasants, and in land use since the very beginning of the establishment of the Household Responsibility System (HRS) in the early 1980s. These major changes include shifts in the imports and exports of agricultural products, a notable leakage of population from agriculture, a gradual reconcentration of agricultural land use within China, and the pursuit to control more arable land overseas in recent years. Being home to approximately 20 percent of the total world population, China has been significantly affected by these changes at the regional and intercontinental levels.

Three Major Agrarian Changes: In Food, Peasants, and Scale of Land Use   Agrarian changes in China became significantly notable after the establishment of HRS. HRS, in its essence, seeks to liberate rural labor from the commune. In the previous Commune Period, the state controlled agricultural production, circulation, and prices so as to provide the cheap raw materials needed for the development of heavy industry. The current HRS now enables peasants to keep the surplus grains in the household after the deduction of the shares for the state and the collective. In other words, peasants, the collective, and the state have reached an agreement on who will get what from the land. Peasants have the right to use the land and keep the surplus; the collective (represented by the village committee) has been empowered to claim some agricultural produce for collective purposes and make adjustments of land allocation among households when necessary (for instance, the increase or decrease of households and family members due to births, deaths, marriages, and so forth); and the state has the right to collect agricultural taxes. As a consequence, grain production has greatly increased since the early 1980s and the Chinese people are basically able to feed themselves, reflected in the drop of imports of main staple foods (in percentage) shown in Figure 11.1.[86]

But this does not mean that the struggle between peasants and the state over "who will get what" has ended, especially when the state has prioritized an urban-centered and industry-first development policy. This policy has at least two consequences: On one hand, resources have been siphoned out of rural areas in the form of agricultural revenues and scissor prices, but agricultural investments from the government are relatively marginal. The net revenue drawn from the agricultural sector amounted to an annual average of 81 billion yuan (US$13.3 billion) from 1979 to 1994.[87] Meanwhile, the average annual agricultural investments from 1976 to 1995 accounted for merely 10 percent of the total financial expenditure.[88] On the other hand, rural populations started to migrate because of a simple reproduction squeeze,[89, 90] or because of growing monetary expenditures on education, housing, medical services, and so forth, in comparison to an increasingly lower land–tiller ratio. The migration of labor used to be strictly controlled to ensure adequate agricultural production and social stability. Peasants were not even allowed to move

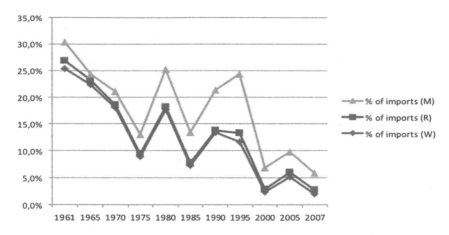

Figure 11.1   Percentage of Imports of Maize (M), Rice (R), and Wheat (W) in Domestic Supply* in China

*Domestic supply = domestic production + imports + storage – exports

Source: Food and Agriculture Organization of the United Nations, FAOSTAT database (FAOSTAT 2013), http://faostat.fao.org.

to cities until 1984, and even then they were required to bring food with them when looking for jobs in urban areas so that they might not be a burden to the city. The number of migrant workers has been on the rise since then, climbing from 59.6 million in 1985 to 253 million in 2011.[91] But this massive rural outmigration has produced an example of the phenomenon of a "left-behind population,"[92] with the result that agriculture is now often seen as a "woman's job" or an "old person's job." Women and the elderly have had to change their agricultural production patterns to deal with their increased workload after the migration of (young) male laborers. According to a recent study in two counties in Henan Province,[93] many young, left-behind women were newly returned migrant workers who had little experience in farming. Furthermore, the majority of households had to reduce their total amount of cultivated land because of the lack of a family labor supply; machines and hired laborers had to be more frequently used in busy farming seasons; the number of domestic animals such as chickens, pigs, ducks, and cattle declined sharply; and more fertilizers were spread in farmland as a result. In short, farmers in the investigated area have been muddling along when it comes to agriculture. Many arable lands have been left fallow or leased out. A process of depeasantization in agriculture is observable.

This brings us to the third major agrarian change in recent years, the reconcentration of agricultural land use. Against HRS's innate tendency of land fragmentation, rural China is experiencing a scale-up in agricultural production unit in terms of land area and agricultural employees. The emergence of agrarian capital is notable in many provinces of China, taking on different forms and cultivating various crops, such as grains, coffee, and cotton.[94] Since 2000, large parcels of land have been leased out and disguised as cooperatives and family farms but are usually supported financially by the local or central government. These cooperatives or family farms generally occupy vast pieces of land (ranging from several hundred Mu[95] to more than 10,000 Mu) and are used to grow vegetables, flowers, or other cash crops, as well as to employ a large number of rural laborers.[96]

In 2000 a national development policy of going global was proposed for agriculture. This policy has provided incentive for agricultural investments overseas. Although there are no exact data on how much land has been leased or sold to Chinese investors or on what terms, it is reported that the Chinese government has been supporting investment by Chinese companies to secure supplies of soy, palm oil, and jatropha, as well as rubber and timber, in countries such as Brazil, Argentina, Angola, the Democratic Republic of Congo, Russia, Kazakhstan, Mozambique, Tanzania, Zambia, the Philippines, Cameroon, Sierra Leone, Cambodia, Laos, Myanmar, Indonesia, and Papua New Guinea.[97] Up until now, overseas agricultural investment occupies merely a small proportion of the total investment in comparison to other industries. Its proportion fluctuated around 1 percent from 2006 on: for instance, 0.9 percent (190 million USD) in 2006; 1 percent (270 million) in 2007; 0.3 percent (170 million) in 2008; 0.4 percent (340 million) in 2009; 0.78 percent (533 million) in 2010.[98] The total stock was $9 billion, or 4.2 percent of the total investment, out of which 60 percent (5.4 billion) either was canceled or was announced but not actually implemented. Thus the potential for agriculture to go global is still fairly high in the eyes of policymakers.

Contestations against the Outlined Agrarian Changes   These agrarian changes have had significant impacts on peasants in China and in invested areas outside of China's borders. With a few exceptions in which peasants succeeded in accumulating some wealth and started small businesses or reinvested in agriculture, the majority of peasants became drifting populations in urban areas or agricultural employees for corporate farms. The peasants' way of production, or peasant farming, is undergoing severe attack from internal and external capital. As a result, peasants are losing control over their land, including over what to produce and how to produce it.

Organized landless peasants' movements and related NGOs cannot be found in China, but that does not mean that contestations and protests are lacking. In many cases, peasants' resistance against land grabbing in China is unorganized and unstructured but also overt, targeting mainly local governments, village committees, or investors with the goal of gaining the support of the public and the upper-level government officials (extreme examples of these protests have included self-immolation). Although some elites have mobilized peasants' movements by collecting signatures for petitions, contacting upper-level government officials utilizing mass media, and negotiating with local governments (much as the Youth League in Wukan village, Guangdong Province, did); mass incidents concerning land in China so far are more issue-based. A permanent peasants' organization was not born out of these movements. At present, there are no national organizations (governmental or nongovernmental) representing peasants. Furthermore, in the last People's Congress, held in March 2012, only three peasant representatives represented the 800 million peasants of China. This unorganized situation explains to some extent the present form and the extent of Chinese peasants' resistance against internal land grabbing.

Likewise, China has been less successful in some countries than others when outsourcing its development. For instance, of 18 Chinese investment deals in Cambodia, involving 105,000 ha of land, 13 deals have aroused strong resistance. Many protests of local villagers have been brought to the district, provincial, and national levels, but according to the Office of the United Nations High Commissioner for Human Rights,[99, 100] these protests were ignored or suppressed by the state or were met with empty promises and bribery. Land grabbing in the Philippines by Chinese investors, however, has been successfully turned down or suspended, such as was the case with telecom giant ZTE in China, which planned to have a 1.24 million ha investment in the Philippines, and the case of the 2007 memorandum of understanding signed between several Philippine government officials and various Chinese investors, which included about 1.4 million ha land investment.[101]

It is not easy to explain why some land grabs and related agrarian changes invoked upheavals whereas others did not, nor why some protests succeeded when others failed. The upsurge of peasants' resistance is perhaps not about how much has been taken away from the oppressors, but about how much is left for the peasants.[102] The interaction between the state, capital, and the peasantry could have greatly influenced the outcome of land grabbing—which is usually a dynamic process and which makes the picture of global land grabbing complicated and fascinating.

Another Way Forward?   As aforementioned, these agrarian changes have aroused great concern over China as a new hub of capitalism, as well as over its rising demand for more feed, fuels, and food (especially meat). The shrinking arable land (more in terms of quality rather than quantity) and agricultural populations have created enormous worries in the society, while coping strategies—scaling-up of agriculture and going global—may produce more problems. Although the current amount and proportion of overseas agricultural investments have not been shocking up to now, it is a worrying trend. It is the persistence of peasants and peasant farming in China as well as landless farmers' and workers' movements that may point to another way forward.

Brazil

Despite Brazil's rapid economic growth into what is now the world's sixth largest economy, complete with a booming agricultural sector, rural poverty and inequality remain at large. More than 25 percent of the rural population lives in extreme poverty, and 9 percent of all farm units control nearly 80 percent of the total cultivated area.[103] Moreover, farm units controlling over 1,000 hectares, which represent just 0.9 percent of total farm units, control 44 percent of Brazil's total farmland area. As the world's leading producer of sugar cane, amounting to 25 percent of world production and second leading producer of soy with 28 percent of total world output, Brazil's agricultural growth has largely been concentrated among the agro-industrial elites.[104] Although this unequal agrarian structure is not a new phenomenon, situating contemporary land-based power relations in the context of previous agrarian reform programs and land-based social struggles provides a better understanding of the current processes and future trajectories of agrarian change.

Background on Brazilian Agrarian Reform   Brazil's agrarian policy has largely been based on the 1964 Land Statute (Law 4504) established during the first military government, which sought to gradually eliminate both small parcels (*minifundios*) and large estates (*latifundios*) to prevent social uprisings.[105] Conflicts and struggles were widespread as the military regime resorted to violence and repression in order to solve land-based social conflict. By the early 1980s, land occupations became the principle means of struggle for social justice, and strong rural–urban worker alliances led to a return to democratic rule in 1985.[106] In 1985 the National Agrarian Reform Plan (*Plano Nacional da Reforma Agrária-Nova Republica*, PNRA–NR) was implemented "to expropriate land with compensation in the interest of social justice."[107] Large estates (*latifundia*) that were deemed unproductive,[108] that degraded the environment, that did not conform to labor legislation or contracts, or that did not serve a social function were to be expropriated by the government and redistributed to the landless.[109] This legislation was actually part of the 1964 Land Statute and remained in the 1988 federal constitution; it continues to be enforced today. The expropriation by compensation process includes long-term payments for the value of land as well as cash payments for improvements, for which the National Settlement and Agrarian Reform Institute (INCRA)—a branch of the Ministry of Agrarian Development (MDA)—is currently responsible.

However, Brazil continues to have one of the world's most highly concentrated landholding structures, with a Gini-coefficient near 0.9.[110] These severe inequalities in land ownership have persisted since the *latifundio*-style agriculture and land tenure system that took shape in the 1960s and 1970s during the military government and the implementation of green revolution agricultural policies.[111] As a response to such unequal land distribution, more than 30 social movements—including MST, the National Confederation of Rural Trade Unions (CONTAG), the Pastoral Land Commission (CPT), and the Brazilian Association for Agrarian Reform—aligned to form the National Forum for Agrarian Reform and Rural Justice. This forum was created to oversee the actions of market-led agrarian reform (MLAR) initiated through a variety of programs by the Cardoso government from 1995 to 2002. During this phase of land reform, Cardoso implemented four different MLAR programs, including the Sao Jose Project, which financed the purchase of 23,400 hectares of land, settling 700 families at an average per family cost of R$6,083, or R$179 per hectare; the *Cedula da Terra*, executed from 1997 to 2002, which resettled approximately 15,000 families on 399,000 hectares of land, at a per-family cost of R$11,975, or R$191 per hectare;[112] and the Land Bank (*Banco de Terra*) and the Land Fund. Law 25, passed by parliament in February 1997, which secured land reform by a national fund constitutionally mandated to finance the purchase of land by rural workers. This law formally incorporated the "voluntary transfer of land purchased under market conditions instead of state-led expropriation" in the national agrarian policy.[113] Banco de Terra was highly criticized by the National Forum for Agrarian Reform and Rural Justice, which argued that Banco de Terra was "transferring agrarian reform into the hands of the 'latifundarios' and local oligarchies."[114] Banco de Terra targeted families with higher incomes and thus was not contributing to the dire inequalities that exist in the Brazilian countryside, only exacerbating problems of unequal access.

Land Reform under Lula   As a member of the Worker's Party (PT), and bolstered by strong support from the MST, President Luiz Inacio Lula da Silva (Lula) campaigned on promises of large-scale, quick agrarian reform. Conversely, Lula also prioritized the need to support the agribusiness sector in order to generate a positive trade balance and fulfill Brazil's external debt obligations. As a result, the Lula administration has continued Cardoso's macroeconomic policies and support for the export sector while also pursuing policies of social inclusion. To understand the dynamics behind these decisions, it is necessary to examine the political environment in which the Lula administration is operating.

Lula was elected with a 61 percent majority but had to enter a coalition government, of which his coalition did not control the congress.[115] This meant that his government consisted of allies and adversaries; the latter of whom have been strongly opposed to agrarian reform. These internal contradictions within the government have been reflected not only in the agriculture ministries, but also in the policies implemented. Lula appointed Miguel Rossetto—a member of the Worker's Party, friend of the MST, and a strong advocate of small-scale agriculture and serious land reform—cabinet minister to oversee agrarian reform. On the other hand, Lula appointed Roberto Rodriguez minister of agriculture. Rodriguez is a well-known supporter of international agribusiness and advocates for large-scale, highly capital-intensive, export-oriented agricultural policies.[116] Due to these conflicting views on land reform and agricultural development, Brazil's agrarian policies attempted to fulfill redistributive promises while pursuing capitalist strategies. The competing models of state-led agrarian reform (SLAR) and market-led agrarian reform (MLAR) have been simultaneously coopted by state actors that have failed to carry out the massive agrarian reform needed to transform the severe inequalities in the countryside.

One of the first actions of the Lula administration was to discontinue the Banco de Terra in 2003.[117] However, redistributive agrarian reform was not a priority for the Lula government. Instead, a campaign was launched to end hunger and cut INCRA's budget for land acquisition through expropriation. In November 2003, the Second National Agrarian Reform Plan (PNRA–II) was launched, which intended to redistribute land titles to 400,000 families in four years.[118] The plan emphasized the need for agrarian reform that includes social and physical infrastructure and access to credit, technical assistance, and marketing channels to accommodate the landless and also provide compensation for lands that were expropriated. The PNRA–II also includes three different land financing programs: the World Bank–funded Land Credit and Poverty Reduction program (CFCP); a new World Bank–financed program called Our First Land (*Nossa Primeira Terra*), aimed at enabling rural youth to purchase farms; and Family Farm Consolidation—a credit line to enable smallholders to expand their holdings and consolidate family farms. The plan expected to settle 400,000 families through expropriation with compensation or state-led agrarian reforms (SLAR) and 150,000 families through the aforementioned forms of land credit (MLAR) in a period of four years, for a total of 550,000 family beneficiaries.[119] Even if the government fulfilled these promises, which it did not (see Chart 11.1), the number of land reform beneficiaries is far from the 1 million demanded by the social movements.

To acquire a piece of land through the MLAR land credit programs, the beneficiaries were required to be landless rural producers or owners of a smallholding, as well as the head of a family, including women. One was also required to have a tradition in agriculture activity; to have shown intention to acquire land through a producer's association; and also to indicate at least one landholder willing to sell one property. Finally, one had also to agree to repay the sum given for the acquisition of the landholding.[120] To start this process, a small producer or landless worker must establish an association collectively and find a financial agent or state land institute with a proposal for a settlement. In this regard, there were no restrictions on the type of property that could be acquired, and as a result, properties that were under- or unused and that could have been expropriated entered the program. This prompted CONTAG to negotiate an agreement with the bank to exclude from the program properties that could be expropriated, establishing the Anti-Poverty Land Credit Programme. Land that could be expropriated was thereafter excluded from the MLAR model.

The benefits of the land credit programs (MLAR) and the expropriation by compensation (SLAR) have been marginal. Of the 150,000 families targeted under the MLAR project from 2003 to 2006, only 35,564 families benefited. This is a mere 23.7 percent success rate in redistributing land through the MLAR approach, partly owing to the price increase in land and the lack of government support in land reform. Land prices increased thanks to the new opportunities for agribusinesses to acquire land.[121] On the other hand, of the 400,000 families who were supposed to be granted a plot of land through expropriation (SLAR), 381,419 benefited.[122] Although the SLAR model seems to have been much more successful, MST critics disagree with the official figures. According to representatives of the MST, "the official figures have been inflated, because they include families who merely received formal titles to land that they were already living on, and families who [later] left the property that they had been granted."[123] Not only has the MST been active critics of the Lula administration and the World Bank programs, but it has also performed land reform activism by claiming unused land and initiating land reform for the people from the ground up.

Brazil's Landless Workers Movement—Movimento Dos Trabalhadores Rurais Sem Terra *(MST)* The MST is the largest social movement in Latin America, consisting of an estimated 1.5 million landless members organized in 23 out of 27 states in Brazil. With 0.9 percent of the landowners controlling 44 percent of arable land, it is apparent that the government has failed to address these inequalities and to implement a thorough model for land reform.[124] The Brazilian Constitution states that land that is unproductive should be used for a "larger social function"—a stipulation that the MST has acted upon with substantial success. Since 1985, the MST has "occupied unused land where [it has] established cooperative farms, constructed houses, schools for children and adults and clinics, promoted indigenous cultures and a healthy and sustainable environment and gender equality."[125] The MST has won land titles for over 350,000 families in 2,000 settlements and has gained prominence and legitimacy in state affairs.[126] The MST opposes the neoliberal model and the agribusiness/ agroexport economy based on free trade, privatization, and commodification of natural resources. In contrast, the MST advocates a model of agriculture based on the family farm and food sovereignty that "prioritizes local production of food for local and national markets, negates dumping, and uses sustainable production practices based on local knowledge."[127] The MST calls for land reform that would guarantee land to 4 million landless families in Brazil through small and medium-sized farms. It promotes intercropping and improved rotations to improve soil quality and preserve the environment. Furthermore, the MST opposes the use of pesticides, advocating production of healthy food through environmentally friendly agricultural practices that use conventional seeds native to Brazil.[128] The MST has been successful in establishing 96 small and medium-sized cooperatives, 1,800 public schools, and literacy and health programs. It has continued to expand its reach in the fight for agrarian reform, a free, sovereign, egalitarian Brazil, and a continent free from the FTAA.[129]

Agroindustrial Bias and "Flex Crops"   Despite the MST's relative success as one of the most radical and progressive rural social movements to affect change, land-based resource wealth is becoming increasingly concentrated. Even with a seemingly more favorable left-leaning government of Lula and Dilma (Worker's Party–PT), relations within the state have continued to enforce an "agro-industrial landlord bias."[130] For example, according to the latest agricultural census, large-scale landholdings over 1,000 hectares, which represent less than 1 percent of Brazil's total farm units, receive more than 43 percent of the government's total agricultural financial expenditures.[131] Investments in flex crop production—crops that have multiple uses and that can be easily and flexibly interchanged according to market conditions in order to avoid market volatility—have increased substantially.[132] For example, in February 2010, Royal Dutch Shell and a Brazilian conglomerate producer of bioethanol, sugar, energy, and foods, Cosan, entered into a joint venture agreement to produce ethanol from Brazilian sugar cane worth $12 billion.[133] Since 1990, monocrop plantation areas for soy have increased 188 percent, for sugar cane 156 percent, and for maize 138 percent.[134] This agroindustrial-induced expansion is increasingly putting a squeeze on the middle peasantry as the average price per hectare of cropland has increased by 430 percent from 1994 to 2010.[135] As land resources become increasingly commodified for a variety of uses (food, fuel, feed, industrial material, conservation), new investors emerge in the agricultural sector (such as Royal Dutch Shell), and so do new accumulation mechanisms (such as agrocommodity derivatives). In the context of volatile and uncertain financial and commodity markets, investors are turning to farmland as a new haven for global investments as they seek "opportunities to earn returns from the production of food and biofuel crops."[136]

Brazil's natural resource wealth as not only a leader in agricultural production but also in the new bioeconomy has led to an influx of new land- and resource-based investments.[137] This new wave of investments requires a new wave of resistance to stop new forms of accumulation, dispossession, and exploitation. The latter must necessarily work to transform relations of production, reproduction, property, and power[138] beyond win–win solutions to govern land and other natural resource grabs.

Trajectories of Agrarian Change: "Win–Win" Solutions, or Business as Usual?

The previous country cases show how as new processes of capital accumulation penetrate rural areas around the world, land concentration and the unequal land-based social relations of access and control are facilitating the expansion of the agro-industrial complex. Following Anna Tsing, it is important to approach property rights not as things, but rather as social relationships.[139] But even beyond the bundle of rights attached to property, it is much more useful analytically to use Ribot and Peluso's access analysis, which "requires attention to property as well as to illicit actions, relations of production, entitlement relations, and the histories of all of these."[140] The history of how these social relationships have developed over time is important to understand the nature, pace, extent, and direction of agrarian change.[141]

However, understanding these changing dynamics and the consequential exploitation, inequality, or impoverishment that may or may not arise as technical problems that can be resolved through a "toolkit of 'good governance'" such as "information, choice, prices, law, and transparency" is problematic.[142] As Li explains, "it takes a complex political economic problem driven by unequal power, and parses it into components that can be addressed by technical means."[143] Although Li makes specific reference to the World Bank's "Rising Global Interest in Farmland" report, as well as its 2008 Agriculture for Development report (WDR08), similar conclusions can be drawn from the World Bank et al.'s "Principles for Responsible Agricultural Investment That Respect Rights, Livelihoods and Resources" (PRAI) or the International Food Policy Research Institute (IFPRI) Code of Conduct (CoC). These strategies rely on a combination of good governance and corporate social responsibility (CSR) mechanisms that fail to address underlying social relations of access and control and existing patterns of production and consumption. As Borras and Franco argue, "a CoC-framed response to land-grabbing is likely to facilitate, not block, further land-grabbing and thus should not be considered, even as a second-best approach."[144] Furthermore, these proposed "solutions" to negative impacts of land-grabbing or large-scale land investments approach such problems in a residual way—that is, taking the view that poor people are poor owing to their inability or their exclusion from market access. The solutions thus rely on integrating people into markets through increased capital investment. However, as we have exemplified throughout, new and continuing forms of capital accumulation lead to an increased concentration of capital, inequality, and various forms of dispossession.[145] Without addressing the underlying relations of production, reproduction, access (including property and beyond), and power, and without transforming unequal structural agrarian formations through zero-sum resource-based transfers, proposed win–win solutions will quickly result in business-as-usual outcomes.

Concluding Discussion

New dynamics of agrarian change, particularly concerning land-based social relations of access and control, present new challenges for the rural poor that require new alternatives and alliances for social justice. Although this newness has been triggered by the aforementioned multiple crises reshaping the international political economy of food and agriculture with new emerging economies and new actors (investors) and mechanisms (agro-commodity derivatives/agro-financialization) for accumulation, the penetration of capital inherent in these new processes exploits the existent, and historically based, land-based social relations.

In this chapter we used case studies from Bolivia, Guatemala, China, and Brazil to illustrate the historical importance of present-day agrarian structures. Although each country's agrarian structure has developed along its own unique trajectory, contemporary dynamics of capital accumulation are exploiting unequal land-based social relations and pointing to similar trajectories of capital-monopolized agrarian change. In Bolivia, a dual agrarian structure took shape throughout over 50 years of an eastern landlord bias, institutionalizing a form of agrarian hegemony among the landed elites of Santa Cruz. Despite a seemingly proreform government with redistributive land policies, new forms of capital are penetrating into the Bolivian lowlands, with Brazilian capital now controlling almost 50 percent of cultivated land.[146] Market-led agrarian reform (MLAR) and associated (freehold) land titling programs have also laid fertile grounds for the flex crop agribusinesses to flourish or spread in Guatemala. To the marginalization of the indigenous peasantry from food, commodities, and credit markets during the previous period of orthodox neoliberalization is added, from the mid-2000s on, marginalization from labor markets and territorial land resources. It is in this context that resistance is growingly framed as defense of territory, which straddles the land to the tiller and food sovereignty frames within. In China, the gradual reconcentration of agricultural land use within the country and the pursuit to control more arable land overseas in recent years to feed an exponential industrial growth is presenting new challenges for the historically marginalized rural poor both inside and outside mainland China. Finally, in Brazil, despite strong demands from rural social movements in 1985 and 2003, MLAR and the continuing agroindustrial bias and flex crop concentration continue to threaten livelihoods of the rural poor and small-scale farmers even as state and corporate actors look abroad for newer, more lucrative investment opportunities.

Although these case studies illustrate similar patterns of reconcentration of land control and access, the importance of their patterning dynamics of the nature of structures and agencies over time cannot be overlooked. We have attempted to highlight the importance of such historical developments in shaping and reshaping current and future agrarian dynamics in the contemporary context of the rapidly changing political economy of agrocommodities, land, and natural resources. In supporting a historically and geographically situated research agenda of contemporary political dynamics of agrarian change, we would like to put forward here two final reflections for further discussion.

On the one hand, we have argued that market-based—and "good governance"–centered—approaches proposed to govern emergent ecologies and social relations in diverse agrarian settings (and sometimes beyond) tend to overlook such historically constituted power dynamics. We therefore subscribe an alternative framework of land sovereignty, defined as "the right of working peoples to have effective access to, use of, and control over land and the benefits of its use and occupation, where land is understood as a resource, territory, and landscape."[147]

On the other hand, though intimately close, we have sketched several ways in which such dominant directions of agrarian change are usually contested, and often resisted, by (indigenous) peasants and rural laborers, male and female, in very diverse agrarian milieus through not only unstructured but even militant struggles. This is why we cannot but stress that outcomes of contemporary world agrocommodity regime change are not stories foretold, but rather the result of multiple politics among, across, and within diverse but historically constituted contending actors at various scales and places.

Notes

1. World Bank, "World Development Report 2008: Agriculture for Development" (Washington, DC: The World Bank, 2007), 3–4.

2. IFAD, "Rural Poverty Report 2011" (Rome: International Fund for Agricultural Development, 2010). www.ifad.org/rpr2011/index.htm

3. Klaus Deininger and Derek Byerlee, "Rising Global Interest in Farmland: Can It Yield Sustainable and Equitable Benefits?" (Washington, DC: World Bank, 2011).

4. ILC, "Tirana Declaration: Securing Land Access for the Poor in Times of Intensified Natural Resources Competition," Global Assembly 2011, May 27, 2011 (Rome:

International Land Coalition, 2011); World Bank, FAO, IFAD, and UNCTAD, *Principles for Responsible Agricultural Investment That Respects Rights, Livelihoods and Resources* (Washington, DC: World Bank, 2010); J. Von Braun and R. Meinzen-Dick, "'Land Grabbing' by Foreign Investors in Developing Countries: Risks and Opportunities," IFPRI Policy Brief, No. 13 (Washington, DC: International Food Political Research Institute, 2009).

5. Saturnino Borras Jr. and Jennifer Franco "From Threat to Opportunity? Problems with the Idea of a 'Code of Conduct' for Land-Grabbing," *Yale Human Rights and Development Law Journal* 13 (2010): 507–523.

6. See Hernando De Soto, *The Mystery of Capital: Why Capitalism Triumphs in the West and Fails Everywhere Else* (New York: Basic Books, 2000).

7. Anna Tsing, "Land as Law: Negotiating the Meaning of Property in Indonesia," in *Land, Property, and the Environment*, ed. F. Richards (Oakland, CA: Institute for Contemporary Studies, 2000), 94–137.

8. Ronald Herring, "Beyond the Political Impossibility Theorem of Agrarian Reform," in *Changing Paths: International Development and the New Politics of Inclusion*, eds. Peter Houtzager and Mick Moore (Ann Arbor: University of Michigan Press, 2003), 58–87.

9. Saturnino M. Borras and Jennifer C. Franco, "A 'Land Sovereignty' Alternative? Towards a Peoples' Counter-Enclosure," Discussion Paper, TNI Agrarian Justice Programme (Amsterdam: Transnational Institute, 2012); Henry Bernstein, Ben Crow, and Hazel Johnson, *Rural Livelihoods: Crises and Responses*, vol. 3 (Oxford: Oxford University Press in association with The Open University, 1992).

10. Solon Barraclough, "The Role of the State and Other Actors in Land Reform," Discussion Paper No. 101 (London: URISD, 1999), ii.

11. A. Haroon Akram-Lodhi, Saturnino M. Borras Jr., Cristóbal Kay, eds., *Land, Poverty and Livelihoods in an Era of Globalization: Perspectives from Developing and Transition Countries* (London and New York: Routledge, 2007), 6–8.

12. Before the International Conference on Agrarian Reform and Rural Development (ICARRD) in 2006 and the World Bank Development Report's (WDR) Agriculture for Development in 2008, the last major international conference on agriculture and land was the World Conference on Agrarian Reform and Rural Development (WCARRD) in 1979.

13. Harriet Friedmann, "The Political Economy of Food: The Rise and Fall of the Postwar International Order," *American Journal of Sociology* 88S (1982): 248–286; Fatoumata Jawara and Aileen Kwa, *Behind the Scenes at the WTO* (London and New York: Zed Books, 2004).

14. Raj Patel, "The Long Green Revolution," *The Journal of Peasant Studies* 40, no. 1 (2013): 1–63.

15. Ibid.

16. Saturnino M. Borras, Cristóbal Kay, and A. Haroon Akram-Lodhi, "Agrarian Reform and Rural Development," in *Land, Poverty and Livelihoods in an Era of Globalization: Perspectives from Developing and Transition Countries*, eds. Akram-Lodhi, Borras and Kay, 13; and see Herring, "Beyond the Political Impossibility Theorem of Agrarian Reform," 58–87.

17. Jonathan Fox, "The Roots of Chiapas," *Economic and Political Weekly* 29, no. 19 (1994): 1119–1122.

18. Akram-Lodhi, Borras, and Kay, *Land, Poverty and Livelihoods in an Era of Globalization: Perspectives from Developing and Transition Countries*, 12–13.

19. Ibid.

20. Klaus Deininger and Hans Binswanger, "The Evolution of the World Bank's Land Policy: Principles, Experience, and Future Challenges," *The World Bank Research Observer* 14, no. 2 (1999): 247–276; Klaus Deininger, *Land Policies for Growth and Poverty Reduction: Key Issues and Challenges Ahead* (Washington, DC: World Bank, 2004); Akram-Lodhi, Borras, and Kay, *Land, Poverty and Livelihoods in an Era of Globalization: Perspectives from Developing and Transition Countries*; Saturnino M. Borras, *Pro-Poor Land Reform: A Critique* (Ottawa, Canada: University of Ottawa Press, 2007).

21. Jennifer Clapp, "Financialization, Distance and Global Food Politics," paper presented at Food Sovereignty: A Critical Dialogue (Ithaca, NY: Yale University, 2013), 2.

22. Saturnino M. Borras, Jennifer C. Franco, Sergio Gómez, Cristóbal Kay, and Max Spoor, "Land Grabbing in Latin America and the Caribbean," *The Journal of Peasant Studies* 39, nos. 3–4 (2012): 850–851.

23. Harriet Friedmann and Philip McMichael, "Agriculture and the State System: The Rise and Decline of National Agricultures, 1870 to the Present," *Sociologia Ruralis* 29, no. 2 (1989): 93–117.

24. Philip McMichael, "A Food Regime Genealogy," *The Journal of Peasant Studies* 36, no. 1 (2009): 139–169.

25. For more on agrofinancialization, see Clapp, "Financialization, Distance and Global Food Politics," 2.

26. Flex crops are "crops that have multiple uses (food, feed, fuel, industrial material) that can be easily and flexibly interchanged: soya (feed, food, biodiesel), sugar cane (food, ethanol), oil palm (food, biodiesel commercial/industrial uses), corn (food, feed, ethanol)"; see Borras et al., "Land Grabbing in Latin America and the Caribbean," 851.

27. Author's calculation based on data from INE 2011 and World Bank 2007, 19: (2,861,330 ha total arable land × 14%) ÷ (660,000 total farm units × 87% smallholders) = 0.698 ha per unit.

28. Instituto Nacional de Estadistica (INE), "Informacion Estadistica" (INE 2012). www.ine.gob.bo

29. IFAD, *Rural Poverty Report 2011*.

30. Kay Borras and Akram-Lodhi, *Land, Poverty and Livelihoods in an Era of Globalization: Perspectives from Developing and Transition Countries*, 1.

31. Instituto Nacional de Estadistica, "Informacion Estadistica."

32. Gabriela Valdivia, "Agrarian Capitalism and Struggles over Hegemony in the Bolivian Lowlands," *Latin American Perspectives* 37 (2010): 67–87.

33. For Kay and Urioste (2007), "the 1953 law legitimated disguised forms of neo-latifundism, under the generic heading of 'enterprise.'"

34. James M. Malloy and Richard S. Thorn, eds., *Beyond the Revolution: Bolivia since 1952* (Pittsburgh, PA: University of Pittsburgh Press, 1971), 165–169.

35. Cristóbal Kay and Miguel Urioste, "Bolivia's Unfinished Agrarian Reform: Rural Poverty and Development Policies," in *Land, Poverty and Livelihoods in the Era of Globalization: Perspectives from Developing and Transition Countries*, eds. Akram-Lodhi, Borras, and Kay, 55.

36. Valdivia, "Agrarian Capitalism and Struggles over Hegemony in the Bolivian Lowlands," 67–87; Enrique Saavedra Ormachea, "¿Revolucion agrarian o consolidacion de

la via terrateniente? El Gobierno del MAS y las politicas de tierras," *Centre de Estudios para el Desarollo Laboral y Agrario* (La Paz, Bolivia: CEDLA, 2007); Kay and Urioste, "Bolivia's Unfinished Agrarian Reform: Rural Poverty and Development Policies."

37. Kay and Urioste, "Bolivia's Unfinished Agrarian Reform: Rural Poverty and Development Policies," 58.

38. *Instituto Nacional de Reforma Agraria.*

39. James C. Scott, *Seeing Like a State: How Certain Schemes to Improve the Human Condition Have Failed* (New Haven, CT: Yale University Press, 1998).

40. Valdivia, "Agrarian Capitalism and Struggles over Hegemony in the Bolivian Lowlands," 73.

41. Instituto Nacional de Reforma Agraria (INRA), *Estado del Proceso de Saneamiento a 10 Anos de vigencia de la Ley 1715* (La Paz, Bolivia: INRA, 2006).

42. From 1996 to 2006, Bolivia had seven different presidents.

43. Kay and Urioste, "Bolivia's Unfinished Agrarian Reform: Rural Poverty and Development Policies," in *Land, Poverty and Livelihoods in an Era of Globalization: Perspectives from Developing and Transition Countries*, eds. A. Haroon Akram-Lodhi, Saturnino M. Borras Jr., and Cristóbal Kay (London and New York: Routledge, 2007).

44. Nicole Fabricant, *Mobilizing Bolivia's Displaced: Indigenous Politics and the Struggle over Land* (Chapel Hill: University of North Carolina Press, 2012), 140.

45. Ibid., 140.

46. Valdivia, "Agrarian Capitalism and Struggles over Hegemony in the Bolivian Lowlands," 74.

47. Miguel Urioste, *Land Governance in Bolivia* (La Paz, Bolivia: Fundacion TIERRA, 2010).

48. INRA, 2010; Daniel Redo, Andrew C. Millington, and Derrick Hindery, "Deforestation Dynamics and Policy Changes in Bolivia's Post-Neoliberal Era," *Land Use Policy* 28 (2011).

49. Ibid., 234.

50. Ibid., 237.

51. Susanna B. Hecht, "Soybeans, Development and Conservation on the Amazon Frontier," *Development and Change* 36, no. 2 (2005): 377.

52. Borras et al., "Land Grabbing in Latin America and the Caribbean"; Deininger and Byerlee, "Rising Global Interest in Farmland: Can It Yield Sustainable and Equitable Benefits?"

53. Miguel Urioste, "Concentration and 'Foreignisation' of Land in Bolivia," *Canadian Journal of Development Studies* 33, no. 4 (2012).

54. "Agricultural Production with High (Maximum) Yields in a Given Area by Means of Soil Treatment and Specialized Farming Practices," Gobierno Departamental Autonomo De Santa Cruz (2009).

55. "Agricultural Production with Moderate to Low Land Use Activity, Little to No Capital Investment, and/or Only Family Labour," Gobierno Departamental Autonomo De Santa Cruz (2009).

56. Urioste, "Concentration and 'Foreignisation' of Land in Bolivia"; Instituto Nacional de Estadistica, "Informacion Estadistica."

57. Gustavo Bonato, "Brazilian Farmland Prices Nearly Quadruple in Last Decade-Study," Reuters (2012). www.reuters.com/article/2012/11/28/brazil-farmland-prices-idUSL1E8MS1UB20121128

58. Deininger and Byerlee, "Rising Global Interest in Farmland: Can It Yield Sustainable and Equitable Benefits?" 17.

59. Borras et al., "Land Grabbing in Latin America and the Caribbean"; Gustavo L. T. Oliveira, "Land Regularization in Brazil and the Global Land Grab," *Development and Change* 44, no. 2 (2013): 261–283.

60. Tony Weis, "The Meat of the Global Food Crisis," *Journal of Peasant Studies* 40, no. 1 (2013): 65–85.

61. Ibid.

62. Carrie Brown-Lima, Melissa Cooney, and David Cleary, "An Overview of the Brazil–China Soybean Trade and Its Strategic Implications for Conservation," *Nature Conservancy Report 2010*. www.nature.org/ourinitiatives/regions/southamerica/brazil/explore/brazil-china-soybean-trade.pdf

63. Alberto Alonso-Fradejas, "Contemporary Land Grab–Driven Agrarian Change from a Multiple Politics Perspective: Insights from Guatemala," LDPI Working Papers, No. 51 (The Hague: The Land Deal Politics Initiative, 2013); L. Grandia, *Enclosed: Conservation, Cattle, and Commerce among the Q'eqchi' Maya Lowlanders* (Seattle: University of Washington Press, 2012); L. Hurtado, "Dinámicas Agrarias y Reproducción Campesina en la Globalización: El Caso de la Alta Verapaz" (Guatemala: F&G Editores, 2008).

64. Borras et al., "Land Grabbing in Latin America and the Caribbean," *Journal of Peasant Studies* 39, nos. 3–4 (2012): 851.

65. Alberto Alonso-Fradejas, "Land Control-Grabbing in Guatemala: The Political Economy of Contemporary Agrarian Change," *Canadian Journal of Development Studies* 33, no. 4 (2012): 509–528.

66. Henry Bernstein, "Labour Regimes and Social Change under Colonialism," in *Survival and Change in the Third World*, eds. B. Crow, M. Thorpe, and D. Wield (Cambridge, UK: Cambridge Polity Press, 1988), 30–49.

67. Stressing that "the emergence of specific labor regimes is not inevitable but the product of politics" (White et al. 2012, 623), we adhere to White et al.'s choice of Bernstein's 1988 definition of labor regimes as "specific methods of mobilizing labor and organizing it in production, and their particular social, economic and political conditions" (Bernstein 1988, 31–32, in White et al. 2012, 622).

68. G. Hart, "Geography and Development: Development/s beyond Neoliberalism? Power, Culture, Political Economy," *Progress in Human Geography* 26, no. 6 (2002): 818.

69. H. Friedmann and P. McMichael, "Agriculture and the State System: The Rise and Decline of National Agricultures, 1870 to the Present," *Sociologia Ruralis* 29, no. 2 (1989): 93–117.

70. Ibid., 95.

71. P. McMichael, "A Food Regime Genealogy," *The Journal of Peasant Studies* 36, no. 1 (2009): 139–169.

72. The 2005 Dominican Republic, Central American, and USA Free Trade Agreement (DR–CAFTA) is paramount in this regard, together with the 1991 MCCA and the 2011 European Union–Central America Association Agreement.

73. That is, new countries of origin of FDI in Guatemala (e.g., Colombia, Nicaragua, and Brazil) and the investments of Guatemalan agribusinesses throughout Central America, in Mexico, and in Brazil (Alonso-Fradejas et al. 2008).

74. Such as the 2005-approved 2005–2015 National Competitiveness Agenda (renewed in 2012 until 2021), the 2008-settled Mesoamerican Biofuel Commission, the 2008–2017 Central American Common Agricultural Policy, the EU's 2003 Renewable Energy Directive, and the USA's 2009 American Clean Energy and Security Act, among others.

75. Part of the Mesoamerican Biological Corridor established in 1997.

76. Launched in 2001 as the Puebla to Panama to Putumayo Plan (PPPP).

77. The Gini coefficient regarding land distribution rose from 0.83 in 1960 to 0.84 in 2003 (INE 2004), meaning that already by 2003, in the onset of the recent rush for land, 78 percent of the arable land was controlled by 8 percent of the landholders.

78. World Bank, "World Development Report 2008: Agriculture for Development" (Washington, DC: The World Bank, 2007a), 138 (emphasis added).

79. It has been discussed elsewhere (Dürr et al. 2010, Alonso-Fradejas et al. 2008, Alonso-Fradejas et al. 2011) how peasant agriculture generates far more employment (per hectare and in absolute terms) and as much as 10 times more territorial wealth, than sugar cane, oil palm, or cattle ranches controlled by corporations and large owners.

80. Understood as "shared understandings and identities that justify, dignify and animate collective action" (Tarrow 1998, 21).

81. Q'eqchi' lawyer and congressmember, June 26, 2013.

82. James C. Scott, *Weapons of the Weak: Everyday Forms of Peasant Resistance* (New Haven, CT: Yale University Press, 1985).

83. Alberto Alonso-Fradejas, "Contemporary Land Grab–Driven Agrarian Change from a Multiple Politics Perspective: Insights from Guatemala."

84. This is how the food sovereignty frame is mutually constitutive of the defense of territory.

85. A major example of strategic alliances forging across grassroots groups and organizations and national rural social movements' organizations lies in the Popular, Peasant, and Indigenous March (*La Marcha Indígena, Campesina y Popular*).

86. There are of course other factors contributing to the increase of grain production, such as the growing use of chemicals and fertilizers.

87. Cheng Guohui, *Abolishing Agricultural Taxes to Return Peasants' National Treatment*, March 9, 2004. www.people.com.cn/GB/guandian/1033/2380445.html

88. Data available at Ministry of Finance, www.mof.gov.cn/mof/zhengwuxinxi/caizhengshuju/200805/t20080519_27197.html

89. A simple reproduction squeeze is the "process of pressure on the reproduction of petty commodity producers as either or both capital and labour, associated with the commodification of subsistence and often leading to depeasantization" (Bernstein 2009, 129).

90. Henry Bernstein, "Notes on Capital and Peasantry," in *Rural Development: Theories of Peasant Economy and Agrarian Change*, ed. John Harris (London: Hutchinson University Library, 1982), 160–177.

91. Data available at National Bureau of Statistics China, www.stats.gov.cn/tjfx/fxbg/t20120427_402801903.htm

92. Jingzhong Ye and J. Murray, *Left-Behind Children in Rural China: Impact Study of Rural Labor Migration on Left-Behind Children in Mid-west China* (Beijing: Social Sciences Academic Press, 2010).

93. A research team from China Agricultural University conducted a study on left-behind population at the request of the World Bank in 2013. The findings followed were drawn from this research. Permission to use these data has been given.

94. Forrest Q. Zhang and John A. Donaldson, "From Peasants to Farmers: Peasant Differentiation, Labor Regimes, and Land-Rights Institutions in China's Agrarian Transition," *Politics and Society* 38, no. 4 (2010): 458–489.

95. 1 Mu = 1/15 hectare.

96. In the same investigation in Henan Province, we observed such cooperatives planted with rice. According to the village leaders, these cooperatives were bankrupt. However, they still remained there due to assistance from huge government grants. Large-scale grain plantations, according to key informants, could not produce as much as peasants' intensive farming. Another investigation in Sichuan in June 2013 proved the same claim, where vegetable production per Mu was markedly lower in an 800 Mu farm than a 50 Mu farm.

97. Irna Hofman and Peter Ho, "China's 'Developmental Outsourcing': A Critical Examination of Chinese Global 'Land Grabs' Discourse," *Journal of Peasant Studies* 39, no. 1 (2012): 1–49.

98. Data available from Ministry of Commerce: www.mofcom.gov.cn/article/gzyb/bolian/

99. UNOHCHR, *Land Concessions for Economic Purposes in Cambodia: A Human Rights Perspective* (Phnom Penh: United Nations Office of the High Commissioner for Human Rights in Cambodia, 2004).

100. UNOHCHR, *Economic Land concessions in Cambodia: A Human Rights Perspective* (Phnom Penh: United Nations Office of the High Commissioner for Human Rights in Cambodia, 2007).

101. GRAIN, "Seized! The 2008 Land Grab for Food and Financial Security," in *GRAIN Briefing* (Barcelona: GRAIN, 2008).

102. James Scott, *The Moral Economy of the Peasant: Rebellion and Subsistence in Southeast Asia* (New Haven, CT: Yale University Press, 1976).

103. IBGE, *Censo agropecuario 2006* (Rio de Janeiro: Instituto Brasileiro de Geographia e Estatistica). www.ibge.gov.br/home/estatistica/economia/agropecuaria/censoagro/agri_familiar_2006/familia_censoagro2006.pdf

104. USDA, "Sugar: World Markets and Trade" (Washington, DC: U.S. Department of Agriculture, Foreign Agricultural Services, 2013a), www.fas.usda.gov/psdonline/circulars/sugar.pdf; USDA, "World Agricultural Supply and Demand Estimates, World Agricultural Outlook Board" (Washington, DC: United States Department of Agriculture, 2013b). www.usda.gov/oce/commodity/wasde/latest.pdf

105. Diana Carmen Deere and Leonilde Servolo de Medeiros, "Agrarian Reform and Poverty Reduction: Lessons from Brazil," *Land, Poverty and Public Action* Policy Paper no. 2 (The Hague: ISS/UNDP, 2005).

106. Ibid.; Stephen Baranyi, Carmen Diana Deere, and Manuel Morales, *Land and Development in Latin America: Issues and Openings for Policy Research* (Ottawa, Canada: North–South Institute/IDRC, 2004).

107. Stephen Baranyi, Carmen Diana Deere, and Manuel Morales, *Land and Development in Latin America: Issues and Openings for Policy Research* (Ottawa, Canada: North–South Institute/IDRC, 2004), 5.

108. Unproductive farms are those classified as not achieving 80 percent of the use of tillable land, or whose yields are below 100 percent of the average per-hectare productivity rates.

109. Gerd Spavorek and Rodrigo Fernando Maule, "Negotiated Agrarian Reform in Brazil," in *Agricultural Land Redistribution: Toward Greater Consensus*, eds. Hans P. Binswanger-Mkhize, Camille Bourguignon, and Rogerius Johannes Eugenius van den Brink (Washington, DC: World Bank, 2009), 294.

110. Sauer Sergio, "The World Bank's Market-Based Land Reform in Brazil," in *Promised Land: Competing Visions of Agrarian Reform*, eds. Peter Rosset, Raj Patel, and Michael Courville (Oakland, CA: Food First Books, 2006), 178.

111. Raj Patel, "The Long Green Revolution," *The Journal of Peasant Studies* 40, no. 1 (2013): 1–63.

112. World Bank, "Implementation Completion Report (CPL-41470)," Report 25973, Brazil Country Management Unit (2003), quoted in *Agricultural Land Redistribution: Toward Greater Consensus*, eds. Binswanger-Mkhize, Bourguignon, and van den Brink (Washington, DC: World Bank, 2009), 295–296.

113. Spavorek and Maule, "Negotiated Agrarian Reform in Brazil," 296.

114. Leonilde Servolo De Medeiros, "Social Movements and the Experience of Market-Led Agrarian Reform in Brazil," in *Market-Led Agrarian Reform: Critical Perspectives on Neoliberal Land Policies and the Rural Poor*, eds. Saturnino Borras, Cristobal Kay, and Edward Lahiff (New York: Routledge, 2008), 90.

115. Deere and Medeiros, "Agrarian Reform and Poverty Reduction: Lessons from Brazil," 18.

116. Angus Wright and Wendy Wolford, *To Inherit the Earth: The Landless Movement and the Struggle for a New Brazil* (Oakland, CA: Food First Books, 2003), 337–338.

117. Spavorek and Maule, "Negotiated Agrarian Reform in Brazil," 297.

118. Deere and Medeiros, "Agrarian Reform and Poverty Reduction: Lessons from Brazil," 17.

119. Leonilde Servolo De Medeiros, "Social Movements and the Experience of Market-Led Agrarian Reform in Brazil," 92.

120. Ibid., 93.

121. Ibid., 95.

122. Mario Osava, "Brazil: No Consensus on Success of Land Reform" (Rome: Inter Press Service International Association, 2007). http://ipsnews.net/news.asp?id news=37053

123. Ibid.

124. IBGE, *Censo agropecuario 2006*.

125. Movimento dos Trabalhadores Rurais Sem Terra (MST), *Brazil's Landless Workers Movement: About*. www.mstbrazil.org/?q=about

126. Ibid.

127. International NGO/CSO Planning Committee for Food Sovereignty (IPC), "Agrarian Reform in the Context of Food Sovereignty, the Right to Food and Cultural Diversity: Land, Territory and Dignity," Issue Paper 5, presented at the International Conference on Agrarian Reform and Rural Development, Porto Alegre, March 7–10, 2006. www.icarrd.org/en/icard_doc_down/Issue_Paper5sum.pdf

128. Joao Pedro Stedile, "The Neoliberal Agrarian Model in Brazil," *Monthly Review* 58, no. 8 (2007). www.monthlyreview.org/0207stedile.htm

129. MST, *Brazil's Landless Workers Movement: About.*

130. Cristobal Kay, "Rural Poverty and Development Strategies in Latin America," *Journal of Agrarian Change* 6, no. 4 (2006): 455–508.

131. IBGE, *Censo agropecuario 2006.*

132. Borras et al., "Land Grabbing in Latin America and the Caribbean."

133. ETC Group, *The New Biomassters* (Ottawa, Canada: ETC Group, 2011).

134. IBGE, *Censo agropecuario 2006.*

135. Sérgio Sauer and Sergio Pereira Leite, "Agrarian Structure, Foreign Investment in Land, and Land Prices in Brazil," *Journal of Peasant Studies* 39, nos. 3–4 (2012): 873–898.

136. Clapp, "Financialization, Distance and Global Food Politics," 9.

137. C. A. M. Santana, D. A. P. Torres, and E. Contini, "Bioeconomy: A Revolutionary Paradigm for Agriculture!?" *Perspective Agricultural Research* (Brasilia: EMBRAPA and Ministry of Agriculture, Livestock and Food Supply, 2012); Sauer and Leite, "Agrarian Structure, Foreign Investment in Land, and Land Prices in Brazil."

138. Bernstein, Crow, and Johnson, *Rural Livelihoods: Crises and Responses.*

139. Anna Tsing, "Land as Law: Negotiating the Meaning of Property in Indonesia," in *Land, Property, and the Environment*, ed. F. Richards (Oakland, CA: Institute for Contemporary Studies, 2002), 94–137.

140. Jesse C. Ribot and Nancy L. Peluso, "A Theory of Access," *Rural Sociology* 68, no. 2 (2003): 157.

141. Borras, *Pro-Poor Land Reform: A Critique*, passim.

142. Tania M. Li, "Centering Labor in the Land Grab Debate," *Journal of Peasant Studies* 38, no. 2 (2011): 292.

143. Ibid.

144. Saturnin Borras Jr. and Jennifer Franco, "From Threat to Opportunity? Problems with the Idea of a 'Code of Conduct' for Land-Grabbing," *Yale Human Rights and Development Law Journal* 13 (2010): 521.

145. David Harvey, *The New Imperialism* (Oxford and New York: Oxford University Press, 2003).

146. Urioste, "Concentration and 'Foreignisation' of Land in Bolivia."

147. Saturnino M. Borras and Jennifer C. Franco, "A 'Land Sovereignty' Alternative? Towards a Peoples' Counter-Enclosure," discussion paper, TNI Agrarian Justice Programme (Amsterdam: Transnational Institute, 2012), 6.

12

The Importance of Process in Achieving Food Sovereignty: Participatory Action Research (PAR) in Coffeelands of Nicaragua

Heather R. Putnam and J. Christopher Brown

This chapter explores the use of a participatory action research (PAR) model to identify community food insecurity dynamics and devise strategies to address them by building food sovereignty. It is based on a case of study of a community food security and sovereignty project involving a second-level coffee cooperative in San Ramón, Nicaragua, and a U.S. nonprofit organization, the Community Agroecology Network (CAN). We argue that the PAR process can result in strategies that favor communities' food security needs and food sovereignty goals. These needs and goals differ in essence from traditional food security strategies; they can be regularly adjusted to better fit the needs of the communities and stakeholders involved and, furthermore, may contribute to resilience through a strengthened participation structure that promotes communication and response. The PAR process as a community food sovereignty tool, however, is limited by difficulties in engaging national-scale and transnational actors that have heavy influence even at the local level, which in turn limits the changes that PAR can effect in mitigating the negative influence that the global food structure has on smallholder coffee growing communities. If PAR is used as a methodology for promoting food sovereignty, it must be complemented by other strategies that engage both global food structures and political processes that weaken local food systems and people's ability to access food.

Food Sovereignty as an Approach to Food Security

Food has not only become a core focus of many civil society organizations, but is also included in the national food and agriculture policies of several nations. Formulated and introduced by the transnational peasant organization La Vía Campesina in 1996, food sovereignty represents an alternative approach to achieving food security in the sense that it focuses on guaranteeing the right to organize and control food systems locally. In comparing food security and food sovereignty, Windfuhr and Jonsén[1] emphasize that food sovereignty is a comprehensive, rights-based approach to achieving food security. This is perhaps the most key distinction between food security and food sovereignty. As Pimbert[2] explains, "The mainstream definition of food security . . . doesn't talk about where that food comes from, who produced it, or the conditions under which it was grown." Drawing on Pimbert's observation, our analysis in this study sought to include contextual factors underlying the processes by which individuals, households, and communities produce and procure food, giving importance to the context and "culture" of food production. The analytical framework used in this study identified 10 indicators drawn from established food security frameworks and combined with food sovereignty indicators, which take into account localized context and culture. Establishing food security must take into account a more complex web of interacting elements that at its core respects the breadth and depth of community participation in defining and shaping their food security.

Existing Approaches to Implementing Food Sovereignty in Rural Communities

The meaning of food security has become more nuanced, expanding beyond food self-sufficiency, beyond the question of national vs. local scale organization, and beyond the radical discourse of participation and power used by civil society groups such as *La Vía Campesina*, placing the idea of sovereignty squarely in the center of the discourse around how to alleviate food and nutritional insecurity. Whereas food security approaches of the 1970s and 1980s focused on food redistribution and strengthening of markets, current discourse focuses on the participation of poor smallholder farmers as the drivers of food security; the end goal is not simply enough food, but rather good nutrition. Contemporary approaches aim to address both the structural and the proximate causes of food insecurity. The 2012 FAO Report "State of Food Insecurity in the World"[3] did argue for increased participation of the poor in economic growth and its benefits and pinpointed agriculture as a key tool for ending hunger and malnutrition, but the FAO's strategies still rely on agricultural development as a way to increase income of the poor (and thus increasing their economic access to food) and to increase employment (also increasing economic access to food), all while promoting radical strategies like small-holder empowerment and participation of the poor. This is still a stark contrast to the food sovereignty strategies and goals promoted by La Vía Campesina and other social movements in building sustainable local food systems to increase local availability and access to food. Other traditional approaches include sub-sidies for seed, production inputs, and even food offered by many national governments—for example, Mexico, through its PROCAMPO and *Oportuni-dades* programs. In the case of Mexico, it has been shown that although food subsidy programs such as *Oportunidades* do alleviate immediate hunger, pro-duction subsidy programs such as PROCAMPO have not actually resulted in diversified production and have not achieved their programmatic goals related to food security.[4] New approaches by other governments have heeded the call for participation by creating municipal level food security committees and other government structures (including Nicaragua and Guatemala) that are part of new legal structures, such as right-to-food laws, that attempt to inte-grate government food security programs and projects into the existing state legal and government structure in varying ways with varying levels of efficacy.

The development and coffee sectors have used approaches couched as community-based, and they generally focus on diversification of production for diversified consumption and income generation. The Coffeelands Food Security Coalition, for example, is focused on a combination of strategies that include improved farming and business techniques, developing additional sources of income through home gardens and diversified crop production, and engaging more effectively with local government to provide assistance to the hungriest of families.[5] The coalition's approach, like others used within the coffee industry, does not explicitly focus on changing the power dynamics of food systems: It is not a food sovereignty approach, as espoused by La Vía Campesina, but rather a food security approach with a focus limited to the farm level that does not really engage with policy at any scale.

PAR and Rural Development

Participatory action research (PAR) emerged in the context of the rise of post-structural social theories, which essentially argue that historical and cultural structures influence how knowledge is produced and thus how we interpret knowledge; poststructuralism emphasizes the difficulty of analyzing struc-ture if we are part of the structure. According to Kinden et al.,[6] PAR "involves researchers and participants working together to examine a problematic situa-tion to change it for the better." PAR treats all participants as competent agents in a collaborative process, incorporating multiple perspectives within a com-munity into the creation of new meanings based on reiterative reflection and action,[7] essentially challenging dominant epistemologies of knowledge. These principles are rooted in critical social science theories and practices, especially feminist poststructuralism and feminist political ecology, as well as emancipatory community-based research processes developed in the 1960s and 1970s in Brazil and contemporaneously in Africa, India, and other parts of Latin America.

Although PAR's early roots extend to post-WWII researchers, most narratives of PAR origins identify the point of conceptual identification of PAR as beginning with the work of Paulo Freire in Brazil in the 1960s and 1970s. That work involved development of methodologies of popular participation in knowledge creation and social transformation processes, especially the creation of consciousness of injustice and of using collective consciousness to inform action, most commonly known through Freire's landmark book *Pedagogy of the Oppressed* (first published in Portuguese in 1968 and in English in 1970). Kinden et al. describe contemporaneous efforts in India that continued and revised the ideas put forth earlier by Mahatma Gandhi to draw on local knowledges and narratives to resist colonial rule. A second wave of PAR took place in the 1980s in the context of a rise in investment in international development; community and rural development contexts still continue to be a major focus of PAR researchers and researchers. Those that add "participatory" to their "action research" projects signal a commitment to the legacies of Freire, Gandhi, and other early PAR practitioners to "political commitment, collaborative processes, and participatory worldview."[8]

The approach is rooted in a cyclical process of looking, reflecting, acting, and sharing between the investigators and the communities involved, resulting in a process of knowledge production in which reflections about actions are constantly monitored and reintegrated into actions in a dialogic process.[9] As Méndez et al. argue, the value of PAR approaches is that "they are done with the participation of communities, produce relevant and necessary data, and facilitate capacity building and support networks."[10]

In work related to rural livelihoods, participatory research has had several manifestations and issues. Participatory Rural Appraisal (PRA), which can be defined as "a family of approaches and methods to enable rural people to share, enhance, and analyze their knowledge of life and conditions, to plan and to act," has many approaches within its family, including activist participatory research, agroecosystem analysis, applied anthropology, field research on farming systems, and rapid rural appraisal (RRA);[11] thus it can be considered a kind of umbrella family of methodologies. PRA parts from RRA in focusing on local ownership of the research process and the designing of actions stemming from local analysis of the problems and issues identified, whereas RRA is a methodology more related to donor elicitation and extraction of information.[12] The valuing of the analytical ability of rural peoples and peasants is a tenet of PRA[13] that informs the present study as well as some of the methodologies PRA traditionally uses, including "they do it" (in which subjects themselves perform the research), stories and case studies, sharing of information and ideas, and, especially, livelihood analysis,[14] the main methodology employed by this study.

Chambers emphasizes that in participatory research, there are different ways that "participation is used"—it can be a cosmetic label used to give a positive face to the work being done without involving real local ownership of the project; it can also describe a coopting process in which participants contribute their time to an outside-led project process; or it can be an empowering process in which the "we" describes project beneficiaries actively involved in decision making.[15]

Potential Benefits of Using PAR to Implement Rural Community Food Sovereignty

PAR permits a more active engagement with local place-based cultural factors, which are often ignored in most food security studies; the FAO has stated that cultural preferences must be taken into account when promoting food security, but the reference is murky and its applicability is unclear.[16] Though food sovereignty social movement discourse addresses cultural preferences explicitly and centrally in its discourse (see La Vía Campesina's 2007 Declaration of Nyéléni), methodologies for studying, evaluating, and working toward food sovereignty are nascent, and they could benefit from the experience of PAR as a field, in terms of specific methods for integrating elements of cultural values and preferences into study design, analysis, and formulation of strategies and actions.

Another potential benefit of PAR as a tool for implementing food sovereignty is PAR's utility in avoiding an overromanticizing of "local" food systems as a solution in what is called the local trap, a tendency in some politico-ecological work to assume that local organizations and locally based actions will inherently produce better results than nonlocal solutions to a problem[17] and a homogenization of the idea of community that also results from this phenomenon. The local trap has indeed manifested in food justice movements. In 1999 Patricia Allen explored the topic of food security and the issues involved in its then-surging links with the local food movement.[18] Citing a movement to promote local food systems as the solution to community food insecurity, she highlighted various problems with local food systems: Although they do increase access to food for low-income consumers, decentralize power over food systems, create a sense of place and pride in place, and promote increased awareness of food systems among producers and consumers alike, the idea of local food systems tends to also homogenize community. They are also driven by ideologies mediated by income, occupation, gender, race, ethnicity, and other factors that can lead to local food system initiatives addressing not the needs of the most disenfranchised residents, but rather the needs perceived by the movement drivers, which can create power imbalances. Allen argued for solutions wherein the problems are identified locally and by a wide array of actors; that address issues of labor (which is often not locally based even in local foods), low wages, and high costs of living; and that especially include complementary state interventions; Allen is essentially arguing that social movements cannot do it alone but must engage with other problems and actors outside the food system. Avoidance of the local trap could potentially come from the PAR methodology of including multiple stakeholder voices from within and outside the direct realm of a given problem in analyzing a problem and defining actions to address it.

PAR methods are appropriate to food sovereignty evaluation and implementation precisely because they maintain a place for local knowledge by involving farmers and community stakeholders in the research process, thereby empowering communities to be stewards of their own community development and community food sovereignty while also benefiting from the knowledges of other stakeholders.

In light of these benefits, it may be argued that PAR has the potential to yield results that (1) are the product of involving farmers in the development of the study, interpretation of the data, and identification of strategies joining indigenous with Western knowledge to address the complex causes of food insecurity and that (2) lead to the development of more sustainable, effective, context-oriented, and culturally and environmentally appropriate strategies for strengthening food sovereignty and enhancing community food security because of its emphasis on local knowledge and practices combined with other knowledges. In the PAR model used in the case study, we emphasized the revitalization of traditional production systems and food cultures, because all of the stakeholders agreed from the outset that this is essential not only for increasing or restoring agrobiodiversity, but also for strengthening local control over food availability and accessibility—which, in turn, is argued to enhance agroecological and cultural resiliency.

Food Security and Sovereignty in Coffeelands

Food insecurity in smallholder coffee-growing communities is a reality that has become a central focus of the fair trade movement, as well as of the specialty coffee industry as a whole. After decades of promoting higher fair trade prices in the interest of economic justice for marginalized smallholder coffee farming families, research in the last 10 years has shown the effects of alternative coffee markets to be uneven. Although farmers participating in fair trade benefit from various positive impacts in education, investment in infrastructure, and lower costs, basic livelihoods factors are not positively affected, and the farmers still suffer low income, high rates of outmigration, and food insecurity.[19] Seasonal hunger is the most common manifestation of food insecurity in coffeelands, although chronic hunger and malnutrition also affect families and especially children under age five in the most vulnerable communities. Transitory food insecurity also occurs in coffee-growing communities as the result of periodic shocks such as extreme weather events or coffee price dips that directly affect the availability of food in the community (as in the case of heavy rains' destroying basic grains crops) or a family's ability to access food economically (as in the case of price dips), according to Caswell et al.'s analysis of the relatively limited body of studies exploring the effects of alternative coffee certifications (including studies of smallholders certified Fair Trade or Organic) on food security.[20]

Seasonal hunger in northern Nicaragua, called in Nicaragua *los meses de las vacas flacas*, or "skinny cow months" (hereafter "thin months"), is experienced in coincidence with three other phenomena as shown in Table 12.1, based on the results of this study: The rainy season between May and November, the period after income from the previous coffee harvest has been spent and cash for purchasing basic foods is scarce, and the period after basic grains have been harvested. Strategies used to mitigate the thin months include limiting the diet to basic grains (risking nutrient deficiencies) or skipping meals altogether (risking caloric deficiency), according to Caswell et al.[21]

Coffee communities' extreme vulnerability to multiple risk factors, including coffee price swings, climate change, degradation of the means of production, and seasonal changes in food prices,[22] lead to vulnerability and lack of resilience to shocks such as occurred during the period of the coffee crisis in 1999–2004, when coffee prices dipped to historical lows, wreaking economic and social havoc in coffeelands. Efforts to mitigate the effects of the coffee crisis in 1999–2004 focused on promoting alternative markets to provide higher and more stable prices to smallholders and decrease smallholder organizations' vulnerability during market swings. These strategies were complemented by development projects aimed at diversifying coffee markets and strengthening coffee quality by improving farmer production practices. Much of these interventions involved collaborations and partnerships between specialty coffee companies and organizations with development organizations and agencies internationally and locally. However, the focus on higher-paying specialty and alternative markets also had the negative, but not unpredictable, effect of farmers' planting more of their land in coffee and less in food;[23] this is a well-documented tendency among coffee farmers of any size when the market experiences an upswing for more than a year at a time, and it reduces smallholder household resilience in the face of subsequent weather or market shocks that affect production yields or prices. PAR can potentially be a critical tool for communities and researchers to identify the long-term effects of sub-jection to these shocks as well as solutions (including increasing and diversify-ing food production, or strengthening local food distribution systems) that will help households and communities be resilient in the face of these often unpredictable shocks.

PAR Principles and Acknowledging Tensions in the San Ramón Case Study

The approach, methods, and methodologies employed in this study are rooted in a history of past experiences of CAN-affiliated researchers in PAR processes and projects over the past 10 years in coffee-growing communities in Central America. With each project CAN researchers have learned new ways of imple-menting the iterative cycle of learning, reflection, and action, adapting the process to different types of relationships and social structures and improv-ing it along the way. After going through and reflecting on two iterations of the PAR cycle with coffee farmer organizations in Matagalpa, Nicaragua, and Tacuba, El Salvador, in the mid-2000s, Bacon et al. reflected and developed a set of five principles for PAR research,[24] listed here with comments on how these principles were implemented in the current case study:

1. "PAR activities can support different ends depending on the values of the organizations and academics involved in the process"; that is, PAR research can also serve conventional purposes, not just community development and environmental conservation efforts. (citing Fox 2004)
2. If people involved in a PAR process want to create an opportunity for more participation they will need to engage the many manifestations of differ-ence . . . recognize the way that cultures arrange these differences into hier-archies, and work to create forums that provide more opportunities for marginalized voices.

In this case study, implementing these particular principles required the explicit focus and involvement of youth and women in the PAR process from the outset, since it is a given that these two groups are the most marginal-ized within the cooperative and community structures, and they are also the explicit beneficiaries of the project itself. The PAR cycle also focused explic-itly on capacity building, by training staff as well as cooperative youth leaders in basic PAR principles, processes, and methodologies.* Although the second

---

*This resulted in the UCA–San Ramón taking on a more leading role in the design and imple-mentation of the 2-year evaluation study that we are currently completing at the writing of this chapter.

principle has guided both the project and research design, we feel that we have not adequately addressed the hierarchy of the cooperative structure itself; the points of consultation with cooperative members and beneficiary families have been limited to workshops in which we share preliminary analyses of data as well as proposed strategies and in which participants agree or disagree or add other insights and ideas to the working document. The tension of hierarchies is something that will require ongoing and complicated dialogue, even as we are conscious of it and know we need to address it transparently.

3. There are tensions between social change and scholarly agendas. . . . Researchers are generally paid by universities and rewarded according to their ability to publish examples of how specific cases advance and/or contradict more general theories . . . [while community participants] are interested in using more general principles to create specific strategies for change"—two very distinct approaches and goals, which must be acknowledged from the outset of any project to achieve an effective process. (citing Fox 2004)

This tension is related to the first principle. Farmer beneficiaries want to know what actions will be implemented immediately to solve their problems of chronic and seasonal hunger, and we researchers seek to understand how their experience will enrich our own understanding of why they are experiencing it in the first place (and publish that knowledge and get paid for it). The tension is also a tension of hierarchy, as one of these distinct interests might be prioritized by whoever has power—more often than not, the researcher.

4. The PAR process is context dependent, often requires more time, and is more complicated than most conventional research.

In San Ramón, Nicaragua, the project included a team of agronomists, project managers, and youth leaders, who have very different needs and approaches in the research process. It also depends on the social structures themselves. In San Ramón the existing cooperative hierarchy required that we consult with varying levels of the structure during each step and iteration, including the UCA–San Ramón board of directors, the staff, the first-level cooperative boards, and the families themselves. Needless to say, this was complicated and time-consuming—and continues to be.

5. The fifth principle reminds all participants to think beyond themselves and their organizations towards playing a part in larger cycles.

This principle is both the hardest and easiest for researchers to remember. It is the easiest because we work with organizations such as the UCA–San Ramón whose daily discourse and language revolves around resistance to the dominant repressive economic model and the need for social change. The difficulty of abiding by this principle arises because on a daily basis we deal with often-competing priorities and interests from different directions, including our donor organization and its requirements and our interests in publishing and disseminating all the work we do—all while keeping in mind the interests of the UCA–San Ramón as an organization primarily committed to commercializing coffee and other commodities.

The Structure of the PAR Process in San Ramón

The basic PAR cycle of Looking→Reflecting→Acting→Sharing, in repeating iterations over time, informed the design of this study, along with the considerations of the guiding principles, actor relationships, actor priorities, and project goals described above. This process is illustrated in Figure 12.1. This chapter encompasses the process up through step 4 in a two-year

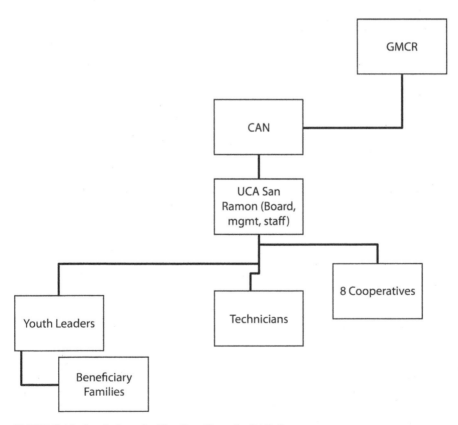

FIGURE 12.1   Actors in the San Ramón PAR Process

PAR process with 59 households in eight first-level coffee cooperatives that are members of the UCA–San Ramón cooperative; step 5, implementing the action plans and monitoring and evaluating change resulting from actions, is part of the second iteration of the PAR process between CAN and the UCA–San Ramón (but is beyond the scope of this chapter). In Figure 12.2, we map the relationships of the actors involved in the PAR process, including the project funder, Green Mountain Coffee Roasters (GMCR), and the families themselves.

The Results of the PAR Process in San Ramón

The initial PAR process with the eight cooperatives and the UCA–San Ramón resulted in a series of negotiations among stakeholders to reach a common understanding of the problem of food insecurity in these cooperatives and of how to take a food sovereignty approach to begin to address the problem.

Previous research had established that food insecurity and reduced food resilience among smallholder coffee farming families are related to overdedication of available land to coffee production, resulting in economic

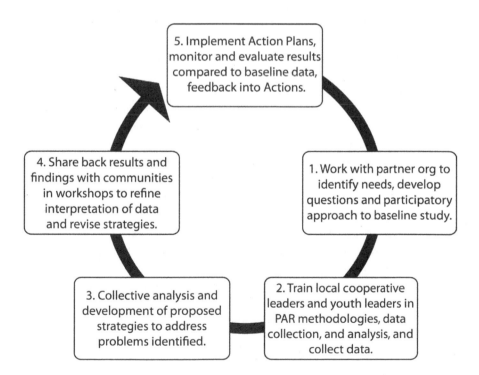

FIGURE 12.2   The PAR Process in San Ramón

overdependence on a single source of income as well as low food production at the farm level.[25] What we found was more complex than a simple inverse relationship between coffee production and food production. In addition, we discovered that this chain of explanation couldn't be reduced to the scale of the farm, community, or cooperative. Explanation must include structural factors that must be taken into account in any strategy proposed to alleviate food insecurity or seasonal hunger in coffeelands.

We found that coffee production and basic grains production is inversely related, consistent with the conclusion that overdependence on coffee as the single cash crop reduces families' ability to grow food for consumption and increases their vulnerability. We also must pay special attention to the specific relationship among the factors of access to land (especially for young people who were children during the Nicaraguan agrarian reform and have since come of age and formed families), production of basic grains only during one season, and lack of production diversity (almost no vegetables and little protein production).

It would be expected that high dependence on coffee as a once-yearly source of income to buy food, combined with less land dedicated to food production, would result in increased periods of scarcity. Higher dependence on coffee is related to lower amounts of land available for food production, but it does not appear to directly result in longer periods of scarcity. Whether a household produces basic grains is indeed related to small parcel sizes, which limit the amount of available land for growing basic grains. A counterexample suggests that other factors are important elements in food security: Even Ramón Garcia Cooperative, which produces almost no coffee, still experiences severe periods of scarcity. Even selling about 50 percent of the grain it produces, it is not able to meet its needs, indicating that the problem for this cooperative may lie with finance cycles and the dependence on a grain market where prices are very low at the time of sale, and thus families must sell a higher proportion of their grains to earn the cash they need. This cooperative also still has low dietary diversity, even though its consumption of protein is higher.

However, regardless of the size of the landholding, balanced dedication to two or more crops for food and/or income leads to longer periods of household provisioning, whereas shorter periods of household provisioning is linked to overdependence on a single cash crop, be it coffee or basic grains. The implication of this finding in particular is that production diversification is critical to increasing local availability and access to enough basic foods.

Other factors identified as contributing to household food insecurity are as follow:

- Loss of local knowledge of seed selection and saving
- Lack of hygienic seed storage infrastructure

- Loss of knowledge of how to prepare and consume local vegetables and fruits
- Lack of access to markets for diverse products
- Low levels of education that inhibit innovation that would increase productivity or other economic opportunities
- Lack of access to road and transport infrastructure
- Lack of water to irrigate during the dry season (limiting production to one season and limiting vegetable production)
- In some cases, gender inequity that limits womens ability to provide for their families (since they are assuming multiple roles as head of household)
- Short-term finance cycles that are high-cost and high-risk for farmers

A complicating fact is that very few fresh fruits are consumed, even in the households where a diversity of fresh fruits is available. This implies that attention must be paid to revitalizing consumption cultures, especially in relation to fruits. Vegetables are also rarely consumed, and this is related in part to the fact that they are hardly produced within the cooperatives. The conclusion reached by stakeholders was that any strategy must include not only promotion of production at the household level, but also education about how to consume vegetables and creation of new cultures of consumption.

The calendar of when households must manage these different factors is critical as well, as shown in Table 12.1, further demonstrating the complexity of household food insecurity. Addressing all or some of these proximate causes in combination can arguably increase households' food security in both the short and the long terms.

Even in light of the complex story of the interrelatedness of coffee and these other factors in contributing to food insecurity, the role of coffee cannot simply be dismissed or underemphasized: Farmers and their families are subject to wide price swings that periodically threaten their livelihoods when prices fall below the cost of production, as they did during the 1999–2003 coffee crisis. Dependence on income from coffee to purchase food and other basic needs, on the one hand, allows farmers to access those foods; but on the other, it can be argued that it also increases their vulnerability to price swings, coffee plagues, and extreme weather events. Any solutions that are promoted must be combinations that address coffee production and income, basic grains production, production diversification, access to water for irrigation, the creation of good food preparation and consumption habits and cultures, and agroecological practices that will preserve the means of production (quality of land) over time for both food and coffee production.

The political ecological analysis of this case study reveals three levels of causality of food insecurity in the cooperatives studied (see Figure 12.3). The proximate causes of insecurity discussed above can be more readily addressed

TABLE 12.1 Calendar of Production, Finance, and Coping Mechanisms

	Event	January	February	March	April	March	April	May	June	July	August	September	October	November	December
Coping mechanisms	Avg. coffee harvest duration	■												■	■
	Pay back coffee credit		■	■											
	Average duration of food harvest	■	■	■	■									■	■
	Plant grains and gardens						■	■							
	Rainy season							■	■	■	■	■			
	Avg. thin months (4.63 mos.)							■	■	■	■				
	Highest food prices								■	■					
	Lowest food prices											■	■		
	Harvest grains and gardens											■	■		
	Limit diet to basic foods							■	■						
	Take out credit from local store or co-op to buy seed or food						■	■	■						
	Skip meals									■	■				
	Borrow money from relatives to buy food									■	■				
	Sell grain to pay back credit											■	■		
	Take out credit to fund coffee harvest													■	■

than the structural causes, which require a sovereignty approach to increase households' resiliency when confronting them. Households and cooperatives are vulnerable to four major structural factors that influence their behavior at the local scale and their ability to respond to their own needs: volatile food prices, extreme weather events, volatile coffee prices, and the persistence of the culture of green revolution technologies.

Smallholder coffee farmers are buffeted by volatile global coffee markets that swing periodically between high and extremely low prices and that threaten family stability, the ability to fully provision a family during the year, and community well-being.[26] They are doubly hit by speculation on the grain markets at the national and international levels that sends prices spiraling downward at the moment of sale, then shooting upward when farmers must purchase grain for food or planting or take out credit for these activities. Farmers are unable to fully engage with these markets as aware participants owing to their lack of information infrastructure and awareness of where to get market information. Instead, they must rely on intermediaries (including the UCA–San Ramón) to purchase their crops or to provide the grains they must buy. The UCA–San Ramón, as a second-level cooperative, has worked to provide a more just and transparent bridge to markets for basic grains and coffee (and, most recently, milk), but the cooperative still is restricted to paying farmers local market prices for these products as they fluctuate as a risk management strategy. However, this is still a great improvement over the prices that middlemen pay or charge for buying or selling these products.

Extreme weather events are perceived by farmers to be related to climate change, and these events are considered the single greatest factor affecting their resilience. The main reasons are that there is little physical or organizational infrastructure to prepare communities or cooperatives for the loss of their crops due to rain, and no risk management strategies exist at those levels, either. Potential strategies would be establishing local grain and food distribution centers that maintain a secure local food supply, local seed banks that can allow farmers to easily replant their basic grains if their crops are destroyed by weather events, and emergency evacuation plans. We argue that risk management strategies such as these—increasing resilience and the ability of families and cooperatives to respond to such conditions without depending on external support—are as important to creating food security at the family and community level as are increasing and diversifying production to increase availability of foods at the local level. Torrential rains tremendously harmed the basic grains harvests of 2010 and 2011. Thus it is imperative that any strategies to alleviate seasonal hunger in these eight cooperatives include weather risk management strategies and food and seed storage strategies to ensure supplies. Risk management strategies are also critical to deal with price swings in basic foods, coffee, and other commodities on which cooperatives, including Ramón Garcia, depend.

Finally, it is clear that the long-term impacts of the green revolution persist among these cooperatives and within the UCA–San Ramón. This has manifested in a number of different ways. At the farm level, widespread usage of agrochemicals has been accompanied by the abandonment of traditional soil conservation and water conservation practices, as well as on-farm fertilizer production. This has resulted in polluted water sources, soil loss over time, loss of soil fertility, and overall environmental degradation. Over time, many farmers have come to see the use of green revolution technologies, like agrochemicals, as "progress"—so much so that they believe traditional or artisanal agroecological technologies to be inferior or irrelevant. This is not true across the board, but the belief persists, especially among the older generation.

Among youth who have been active in the UCA–San Ramón's environmental education campaigns or youth groups, there is less buy-in to the belief that "modern" technologies are the way to go. However, this story has an irony to it: Although the UCA–San Ramón has invested personnel and capital in environmental education and capacity building in organic production techniques among its members, it also continues selling NPK fertilizers to its members out of its offices, and its field technicians continue to prescribe the use of these chemical fertilizers to farmers. I have noticed over the years a stout resistance among the field technicians to organic techniques and to agroecology; it is clear that the technicians themselves have been trained and inculcated as well into the culture of the green revolution, and it is difficult for them to reject all the training they received in agronomy school. However, this is the contradiction and challenge for the present, and one that the staff and managers of the UCA–San Ramón know well. In pursuing food security among its member cooperatives, the UCA–San Ramón will need to confront its own role in promoting continuing environmental degradation even as it promotes health programs, education projects, and environmental campaigns among its members.

These are the five major structural factors affecting food insecurity that must serve as an umbrella for any way we think about dealing with the proximate causes of food insecurity; these must also be at the center of any strategies to promote self-determination and sovereignty. Beyond the major structural and proximate causes discussed above, there exist other relationships, politics, and ideas that may contribute to mitigating or worsening the ability of the 59 households to be food-secure throughout the year, consume a nutritious diet, and be sufficiently resilient in the face of weather and economic shocks. Finally is the increasingly powerful cultural imposition of transnational food companies who push processed foods, especially on children. The effects of this are evident in children's preferences toward processed snacks often sold in local schools themselves in the communities in question.

In other factors (so named because their effects are uneven and inconsistent) are the Nicaraguan state's increasing interventions in the area of rural food security, often in partnership with international social movements like *Campesino a Campesino* that are dedicated to strengthening local control over food systems and promoting food sovereignty at the community level. The state's fostering of this movement along with the establishment of government structures dedicated to food security at the national, departmental, and municipal scales is promising even though its impacts are uneven; only three of the Food Security Law–mandated 153 municipal food security committees are currently active and functioning (San Ramón municipality is among the three), but in those three, citizen participation has been active in the last two years. The efficacy of the Food Security Law is also limited by its reliance on the FAO food security framework, which relies on a neoliberal framework that privileges the strategy of increasing agricultural production for income generation as mentioned earlier, rather than seeking to address many structural limitations to food insecurity. Those limitations are noted in Figure 12.3, including volatile food prices, extreme weather events, and the persistent power of green revolution culture.

A final factor affecting food security is the contradictory nature of the specialty coffee industry, a factor that produces uneven results, along with government structures and laws governing food security (see Figure 12.3). On the one hand, the industry has stepped up to investigate the causes of, and find solutions to, the problem of persistent food insecurity in the communities it sources coffee from, and it should be congratulated for this. The coffee industry partnered with the international development industry to focus primarily on production diversification and increased market opportunities at the local level, however, and, as Colleen Bramhall of the Corporate Social Responsibility area of GMCR has mentioned to us, the industry needs to engage more with the governments of the countries where they work. We argue that the industry needs to also pay closer attention to the structural causes of food insecurity and engage with its own relationship to these factors.

Results of the PAR Process

The PAR process of this diagnostic study culminated in sharing back the preliminary analyses with the various stakeholders at the UCA–San Ramón. We performed five workshops with the Board of Directors and staff of the organization, with the youth leaders as a group, and with the project beneficiaries of the eight cooperatives. In these workshops, participants gave input into interpretations of the data that we offered, sometimes agreeing and sometimes offering alternative interpretations. All of their input was integrated into the final interpretation of the data, the identification of problems and of specific actions to address the problems.

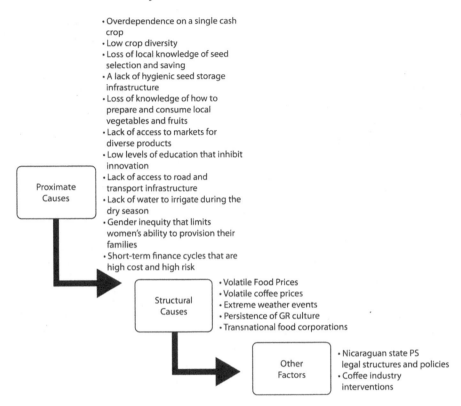

FIGURE 12.3 The Chain of Explanation of Food Insecurity in Eight Smallholder Coffee Cooperatives

The resulting five-year action plan addressed a major portion of the problems identified in a comprehensive way. Moreover, the board of directors of the organization voted in 2012 to adopt the five-year action plan as the UCA–San Ramón's Five-Year Food Security Strategic Plan, to be implemented eventually among all of its member cooperatives as needed. Although the management was resistant to individualized cooperative action plans, actual implementation of the plan has involved individualized actions organized informally:

- Cooperatives with the most female heads of household are part of efforts to reduce vulnerability.
- Cooperatives experiencing difficulties with the supply of water are part of efforts to develop irrigation systems.

The strategic plan that resulted from the PAR process offers insight into the vision of the UCA–San Ramón, the project beneficiaries, and the CAN researchers. Desired outcomes mentioned in the plan are focused on increased and expanded food production, a strong implementation of sustainable agro-ecological food production practices, revaluing and disseminating sustainable traditional production practices as well as food preparation and consumption practices, relinking local food production and local food preferences, increasing and diversifying leadership roles and income generation opportunities for women and youth in the cooperatives. The desired outcomes are geared toward reducing dependence on external food sources, strengthening local control over food access and availability, and bolstering women's and youth leadership in the food system, but they do not include outcomes related to changing power structures in the global food system that create dependencies and inequities in the first place. Including these kinds of outcomes into a cooperative strategic plan would of course be complicated, but without them the plan is limited in effecting deep social change outside the scope of the cooperative, unless the strategies used include engaging with wider social movements, policy, and other scalar relations.

The strategies identified to reach the desired outcomes in five years include production diversification and improvement of agroecological practices to improve availability of foods at the family and cooperative levels; increased access to, and availability of, diverse and nutritious foods, as well as promotion of the sustainability of local food systems; and the strengthening of cooperatives with a focus on the participation and leadership of women and youth in the base cooperatives. Echoing the desired outcomes laid out in the plan, the strategies are exclusively focused on enhancing existing, and building new, local organizational structures to support changes that will result at the cooperative scale in more sustainable production practices, heightened local food accessibility and availability, and increased capacity of youth and women to manage local food systems. In essence, the priority of the PAR partnership and the resulting strategic plan is to delink the local structures (cooperatives, in this case) from global factors and replace dependency on food and agricultural inputs with self-dependence.

Food Sovereignty and Resilience in the Face of a New Crisis

The issue of food resilience has become an urgent topic in the coffee world and especially coffee growing communities in the last five months, as Central American coffee fields have been destroyed by a disease called *la roya*, or coffee leaf rust. The disease is normally present in coffee fields in minor amounts, and farmers simply pick off affected leaves to manage the disease. For reasons not well understood, *la roya* has hit coffee fields this year in Colombia, Guatemala, Nicaragua, Honduras, and Costa Rica in "one of the worst outbreaks . . . in memory" according to the *New York Times*.[27] In northern Nicaragua, the cooperative PRODECOOP has cited 80 percent loss of income during the

2012–2013 coffee harvest, and regionwide the disease is expected to halve harvests across the board. This means not only a supply crisis for the coffee industry next year, but also a crisis for those families that depend on coffee as their main source of income to purchase food for the year. The *la roya* crisis over the next two years will be a testing ground for everything we have implemented so far to improve food security and resilience with and among smallholder coffee farmers, and the crisis will show us where we should focus attention to assure the survival and prosperity of the families with whom we work.

Conclusions: PAR as a Food Sovereignty Implementation Tool

At the beginning of this chapter we argued that PAR has the potential to yield results that (1) are the product of involving farmers in the development of the study, interpreting the data, and identifying strategies joining indigenous with Western knowledge to address the complex causes of food insecurity and that (2) lead to the development of more sustainable, effective, context-oriented, and culturally and environmentally appropriate strategies for strengthening food sovereignty and enhancing community food security because of its emphasis on local knowledge and practices combined with other knowledges. The PAR process in this case study resulted in strategies that addressed issues of local control over food systems, including access to the means of production (seeds, water), leadership of youth and women in food systems management, and diversified production for consumption and income generation. The collectively devised and approved strategies join the values of the different participants in the process and reflect the respective strengths of, and relationships among, the different stakeholders involved, rather than imposing one set of values of one actor (e.g., income generation is the way to increase access to food). In this way the strategies differ from those used by Nicaraguan government programs as well as many development agencies.

A major limitation of this process was its exclusive focus on the scale of the cooperative, the household, and the farm. This is a limitation because although strategies identified through the process are meant to increase household food resilience to environmental and economic shocks, they do not really address how these same households are affected daily by national and international policies, transnational corporations and agencies, and other structures outside the realm of their direct control. The process, in effect, ignored the roles of actors at other scales besides the local, as well as possible innovations lying outside the local. The question arises how a PAR process promoting food sovereignty can engage actors beyond the local scale, and how they might be influenced.

How applicable are the strategies and lessons learned in San Ramón to other places? In light of what we know about the variability in causal dynamics of food insecurity and seasonal hunger among eight cooperatives lying in the same municipality, we must assume that in other countries the dynamics may present similar or even greater variability; we would be wasting time and resources if we tried to apply the same set of strategies to communities in another country. Promoting rural food security and sovereignty thus requires a *process* that emphasizes communities' needs, rather than a defined set of strategies, seeing that we already know that one set of strategies is not applicable from place to place. Food sovereignty is the approach, and PAR is a tool to implement this approach, even with its recognized and unresolved tensions of interests, power, and values. It is the PAR process that is applicable. Locally appropriate and culturally preferred strategies can be decided on by participants themselves. Civic and political structures and dynamics at various scales can be taken into account and integrated into the process. We are convinced of this because of our experiences in various places. At the same time that we began the project in San Ramón, Nicaragua, we also launched the project in the mountains of Veracruz, Mexico. It is beyond the scope of the present chapter to go into much detail about the differences; it will suffice to mention a few: Regarding social organization, we work with a local nonprofit there, not a producer cooperative, with Mexican party politics affecting everything we do. The altitude and climate of the region restricts what can be produced there in a number of ways. The human organizational scalar relationships were also different: The coffee farmers we work with there were not organized into a cooperative when we started. They did not have direct market linkages, but they did have linkages with development organizations. Moreover, the PAR process itself unfolded differently than in Nicaragua. We had begun with exactly the same general project blueprint as in Nicaragua, but the work we did together changed as the PAR process progressed. Today the project has distinct goals, strategies, and actions from the San Ramón project. It has its own definition of success as well. We have learned that the process can be applied in different places and that it leads to locally appropriate, locally defined, actions. This has its challenges and critiques and arguably has not led to generalized understandings that can be globally applied, but this is the future of this kind of work: decentralization and situation-appropriate collaboration guided by experimentation, participatory monitoring of results, collective reflection, and sharing. It might seem as if the results will be small-scale, but it could also turn out that one of these days we will create a viable model that truly is sovereign and independent of transnational green revolution–oriented companies. What the decentralized process encourages is the pursuit of a number of strategies, each of which we can present to the world as being possible. So far the dominant model has simply dictated one standard way of producing food, and it has not resulted in eradicating hunger and poverty at any scale, but has instead increased farmer vulnerability. What do we have to lose?

Notes

1. M. Windfuhr and J. Jonsén, *Food Sovereignty: Towards Democracy in Localized Food Systems* (Warwickshire, UK: ITDG Publishing, 2005), 23–24.

2. Michel Pimbert, *Towards Food Sovereignty: Reclaiming Autonomous Food Systems* (London: International Institute for Environment and Development, 2009), 50.

3. Food and Agriculture Organization (FAO). *The State of Food Insecurity in the World 2012*, FAO. www.fao.org/news/

4. Mauricio Merino, "Agricultural Subsidy Programs: The Rationale and Irrationality of a Poorly-Designed policy," in *Subsidizing Inequality: Mexican Corn Policy since NAFTA*, eds. Jonathan Fox and Libby Haight (Santa Cruz: Woodrow Wilson International Center for Scholars, University of California–Santa Cruz, 2010), 56.

5. "Coffee Industry Leaders Unite with Mercy Corps and Aldea Global to Help Nicaraguan Coffee Farmers Combat Seasonal Hunger," After the Harvest. http://aftertheharvestorg.blogspot.com

6. Sara Kinden, Rachel Pain, and Mike Kesby, "Introduction: Connecting People, Participation and Place," in *Participatory Action Research: Approaches and Methods*, eds. Kinden et al. (London and New York: Routledge, 2007), 1.

7. Kinden et al., "Introduction," 7.

8. Kinden et al., "Introduction," 10.

9. Christopher M. Bacon, V. Ernesto Méndez, and Martha Brown, "Participatory Action-Research and Support for Community Development and Conservation: Examples from Shade Coffee Landscapes of El Salvador and Nicaragua," Research Brief #6 (Santa Cruz: Center for Agroecology and Sustainable Food Systems (CASFS), University of California–Santa Cruz, 2008), 2.

10. Mendez et al., "Effects of Fair Trade and Organic Certifications on Small-Scale Coffee Farmer Households. . . ." *Renewable Agriculture and Food Systems* 25 (2010): 371.

11. Robert Chambers, "The Origins and Practice of Participatory Rural Appraisal," *World Development* 22, no. 7 (1994a): 953–956.

12. Robert Chambers, "The Origins and Practice of Participatory Rural Appraisal," *World Development* 22, no. 7 (1994a): 956.

13. Robert Chambers, "Paradigm Shifts and the Practice of Participatory Research and Development," Institute of Development Studies Working Paper 2, (Institute of Development Studies, 1994b), 1255.

14. Robert Chambers, "The Origins and Practice of Participatory Rural Appraisal," *World Development* 22, no. 7 (1994a): 959–960.

15. Robert Chambers, "Participatory Rural Appraisal (PRA): Analysis of Experience," *World Development* 22, no. 9 (1994c), 1253.

16. William Schanbacher, *The Politics of Food: The Global Conflict between Food Security and Food Sovereignty* (Santa Barbara, CA: Praeger, 2010), 10.

17. Christopher J. Brown and Mark Purcell, "There's Nothing Inherent about Scale: Political Ecology, the Local Trap, and the Politics of Development in the Brazilian Amazon," *Geoforum* 36 (2005).

18. Patricia Allen, "Reweaving the Food Security Safety Net: Mediating Entitlement and Entrepreneurship," *Agriculture and Human Values* 16 (1999).

19. Bacon, Mendez, and Brown, "Participatory Action-Research and Support for Community Development and Conservation."

20. Martha Caswell, V. Ernesto Méndez, and Christopher M. Bacon, "Food Security and Smallholder Coffee Production: Current Issues and Future Directions," ARLG Brief #1, Agroecology and Rural Livelihoods Group (ARLG) (Burlington: University of Vermont, 2012), 5. www.uvm.edu/~agroecol/?Page=Publications.html

21. Ibid.

22. Ibid., 1.

23. Ibid.

24. Bacon, Mendez, and Brown, "Participatory Action-Research and Support for Community Development and Conservation," 11.

25. Caswell, Mendez, and Bacon, "Food Security and Smallholder Coffee Production."

26. Ibid.

27. Emma Bryce, "Fighting Off the Coffee Curse," in *Green: A Blog about Energy and the Environment* (*New York Times*, February 8, 2013).

Index

About the Contributors

ALBERTO ALONSO-FRADEJAS is a PhD researcher at the International Institute of Social Studies in The Hague and is a Research Fellow of the Guatemalan Institute of Agrarian and Rural Studies (IDEAR) and of the Transnational Institute (TNI) in Amsterdam.

SATURNINO M. BORRAS JR. is an Associate Professor at the International Institute of Social Studies (ISS), The Hague, The Netherlands, an Adjunct Professor at China Agricultural University in Beijing, and a Fellow of the Amsterdam-based Transnational Institute (TNI) and California-based Food First.

J. CHRISTOPHER BROWN is an Associate Professor of Geography and Environmental Studies at the University of Kansas, as well as he is also Director of the Environmental Studies Program. His work spans ecology and biogeography, political ecology, and moral geography. His current projects include studies of environmental governance along the mechanized agricultural frontier of Amazonia; social movements, civil society, and the environment; and farmers' land-use decisions vis-à-vis changes in the biofuel economy in Brazil and the U.S. Great Plains. Among his publications are articles in the *Journal of Biogeography, Ambio, Comparative Political Studies, Latin American Research Review, Political Geography, Progress in Development Studies*, the *Professional Geographer*, and *Geoforum*.

SARA B. DYKINS CALLAHAN is an Instructor of American Studies and codirector of the Food Studies Certificate program at the University of South Florida. She is a performance studies scholar interested in the intersection of performance studies with food studies, theories of place/space, performances of pain and suffering, and lived experiences of class.

DOUGLAS H. CONSTANCE is Professor of Sociology at Sam Houston State University. His degrees are in Forest Management (BS), Community Development (MS) and Rural Sociology (PhD), all from the University of Missouri. His research area is the community impacts of the globalization of the agrifood system and alternative agrifood systems. He has written numerous journal articles, book chapters, and books on these topics. He is Past President of the Southern Rural Sociological Association (2003) and the Agriculture, Food, and Human Values Society (2008). He currently serves as Editor-in-Chief of the *Journal of Rural Social Sciences*.

ANNETTE AURÉLIE DESMARAIS is Canada Research Chair in Human Rights, Social Justice, and Food Sovereignty at the University of Manitoba. She is the author of *La Vía Campesina: Globalization and the Power of Peasants* (2007), which has been published in French, Spanish, Korean, Italian, and Portuguese. She also coedited *Food Sovereignty: Reconnecting Food, Nature, and Community* (2010) and *Food Sovereignty in Canada: Creating Just and Sustainable Food Systems* (2011). Before obtaining her doctorate in Geography, Annette was a farmer in Canada for fourteen years. She also worked providing technical support to La Vía Campesina for a decade.

DELL deCHANT is a Master Instructor in the Department of Religious Studies at the University of South Florida, where he has served for over 25 years. He is the author of three books, more over 30 articles in professional publications, and chapters in ten books. His specialization is religion and contemporary cultures. His recent research focuses on the contemporary ecological crisis as it manifests in American popular culture and religion. deChant is Chair of the Environmental Committee of the City of New Port Richey, is a member of the Ecology Florida board of directors, and serves on steering committee for Friendship Farms & Fare.

GRACE GERSHUNY is currently an Instructor in the Green Mountain College (VT) MA program in Sustainable Food Systems and works with MA students through Prescott College (AZ). She has taught about all aspects of alternative agriculture and food system issues at the college level for many years, in affiliation with the Institute for Social Ecology (Plainfield, VT). She is a regular contributor for the *Organic Standard*, an online publication aimed at organic policy professionals, and is coauthor of the classic text on ecological soil management *The Soul of Soil*. In the 1990s Grace served on the staff of the USDA's National Organic Program and was a principal author of its first, much maligned, proposed rule. She received her MA in Extension Education from the University of Vermont in 1982, with a self-designed concentration in Ecological Agriculture.

MARY HENDRICKSON is Assistant Professor of Rural Sociology at the University of Missouri. She has spent 15 years working to create local food systems through the University of Missouri Extension. She currently teaches courses on sustainable agriculture and food systems. Her research focuses on understanding the structure of the global food system and helping farmers, eaters, and communities create sustainable alternatives.

PHILIP H. HOWARD is an Associate Professor in the Department of Community Sustainability at Michigan State University. He is a member of the editorial board of *Agriculture and Human Values*. His research interests focus on structural changes in food systems, consumer interests in food ecolabels, and data visualization.

JOANN LO is Executive Director of the Food Chain Workers Alliance, a national coalition of unions, worker centers, and advocacy organizations throughout the food system. Since graduating from Yale University with a degree in environmental biology in 1997, she has worked as a labor and community organizer and director of labor alliances. She currently serves on the Leadership Board of the Los Angeles Food Policy Council, the City of Los Angeles's Sweatfree Advisory Committee, and the Enlace Institute Advisory Board.

MARÍA ELENA MARTÍNEZ-TORRES is researcher and Professor in Society and Environment at the Centro de Investigaciones y Estudios Superiores en Antropología Social–Unidad Sureste (CIESAS–Sureste) in Mexico and author of *Organic Coffee: Sustainable Development by Mayan Farmers* (Ohio University Press, 2006).

BEN McKAY is a PhD candidate at the International Institute of Social Studies (ISS) in The Hague and is part of the research program Political Economy of Resources, Environment, and Populations Studies. He is currently researching the rise of BRICS countries and its implications for global agrarian transformation, with a specific focus on the rise of the Brazilian state and capital and attendant influence on agrarian transformation in South America, specifically in Bolivia.

R. DENNIS OLSON, a Senior Research Associate at the United Food & Commercial Workers International Union in Washington, DC, advocates fair labor standards and works on agricultural and trade issues. Olson coauthored a UFCW report, *Ending Walmart's Rural Stranglehold*, that made recommendations for curtailing buyer power abuses in food supply chains. Olson worked as a policy analyst for the Institute for Agriculture and Trade Policy, where he wrote "Hard Red Spring Wheat at a Genetic Crossroad," a chapter in *Controversies in Science and Technology*. He also worked as a community organizer and lobbyist on agricultural and conservation issues.

HEATHER R. PUTNAM is Associate Director of the Community Agroecology Network (CAN) in Santa Cruz, California. She has spent over a decade working with coffee farmer organizations in Central America, Uganda, and Brazil to promote participatory rural development processes. Her research interests include participatory action research, food systems, food security and sovereignty, rural livelihoods, and cooperativism.

PETER M. ROSSET is a researcher and Professor in Agriculture, Society, and the Environment at El Colegio de la Frontera Sur (ECOSUR) in Mexico and a researcher at the Centro de Estudios para el Cambio en el Campo Mexicano (CECCAM). He is also co-coordinator of the Land Research Action Network (www.landaction.org).

WILLIAM D. SCHANBACHER is an Instructor of Religious Studies at the University of South Florida. He is the author of *The Politics of Food: The Global Conflict between Food Security and Food Sovereignty* (Praeger, 2010). His research interests include ethics and the global food system, religion and food, human rights and theories of justice, and liberation theologies.

BRIAN TOKAR is an activist and author, the Director of the Vermont-based Institute for Social Ecology, and a lecturer in Environmental Studies at the University of Vermont. He is the author of *The Green Alternative*, *Earth for Sale*, and *Toward Climate Justice*, has edited two books on the politics of biotechnology, *Redesigning Life?* and *Gene Traders*, and has coedited the recent collection *Agriculture and Food in Crisis: Conflict, Resistance, and Renewal* (Monthly Review Press).

CHUNYU WANG is an Associate Professor at the College of Humanities and Development Studies (COHD), China Agricultural University. She is a coauthor (with Saturnino Borras and Jennifer Franco) of *The Challenge of Global Governance of Land Grabbing* (Globalization, 2013). Her research interests include rural transformation, county governance and planning, rural politics, and land grabbing. She can be e-mailed at wangchyu@cau.edu.cn.